The Science of Attitudes

The Science of Attitudes is the first book to integrate classic and modern research in the field of attitudes at a scholarly level. Designed primarily for advanced under-graduates and graduate students, the presentation of research will also be useful for current scholars in all disciplines who are interested in how attitudes are formed and changed. The treatment of attitudes is both thorough and unique, taking a his-torical approach while simultaneously highlighting contemporary views and con-troversies. The book traces attitude research from the inception of scientific study following World War II to the issues and methods of research that are prominent features of today's research.

Researchers in the field of attitudes will be particularly interested in classic and modern research on the organization, structure, strength, and function of attitudes. Researchers in the field of persuasion will be particularly interested in work on atti-tude change focusing on propositional and associative learning, metacognition and dynamic theories of dissonance, balance and reactance. The book is designed to present the integration of the properties of the attitude with the dynamic consider-ations of attitude change. *The Science of Attitudes* is also the first book on attitudes to devote entire chapters to work on implicit measurements, resistance to persuasion, and social neuroscience.

Joel Cooper has been on the Psychology faculty at Princeton University since obtaining his Ph.D. from Duke University. He is past editor of the *Journal of Exper-imental Social Psychology*, is the author of several books, and co-editor of a major handbook in social psychology.

Shane F. Blackman received his bachelor's degree in psychology at the University of Chicago and his Ph.D. from Princeton University in psychology and public pol-icy. His scholarship has focused on attitudes, naïve realism, and social policy.

Kyle T. Keller received his Ph.D. in psychology from Princeton University and his bachelor's degree at the University of Arizona. He contributed to research in cogni-tive dissonance, choice, and choice behaviors. Kyle was selected as a Fellow of the Princeton Energy and Climate Scholars.

The Science of Attitudes

Joel Cooper
Shane F. Blackman
Kyle T. Keller

Routledge
Taylor & Francis Group

NEW YORK AND LONDON

First published 2016
by Routledge
711 Third Avenue, New York, NY 10017

and by Routledge
2 Park Square, Milton Park, Abingdon, Oxon OX14 4RN

Routledge is an imprint of the Taylor & Francis Group, an informa business

Library of Congress Cataloging-in-Publication Data
Cooper, Joel.
    The science of attitudes / Joel Cooper, Shane Blackman, Kyle Keller.
        pages cm
    Includes bibliographical references and index.
    1. Attitude (Psychology)   2. Attitude change.   I. Blackman, Shane
J.   II. Keller, Kyle.   III. Title.
    BF327.C665 2016
    152.4—dc23
    2015007593

ISBN: 978-1-138-82078-4 (hbk)
ISBN: 978-1-138-82079-1 (pbk)
ISBN: 978-1-315-71731-9 (ebk)

Typeset in Stone Serif
by Apex CoVantage

Printed and bound in the United States of America by Publishers Graphics,
LLC on sustainably sourced paper.

CONTENTS

PREFACE

This book is about attitudes. Everyone has them. We have attitudes about important world issues, about the mundane objects in our everyday life, and about the people who comprise our social world. The attitude concept has been the most studied concept in the history of social psychology. It is a topic covered in psychology courses, from the basic introductory class to the graduate level. Yet, with all the attention paid to attitudes, the current book was born of a teaching need. We found it difficult to teach a responsible course on the social psychology of attitudes without compiling a unique curriculum of ideas, references and concepts. This volume is designed to provide students, teachers and scholars with the overarching framework that unifies the exciting field of attitudes and persuasion and also brings to life the scientific approach to the discipline.

When psychologists first began to study the attitude, they could only imagine that some day researchers would be combining people's verbal judgments with information gathered from implicit measures and from brain activity. Now, modern attitude research uses a panoply of traditional and innovative methods to form a more complete picture of how people form and change attitudes. From its inception, the study of attitudes in psychology meant applying the scientific research method. This book begins with an analysis of how attitudes first came to be studied and shows the changing perspectives that occurred over the course of time. We use a historical approach to trace the changing methods, theories and assumptions that guided research in attitudes and attitude change. The book gives the reader a foundation in the classic approaches that prepares the way for an appreciation of current issues and cutting edge methodologies. We show the reader how contemporary issues complement classic approaches and how newer implicit measures and fMRI technology complement more traditional measures in the field of attitudes.

No book can be written without the help of numerous people. We wish to acknowledge and thank the many people who by reading, criticizing, commenting, typing, taking photos and otherwise offering their assistance to allow us to complete this book. We specifically acknowledge Paul Bree, Matthew Kugler, Christine McCoy, Allison Fleming and Barbara Cooper for their valuable assistance. We also could not have completed the book without the helpful criticisms and suggestions offered by Russell Fazio, Michael Olson and other anonymous reviewers.

CHAPTER 1

The Meaning and Measurement of Attitudes

A young girl walked off her school bus, fearful that her school would close. She was twelve years old, and nothing had been more important in her young life than her education. Her hopes and dreams were threatened by an edict from the Taliban militia: All schools serving girls must be shut and boarded by January of 2009. As a child growing up in the Swat Valley of Pakistan, Malala Yousafzai's schooling had been frequently interrupted by the militias, hostile to the belief that girls might receive a formal education. "How dare the Taliban take away my basic right to education?" she had said to a public meeting of reporters when she was 11 years old.

Malala's attitude toward education would cause her both trauma and triumph. Trauma occurred on October 9, 2012, when Taliban gunmen boarded her school bus and shot her with a single bullet to the head. They made clear that she had been targeted for her outspoken commitment to girls' education. But Malala survived and, following a difficult recovery, emerged to a triumphant standing ovation at the General Assembly of the United Nations. She concluded her remarks by saying,

> Dear brothers and sisters, we want schools and education for every child's bright future . . . we must not forget that millions of people are suffering from poverty, injustice and ignorance. We must not forget that millions of children are out of schools. We must not forget that our sisters and brothers are waiting for a bright peaceful future. So let us wage a global struggle against illiteracy, poverty and terrorism and let us pick up our books and pens. They are our most powerful weapons. One child, one teacher, one pen and one book can change the world. Education is the only solution. Education First.
>
> (*NY Times*, July 12, 2013)

Malala Yousafzai was awarded the Nobel Peace Prize in 2014.

Attitudes matter. Throughout the history of the world, people have taken extraordinary steps to support a set of attitudes and beliefs to bring about a better world. Gandhi, Nelson Mandela and Martin Luther King Jr. led societies to new views of human freedom and dignity by their written words and their behavior. Every day, people take action to advocate for social justice. They persuade and organize in the service of bringing about a world that is closer to the paragon in which they believe.

Attitudes matter in our daily lives as well. The way we think of our world is largely determined by our attitudes. From the major political issues of the day to the mundane evaluations of the food on our breakfast tables, it is difficult to envision a world without them. They are reflections of our likes and dislikes, our preferences and our evaluations. It seems virtually impossible to describe our social lives without considering our attitudes. This book is devoted to organizing in a coherent fashion the main tenets of what the science of psychology has learned about attitudes. We will examine how our attitudes are structured, how they are measured and the functions they serve. We will consider the effectiveness of ways to change attitudes in the form of persuasion, and also the ways that allow people to resist persuasion. We will consider the relationship of our attitudes to our behaviors, both as causes and consequences of behavior, and finally discuss the emerging knowledge relating attitudes to electrochemical changes in our brains.

A BRIEF HISTORY OF THE STUDY OF ATTITUDES

The scientific study of the attitude has a long and storied history. Although the science of social psychology is only a little more than a century old, Thomas and Znaniecki wrote in 1918 that social psychology was essentially the study of the attitude. It was not always so. The first usage of the word attitude in the English language was recorded in the 17th century, when it was adapted from the French. Its meaning was not at all what psychologists describe today. If you referred to a person's attitude, you would be referring to their posture rather than a psychological concept. The first known link to psychology entered the language in 1725, when attitude referred to a posture of the body that reflected a mental state. It was not until 1837 that etymologists found a use of the word to refer to an opinion or a feeling about an object. Advance the clock only 80 years and Thomas and Znaniecki (1918) could declare the study of the attitude to be the essence of the fledgling science of social psychology.

Although the term *attitude* to describe people's mental states toward an object or issue is relatively newly minted, the art of persuading people to change those mental states is as old as civilization. It was the profession of the Sophists in ancient Greece to teach citizens how to argue and persuade. Aristotle considered persuasion in great detail in *Rhetoric*. The Roman forums relied on debate and persuasion in the running of the empire. It is not that scholars were unaware that people held opinions but, as art gave way to science, they needed a more precise way to conceptualize people's opinions and so the relatively new term, attitude, rose to prominence.

The scientific study of attitudes was facilitated by the development of methods to assess them. L.L. Thurstone, Rensis Likert, Louis Guttman and Charles Osgood provided increased sophistication to the scales used to study attitudes. With the publication of attitude measurement techniques, the volume of empirical research in attitudes exploded. By 1935, Gordon Allport declared the attitude to be "the most distinctive and indispensable concept in contemporary American social psychology" (Allport, 1935, p. 198). From the perspective of the 21st century, it is clear that Allport's assessment remains true, with the caveat that the qualifying term "American" is no longer required. A literature search using "attitude" as the search term yields more than 65,000 articles, chapters, books and dissertations.

Attitudes express our evaluations, influence our perceptions and guide our behavior. A matter of practical and theoretical concern is how to alter them. Political candidates know that people's attitudes toward them, and possibly the issues they represent, predict their voting behavior. Commercial marketers know that people's attitudes toward a product predict their purchasing behavior. Leaders of mass movements know that people will sacrifice a great deal in support of attitudes they find powerful and important. Finding the principles that govern the creation and change of attitudes has been the focus of a healthy proportion of those 65,000 entries in the psychological literature.

A Tale of Two Traditions: Attitudes and Attitude Change

Persuasion is both an art and a science. As an art form, it relies on intuition. Many political candidates, political consultants and advertising agencies are adept at convincing their audiences without being able to articulate the principles that underlie the persuasion. Just as artists paint a picture that can be striking for its beauty, some persuasive communicators effectively convince their audience with the subtlety of their words or the beauty of their images. When a young man named Volney Palmer opened the very first advertising agency in Philadelphia in 1843, instinct and intuition were the tools of his trade (Pratkanis & Aronson, 2001). The science of persuasion had not yet begun.

The science of persuasion, in contrast to the intuition of persuasion, relies on the *systematic investigation of underlying principles that lead to attitude change*. The first programmatic effort to examine attitude change systematically was conducted by a group of investigators at Yale University in the 1940s. The group was convened by the United States government, responding to what it perceived to be a dilemma of public opinion. Toward the end of WWII, after the surrender of the European Axis powers, the government was concerned about persuading its citizens that the war in the Pacific theater of operations would be both lengthy and difficult. Worried that people would believe that a successful end to the war was inevitable, the government was determined to persuade them that sacrifice remained essential.

They convened a group of social scientists, funded by the U.S. Army's Information and Education Division, to engage in the systematic scientific investigation into the principles of persuasion.

The accomplishments of the Yale Attitude Change and Communication Program were vast, and we will examine them in detail in Chapter 4. It is interesting to observe, however, that the vast literature on persuasion gave little attention to what was meant by an attitude. Investigators examined the principles of persuasion by using concepts such as opinions, beliefs and attitudes interchangeably. Hovland, Janis and Kelley's (1953) major volume, reporting results of the early work, was entitled *Communication and persuasion: Psychological studies of opinion change*. The word *attitude* does not appear. It was as though an attitude was anything that was measureable by a scale. Issues that served as targets for attitude change ranged from whether people thought that Prohibition was a good policy to whether people believed the Soviet Union could build a nuclear submarine. The application of scientific methodology to studies of persuasion and the growth of new theories to predict change fueled a long and exciting period of study in attitude change. Being certain of what we mean by an attitude has had a more deliberate growth.

Why Study Attitudes?

Social scientists study attitudes because they are psychological structures that provide insight into human thought and behavior. Understanding the principles that underlie attitudes and attitude change tells us a great deal about human development, learning and motivation. We also study attitudes because they are a bridge to human behavior. It is reasonable to believe that people's behavior is affected by their attitudes. Therefore, understanding attitudes provides insights into people's behavior. Understanding how attitudes *change* can provide insight for changing behavior.

Imagine a candidate for political office who hopes to persuade people to vote for her. By changing people's attitudes toward the issues she stands for, it seems reasonable that people will be more likely to cast their ballot for her. Similarly, a business that hopes to improve its profits may hope to persuade people to adopt positive attitudes toward the product it manufactures. As a practical matter, being able to persuade people to adopt and/or change their attitudes is an important enterprise and a scientific approach to understanding the principles that underlie persuasion facilitates that enterprise.

The attention that social scientists have paid to the study of attitudes has produced important theories and results. Yet anomalies in the findings have raised questions about the basic assumptions underlying the attitude concept. For example, attitudes do not *always* predict behavior. In one important illustration that we shall consider in more detail in Chapter 6, LaPiere (1934) asked shopkeepers about their attitudes toward serving Chinese couples in their places of business. This was an era in which anti-Chinese sentiment was strong in the United States. Almost unanimously, shopkeepers expressed negative attitudes toward serving Chinese couples and reported their intention to refuse them service. Yet LaPiere escorted a Chinese couple on an automobile trip covering more than 10,000 miles, stopping at 251 hotels and restaurants. He found that, despite the attitudes that the proprietors reported on the questionnaires, 250 of the 251 establishments gave full and polite service to the couple.

Anomalies can be useful because they lead to more focused attention on resolving them. Following LaPiere's report, many social psychologists turned their attention to studying the structure, meaning and function of attitudes. This attitude tradition was more precise than the attitude change literature in identifying some of the underlying concepts that make attitudes more or less predictive of behavior. Because all attitudes are not created equal, asking people for their attitude about a cereal, a candidate or tooth brushing on an attitude scale may miss some important differences among those attitudes. For example, some attitudes are stronger than others and have greater impact on behavior. Attitude strength, in turn, depends on such questions as how the attitudes were formed, how easily they can be activated from memory and the consistency of the various components that comprise the attitude. We will discuss these issues in the following chapter and then consider the functions that they serve in Chapter 3. We will now turn our attention to considering what we mean by an attitude.

Defining the Attitude

Social psychology has made enormous progress in understanding the underlying structure and function of attitudes, as well as developing empirically based theoretical perspectives on how to change them. There has been less consensus about how to define them. We will adapt a definition of attitudes proposed by Zanna and Rempel (1988):

>An **attitude** is the categorization of a stimulus object along an evaluative dimension.

Zanna and Rempel went on to propose that the evaluation itself is a result of affective information, cognitive information, information about behavior, or some combination of the three.

The critical notion in the definition of attitudes is *evaluation*. When we evaluate a stimulus object, we are making a summary judgment about its value or worth along a positive/negative dimension. This can be done as an absolute judgment, such as "I think my elected official is good" or it can be a relative judgment, such as "I think my elected official is better than my neighboring elected official." As the number of categories increase from merely good versus bad to express gradations of good and bad, we then have an ordinal scale for expressing our evaluative judgments.

Although most scholars agree that attitudes are evaluations, they do not always agree on what is meant by evaluation. One widely cited definition of attitudes was placed into the literature by L. L. Thurstone (1946). He declared that attitudes were "the intensity of positive or negative affect for or against a psychological object" (p. 39). Note that the difference between the two views is that our proposed definition uses the term evaluation while Thurstone used the term affect. We construe affect to be an emotive experience: When you feel happy, you experience affect; when you feel sad, you experience affect. Although your affect may be one basis for your evaluation of an attitude object, it may not be the only one. Consider ice cream: Merely looking at a cold, creamy dish of chocolate ice cream may make you experience delight. Without question, you feel happy and delighted. At the same time, you know that ice cream will not help you lose the five pounds you have been trying to lose, and that the fat and sugar content will not be good for your health. So what is your attitude toward the ice cream? Your affective response is certainly positive, but is tempered with what you believe about its health consequences. Asked about your *attitude* toward ice cream, your evaluation will be a complex judgment based upon a combination of the factors you have considered.

Other scholars have proposed that affect, cognition and behavior are all intrinsic aspects of the attitude concept (Rosenberg & Hovland, 1960; Zimbardo & Ebbesen, 1970). In this tripartite view, an attitude must include a tendency for a person to act in a way that corresponds to his or her cognitive beliefs and affective experiences. For example, Droba (1933) suggested "an attitude is a mental disposition of the human individual to act toward or against something in the environment" (p. 309). In this view, your attitude about chocolate ice cream is positive to the extent that your emotional experience, your beliefs about the ice cream *and* your behavior toward it are all positive. Insisting on the behavioral tendency as part of the definition of attitude raises the following question: If you know that ice cream makes you feel good but you never eat it, is it legitimate to say that you have a positive attitude toward ice cream?

We believe the answer to that question is yes. We concur with many attitude researchers (e.g., Alberracin, Zanna, Johnson and Kumkale, 2005; Zanna & Rempel, 1988) who suggest that to include behavior in the definition of attitudes pre-judges some of the most fascinating and important questions in attitude research: Under what circumstances do attitudes predict behaviors? Under what circumstances do behaviors predict attitudes? Under what circumstances are behaviors predicted by purely emotional experiences independent of any logical thought? These are empirical questions whose answers have shed light on many fascinating issues. As we present some of the classic research on attitudes in the forthcoming chapters, we will see that people's evaluative judgments are *sometimes* based upon their behavior toward an attitude object, *sometimes* on their thoughts and *sometimes* on their emotive experiences—and, most often, on some weighted combination of the three. To constrain attitudes by defining them as necessarily based on all three components acting in unison is to eliminate some of the most interesting research questions about attitudes. Using a working definition of attitudes as a summary evaluation that takes into account any or all of the three sources of information (affect, behavior and cognition) affords the most flexibility in studying attitudes.

The definition of attitude we are adopting also takes no position about the stability or permanence of an attitude. An attitude may or may not be stored in memory, ready to be used when interacting with an attitude object. A person may have an often-used, well-rehearsed attitude toward chocolate ice cream that serves her well whenever she approaches it. She sees it and she evaluates it positively with no hesitation. Another person may have to consider each interaction with the ice cream anew, depending on how she feels at the moment, the time of day, her weight loss goals and so forth. Presumably, attitudes that are stored in memory may be more stable, predict behavior more consistently and lead to quicker reactions about the object than attitudes that are inferred at the moment (Fazio, 2001). However, this is a research question rather than a definitional question and we shall examine some of that research in the next chapter.

Attitude Measurement

Attitude assessment in the 21st century is a multi-billion dollar business. Preceding any election, opinion polls abound. Those polls measure people's attitudes on a weekly or even daily basis. They may be conducted by personal interviewers, by phone, by mail or by internet. Following televised debates, attitudes can be assessed within minutes of the debates. The profession of attitude assessment is exemplified in marketing and consulting firms whose expertise is to assess people's attitudes toward commercial products and advertisements, as well as political issues and candidates.

Measurement is not a simple issue. Despite the sophistication of polling and attitude assessment techniques, more than one candidate has been misled because voters' attitudes were assessed poorly. In a famous illustration, Republican candidate Thomas E. Dewey was advised to stop campaigning weeks before the 1948 U.S. presidential election because polling data had shown that an overwhelming majority supported his candidacy. Worried that the only thing he could accomplish by continuing to campaign was to stumble, he left for Europe with weeks remaining in the campaign. On the day of the election, November 2, 1948, Harry S. Truman became the 33rd president of the United States, upsetting Dewey by more than two million votes. It may never be known if Truman 'came from behind' during the final weeks of the campaign or if the polling agencies simply measured the voters' attitudes incorrectly.

The Stimulus Object

How one assesses attitudes is partly a function of what you want to know. We assess people's evaluation of a **stimulus object**, by which we mean almost anything about which people can form evaluations. A stimulus object (sometimes called the *attitude object)* can be a person, an animate or inanimate object or a topical issue. If people can evaluate the stimulus object on a good/bad dimension, then it can serve as the basis for an attitude. One of the primary concerns of attitude researchers is to identify the stimulus object properly. Put another way, it is imperative to decide what it is that you really want to know.

Imagine that you want to run for political office. Your supporters tell you that you have a certain charm or charisma, but you also want to be certain that your own attitudes about local and national issues are consistent with those of your electorate. In this hypothetical scenario, you decide that expanding preschool opportunities for economically disadvantaged children is your top priority and you want to assess the attitudes of your potential constituents. You decide to conduct a poll in which you will ask people about their attitudes. Before you can construct a scale, you need to make an important decision: What is the stimulus (i.e., attitude) object? Do you want to know whether people are in favor of preschool education in general, or do you want to know whether they favor a specific proposal currently before their legislature? Do you want to know if they favor public *funding* of preschools or just having a system that might be funded at some time in the future? Or, perhaps you want to know how favorable your potential constituents are toward helping disadvantaged children as a category of people. You may well find different evaluations or attitudes, depending on how you construe the attitude object.

In the pages that follow, we will discuss a number of techniques that researchers have frequently used to assess attitudes. Here we pause to note a scientific imperative: Questions must be asked in a way that does not 'push' the answer to the question. For example, if a respondent answers a question such as, "Do you agree with a social policy that takes care of children, or would you rather have them grow up without an education?" you are likely to find what you might mistakenly construe as attitudinal consensus for preschools. However, the phrasing of the question may have pushed people toward that answer because they do not want to see children wandering the streets without an education. That nonetheless may be quite different from a positive evaluation of a particular education assistance program currently before the legislature.

In science, researchers must have no vested interest in the outcome of an attitude questionnaire. If they phrase a question that pushes or leads people toward a particular answer, it will only serve to weaken the meaningfulness of results they obtain in their research. Sometimes, however, 'push' or leading questions are used deliberately for politicians or pundits to make a particular point. The wording of questions can push people to appear to support a pundit's particular viewpoint or make it appear that a particular candidate is favored by a greater proportion of the electorate than is really the case. The science of attitude research strives to make certain that attitudes are measured, not pushed.

Explicit Attitude Assessments

Measurement *is the assignment of numbers to objects according to rules* (Stevens, 1946). Typically, scientific research assesses attitudes by measuring and assigning numbers so that comparisons can be made. A person may be relatively favorable to expanded preschool education for children. We may discover this by asking an explicit question that assigns a number that can be used to compare against a standard. For example, a person's attitude measurement may be greater than the mid-point on a favorable/unfavorable dimension or it may be greater than the number that other people marked on the favorable/unfavorable dimension.

How do we obtain these numbers, and how certain are we that the numbers represent people's evaluations? Arguably, the dawn of the age of scientific attitude research began with L. L. Thurstone's classic article whose main thesis (and title) was the pronouncement that "attitudes can be measured" (Thurstone, 1928, p. 529). It seems ironic from the perspective of modern psychology that there was a time that attitudes were thought to be unmeasurable. But that was the case in the early part of the 20th century. Thurstone argued that, contrary to the prevailing assumption, numbers could be assigned to attitudes in a scientifically valid manner. He likened the problem of measuring a multi-faceted concept like an attitude to measuring a multi-dimensional object like a table.

> . . . Measuring an ordinary table is a complex affair, which cannot be wholly described by any single numerical index. So is a (person) such a complexity, which cannot be wholly represented by a single index. Nevertheless, we do not hesitate to say that we measure the table.
>
> (Thurstone, 1928, p. 531)

The Thurstone Scale

Thurstone advanced a technique to assess attitudes that now bears his name. He reasoned that people's attitudes are given expression in the form of specific opinions that they would endorse about a stimulus object. To use a modern example, people who endorse an opinion statement like "All children should have access to an education when they are young" are likely to have attitudes that are supportive of publicly funded preschools. People who endorse statements like "Children should begin formal schooling at age 6" are more likely to have negative attitudes about a public preschool program.

Constructing a Thurstone Scale requires several steps. The first is to ask a large number of people to generate opinion statements like the previous ones. Further examples might be "Preschool for all children is too expensive," and "Preschool for all children is a moral responsibility of a society." A researcher can gather hundreds of statements, but the goal of Thurstone's method is to turn them into a scale. This requires that there be a scale of measurement such that people's attitudes can be legitimately compared. To create the scale, the opinion items that were generated by the first large group of respondents are shown to a different group of respondents, who are asked to separate the items into 11 piles. One pile will contain all of the opinion items that they judge to be extremely supportive of preschools for the disadvantaged, another pile will contain all of the items that are extremely anti-preschool, and yet another pile will be neutral, neither favoring nor opposing preschools for the disadvantaged. Therefore, based on the judges' ratings, there will be 5 units of pro-preschool that vary in intensity with equal intervals from extreme to moderate and five of anti-preschool also ranging from extreme to moderate and one neutral point. The important operation that allows the scale to have units of measurement is the judges' separation of the opinion statements into the 11 equal units.

A Thurstone scale can be created for any topic on which people can make evaluative judgments. Respondents simply indicate which of the statements they endorse, with the mean of the endorsed statements constituting a numerical representation of the respondent's attitude. The scale in Figure 1.1 illustrates a hypothetical Thurstone scale that may have been constructed for determining people's

PLEASE INDICATE WHETHER YOU AGREE OR DISAGREE WITH EACH ITEM
1. Free preschools for the poor are socialist
2. The Head-Start preschool program has been a failure
3. Taxes are too high to support preschools for everyone
4. People should pay for their own children's preschool
5. Nations that have preschools have poor education systems
6. Children can get by without preschools
7. In the long run, we all pay for children who are uneducated
8. People cannot be sure that public education will always be available
9. My child needs a free preschool program
10. Poor children can only succeed if preschools are available
11. Providing education from birth to adulthood is a moral obligation for society

FIGURE 1.1 *Example of a Thurstone scale for measuring attitudes towards preschool education. Participants respond by indicating which statements they endorse.*

attitudes toward preschool for disadvantaged children. If John decides that he endorses items numbers 6, 7 and 8, we can assign him a number on the scale that is the mean (=7) of the items he endorsed. That number can be used to test differences among individuals or among groups of people who take the scale.

Thurstone scaling is an important technique in attitude measurement, partially because of its historical importance. As we pointed out, social scientists were eager to study people's attitudes but, until Thurstone's paper, they did not have a psychometrically reliable method for studying them. A second reason for the importance of Thurstone scales is that they could be developed to study attitudes about any attitude object. Thurstone scaling is still used in modern social psychology, although not to the degree that the scales that succeeded it are used.

The Likert Scale

One drawback of constructing an attitude scale using Thurstone's procedure is the cumbersome nature of the approach. By drawing on hundreds of people to generate a list of statements, Thurstone hoped to avoid having an unrepresentative set of statements to rate. By recruiting another hundred or so judges to rate the statements for their level of support for a stimulus object, he hoped to create consensual units for the scale that respondents could endorse. The burden on researchers each time they wished to study an issue seemed nearly prohibitive.

Rensis Likert (1932) suggested a simpler method. Not only was he seeking a scale that would be easier to use, but he also was concerned with Thurstone's assumption that asking a large number of judges to rate a large number of statements solved the potential problem of having biased or unrepresentative issues. His simpler method involved generating 'judgments' with which people could agree or disagree at various strengths.

A Likert item on pre-school education would look like the following:

"A modern democracy should have a system of free preschools for disadvantaged children."				
1	2	3	4	5
Strongly Agree		Undecided		Strongly Disagree

FIGURE 1.2 *Example Likert scale for measuring attitudes towards preschool education. Participants indicate their response by circling a number on the scale.*

Respondents are asked to choose the degree to which they agree or disagree with the item using a 5-point scale like the one pictured in Figure 1.2.

Note the differences between Likert's and Thurstone's methods. Thurstone asked people to endorse statements of beliefs toward an attitude object that had been pre-rated by a group of judges to fall equally along a value continuum. Likert asked people the degree to which they agreed or disagreed with a judgment that contained value statements such as "should" or "ought to." The judgment items were created by the investigator to be reasonably associated with the attitude object. We should note that Likert did not recommend that attitudes be measured by single items. In order to assess prejudicial attitudes, for example, Likert and his colleagues generated many 5-point judgment items related to racial prejudice, which they then summed to create a scale score. Today, investigators are more likely to use Likert *items* rather than Likert *scales*. Whether several Likert items should be summed to form a single scale score is considered an empirical question. Statistical techniques (e.g., Cronbach's alpha; Cronbach, 1951; Cronbach & Shavelson, 2004) are applied to the items in combination to see if it is appropriate to combine them into a single scale.

Semantic Differential

Several other techniques have been advanced that continue to be used today. Osgood and his colleagues (Osgood, 1962; Osgood, Suci, & Tannenbaum, 1957) proposed that any concept could be described along three major semantic dimensions—its evaluation (good/bad), its potency (strong/weak) and its activity (active/passive). To demonstrate this, Osgood et al. (1957) chose more than 70 adjective pairs from Roget's Thesaurus and asked people to rate a wide variety of objects on those pairs of adjectives. When the ratings were collected, the investigators subjected the results to a statistical technique known as a factor analysis, which identifies the underlying dimensions of the ratings. Regardless of culture or language, the factor analysis identified three factors: Good versus bad (evaluation), strong versus weak (potency) and active versus passive (activity).

When used as a measurement technique, people are asked to assess an attitude object on 7-point evaluative scales on each of the three dimensions. An attitude object is identified (e.g., 'preschool education' or 'poor children') and respondents are asked to rate the object on scales that capture people's evaluations along the three dimensions (See Figure 1.3). In practice, attitude researchers do not frequently

ON THE SCALES BELOW, PLEASE DESCRIBE YOUR REACTIONS TO PRESCHOOL EDUCATION		
Powerful	/ / / / / / / / /	Powerless
Strong	/ / / / / / / / /	Weak
Good	/ / / / / / / / /	Bad
Positive	/ / / / / / / / /	Negative
Quick	/ / / / / / / / /	Slow
Rapid	/ / / / / / / / /	Sluggish

FIGURE 1.3 *Example of a semantic differential scale for assessing attitudes towards preschool education. Participants indicate responses by placing a mark in the appropriate box.*

assess all three dimensions that Osgood et al. (1957) specified. More typically, it is used as single evaluative (good/ bad) item and, when used that way, is a slightly more elaborated version of the Likert technique.

Levels of Measurement

What are we asked to do when we respond to an attitude scale? As we have seen, we can be asked to endorse statements, agree or disagree with judgments and evaluate a statement on a good/bad semantic differential. Here, we will focus not on the questions of an attitude scale but rather on the response categories. The levels of measurement implied by different types of response categories are also referred to as different types of scales.

The Nominal Scale

The most basic level of measurement is the nominal scale: Nominal (also known as categorical) scales simply record whether the measured variable is falling into one of a number of categories. The categories themselves do not have to be arrayed in any particular order. For example, imagine that a polling organization wants to know whether more people in Arkansas are liberal or conservative. They may ask respondents to answer a question like, "What would you consider your political orientation?" allowing people to choose liberal or conservative. This scale is nominal because it only places people into categories. It does not assess their degree of conservatism or liberalism, only whether they place themselves in the liberal or conservative column. This level of measurement can be useful, depending on what the researcher wants to know. For example, determining that 68% of Arkansas residents describe themselves as conservative whereas 32% describe themselves as liberal may be just what the researcher wanted to know. Alternatively, the researcher might want to know if liberalism/conservatism differs between states in the United States, so the researcher asks the same question of people in Massachusetts. The poll shows that the percentages reverse in Massachusetts, such that 68% consider themselves liberal and 32% consider themselves conservative. The investigator can perform statistical analysis of the nominal data and conclude that liberal versus conservative attitudes differ significantly between the two states.

Ordinal Scales

Typically, researchers who are interested in studying attitudes want to use scales that allow a measurement of the *degree* to which something is true. The next higher level of measurement is the ordinal scale, which takes advantage of rank ordering. What we know in an ordinal scale is that one category is numerically higher than another category, although we do not know by how much. In a particular ordinal scale, 3 is bigger than 2 and 2 is bigger than 1, but 3 minus 2 does not equal 1.

Suppose that we want to find out if social class affects people's liberal versus conservative attitudes. We might ask people to declare if they feel they are in the lower class, working class or upper class. In this case, the categories have a limited arithmetic meaning. In terms of wealth, upper class has greater wealth than middle class, which has greater wealth than working class. Because the magnitude of the three classes is ordered in terms of income perception, we describe this as an *ordinal scale*. We might find that as income rises from lower to upper class, people's attitudes become more liberal. In this example, liberal and conservative are still nominal variables, but social class is measured on an ordinal scale. This time, if we assign a number 1 to the lower class, 2 to the middle class, and 3 to the upper class, the numbers do have meaning. A 3 is a higher income score than a 2, which is higher than 1, but it would be incorrect to assume that their intervals are equal (3 minuses 2 does not equal 1).

Equal Interval Scales

The most frequently used scale in attitudes research adopts the assumption that the difference between points on a scale occur at equal psychological intervals. Thurstone's most enduring insight was that judges could place opinion statements along a continuum where the intervals would be equal. Similarly, Likert's five-point scale was based on the assumption that the difference between each mark on the scale represents an equal psychological interval for the respondent at all points along the scale. The difference between a 3 and a 2 on the scale is assumed to be equal to the difference between a 4 and a 5; the difference between 5 and 7 is twice the distance between 5 and 6. The great advantage of equal interval scales is that responses (i.e., the numbers) can be added, subtracted and averaged, and one can determine their standard deviation. This allows for a host of statistical analyses that cannot be conducted on nominal and ordinal scales. Common examples of interval scales include the Fahrenheit and Celsius scales, which measure temperatures.

Ratio Scales

The final level of scaling is called ratio scaling. Ratio scales add one requirement to those of interval scaling: They must have a meaningful 0 point. Fifty degrees Celsius is not twice as hot as 25 degrees; the Celsius scale sets its 0 point at the temperature at which water freezes rather than the temperature that signifies a complete absence of heat. The Kelvin scale did exactly that, however, and 50 degrees Kelvin is twice as hot as 25 degrees Kelvin, though it still is not t-shirt weather. Many physical properties are measured on ratio scales. Examples include: height, weight, distance and energy. Explicit attitude measurements rarely use ratio scales. It is typically not meaningful to draw conclusions about people being 'twice as liberal' or 'half as conservative', which would be the rationale for developing a ratio scale in attitude measurement.

Problems with Explicit Measures

For nearly a century, attitudes have been assessed with explicit measures much like the ones we have described so far. Thurstone's proclamation that attitudes could be measured showed social scientists how they could assign numbers to the evaluation of psychological objects and how they could use the psychometric properties of the equal interval scale to make comparisons between or among groups. Further debates have led to simpler and easier-to-use scales, but the confidence that attitudes can be measured has not waned.

Nonetheless, attitude measurement has been shadowed by a persistent concern: Can even the best attitude measurement be a valid indicator of a person's attitude if he or she is inclined not to tell the truth? A yardstick can be used to measure someone's height but its meaning will change if the person slumps his shoulders and bends his knees. Similarly, a Likert scale has meaning as an indicant of a person's attitude only if he or she responds honestly. If the response is distorted, it fails to serve as a meaningful measure, just as the yardstick fails to measure the slouching person's true height.

Why would respondents fail to respond honestly to an attitude scale? Suppose we wanted to assess people's attitudes about a day care system for impoverished children in society. You design one or more Likert items to assess respondents' attitude toward preschool education for the disadvantaged, such as the items in Figure 1.2. People can choose a number from 1 to 5 that best represents their attitude toward the issue. Their answers will be determined in large part by their true attitude toward preschools. However, they also may be reluctant to tell you, the researcher, what their attitudes are. Suppose the respondent is not in favor of universal preschool education but is responding at a university campus where she believes it is likely that most people support a free system. She may not be willing to reveal her attitude for fear of social disapproval by anyone viewing her questionnaire. Another respondent may be unwilling to admit to himself that he holds an attitude that is contrary to what is socially expected. Asking people to rate their attitudes on a measurement scale will provide a number. The question is whether the number will be a valid measure of the attitude you sought to assess.

The psychologists who created measurement scales were aware of this issue but accepted it as an unavoidable problem. Thurstone (1928), while describing his measurement, stated, "We shall assume that an attitude scale is used only in those situations in which one may reasonably expect people to tell the truth about their convictions or opinions" (p. 534). The solution that Thurstone offered was to use attitude scales only in contexts in which people did not feel constrained to offer a response that was not true.

Dishonesty can be minimized in a number of ways. Attitude items need to be framed in ways that do not seem as though there is a correct, or socially approved, answer. As Thurstone and Likert advised, honest responses can be facilitated by the social context, such as the anonymity of the responses. The tendency to provide answers in a socially desired direction has been found to be a reliable individual difference, and a number of scales have been developed to assess people's inclination to provide socially desirable rather than truthful answers (Crowne & Marlowe, 1960; Fischer & Fick, 1993).

Beyond Dissimulation

Modern research in the assessment of attitudes has identified an array of issues that researchers need to keep in mind in addition to whether the respondents are telling the truth. Schwarz (1999; 2007) has argued that asking people to respond to items on a scale has some of the properties of a conversation between questioner and responder. The responder assesses the meaning of a question from its context in addition to the precise wording of the question. If a question about support for publicly funded day care is preceded by a question about attitudes toward philanthropy, support for day care may be different than if the question was preceded by a question about fiscal responsibility. The preceding question may establish a context that affects the way day care is perceived and interpreted.

A properly asked question on an attitude scale also needs to consider the way in which possible answers are depicted. A Likert-type item might ask people to respond to the following statement: "Our government should sponsor a system of free day care for needy children." That item might be followed by a response scale that allows people to answer in gradations from 1 (strongly agree) to 5 (do not agree at all). Or the same 5-point response scale may be labeled 1 (strongly agree) to 5 (strongly disagree). Are they the same? Some recent studies show that, although both are 5-point evaluative scales, respondents may interpret these scales quite differently. This is especially an important question to consider when comparing across studies or across groups of people (Uskul, Oyserman, Schwarz, Lee, & Xu, 2013). In addition to deciding on the labels that anchor the response scale, another decision that a researcher needs to make is how many gradations to use on the evaluation scale. In Likert's own research, he typically used a 5-point response scale, but occasionally used a different number. Is there an appropriate number of gradations and does it matter? Although there has been no consensus on the appropriate number to use, Smallman, Becker and Roese (2014) found that the number of gradations might not be symmetrical for liked vs. disliked attitude objects. Respondents preferred to have a greater number of gradations to express their liking or agreement with an issue than for expressing disagreement.

Asking for people's attitudes using explicit attitude measures such as Likert scales continues to be the most frequently used assessment method. It is only important to bear in mind that, in addition to the possibility of dissimulation, attitude scales can be sensitive to the testing and cultural contexts in which they are administered as well as to the response alternatives from which people are allowed to choose (Lee & Schwarz, 2013). The importance of these issues is greater to the extent that the researcher's question requires a comparison across studies and populations.

Implicit Attitude Assessments

The scientific study of attitudes took a dramatic turn during the past several decades with an explosion of techniques designed to assess attitudes at an implicit level (see Petty, Fazio, & Briñol, 2012; Wittenbrink & Schwarz, 2007). *An implicit measure is an assessment of attitudes that occurs outside a person's conscious awareness or control.* The difference between an explicit measure and an implicit measure may be likened to the difference between asking a child to estimate his temperature on a scale from 98 to 102 degrees, compared to using a fever thermometer. Even if the child is adept at knowing his own temperature, his desire to skip school the next day may cause him to explicitly state a temperature somewhat higher than he genuinely believes. An implicit attitude measure tries to simulate the fever thermometer rather than the self-report by obtaining a measure that is unaffected by the respondent's desire to present himself in a particular way. The interest in measuring attitudes with implicit measures has been enthusiastic, buoyed by the development of new and innovative techniques. The burgeoning interest in implicit approaches will be discussed in its own chapter later in this book (see Chapter 9), but we will foreshadow some of the major developments here.

Physiological Measures

The nervous system of the human body often responds to stimuli in automatic ways, that is, without conscious control or intention. We are all familiar with the startle response: A sudden loud sound has measurable effects on the body's autonomic nervous system that precede conscious deliberation. No matter how much we would like to appear 'cool' and unperturbed by a sudden backfire of a truck, our respiration, skin conductance and heart rate will be affected. To the extent that bodily responses reveal our evaluations of stimulus objects, they can serve as indicants of people's evaluations. We call such measures implicit because they bypass people's conscious considerations, which can cause ambiguities with explicit measures. Concerns over the socially correct attitude evaluation can be eliminated if the body responds to an attitude object the way a fever thermometer responds to temperature.

There is no consensus about physiological measures that can replace explicit attitude scale in all instances. Nonetheless, there are some exciting examples of measures that have proved useful in particular circumstances. For instance, Hess (1965) examined pupillary dilation in response to an attitude object. He noted that the more attractive an object was, the more the pupils dilated. Therefore, pupil dilation can serve as a measure of people's evaluation of an attitude object.

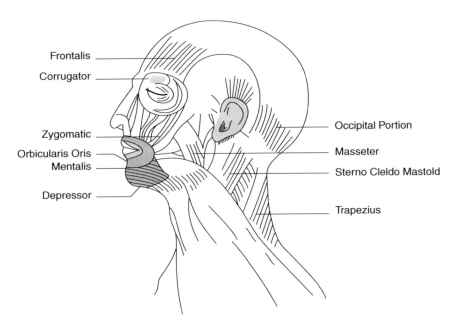

Frontalis
Corrugator
Zygomatic
Orbicularis Oris
Mentalis
Depressor

Occipital Portion
Masseter
Sterno Cleldo Mastold
Trapezius

FIGURE 1.4 *Muscle groups of the face that are used for EMG recordings when assessing attitudes.*
Source: Cacioppo, J.T., & Petty, R.E. (1981c). Electromyograms as measures of extent and affectivity of information processing. *American Psychologist, 36*(5), 441. Reprinted with permission.

Cacioppo and Petty (1981c) introduced facial electromyography (EMG) as a measure of attitudes. They noted that portions of our faces show greater muscle activity when we are pleased than when we are displeased. Positive evaluations cause the muscles (see Figure 1.4) that control smiling (the zygomaticus group) to tighten while the muscles that control frowning (the corrugator supercilli group) relax. Negative evaluations, on the other hand, lead to activation of the corrugator muscles associated with frowning and a relaxation of the zygomatic muscles associated with the experience of smiling. The activation of the different muscles is automatic and often undetectable either by an observer or the respondent. However, EMG recorders attached to a person's face can show both the direction and the intensity of the response (Cacioppo, Petty, & Geen, 1989; Larsen, Norris, & Cacioppo, 2003; Witvliet & Vrana, 2007).

Implicit Cognitive Measures
Some of the most exciting developments in implicit measurements have come in the area of cognitive responses. We consider an implicit measure to be cognitive to the extent that it relies on associations stored in memory to serve as an indicator of an attitude. As an example, let us consider how we might determine people's

attitudes toward the poor, who are the potential recipients of the proposal to provide publicly supported preschools. If we pose an explicit question to respondents, such as asking them how favorable they are toward poor children on a 5-point scale, people may experience pressure to express positive attitudes. As we have seen, even those who have negative evaluations of poor children may be hesitant to express them and even hesitant to admit such attitudes to themselves. Nonetheless, stored in their memories is their true evaluation of the category. Implicit cognitive measures make use of these automatic, uncontrollable evaluations by measuring the impact of those attitudes on other evaluative responses.

Let us make this clear by adapting a method introduced by Fazio and his colleagues (Fazio, Sanbonmatsu & Kardes, 1986) to examine attitudes toward poor children. In this method, we will not ask the respondent to state her attitude toward the poor; rather, we will show respondents a picture of an economically disadvantaged child. The respondent has an immediate and automatic evaluation of the child, whether or not they are willing or able to express it. Now the researcher shows an unrelated word on the computer screen that is either positive (e.g., a rose) or negative (e.g., a thorn) in valence. People are asked to categorize the word as either positive or negative as quickly as they can. If people harbor negative evaluations of the disadvantaged child, they will be slower in reacting to a positive word that followed the picture of the child and faster to respond to a negative word. In other words, the degree to which the automatic evaluation aroused by the picture of the disadvantaged child is consistent with the word that then follows on the screen, the more it will facilitate responses to the word. Quick reaction times to evaluatively consistent pairings are indicative of the attitude (Fazio et al., 1986). In this particular case, if quick reaction times follow from the pairing of negative words with the picture of the poor child and slow reaction times follow from the pairing of positive words with the attitude object, we can conclude that the respondent holds a negative attitude toward disadvantaged children.

The use of implicit assessments that rely on automatic cognitive associations has become a very important development in the study of attitudes. Arguably the most influential method is the *Implicit Association Test (IAT)* (Greenwald, McGhee & Schwartz, 1998; Nosek, Greenwald & Banaji, 2005). The IAT uses the speed of associations to assess relative attitudes toward two categories. If you wanted to know people's attitudes toward the elderly compared to the young, or people's attitudes toward Blacks compared to Whites, the IAT provides a reliable reaction time approach to assess the comparison.

Implicit measures have become important not only because they provide an alternative way to measure attitudes, but also because they raise core issues about the meaning of an attitude. Do we have implicit attitudes that differ from our explicit attitudes or do we have implicit and explicit ways to assess a person's single, underlying attitude? These issues will be discussed in Chapter 9.

Summary and Conclusion

Attitudes are essential and ubiquitous to the study of social psychology, or the study of human behavior more generally—one need look no further than the great lengths to which advertisers and politicians go to persuade others to see the importance of the attitude construct in daily life. Attitudes can be defined as evaluations of stimulus objects or more formally as the categorization of an attitude object along an evaluative dimension. The study of attitudes became a scientific enterprise when Thurstone and his contemporaries provided a way to measure them. Since then, researchers have made significant strides at improving the fluency, parsimony and predictive validity of attitude measurement. Explicit assessments using equal interval scales, for example, allowed researchers to describe numerical representations of people's attitudes and to perform the statistical tests needed to compare attitudes between groups.

Methodologically, Likert scales and semantic differentials replaced Thurstone scales in modern social psychology because of their ease of construction and use. Because people are not always able, or willing, to express their attitudes accurately or honestly, psychologists have sought alternative means to measure attitudes. The recent development of implicit measures, such as the IAT, has made major strides to address this problem (Chapter 9). In addition, methodological advancement has given researchers an ever-expanding toolbox of physiological measures, such as facial EMG and neurological measures (Chapter 10), with which to gain insight into the processes of evaluation and attitude change. While the best practices for measuring attitudes constantly evolve, the importance of the attitude construct remains a dependable constant.

THE PLAN OF THIS BOOK

The goal of this volume on attitudes and attitude change is to give the reader grounding in classic and modern approaches to the study of attitudes. Even a book devoted entirely to this topic must be selective. This literature on attitudes comprises more than a century of science and, as we noted previously, is spread across more than 65,000 articles and books. The present book will provide the reader with a background in the attitude concept and examine the processes of attitude change. In this chapter, we have examined the ways in which social scientists learned to measure attitudes against a backdrop of what we mean by an attitude.

Chapter 2 examines how attitudes are structured. Although all attitudes are manifested by an evaluation of an attitude object, not all attitudes are the same. Some attitudes are held confidently, some tentatively. Some attitudes strongly predict behavior but others do not. Some attitudes show consistency across various components, while others show little consistency. These differences are referred to as structural differences in attitudes and have led to considerable interest in theory and research.

Chapter 3 asks the question of why we have attitudes. What purpose is served by having attitudes toward issues and objects in our environment? We will demonstrate that attitudes serve many functions, ranging from protecting self-esteem to organizing the world around us. Knowledge of the many functions that attitudes play in our lives provides insight into why we struggle to maintain our attitudes and the most effective ways to induce attitude change.

Chapters 4 and 5 analyze how our attitudes change. From political candidates asking for our vote to commercial advertisers asking for our loyalty (and money), the act of persuasion is a powerful one in our society. Our approach is historical. Chapter 4 is devoted to the classic issues in persuasion, focusing in turn on the communicator's role, the communication's effectiveness and the audience's receptivity to persuasion. Message learning and cognitive response theories form the backdrop for the classic research. Chapter 5 presents the last several decades of research in attitude change, which shifted the focus from single process views of persuasion to productive dual-process views. The emphasis on dual processes in persuasion helped to clarify some of the earlier work in attitudes and provided a more complete understanding of the principles of attitude change.

Chapter 6 and 7 examine the relationship of attitudes and behaviors. In Chapter 6, we re-examine the role that attitudes play in predicting behavior. Thought by some scholars to be part of what is meant by attitudes, research results began to accumulate that attitudes were not always precursors to behavior. We present the debate on the relationship between attitudes and behavior, focusing on theory and research that examine the conditions under which behaviors can be predicted from knowledge of people's attitudes.

In Chapter 7, we look at the other side of the attitude-behavior relationship. Rather than considering attitudes to be cognitive structures that help people determine how to act, Chapter 7 considers the research that shows that the knowledge of how we act can create and change our attitudes. We focus on theories of behavior-attitude consistency, with emphasis on the theory of cognitive dissonance. The chapter presents the development of dissonance and related theories, concluding with the current state of dissonance research.

In Chapter 8, we look at people's ability to resist persuasion. We take the position that resistance is more than the absence of persuasion. To the contrary, it is an active process that allows us to maintain the stability of our evaluations and avoid the potential chaos of changing our attitude in response to every persuasive appeal in our environment.

Chapter 9 is devoted entirely to the rapidly growing interest in implicit measurements. We focus on an array of new methods that have allowed social psychology to tackle sensitive issues like prejudice, which had been difficult to assess using the explicit techniques that we described in this chapter. We show some of the reasons for the excitement and also discuss some of the limitations. In particular, we present the debate on whether implicit and explicit measurements are different ways to assess people's attitudes or whether implicit and explicit measurements assess qualitatively different attitudes.

Chapter 10 connects research in attitudes to the burgeoning field of study known as social neuroscience. We discuss research progress using fMRI and EEG technology, showing the relationship between what we know about the timing and localization of brain activity to issues of attitude measurement and change. We also consider contributions from parallel-distributed-processing and constraint-satisfaction connectionist modeling to the study of attitudes. It is a speculative chapter because of the rapidly changing state of knowledge and the rapidly changing procedures that are used to study attitude processes in the brain. The current state of knowledge in this latest research frontier is presented in this chapter.

CHAPTER 2

Attitude Strength and Structure

Not all attitudes are created equal. They differ along several dimensions, the most apparent of which is valence. People evaluate attitude objects with different degrees of positivity and negativity, and those are the differences that are assessed with the scales we described in the previous chapter. However, even when people hold the same level of evaluation, their attitudes may still differ in their component structure and their strength. To foreshadow our more detailed discussion in this chapter, we refer to the structure of an attitude as an analysis of an attitude's components and the strength of an attitude as an analysis of how influential the attitude is in guiding behavior and resisting persuasion.

ATTITUDE STRENGTH

When people tell you that they feel passionately about a particular issue, that they will never change their attitude and that they have taken action in support of their attitudes, you have an intuitive idea that the person's attitude is a strong one. In this chapter, we will consider more formally what we mean by the concept of attitude strength and present evidence for the importance of the concept. Strong attitudes have many properties that weak attitudes do not have (Bassili, 2008). For example, strong attitudes come to mind more quickly than weak attitudes (Fazio, 1995; Holland, Verplanken & van Knippenberg, 2002), are more resistant to persuasion (Eagly & Chaiken, 1995; Krosnick & Petty, 1995) and tend to be more extreme. They are more likely to pervade people's behavior and influence the way people process information.

The **strength of an attitude is defined by its durability and pervasiveness**. The more durable the attitude, the more resistant it is to change when subjected to a persuasive message or to new information. The more durable attitude is also more likely to persist over time rather than be a momentary construction that is conjured when people are asked about their attitudes. Pervasiveness of an attitude implies that the attitude has significance for panoply of other psychological structures and activities. Someone with a strong attitude is likely to construe other attitude objects in relationship to the strong attitude. Consider two people, Jane and Mary, who are asked about their attitudes toward a novel object—let us say, wind farms for generating electricity. Both Jane and Mary hold many similar attitudes about a variety of issues. They both are in favor of a clean environment; they both endorse economic frugality and they are both in favor of solar energy as a replacement for carbon-based energy. However, Jane's attitude toward a clean environment is a strong one. It pervades the formation of other attitudes. Although the start-up cost of a new wind farm might be high, and emphasizing wind over solar power may negatively impact solar's development, her attitude toward the clean environment will control her new attitude toward wind power. On the other hand, Mary's attitude about a clean environment is less strong. It will influence her new attitude, but not more substantially than, say, her fiscal attitudes. Jane will be more likely than Mary to form a positive attitude toward wind farms because of their relationship to her strongly held attitude about a clean environment.

There are other consequences of Jane's strong attitude toward the environment. It would be more difficult to persuade Jane to change her attitude, she will consider the attitude object (the environment) to be more important to her and she will be more likely to construe ambiguous information about the importance of green technology as information in support of her position. Jane will also be more likely to take action in support of a clean environment. Note that Jane and Mary both favor a clean environment, but differ in strength of their attitudes about the environment.

Direct Experience and Attitude Strength

What makes some attitudes stronger than others? Research has identified several factors. One issue to consider is how a given attitude was formed. On one hand, we can read about an attitude object, ponder its conceptual boundaries and think about how it relates to other attitudes. On the other hand, we can have **direct experience** with a stimulus object and form our attitudes on the basis of that experience. Regan and Fazio (1977) suggested that direct experience with an attitude object would increase the strength of attitudes toward the object in the sense that it would pervade and predict people's behavior toward the object. The researchers took advantage of a housing crisis at Cornell University, which occurred in the mid-1970s when there was insufficient dormitory space to house undergraduate students. Regan and Fazio (1977) asked Cornell undergraduates to state their attitudes about how well the university was responding to the crisis. Some of the students had direct experience with the housing crisis. At the time of the study, some were sleeping in beds set up in dormitory lounges. Other students had been assigned to permanent housing and therefore had no direct experience with the housing crisis. In a survey, all students expressed similar attitudes; they were equally critical of the university's handling of the housing shortage. All of the students in the study were then asked if they wished to take some action to help alleviate the crisis. Those who had direct experience with the crisis were more likely to volunteer to behave in ways consistent with their attitude than those who had no such experience. For this group of students, their attitude toward the housing crisis demonstrated greater strength in that it influenced their behavior.

In a subsequent study, Fazio and Zanna (1978) assessed students' attitudes toward participating in psychology experiments. Direct experience with the attitude object (psychology studies) was assessed by merely counting the number of prior studies in which the students had participated. Fazio and Zanna then gave the students the opportunity to participate in future psychology studies. They found that the students' attitudes toward participating in experiments predicted their actual rate of volunteering for future studies as a function of direct experience. The more studies the students had been in, the more strongly their attitudes predicted their volunteering behavior.

Elaboration and Knowledge

The strength of an attitude is related to the amount of knowledge and reasoning that comprise the foundation of an attitude. Petty and Cacioppo (1986) proposed that people form attitudes as a function of the degree of **elaboration** they use to consider the facts and arguments that support a particular position. In Chapter 5, we will consider their theoretical position in detail as we examine the psychological forces that lead to persuasion. One of the key findings in the rich research tradition surrounding their Elaboration Likelihood Model (ELM) is that attitudes formed on the basis of careful scrutiny and logical reasoning are more resistant to change than attitudes formed on the basis of a less well-reasoned process. One person may support a candidate for election because the candidate has a pleasant smile and kisses babies nicely; another person may support the same candidate based on an analysis of the candidate's positions, prior behavior and personal background. Both people intend to vote for the candidate. However, confronted with new information that casts doubt about the candidate or extols the virtue of her opponent, the person whose attitude was formed by elaborating and processing the available information will be more likely to resist the new persuasive appeal.

Haugtvedt and Petty (1992) conducted an experiment to test the notion that elaboration leads to greater persistence of an attitude. They tested two groups of people who differed on their 'need for cognition.' Need for cognition is an individual difference variable that distinguishes between those people who generally use thoughtful processing (people high in the need for cognition) from those who rely on more fleeting aspects of an issue (low in the need for cognition). The experimenters presented both groups with advertisements extolling the virtues of a new answering machine. A test conducted shortly after exposure to the advertisements showed that both groups had formed positive attitudes toward the answering machine. As the data in Figure 2.1 show, when they were brought back two days later and asked about their attitudes, the group that habitually used greater message elaboration (i.e., those high in need for cognition) continued to show positive attitudes, whereas the group low in need for cognition reported a reduction in their positive attitudes. The higher elaboration of information in the high need for cognition group resulted in greater attitude durability, a marker of high attitude strength.

In addition to making predictions based upon measurable differences among people, such as their naturally occurring need for cognition, social psychologists also rely on systematically altering the level of a variable in the situation. To this end, Chaiken (1980) obtained evidence for the durability of attitudes following elaboration by varying the degree to which participants expected to defend their attitude in an interview. Having to rehearse their new attitude in anticipation of the interview led to greater scrutiny of the information supporting the attitude, which in turn resulted in greater durability. Similar findings have been reported by Mackie (1987) and by Boninger, Brock, Cook, Gruder and Romer (1990).

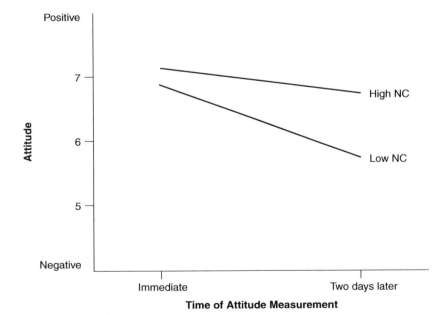

FIGURE 2.1 *Attitudes towards the answering machine as a function of individuals' need for cognition and the time of attitude measurement.*
Source: Haugtvedt, C. P., & Petty, R. E. (1992). Personality and persuasion: Need for cognition moderates the persistence and resistance of attitude changes. *Journal of Personality and Social Psychology, 63*(2), 308–319. Reprinted with permission.

A related perspective on the role of knowledge was offered by Woods, Rhodes and Biek (1995), who suggested that the amount of information that people can draw upon to support their attitudes will determine its strength. They define **working knowledge** as *the amount of attitude-related information that people can retrieve from memory* (Wood et al., 1995, p. 285). People with a high degree of working knowledge can access an extensive store of attitude-relevant beliefs and prior experiences, whereas people with lesser working knowledge possess a relatively impoverished base of information concerning the attitude object. The notion that working knowledge of an attitude object determines its strength is similar to message elaboration. However, the working knowledge perspective takes no position on how much elaboration was used to create the attitude: Working knowledge is solely a function of how much information people can access when asked about their attitudes.

In one research study examining the role of working knowledge on attitude strength, Biek, Wood, Nations and Chaiken (1993) first assessed participants' attitudes toward protecting the environment. They then asked people to list all of the beliefs they could muster as well as recall all of their behavior regarding the protection of the environment. In the next step, participants were subjected to a persuasive message arguing against environmental protection. People resisted the persuasion as a function of the amount of information that they had generated in the working knowledge task. The higher the number of beliefs and behaviors that were accessed from memory, the more resistant people were to the counterattitudinal communication. In a conceptually similar study, Biek, Wood and Chaiken (1996) found that, for students who were fearful of contracting AIDS, the amount of working knowledge they had strengthened their existing attitude about the high risk of contracting AIDS and enabled them to resist a persuasive message arguing that the risk of AIDS was actually low.

Vested Interest Influences Attitude Strength

Our attitudes toward stimulus objects have hedonic consequences. There are some evaluations that we find more important than others in the sense that they bring us pleasure or pain. We can refer to this as a continuum of **vested interest**. According to Crano and his colleagues (1995; Crano & Prislin, 1996), people hold their attitudes more strongly to the extent that they reflect vested interest. Considering what we now know about attitude strength, the vested interest hypothesis suggests that *attitudes that hold personal hedonic consequences for people will be more durable, more resistant to attack and more likely to influence behavior.*

Let us consider a study that demonstrates the link between vested interest and people's willingness to take action to support their attitude. Siveck and Crano (1982) studied students' reactions to a referendum on the legal drinking age. At the time the study was conducted, the minimum legal age for drinking was 18 in the state of Michigan. The referendum asked voters if they wanted to change the age to 21. Siveck and Crano polled students at Michigan State University and found that 80% opposed the change. Selecting only those students who expressed attitudes contrary to the proposal, the researchers had three groups that did not differ in their degree of opposition to the proposal but did differ in their degree of vested interest. Twenty-one-year-old students had little vested interest in the change because it would not affect them. Nineteen-year-olds had a much higher degree of vested interest because, if the referendum were to pass, they would have two years in which they could not drink (legally), and 20-year-olds had a milder degree of vested interest. The dependent variable in this study was a measure of the degree to which the students' anti-referendum attitudes affected their behavior. Specifically, they were asked if they were willing to join a group constituted to oppose the referendum and make telephone calls to persuade residents to vote against it. Despite their similar scores on measures of their attitudes, students with a low vested interest were not as interested in taking action (12%) as those with a moderate vested interest (26%). Students with a high vested interest (the 19-year-olds) were far more willing to follow their attitudes into action (47%). In the language of attitude strength, those with high vested interest had considerably stronger attitudes than those with less of a vested interest, despite the fact that their level of disagreement with the referendum was equivalent.

In a subsequent study, Crano (1983) showed that vested interest in an attitude issue leads people to believe that other people share their attitudes. In a study that tested students' attitudes toward a proposal that would have caused their tuition rates to rise, those who were more affected by the proposal assumed there was a much greater consensus of attitudes on campus than those who had less of a vested interest. Crano speculated that the false consensus bias was in the service of making their attitudes more resistant to change, which is another important feature of attitude strength.

What makes an attitude 'vested'? According to Crano (1995), *people feel vested in their attitudes to the extent that the attitude brings them pleasure or pain—i.e., has hedonic consequences*. Several factors are likely to affect the degree to which attitudes are vested, but for any individual the answer to the question is ultimately subjective. Vested interest is related to attitude importance. Typically, any issue that a person feels vested in is meaningful to that person. Telling Michigan State students that they might not be able to have a legal drink for several more years addressed something important to them. However, while vested interest in an attitude object makes the attitude important, not every important attitude is vested. People may agree that a revolution in a Middle Eastern country is an important issue, but still not feel hedonic relevance. Vested interest is also related to rewards and punishments, but is not always the same. People may adopt an attitude toward a candidate in an election because a significant person in their lives approves of that candidate. Agreeing with the significant person is pleasing and rewarding. Nonetheless, people who form their attitudes for that reason may not necessarily feel the hedonic investment in that candidate. In the end, the notion of vested interest is a subjective experience of pleasure or pain. To the extent that people feel such hedonic involvement, their attitudes are imbued with vested interest and will manifest the characteristics of strength, such as durability and pervasiveness.

Attitude Importance

Concepts that bear similarity to vested interest have also received considerable attention for the role they play in affecting attitude strength. The importance of an attitude has also been linked to attitude strength (Boninger, Krosnick, Berent, & Fabrigar, 1995) independent of its role in created vested interest. **Importance is defined as the subjective sense of concern, caring and significance a person attaches to the attitude**. Recall that a marker of attitude strength is its ability to predict behavior. Jaccard and Becker (1985) showed that the more importance people ascribed to their attitudes about birth control, the more likely they were to act in accordance with those attitudes. Another marker of strength is an attitude's durability. Krosnick (1988) found that people's attitudes toward political candidates remained stable over the course of a five-month period to the extent that they had rated their attitude as personally important at the beginning of the period. Moreover, this was particularly true during the end of a long presidential campaign, when personally important attitudes toward the candidates allowed voters to withstand a barrage of counterattitudinal messages from the opposing side.

Attitude Extremity

The **extremity** of an attitude is also related to its strength (Abelson, 1987; 1995; Bassili, 2008; Judd & Bauer, 1995). People who hold more extreme attitudes are more likely to take action based on those attitudes (Petersen & Dutton, 1975) and view information through a lens that processes ambiguous information as consistent with their attitudes. For example, Judd and Johnson (1981) found that people with extreme attitudes are likely to overestimate the degree to which other people also hold extreme attitudes. Similar to Crano's (1983) study, Allison and Messick's (1988) study found that people with extreme attitudes fall prey to the false consensus effect, believing that far more people agree with them than is actually true. Both the overestimation error and the false consensus bias are in the service of strengthening our attitudes—i.e., making them more durable and preserving them against attack.

In the illustration of Mary's and Jane's attitudes toward a clean environment with which we opened this chapter, we stipulated that Jane's attitude was stronger than Mary's, yet both were pro-clean environment. One basis for the difference in the strength of their attitudes may have been based on Jane's more extreme attitude compared to Mary's more moderate one. But need it be that the extremity of their attitudes must differ in order to have two different levels of attitude strength? Without in any way diminishing the importance of attitude extremity in affecting attitude strength, the answer to that question is no. Mary and Jane can each use a '4' on Likert scale as an honest response to a question about how much they favor pro-environmental policies. From the concepts we have discussed so far, Jane's attitude can be stronger because it is more important to her, because she is more vested in the outcome or because she had direct experience with aspects of the environment.

Attitude Certainty as a Validity Marker

Attitude strength is also bolstered by how certain people feel they are about their attitude. **Attitude certainty is defined as a subjective sense of conviction or validity** (Gross, Holtz, & Miller, 1995; Tormala & Rucker, 2007). Certainty differs from concepts such as importance or vested interest because it is not based upon hedonic feeling states or affective reactions such as the degree of caring or concern. Rather, it is an experience of believing that your attitude is correct. Petty, Briñol and DeMarree (2007) refer to certainty as a "meta-cognitive marker." It is an experience you have when you think about your attitude. Consider your attitude toward protecting the environment. You have access to your evaluation and you have access to the degree of certainty you have about that evaluation. Certainty serves as an index of the validity of your evaluation. Mary's attitude toward protecting the environment may be a '4,' as we have presented it above, but she may have reached that conclusion by having read one article about environmental pollution in a popular magazine. She may 'tag' her attitude with a low validity marker. She is pro-environment, but she is not nearly as certain of the validity of her attitude as is Jane, who has studied the issue at great length, read opinions from both sides of the debate and discussed the consequences of environmental policies with friends and scholars. Jane may tag her pro-environmental attitude with a high validity marker: She is certain.

In the metacognitive approach, both the evaluation and the validity marker are stored in memory (Bassili, 1996; Wells, Olson, & Charman, 2003). When an evaluation is called for, not only does the pro-environmental evaluation come forward but so too does the validity marker of certainty. According to the metacognitive approach, evaluations that are accompanied by indicants of high certainty are also characterized by stability and durability—i.e., by attitude strength.

What provides people with the evidence they need to decide their metacognitive certainty? One answer is the speed with which people can generate an attitude toward an object (Tormala, Clarkson, & Henderson, 2011). Imagine that someone asked you about your attitude toward global warming. Your response may come very quickly. You are against global warming, and it only takes microseconds for you to retrieve your attitude from memory and give it voice. Alternatively, your answer may come quite slowly as you search your memory for the many facets of the issue and conclude that you are against global warming. Your answer to the attitude question will give expression to the direction and extremity of your attitude. All else being equal (i.e., the attitude is held with the same degree of extremity and so forth), the amount of time it took to provide your answer will give you a clue about how certain you feel about the attitude.

The effect of speed of response is interestingly complex. Tormala et al. (2011) asked participants to express their attitudes toward a number of topics. They measured the speed of response, but manipulated the feedback they gave to the participants. Some participants were falsely given a speed and informed that they were relatively slow compared to the average participant's response. Others were given false feedback in the opposite direction, being led to believe that they were relatively quick. Tormala et al. (2011) found that when people were expressing attitudes that they already held, then quick reaction times gave them the subjective feeling of certainty. Conversely, if they were expressing attitudes about a novel attitude object, then the longer they were led to believe it took them to express those attitudes, the more certain they felt about those attitudes. So, the feeling of certainty is affected by how quickly people think they expressed their attitudes. The greater the feeling of certainty, the stronger the attitude.

One Indicant or Many?

The everyday connotations of terms like certainty, extremity, importance and vested interest suggest a degree of overlap. Research has shown that the concepts we have presented do share some common properties, but are not merely synonyms for each other (Krosnick, Boninger, Chuang, Berent, & Carnot, 1993; Visser, Bizer, & Krosnick, 2006; Visser, Krosnick, & Simmons, 2002). Visser et al. (2002) examined the degree of importance and certainty that respondents reported about a variety of policy issues and candidates for public office. As expected, they found that both concepts related to attitude strength but they did so in different ways. For example, the importance that people attached to their policy attitudes predicted their voting behavior, but certainty did not. Certainty, more than importance, predicted the degree to which people were interested in and attended to the issues.

Krosnick et al. (1993) asked people to indicate their attitudes about issues like increased defense spending in the United States. They also collected multiple measures of the strength of that attitude, such as its certainty, importance, knowledge, information elaboration and extremity. They found only moderate correlations among the various measures of strength, meaning that the measures were not redundant. Although they were all related to each other, and presumably to attitude strength, they each captured an independent aspect of the puzzle.

Attitude Accessibility

We have defined attitudes as summary evaluations of attitude objects. Although some attitudes may be constructed at the moment that you are asked for evaluation (Schwarz, 2007; Wilson & Hodges, 1992), most of your attitudes are stored in memory from prior experiences (Albarracín, Wang, Li, & Noguchi, 2008; Fazio, Chen, McDonel, & Sherman, 1982; Fazio, 1995). You may have had an interaction with an attitude object at some time in the distant past or have thought about an issue at one time or another. These evaluations are stored in memory and can be retrieved when you confront the attitude object. If someone were to ask for your attitude about a chocolate ice cream cone, your past history with such a stimulus would bring forward (for most of us) a positive evaluation. You may have less of a history with a maple walnut ice cream cone, but the elements for an evaluation are still stored in memory. Your attitudes may be similarly positive, but it will be much easier to access your memory for how you feel about the chocolate cone than the maple walnut.

In this view, the strength of an attitude is conceptualized as the *strength of the association between the evaluation and the attitude object*. The strength of the association is measured by the speed with which an evaluation comes to mind after exposure to the attitude object. One of the elegant features of an attitude accessibility model is that it can be assessed objectively with a measure of reaction time: The quicker the reaction time, the stronger the attitude.

Attitude strength is conceptualized as a continuum. On one end of the continuum are attitudes that have rarely been activated. When exposed to an attitude object, people with a weak attitude may have to consider their various beliefs, past interactions and affective reactions to infer an evaluation. This will take time and lead to a lengthy reaction time to respond. On the other hand, people with strong attitudes will respond very quickly. Most likely, their attitude has been accessed previously because it is an attitude they consider important or perhaps because their evaluation of this object is a central component of their orientation to the world. In one of our previous examples, chocoholic ice cream lovers will feel strongly about a chocolate ice cream cone. If asked to evaluate the ice cream cone as quickly as possible, their evaluations will be nearly instantaneous. However, asked the same question about maple walnut, they may need to recall any past interactions with that flavor before expressing their evaluations. Their reaction times will be slower than their reaction times toward chocolate, and we can conclude that they have a stronger attitude toward chocolate than maple walnut. We can expect similar differences in reaction time for Jane's and Mary's attitudes toward the issue of a clean environment. Jane, whose attitude is stronger than Mary's, will respond more rapidly to a question asking her evaluation of clean environment policies than will Mary, even though they had the same degree of support for the issue.

Practice Makes an Attitude Stronger: The Role of Rehearsal

What makes some attitudes more accessible, and therefore stronger, than others? Fazio (1995) suggests that one major factor causing attitudes to be accessible is **rehearsal**. Making an attitude more accessible in memory is partly a function of *the number of times it is brought to mind*. The more frequently an attitude is activated, the more accessible it becomes. If people frequently think about the environment, for example, then their evaluations will be activated. More activation leads to greater accessibility and very speedy reaction times. Note that the attitude does not have to be extreme. Moderate attitudes can also be rehearsed and they, too, will become stronger. The more accessible the attitude, regardless of its extremity, the stronger they are and the more likely they are to guide behavior.

Powell and Fazio (1984) asked participants to respond to a series of attitude items on attitude scales either once, three times, six times, or not at all. Then, in what was said to be a second experiment, a different investigator asked the participant to help test an allegedly new type of attitude technique. The participant was instructed to look at a phrase (the attitude object) on a computer screen. For example, one stimulus object was "gun control" and was followed by a simple question: "Good?" The participant's task was to press a Yes button or a No button as quickly as possible to indicate her attitude. Powell and Fazio found that the more often the participant had rehearsed her attitude toward gun control, the faster she was at responding to the final question. Moreover, as predicted, the effect of rehearsal on reaction time occurred regardless of whether the participant had an extreme or a moderate attitude toward gun control. The results, depicted in Figure 2.2, also showed that the participant's attitude toward gun control did not change as a function of the rehearsal. People who were against it on the first attitude measure were still against it; people who were in favor were still in favor of it. Rehearsal simply made the attitude more accessible, which is to say that rehearsal made the attitude stronger.

Are accessible attitudes also likely to affect behavior? One of the essential qualities of a strong attitude is that it is pervasive, affecting thought and behavior. Powell and Fazio's study showed the impact of rehearsal on accessibility, as measured by reaction time. Fazio, Powell and Williams (1989) went further by examining whether rehearsal affects both accessibility (reaction time) *and* behavior. They asked participants to express their evaluation of 100 familiar consumer products. Participants were asked to decide whether they liked or disliked an item as quickly as possible by pressing an appropriate computer key. The reaction times were recorded. In

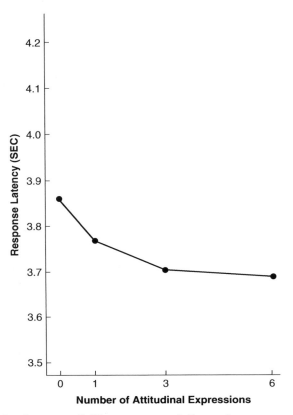

FIGURE 2.2 *Attitude accessibility, measured through response latency, as a function of repetition.*

Source: Powell, M.C., & Fazio, R.H. (1984). Attitude accessibility as a function of repeated attitudinal expression. *Personality and Social Psychology Bulletin*, 10(1), 139–148. Chicago. Reprinted with permission.

a second part of the study, the investigators chose ten of the items and placed them on a table in front of the participant. The items were recognizable snack items, such as Fritos corn chips or a can of 7-Up. The participants were told that as a token of their appreciation, the company sponsoring the research was allowing the participant to take home any five of the ten items.

The question in this research is whether reaction time affects behavior. That is, would people be more apt to choose a snack that they responded to more quickly with the evaluative word "like" than a snack whose evaluation took longer? In conceptual terms, stronger attitudes should predict behavior such that fast reaction times should predict participants' choice of snacks. If reaction times are correlated with degree of liking (and they are), any result that showed quick reaction times leading to behavioral choices could simply be a function of greater liking—i.e., more extreme evaluations—rather than attitude strength. Accordingly, the investigators chose a novel way to analyze the data. For each snack that participants liked, the investigators divided the participants into those who had quick, moderate and slow reaction times. That is, they chose all of the participants who liked a particular snack, say M&Ms, at a particular level of extremity—e.g., a 6 on a 10-point attitude scale—and divided those participants into a quick, moderate and slow reaction time groups. Overall, three groups of participants were created by this procedure. For each snack item, there was a group with a strong attitude, a moderate attitude and a weak attitude toward that item. The extremity of the attitude was the same.

The results of the study showed that people's behavior was influenced by attitude strength. The reaction time measure showed that people's final choices of which snacks to take home with them were predicted by the speed of the reaction times. It was also interesting to note that people with weak attitudes seemed to be affected by factors other than their attitudes. The ten snacks were arrayed in two rows of five for the final behavioral choice. People with weak attitude were influenced by the positioning of the products. They tended to choose snacks in the first row directly in front of them. People with strong attitudes were not at all influenced by positioning effects and made their behavioral choices consistent with their attitudes.

Rehearsal is not the only basis for heightened attitude accessibility. When we search our memories for evidence about our attitudes toward an object, we are also sensitive to the type of information we discover. Some of us may be more certain about our attitudes if we engaged in a great deal of thinking about an issue. For example, when considering our attitude about the environment, we may remember that we systematically evaluated research reports and, from those reports, came to the conclusion that the environment was badly in need of protection. Such people will trust evaluations made in that manner and find the memory of that systematic elaboration as diagnostic of their true attitude. Belief in the diagnosticity of how they formed their attitude will make the attitude more accessible and likely to show the characteristics of stability and durability that are the hallmarks of attitude strength.

Other people may be more persuaded by the diagnosticity of different types of information. Having smelled a rose, for example, is sensory stimulation that supports a positive evaluation of this fragrant flower. It is hard to dissuade someone from feeling positively about the rose by providing information about its acidity. Sensory information can be a powerful root of accessible attitudes. Wu and Shaffer (1987) found that individuals whose attitude toward a particular peanut butter was based on a sensory experience were more resistant to changing their evaluations than individuals whose attitudes were formed based on information they had read. Not surprisingly, other research has identified additional types of information that lead to greater attitude accessibility, including emotion (Fazio & Powell, 1992) and behavior (Fazio, Herr, & Olney, 1984). There is no one-size-fits-all for the type of information that leads to greater accessibility. People are guided by whatever type of information they find more diagnostic. If we search our memories and find our evaluations based on information we can trust, then we are likely to pull those evaluations into consciousness very rapidly—and these are our strong attitudes.

Attitude Strength and Electoral Politics

Fazio and Williams (1986) examined the role played by attitude strength in predicting voting behavior during the U.S. Presidential election of 1984. Incumbent President Ronald Regan was running for re-election against Democratic challenger Walter Mondale. Participants volunteered to be interviewed as part of a political survey. They were asked to respond as quickly as possible to a number of attitude items relevant to the upcoming election. Two critical items asked for their responses on a 5-point rating scale about whether they thought Ronald Reagan or Walter Mondale would make a good president.

The central question was whether the speed of responding to the Mondale/ Reagan question predicted anything beyond what was predicted by the participants' responses to the 5-point rating scale. Responses to two major events provided the answers. A few weeks prior to the election, the candidates appeared in nationally televised debates. Following the second debate, respondents were contacted and asked who had performed better in the debates. Not surprisingly, the results showed that people's ratings of the two candidates were consistent with their perception of who won the debates. People who thought Mondale was the better candidate also thought he performed better than Reagan, while people who supported Reagan found him to be the best debater. People used their attitudes as a filter to process the information they observed in the debates to find evidence for their own candidate's superiority. Moreover, as the investigators predicted, the strength of the attitude made a significant difference as well. People with more accessible attitudes, as measured by short reaction times, were significantly more likely to believe that their candidate won the debate. In an extension of this phenomenon, the investigators also asked respondents who they thought had performed better during the vice-presidential debates between Republican candidate George H.W. Bush and Democratic candidate Geraldine Ferraro. The accessibility of attitudes toward the presidential candidates predicted people's assessment of the vice presidential candidates. The more quickly their attitudes came to mind about the presidential candidates, the more likely they were to perceive the candidate of their preferred party to be the winner of the vice presidential debate.

Of course, the essence of a political campaign is the voting. Participants were contacted two days after the election and were asked for whom they had voted.

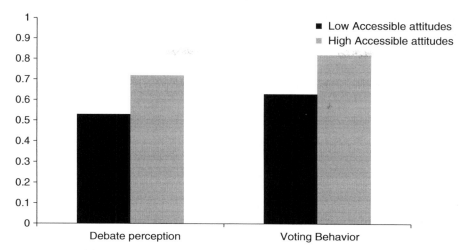

FIGURE 2.3 *Did my candidate win and whom did I vote for? Correlations of attitude accessibility with debate perception and voting behavior.*
Source: Fazio, R. H., & Williams, C. J. (1986). Attitude accessibility as a moderator of the attitude–perception and attitude–behavior relations: An investigation of the 1984 presidential election. *Journal of Personality and Social Psychology*, 51(3), 505. Reprinted with permission.

Attitude accessibility predicted voting behavior: The more rapid the response to the initial questions concerning the two candidates, the more likely people were to actually vote for the candidate of their choice. The relationship of attitude accessibility to the perception of the presidential debates as well as voting behavior is depicted in Figure 2.3.

Bassili (1993; 1995) also studied the impact of response latencies toward a preferred candidate on voters' likelihood of their actually voting for that candidate. He assessed response latencies from large, nationally representative samples in subsequent elections. He found that response latencies in people's responses to questions about their voting intentions were dramatically related to their actual voting behavior. The probability that a potential voter would actually cast a ballot for the person they indicated they were most favorable toward dropped by about 8% for every second of delay it took to respond.

Accessible Attitudes Are Automatically Activated

A hallmark of the attitude accessibility approach is that attitudes are activated from memory *automatically*. According to Fazio (1995), the activation is automatic in that the attitude is activated effortlessly and inescapably. We do not have to consciously and deliberately search our memories to know how we evaluate an object. The stronger the attitude, the more automatic is the response. To demonstrate this,

Fazio, Sanbonmatsu, Powell and Kardes (1986) adapted a priming technique originally used to show automatic activation in cognitive psychology (e.g., Neely, 1977). The presentation of a priming stimulus activates processes that facilitate or inhibit responding. For example, suppose that people are asked to see a string of letters and decide if they form a word or not. To the extent that they have been exposed to a prime such as "bird," then people show greater speed recognizing that the letters *r-o-b-i-n* form a word. Automatically and without conscious thought, the prime facilitates an appropriate response.

Fazio et al. (1986) used this logic to assess the automatic activation of strong attitudes. They reasoned that if people hold a strong positive (or negative) attitude toward an object, then showing people that object would facilitate their speed of identifying a completely different positive (or negative) word. The researchers identified several attitude objects that respondents had evaluated as good or bad and did so quickly (i.e., a strong attitude) or slowly (i.e., a weak attitude). Later, the participants were asked to classify an adjective that was obviously positive or obviously negative. The results showed that holding strong attitudes about the attitude object facilitated responses to adjectives that were similarly valenced. In other words, if people held strong positive attitudes toward an object such as "chocolate," it caused them to respond more quickly to any positive adjective and more slowly to any negative adjective. This is consistent with the idea that the attitude object automatically evoked a valenced evaluation that affected people's subsequent judgment of the valenced adjective. And this occurred without participants intending or trying to evaluate the attitude object.

Attitudes as Contextual Constructions

Some contemporary researchers have questioned the premise that people *have* attitudes at all (Schwarz, 2007; Schwarz & Bohner, 2001; Wilson & Hodges, 1992). No one doubts that people evaluate. The question that has concerned researchers is the degree to which people's attitudes transcend the immediate circumstance in which they are assessed. On one end of the continuum is evidence that people carry with them dispositions to evaluate attitude objects with a certain degree of positivity. Hepler and Albarracín (2013) showed that people's disposition to evaluate objects positively or negatively transcends specific knowledge. Their research suggests that attitudes toward novel objects can be predicted from knowledge of measured dispositional tendencies, which argues that attitudes transcend time and situation. On the other hand, Schwarz (2007) argues that it is more "parsimonious to think of attitudes as evaluative judgments, formed when needed, rather than as enduring personality dispositions" (p.639).

The contextual view of attitudes is that people's evaluations of objects are affected by the attitude object and by a number of other factors present when they think about the attitude object. Attitudes vary with how people construe a particular issue or object (Ramsey, Lord, Wallace, & Pugh, 1994), their mood at the time of assessment (Forgas, 2007; Schwarz & Clore, 1983; 2007) and even their bodily states (Ferguson & Bargh, 2007; Niedenthal, Barsalou, Winkielman, Krauth-Gruber, & Ric, 2005).

In *attitude representation theory*, Lord and Lepper (1999) suggest that people express attitudes toward an object based on a mental representation of an exemplar. Suppose a person were asked about his attitude toward soccer/football. A respondent may generate a mental image of an exciting game at the World Cup and answer that he is a great fan of soccer/football. Later, the same respondent may generate a different example, perhaps one of a dull game in which his team was outscored 7 to nil. Or the same respondent may generate an image based upon a childhood game that he once played and express an entirely different attitude. Attitude representation theory makes the claim that there exists a basic attitude toward an object such as soccer/football, but it will be affected by the particular representation that the person conjures. The more stable or similar the representations that are generated, the more consistent the attitude will be.

In one study based on attitude representation theory, Sia, Lord, Blessum, Thomas and Lepper (1999) asked people about their attitudes toward a series of social categories, including the category 'politicians.' The respondents were asked to name a representative exemplar from each of the categories. A month later, the participants were contacted and asked again about their attitudes toward politicians. Some of the respondents were primed with the name of the original exemplar that they had designated in the first part of the study. In two other conditions, they were primed with a politician whom they liked better—or worse—than the originally named politician. Sia et al. (1999) found that attitudes toward politicians remained stable if the exemplar in the two sessions was the same. Attitudes became more (or less) positive if the exemplar primed in the second session was more (or less) positive than the exemplar used in the first session. In Sia et al.'s view, attitudes combine stability and context, depending on the representation of the exemplar that comes to mind. Lord, Paulson, Sia, Thomas and Lepper (2004) extended this work in a subsequent study. They showed that people who relied on the same representative exemplar of an attitude category (e.g., George Bush as an example of a politician) were less persuaded by a message that attacked their attitudes about politicians than were participants who thought of different exemplars (e.g., George Bush and Angela Merkel) before exposure to a persuasive message.

Gawronski and colleagues (Gawronski, Rydell, Vervliet, & De Houwer, 2010; Gawronski, Ye, Rydell, & De Houwer, 2014) suggest a different approach to the role that social context plays in keeping attitudes stable. According to their model, people form their attitudes within a particular context and those attitudes remain generally stable across time and context. On the other hand, new information in the form of compelling information or different exemplars can create a different evaluation but will not override the existing attitude unless the evaluation is measured in the context in which the new information was received. Consider the following example: Let us say that a student has a generally positive attitude toward professors. Her initial experiences at university were positive, and she found her professors intelligent and kind. However, she learned from a friend that a zoology professor at a different university had confessed to plagiarism. With that professor and that other university in mind, she may express a negative evaluation of professors. Can it be said that she has constructed a new attitude toward professors, or has she evaluated this particular exemplar of the category 'professors'? Gawronski et al. (2014) suggest that the answer to that question rests with the context in which subsequent evaluations are made. Their evidence shows that the student's attitudes toward professors will remain true to her original positive attitude unless the context of the subsequent evaluation reminds the student either perceptually or conceptually of the second professor. To the extent that the student thinks about professors in the context in which she originally formed her positive attitude *or* in a brand new context, her attitude will remain stable, consistent with a dispositional approach to attitudes.

In general, research demonstrates both variability and consistency in people's reported attitudes. From one perspective, stability of attitudes across time and context reflects an attitude's intrinsic strength whereas non-stable attitudes lack the aspects of strength that we have discussed in this chapter. The contrasting point of view is that conceptualizing attitudes as a stable psychological structure lacks parsimony because it must invoke a principle of attitude weakness to explain variability (Schwarz, 2007). Attitude representation theory finds a middle position in the continuum by positing a potentially stable attitude that is occasionally modified by different construals of the attitude object. Stability or instability can be the consequence, not because the attitude is invented freshly for every occasion but because the meaning of the attitude object may change depending on the context in which it is measured (Gawronski et al., 2014) or by the way it is cognitively represented (Lord et al., 2004).

ATTITUDE AMBIVALENCE

If you were to ask someone for her attitude about the Rolling Stones as a music group and she responds with a 4 on a 7-point scale, how should we understand her evaluation? If 1 is negative and 7 is positive, 4 seems neutral. Sometimes, that is the best way to construe the meaning of the score. Our respondent may not be familiar with *Stones'* music or, if she is, it leaves her unenthused. Another possibility exists, however. She may love *the Stones* on many dimensions but dislike them on other dimensions. She may feel passionately that *the Stones* revolutionized music, are fun to listen to and even more fun to see in concert. On the other hand, she may be weary of the old songs and dislike not hearing anything new in concerts. In some ways, she would like to rate *the Stones* with a 6 on the attitude scale but in other ways, she can only muster a 2. When she is asked to place her evaluation on a single 7-point scale, her mental arithmetic arrives at the reasonable number of 4. However, it would be misleading to think she is neutral. To the contrary, she is *ambivalent*.

Many decades ago, researchers studying conflict raised the issue of ambivalence, differentiating it from simple neutrality (Miller, 1944; Mowrer, 1960). Kaplan (1972) was one of the first scholars to suggest a scale for measuring it (see also Thompson, Zanna, & Griffin, 1995). Rather than asking evaluative questions using a single scale that varied between positive and negative, he suggested using two scales—one for the rating of a person's positive evaluation and another for assessing the person's negative evaluation. Kaplan asked respondents, "Considering only the positive qualities of (a particular attitude issue), evaluate how positive its positive qualities are on the following 4-point scale," and asked the identical question about the same attitude issue asking solely about negative qualities. The level of ambivalence was derived from the absolute value of the difference between the two scales.

In order for an attitude to be considered highly ambivalent, the negative and positive evaluations need to be similar. If an attitude has high positive scores and weak negative scores, or vice versa, it is not a highly ambivalent attitude. A second feature of a highly ambivalent attitude is the intensity of the two evaluative scores. Given an attitude about which people have similar positive and negative scores, the ambivalence will be a function of how extreme the scores are. An attitude measure on which people score +4 for its positive evaluation and +4 for its negative evaluation reveals more ambivalence than an attitude whose scores are both +2. Several formula have been advanced for the precise calculation of ambivalence (Larsen, Norris, McGraw, Hawkley, & Cacioppo, 2009; Thompson et al., 1996; Priester & Petty, 1996) but all maintain the essence of ambivalence being a strong and opposite set of reactions to an attitude object. An interesting features of attitudes assessed for their positive and negative evaluations is that, typically, the two evaluations correlate only moderately. Assessing positive evaluations is not simply the inverse of the negative evaluations. Instead, they capture unique experiences of people's reactions to ambivalence.

Ambivalence has a multi-faceted impact on people's attitudes, thoughts and behaviors. Ambivalence in racial attitudes has been shown to increase the extremity of people's reactions to minority group members in both directions, depending on the situational context (Hass, Katz, Rizzo, Bailey, & Eisenstadt, 1991; Katz & Hass, 1988). Ambivalence has also been associated with increases in message processing (Clark, Wegener, & Fabrigar, 2008; Maio, Bell, & Esses, 1996) but generally weakens attitude strength. For example, Conner, Sparks, Povey, James, Shepherd and Armitage (2000) found that ambivalence weakened the relationship of attitudes to behavior. They found that the more ambivalent people were about their attitudes toward losing weight, the weaker the relationship between their attitudes and action designed to lose weight. Jonas, Broemer and Diehl (2000) discovered that attitudes high in ambivalence were less stable over time and more susceptible to influence.

Ambivalence has subtle effects on the information people seek. In general, research has shown that people engage in *selective exposure*—that is, we seek information consistent with our attitudes and avoid information that is inconsistent (Festinger, 1957; Fischer, Jonas, Frey, & Schulz-Hardt, 2005; Smith, Fabrigar, & Norris, 2008). Moreover, the strength of our attitudes is related to our tendency to engage in selective exposure such that stronger attitudes predict greater selective exposure effects (Brannon, Tagler, & Eagly, 2007). When our attitudes are ambivalent, strength is lower but, as with other aspects of attitude ambivalence, the effects on selective exposure are more intriguing. People with unambivalent—and therefore stronger—attitudes are more likely to seek information consistent with their overall evaluation, but only if they are familiar with the information or knowledgeable about the issue. If the information is novel or if people are relatively unfamiliar with the issue, then those with ambivalent attitudes are the ones more likely to seek information (Sawicki, Wegener, Clark, Fabrigar, Smith, & Durso, 2013).

The Experience of Ambivalence

When people hold attitudes that are both negative and positive, we can expect that the resulting experience will be psychologically unpleasant, especially when they are aware of the ambivalence (van Harreveld, van der Pligt, & de Liver, 2014). Earlier, we considered a woman whose attitude toward music made her feel ambivalent toward *the Stones*. When she considers her evaluation of *the Stones*, we can expect that the conflicting negative and positive evaluations will leave her in an unpleasant psychological state. Indeed, researchers have found that when people's measured attitudes on a Kaplan-like scale show a high degree of ambivalence, they feel subjectively uncomfortable (Priester & Petty, 1996; Thompson et al., 1996). Surprisingly, though, the correspondence between measured ambivalence and psychological discomfort (i.e., *subjective* ambivalence) is only moderate, with correlations of approximately r=.40.

The subjective experience of ambivalence increases when people hold ambivalent attitudes but believe that they *should* hold an unambivalent attitude for or against the attitude object (DeMarree, Wheeler, Briñol, & Petty, 2014). The person who is ambivalent about *the Stones* may feel more of the subjective state of ambivalence when she considers her attitude about a Maserati automobile. As someone who has very positive attitudes about the environment, she feels she should dislike any automobile that is not gasoline efficient. Yet, she also knows that she likes the speed and power of the Maserati. The results of research by DeMarree et al. (2014)

suggest that this person will feel more of the subjective experience of ambivalence as she considers her attitude toward the automobile than she will about music groups. Even if the objective measurement of ambivalence is the same for both attitude objects, the feeling that she *should* hold a particular attitude characterizes her evaluation of the Maserati and will lead to greater subjective ambivalence.

Subjective ambivalence is also increased when the two evaluations of the attitude object are accessible at the same time (Newby-Clark, McGregor, & Zanna, 2002). As we saw previously when discussing contextual and dispositional attitudes, different contexts can sometimes lead to different evaluations of objects. This can be true about ambivalent attitudes as well. Someone may be ambivalent about the topic of abortion and score high on a scale of objective ambivalence. However, when the person thinks about the issue of abortion, he may sometimes think of the reasons he opposes abortion and at other times think of the reasons he supports a woman's right to choose. That is, one of the two poles of his ambivalent attitude may be more accessible at one time while the other pole is more accessible at other times. In a series of studies measuring and manipulating the accessibility of both sides of the abortion issue, Newby-Clark et al. (2002) found that the more that the two sides of the issues were simultaneously accessible, the more objective ambivalence translated to the unpleasant feeling state of subjective ambivalence.

Van Harreveld et al. (2014) suggest that people who hold ambivalent attitudes toward an object would prefer to be able to "sit on the fence." The contradictory aspects of their evaluations would lead them to behave in very different ways if they had to make a choice. Sitting on the fence may not be entirely comfortable, but it allows people to avoid the contradictory behavioral implications of their actions. If they know that they will have to climb off the metaphorical fence, then felt or subjective ambivalence—experienced as unpleasant discomfort—is high. In one research example, de Liver (2007) established ambivalent attitudes by giving participants evaluatively incongruent information about a job candidate. Half of the participants thought they would have to make a decision about whether to hire the applicant while the other half only had to evaluate the candidate's writing skills. The group that had to act on their ambivalent attitude reported greater tension and subjective ambivalence than the group that did not expect to make a choice. Subsequent research using skin conductance as a measure of physiological arousal found greater arousal when people had to act on their ambivalent attitudes rather than merely hold them (van Harreveld, Rutjens, Rotteveel, Nordgren, & van der Pligt, 2009).

Attitudes Can Distort Memory

Attitudes affect what we remember and recall. A person who is almost always favorable to the Liberal Party in her country may find it difficult to remember any occasions when she voted for the Social Democrats, even though she may have done so on a small number of occasions. Her attitudes serve to direct her memory about her past history so that she remembers her past selectively. It may be that her selective recall serves to maintain a consistency between her attitudes and her behavior (as she recalls it, at least). We shall see in several of the ensuing chapters in this text that people are motivated to see their attitudes and behavior as consistent. In addition, her attitudes may guide her recollection so as to provide further support to bolster and strengthen her pro-Liberal attitude.

McDonald and Hirt (1997) led participants to form a positive or negative attitude about a fictitious fellow student, "JW." The participants were shown JW's grades from his midterm exams as part of a larger folder of information. They were also led to believe that there was a good chance that JW would either improve his academic performance during the year or, in another condition, that his grades would begin to slide. After a delay, participants were asked to recall JW's grades. Participants who had a positive attitude toward JW misremembered his midterm grades such that it made improvement most likely, whereas participants with a negative attitude distorted JW's grades in the opposite direction.

Other investigators looked at the effect of attitudes on memory by first persuading people to change their existing attitudes by means of a persuasive communication (Lydon, Zanna, & Ross, 1988; Ross, McFarland, & Fletcher, 1981; Sherman & Kunda, 1989). They then examined whether people distort their recollections of their own past behavior to strengthen and support their changed attitudes. For example, Ross et al. (1981) worked with an attitude issue that most people strongly support—the act of brushing one's teeth after every meal. However, Ross et al. had some participants read a persuasive message that argued against that practice. The message noted that brushing with abrasive toothpaste causes erosion of the enamel, which in turn may lead to infection and ultimate tooth loss. Other participants read a message supporting the practice of frequent tooth brushing. All participants were asked to reach into their own recent history and recall the number of times that they had brushed their teeth during the prior two weeks. Participants exposed to the anti-tooth brushing message became less favorable to tooth brushing and recalled fewer occasions at the sink (about 28 tooth brushing occasions) than those who had read the pro-tooth brushing message (recalling 36 occasions of tooth brushing). Similarly, Sherman and Kunda (1989) reported that people who were convinced to hold highly positive or negative attitudes about the value of caffeine recalled their own caffeine consumption as consistent with their newly changed attitudes. Lydon, Zanna and Ross (1989) found that people recalled fewer occasions of engaging in strenuous physical exercise after being persuaded that strenuous exercise was not good.

Politics, Elections and Memory
Thus far, we have seen that attitudes affect people's autobiographical memory and their memory for information about the performance of others. Young, Ratner and

Fazio (2014) proposed that people's political attitudes can influence their perceptual memory in ways that support and strengthen their political evaluations (see also Caruso, Mead, & Balcetis, 2009). The U.S. presidential election of 2012 was fought largely in just a few battleground states, including the state of Ohio. Campaigning for votes, the Democratic and Republican parties and their supporters saturated the

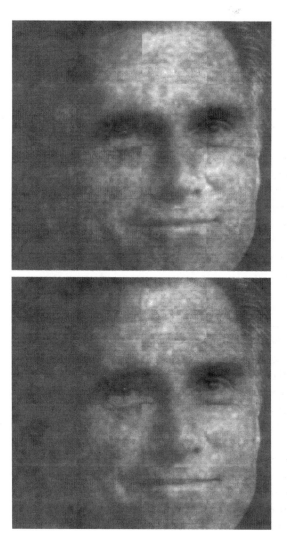

FIGURE 2.4 *Image of Mitt Romney generated by participants who identified as Democrat (above) and Republican (below).*

Source: Young, A. I., Ratner, K. G., & Fazio, R. H. (2014). Political attitudes bias the mental representation of a presidential candidate's face. *Psychological Science*, *25*(2), 503–510. Reprinted with permission.

media with advertisements, usually depicting the images of the candidates. Young et al. (2014) speculated that the visual images of the candidates that voters store in memory might differ subtly depending on the perceivers' attitudes. Focusing on Governor Romney, Young et al. (2014) had participants examine two images of Romney's face that differed, ever so slightly, by the noise pattern across the faces (see Dotsch, Wigboldus, Langner, & van Knippenberg, 2008; Todorov, Dotsch, Wigboldus & Said, 2011, for a more detailed description of this method). Their task was to decide which image was a truer representation of Romney's real face. After 450 trials, the chosen photographs were combined into a final image representing the participant's memory of what Mitt Romney looked like.

Republicans' (pro-Romney) and Democrats' (anti-Romney) visual representations are shown above in Figure 2.4. They have considerable overlap, such that any U.S. voter in 2012 would recognize either picture as Mitt Romney. But they are not the identical and the differences are informative. When a separate group of participants were asked to rate the two photographs on a number of trait dimensions, the image generated by Republicans was rated as more *trustworthy* than the Romney image that had been generated by Democrats. Apparently, those with a pro-Romney attitude remembered a face that did indeed seem more trustworthy than the image generated by those who were against Romney. The visual memory of his face strengthened Democrats' attitude about Romney by visualizing him as an untrustworthy person, while Republicans' visual representation supported their pro-Romney attitude.

THE COMPONENT STRUCTURE OF ATTITUDES: THE RELATIONSHIP AMONG ELEMENTS

Consistency among Attitude Components

When we use the term **attitude structure**, we are referring to the *relationships among the attitude's internal components*. As we have stressed, attitudes are overall evaluations of a stimulus object and, as depicted in Figure 2.5, those evaluations are based on people's beliefs, behavior and feelings. In order to form an evaluation, people may combine the various factors in different ways. Some people may find that they emphasize one attitude component over others when forming their attitude about a particular object, while others may find that that they combine factors relatively equally. Some people may find that the components of their attitudes all point in the same direction, while others may find that the components pull in opposite directions. Attitudes may appear similar in direction and intensity but be quite different in their structure—that is, in the way in which the component features combine. Attitude structure has a profound influence on attitude strength because the more consistent the components, then the more durable, stable and resistant

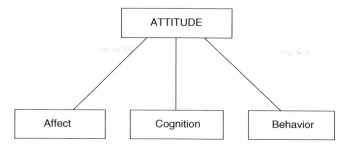

FIGURE 2.5 *The component structure of an attitude.*

the attitude is to persuasion (Bargh, Chaiken, Govender, & Pratto, 1992; Chaiken, Pomerantz, & Giner-Sorolla, 1995; Eagly & Chaiken, 1995; Petty et al., 2003).

Let us consider two hypothetical voters, William and Robert, who are trying to evaluate candidates for political office. William may analyze the situation like this: He knows that he agrees with the Independent Party's candidate on a number of relevant issues and feels good when he hears the candidate's soaring rhetoric, recalling he voted for this candidate in a prior election. William's overall evaluation—i.e., his attitude toward the candidate—is positive and is based on a number of components, which, in this particular case, are consistent.

By comparison, consider Robert's analysis. He may also have voted for the Independent Party's candidate in the past, may also believe in what the candidate believes, but the candidate's rhetoric or appearance just make this person feel uncomfortable. In his final evaluation, Robert may or may not be as positive as William toward the candidate. The overall evaluation would depend on the way the two voters weight the different aspects of their evaluation. If Robert, who has some negative affective reactions to the candidate, combines the behavioral, belief and affect components in a linear, arithmetic fashion, his attitude will be less positive than William's. He will be favorable toward the candidate based on beliefs and past behavior, but that evaluation would be diminished by his negative affect. However, Robert may combine elements in a very different way. He may decide that when it comes to forming an evaluation of a political candidate, it is the cognitive (i.e., belief) component that is most important. Robert may reason that a candidate who believes in what Robert believes is the candidate most worthy of support. His attitude toward the candidate may be just as positive toward the candidate as William's, even though there is inconsistency among the elements within his attitude.

Eagly and Chaiken (1998) suggest that the strength of an attitude is a function of its **intra-attitudinal consistency**. Intra-attitudinal consistency is best assessed by examining the relationship of each component with the overall evaluation of the attitude object. In the case of our two voters, William and Robert held the same overall evaluation of a particular candidate but, unlike William, Robert experienced inconsistency. For Robert, his overall evaluation was consistent with his cognitive belief system, which Eagly and Chaiken would refer to as a high level of *evaluative-cognitive consistency*. Similarly, his *evaluative-behavioral consistency* is high. However, his *evaluative-affective consistency* is low. Inconsistency creates a relatively weak attitude. Robert knows which candidate he favors. He is not ambivalent, vacillating between supporting his candidate or the opponent. However, research suggests that Robert's attitude will be less strong than William's, by which we mean that it is more susceptible to persuasion, takes more time to come to mind (i.e., is less accessible) and is less likely to endure.

Affect and Cognition

Empirical research has supported the notion that the strength of an attitude is related to the consistency of its affective and cognitive components. If the components are inconsistent with the overall evaluation, attitudes are weak and unstable (Chaiken, Pomerantz, & Giner-Sorolla, 1995). Some studies have focused specifically on the link between affect and evaluation (Abelson et al, 1982; Lavine, Thomsen, Zanna, & Borgida, 1998; Rosenberg, 1968; Stark, Borgida, Kim, & Pickens, 2008). Stark et al. (2008) for example, examined attitudes toward harm reduction in public health anti-smoking campaigns and found that the degree of affective-evaluative consistency was the best predictor of strong anti-smoking attitudes. Lavine et al. (1998) examined United States national opinion polls from the elections of 1980, 1984, 1988 and 1992. In each case, they found that affective-evaluative consistency was the best predictor of overall candidate evaluations and voting behavior.

Others have found evidence linking evaluative-cognitive consistency to attitude strength (Eagly, Mladinic, & Otto, 1994; Norman, 1975). Huskinson and Haddock (2006) reported evidence for both types of structural consistency. They created a measure of individual differences in people's tendency to have attitudes that are consistent with their affective and/or cognitive components. They then assessed the accessibility of people's attitudes toward a new set of stimuli (various countries such as Indonesia, France and Italy). They found that people who were chronically high in both evaluative-affective *and* evaluative-cognitive consistency (people referred to as dual consistents) had more accessible—and therefore, stronger—attitudes toward the novel stimuli than dual inconsistents, i.e., people low in both types of consistency.

People tend to protect their attitudes from attack differently if their summary evaluations are more a function of affect than cognition (Petty et al., 2003). People whose attitudes are based on cognitions tend to remember attitude inconsistent information better than attitude consistent information, whereas people whose attitudes are more consistent with their affect tend to remember attitude consistent information (Chaiken et al., 1995). When attitudes are based on cognition, people resist attack by processing and refuting the information that could be used to oppose their evaluations. On the other hand, when attitudes are based on affect, people avoid counterattitudinal information, choosing to buttress their attitudes with consistent information.

How Does Affect Influence Attitudes?

We probably know more about how people are persuaded by cognitions or belief than we do about how people are persuaded by affect (Petty, Fabrigar, & Wegener, 2003). One possibility for the difference is that there is a direct effect of emotions on attitudes. That is, when an object makes us feel a positive emotion, the emotion leads to a positive attitude. A more subtle possibility is that we avoid basing our attitudes on our positive or negative emotions but use our emotions to guide a search for cognitions. Finding the appropriate cognitions would allow us to have a positive attitude in the case of a positive emotion and a negative attitude in the case of a negative emotion. Recent research shows support for the both the direct and indirect influence of affect on our attitudes. Bodur, Brinberg and Coupey (2000) assessed people's emotional responses and their beliefs about HIV and AIDS. They found that attitudes about HIV/AIDS were directly related to their emotions. However, additional predictive power was produced by considering the indirect route—i.e., the impact of people's emotions on their cognitions and then on their attitudes. Emotions influenced people's specific beliefs about the efficacy of AIDS prevention behaviors, such as the use of condoms and sexual abstinence. Those beliefs, in turn, influenced people's overall attitudes toward HIV/AIDS.

Learning new attitudes. In most cases, we develop attitudes through a combination of beliefs and emotions. It is reasonably apparent how we might have come to develop attitudes that are based on cognition. If you are interested in purchasing a car, for example, you might research a number of different cognitive elements associated with a particular car. You might check its price, its fuel economy, its acceleration and its handling. Having a belief about each of these items and knowing how you evaluate each the items, you can form an overall attitude about the car. In this case, emotion has little to do with the final attitude. It is a matter of assembling and evaluating the relevant cognitive elements. It may be less apparent how a person forms an attitude from emotion, with little impact by belief.

One way in which people may form attitudes based primarily on affect is through association with a stimulus that is emotionally pleasant or unpleasant. One well known technique, which pairs a neutral stimulus with one that has emotional valence, is classical conditioning (Pavlov, 1927). Although it is typically studied with infrahuman models, it has also been used to create attitudes toward a variety of issues in humans, such as nationalities (Staats & Staats, 1958). Zanna, Kiesler and Pilkonis (1970) paired attitude objects with turning on or turning off an electric shock (negative and positive emotions, respectively) and found that people's overall evaluation of the formally neutral words was affected by their experience.

Kim, Lim and Bhargava (1998) used a classical conditioning approach to create attitudes toward a fictitious business establishment—L Pizza House. They paired L Pizza with a picture of an exceptionally cute kitten. Pretesting had shown that participants felt positive emotions toward the kitten but that the kitten was completely unrelated to any beliefs about pizza. The results of the experiment showed that the pairing of L Pizza with the picture of the kitten created positive attitudes toward L Pizza without affecting any beliefs about the brand. When asked to rate whether they thought L Pizza was tastier, delivered more quickly, or had better toppings, participants did not believe that L Pizza was better in any way. They just had more positive attitudes toward the product.

In Chapter 9, we will consider the burgeoning field of research known as evaluative conditioning (de Houwer, Thomas and Baeyens, 2001; Gawronski & Bodenhausen, 2006). Like classical conditioning, evaluative conditioning stresses the juxtaposition of an attitude object with an emotional stimulus and has generated considerable interest in the formation and change of attitudes.

Subjective Assessments of Cognitions and Emotions

In many areas of psychological life, what we believe we do is not isomorphic with what we really do. Someone might think she is generous but actually gives very little to charity. Another might believe she behaves shyly in social situations but is actually outgoing and gregarious. See, Petty and Fabrigar (2008; 2013) suggested that there may also be a distinction between what people believe they do and what they actually do when it comes to whether their beliefs or their cognitions are the basis of their attitudes. Some people feel that their attitudes are based on their emotions, although there may be very little evidence for it. Others may feel that their attitudes are based on their beliefs but objective measures may not confirm that. See et al. differentiated what they described as people's *metas*—that is, their beliefs about the bases of their attitudes and the structural bases of their attitudes—as assessed by objective methods.

In their initial study, See et al. (2008) told participants that they were assessing how people make decisions. They measured the structural prosperities of a series of attitudes by asking objective questions about their thoughts and emotions. They also asked participants the *meta* question: i.e., asked them to speculate on whether their attitude toward a topic was based on emotion or beliefs. They then gave participants paragraphs that they could choose to read about the attitude topic. One of the paragraphs emphasized cognitive information while the other addressed affective bases. See et al. found that people who had affective *metas*—that is, who believed that their attitudes were primarily affective, spent more time reading affective information than cognitive information. The reverse was true of people with cognitive *metas*. They spent more time reading the belief based paragraph.

Moreover, the actual structural basis of attitudes did not predict reading time and was not correlated with the *meta* basis. In subsequent research, See et al. (2013) demonstrated that the structural and *meta* bases of attitudes led to different cognitive activities. They found that people whose *meta* bases were affective spent more time and had more interest in reading affective material but that people whose actual, measured structural bases were affective were quicker (i.e., spent less time) reading the affective material. They surmised that people use their structural bases for efficiency of processing information, but use their *meta* bases as an expression of their interest.

Although most of the empirical work on attitude components has focused on beliefs and affect, there is ample evidence that the consistency of behavior with evaluation is also an important component. Much of this work has come from research on factors that influence attitudes to change and thus are not often addressed in discussions of attitude components. Considerable research has shown that people are strongly motivated to ensure consistency between their evaluations of an attitude object and their behavior toward that object. We will address this research more completely in Chapters 6 and 7, when we examine the relationship between behavior and attitudes. From research conducted under the rubric of cognitive dissonance theory (Festinger, 1957), we know that people who are induced to act inconsistently with their overall evaluation of an attitude object will act to restore consistency. Most often, evaluations will change to accommodate the behavior. Sometimes, the behavior can be modified to restore consistency with the evaluation (Stone, Aronson, Cain, Winslow, & Fried, 1994). In either case, people prefer behavioral-evaluative consistency to inconsistency (see Cooper, 2007, for a review.) Further support for the importance of structural consistency that includes behavior comes from data that show that people tend to reconstruct their memory of past behaviors to ensure greater evaluative-behavioral consistency (Ross, 1988) and recruit memories of past behaviors that are consistent with a newly formed attitude in order to strengthen that attitude's stability over time (Lydon, Zanna, & Ross, 1988).

Models of Attitude Structure

Fishbein's Expectancy-Value Model: A Cognitive Approach
Social psychologists have constructed a number of models to express the dynamic relationship between the attitude and its components. The models address the degree to which attitudes can be predicted from knowledge of the components and whether changes in components can predictably affect changes in overall attitudes. One of the most influential views is the expectancy-value model of attitudes (Fishbein, 1967). This model holds that the attitude is a linear combination of beliefs, values and the expected probability that the attitude object actually has that value. For example, consider that you are asked about your attitude toward electric

automobiles. You can think about the many attributes of the all-electric. For example, the electric car uses no gasoline. Is this good or bad? Good, you think. Next, you think that electric cars are small. Is this good or bad? Bad, you think. Then you think that electric cars are slow. Is this good or bad? Bad, you think. Electric cars will reduce your country's involvement in the affairs of Middle Eastern countries. This, you think, is very good.

Fishbein (1967) proposed that an attitude toward a particular object can be predicted from the sum of its component parts. In this illustration, the electric car is the attitude object. One of your beliefs about the car is that it uses no gasoline. Your evaluation of using no gasoline is that it is a good thing. If this were the only aspect of your belief about the electric car, expectancy value theory would simply multiply your belief that it uses no gasoline by your evaluation of that component's value and predict that you would be very positive toward the electric car. As we proposed in the illustration, however, the thought that the car uses no gasoline is not your only thought about the electric car. Each of the other components also has a value, some of which are positive and some of which are negative. Moreover, you may not be fully certain that the electric car actually has the attribute in question. Did you not hear somewhere that there is also a small gasoline engine in the car?

The expectancy-value model of attitudes is based on the combination of the belief and evaluation in the following way: $A_0 = \text{sum } b_i (e_i)$. In the equation, A_0 is the attitude toward the object, which will be calculated by adding every belief the person has about the object (b_i) expressed as the subjective probability that the attitude object really possesses attribute 1 multiplied by the evaluation (e_i) of that attribute. Fishbein proposed that summing the beliefs multiplied by their associated evaluations produces an overall evaluation that approximates people's overall attitude toward the attitude object.

Note two features of the expectancy value model. First, it is almost exclusively based upon one element of attitude structure—namely, cognition. It is calculated as the beliefs about the attitude object, each belief weighted by its value. The term value in this model is an evaluation of the particular attribute so we may say that the A_0 is an attitude that itself was formed by relationship to other attitudes. Second, the cognition or belief about the attributes of A_0 does not need to be accurate. The person merely needs to believe they are accurate with a certain probability for it to be relevant in forming the overall attitude.

Affect and Beliefs in Expectancy-Value Models

Rosenberg (1960) proposed an expectancy-value model that focused on the importance of the affect component. He proposed that an attitude is comprised of a belief about the likely consequence of an attitude object and the degree of affect expected from those consequences. Suppose you are asked about your attitude toward publicly supported pre-schools for the disadvantaged. You have a belief that increasing the number of people receiving an early education will lead to greater diversity in the middle class. How does that make you feel? What affect does that generate? Let us suppose that generates positive affect. You also believe that spending money on a system of pre-school education will increase the national debt. This generates negative affect. Rosenberg (1960) proposed that an attitude is a combination of the probability that each of your beliefs is true, multiplied by the intensity and direction of the affect. In the preceding example, if I am pretty certain about my diversity belief (say 8 on a 1–10 scale) and my affective response to that consequence is intense (say +9 on a scale of–10 to +10), then the contribution to my attitude can be expressed as a score. Similarly, my negative affect toward increasing the national debt is –5 and my belief that a system of pre-school education will actually lead to greater debt is +5. On the basis of these two beliefs and associated affect, I can give myself an attitude score of +47 (+72 for the first affect/belief combination and –25 for the second). What this tells us is that we can expect my overall evaluation of a pre-school education system for the economically disadvantages will be relatively positive.

Rosenberg (1956) asked participants to rate a series of consequences for a number of attitude objects, one of which was people's support for allowing free speech to Communist speakers (a controversial issue at the time). Participants were asked how likely it was for free speech for Communists to lead to the overthrow of democracy, how likely it was for free speech to strengthen civil liberties and so forth. After providing a probability rating for each of those cognitive beliefs, the participants indicated their affect toward those consequences. On a separate task, participants were asked to provide their overall evaluation score of the attitude object—that is, they were asked for their attitude toward the same attitude issues for which they had provided the belief and affect scores. Rosenberg found that overall attitudes were well predicted by consideration of its structure. The multiplication of the probability of the consequence and the affect associated with it correlated with the attitude scores of the many attitude objects that the participants rated.

Horizontal and Vertical Structures: The Syllogistic Model of Attitudes

Jones and Gerard (1967) proposed a more elaborate system for the structure of attitudes, which also uses a combination of beliefs and values to understand the composition of attitudes. They conceived of an attitude as a logical syllogism in which attitudes are deduced by the rules of inference. Students who are familiar with inference rules from philosophy and logic will be familiar with the concept of the syllogism, which prescribes a logical way that we deduce conclusions. The Merriam-Webster Dictionary defines the syllogism as a deductive scheme consisting of a major and a minor premise and conclusion, as in "every virtue is laudable; kindness is a virtue; therefore, kindness is laudable."

The syllogistic model begins with a belief about an attitude object or issue. To adapt one of Jones and Gerard's examples, consider Mrs. Brown's attitude toward her town adding fluoride to its drinking water. She believes that fluoride improves children's teeth. This is a belief about the relationship of fluoride to tooth decay, based on what she has read or heard. Mrs. Brown will now combine her belief with the value she places on saving children's teeth. Assuming she feels joyful about improving children's teeth, she will deduce her attitude toward her town's putting fluoride in the drinking water is quite favorable.

Major Premise: Fluoride fights tooth decay in children's teeth

Minor Premise: Fighting tooth decay is good

Attitude Conclusion: Therefore, fluoride in drinking water is good

The Vertical Structure of an Attitude

In most cases, an attitude toward an object consists of more than one syllogism. Why does Mrs. Brown put a positive value on fighting tooth decay? That value is the outcome of a prior syllogism, perhaps like the following:

Major Premise: Children suffer great discomfort from tooth decay

Minor Premise: Children's suffering is bad

Attitude Conclusion: Therefore, fighting tooth decay is good

The minor premise in the first syllogism (fighting tooth decay is good) is a result of the prior syllogism, whose attitudinal conclusion provided the value statement for the syllogistic reasoning that led to the evaluation that fluoride is good.

The attitude about fluoride can lead to other attitudes downstream. Suppose Councilman Fox is running for re-election to the town council and Mrs. Brown needs to consider her attitude toward the councilman. She knows that Councilman Fox opposes having the government add fluoride to the drinking water. Mrs. Brown will combine her knowledge that Councilman Fox opposes fluoride (her major premise) with her value that opposing fluoride is bad (her minor premise) and draw the attitudinal conclusion that Councilman Fox is bad. As Figure 2.6 depicts, the minor premise (i.e., the value statement) of the syllogism had its roots in a prior

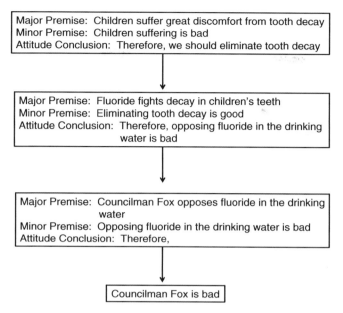

FIGURE 2.6 *An example of a vertical syllogism leading to an attitude toward Councilman Fox.*

syllogism. The greater the number of syllogisms that are used to generate an attitude, the larger is the attitude's *vertical structure*.

The vertical structure of an attitude constitutes an extended set of reasoning, conducted either consciously or non-consciously. A deep vertical structure of an attitude does not make an attitude stronger. Indeed, if a person's attitude is a function of many syllogisms, such that each is a function of the syllogism that precedes it, then the attitude is subject to attack. Convincing someone that their premise about fluoride being conducive to healthy teeth is wrong means the entire chain of reasoning that culminated in the negative attitude toward Councilman Fox crumbles with it. Like the proverbial 'house of cards', when any element in a vertical structure is removed from the chain of reasoning, the house—impressive as it may have been in its construction—will fall.

The Horizontal Structure of an Attitude

Attitudes gain their strength from their *horizontal structure*. The horizontal structure refers to the number of independent syllogisms that lead to the same conclusion. Let us examine our attitude toward Councilman Fox again by examining the horizontal structure depicted in Figure 2.7.

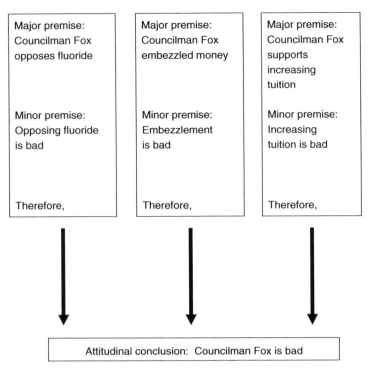

FIGURE 2.7 *An example of a horizontal syllogism leading to an attitude toward Councilman Fox.*

This time, the vertical structure is reinforced by a significant horizontal structure. In addition to our negative evaluation of Fox being based on his stance toward fluoride, there are several other issues he supports. Each of those syllogisms leads to Mrs. Brown's having a negative attitude toward him, but none of the syllogisms relies on the others. If she is wrong about fluoride, she still maintains her negative attitude because of his embezzlement crimes and his support for raising tuition rates at the state university.

In general, Jones and Gerard's view of attitude structure presents a picture of the components of an attitude that rely on a belief about the attitude object and the value placed on an attribute to which it is connected. This combination provides a glimpse at how attitudes develop, as well as the structure that holds them in place. Attitudes with broad horizontal structure are most likely stronger than attitudes that only possess vertical structures. They may be more accessible because they are connected to more stimuli that bring the attitude to mind, and they are more resistant to attack because of the number of routes that lead to the same conclusion.

Conclusion

In this chapter, we noted that all attitudes are not the same. Although people's attitudes are reflected by the measurement of how they categorize a stimulus object along an evaluative dimension, attitudes differ in their strength and their structure. Interest in structural components of attitudes precedes more recent interest in strength. Nonetheless, analyses of how the components of an attitude fit together not only predict subsequent and related attitudes, but also predict outcomes that have considerable bearing on the more recent interest in attitude strength.

The strength of an attitude is defined by its durability, which includes its stability over time and its resistance to persuasion. It is also defined by its pervasiveness, which includes its impact on behavior and other mental processes. Strong attitudes are related to the extremity of a person's positions but they are not isomorphic with extremity. Strong attitudes at any level of extremity, though, tend to be derived from direct experience with an attitude object and are related to the attitude's accessibility, importance and certainty. Ambivalent attitudes tend to be less strong than unambivalent attitudes. In addition, attitudes in which people have a hedonic vested interest tend to be strong as are those in which people have invested a good deal of effortful thought. These determinants of attitude strength have important downstream consequences: research has shown that strong attitudes resist counter-persuasion, influence our thoughts and behaviors and do so over a long period of time. Research on attitude strength, furthermore, has near-ubiquitous application to other areas of attitudes research, including persuasion and the attitude-behavior relationship, as we will see in subsequent chapters of this book.

CHAPTER 3

The Functions of Attitudes

We noted in the beginning of this volume that people have myriad attitudes that help them evaluate the world around them. We have addressed the question of how attitudes are assessed and how they are structured. We now turn to a fundamental question that lies beneath the surface of any analysis of attitudes: Why? Why do attitudes form and what purpose do they serve? When we ask these questions, we address the fundamental issue of **attitude function**.

Most of our characteristics can be attached to a purpose that they serve. Our hearts pump oxygenated blood through our body, which is a good thing considering that our cells need the oxygen to remain alive. The hair on our head helps to insulate us from the rays of the sun and protect us from the cold. Our mental apparatus is also attached to important purposes. For example, it is useful that we are attracted to certain foods because their nutritional value allows us to function through life. Occasionally, this purpose is belied by our becoming overly interested in foods with too high caloric content but, by and large, our psychological experience of taste and our ability to survive are intertwined.

Attitudes are psychological constructs that enable us to evaluate the objects in our environment. We know those evaluations are important to help us choose everything from our preferred breakfast cereal to our preferred presidential candidate. We know that there are systematic ways to influence those attitudes, and we shall be spending considerable time on various theoretical models that allow us to understand how that change comes about. In the current chapter, we shall consider this fundamental question of why we evaluate, that is, why we have attitudes, by considering the functions that they serve.

THE FIVE (PLUS OR MINUS) FUNCTIONS OF ATTITUDES

Smith, Bruner and White (1956) were among the first to address the question of why people have attitudes or opinions. They concluded that the function of an attitude is to aid us in fulfilling a fundamental set of motivations. They specified three major functions that they termed object appraisal, social adjustment and externalization. Katz (1960) expanded the analysis of attitude functions by considering four functions—the utilitarian, ego-defensive, value-expressive and knowledge functions. As Katz and others (e.g., Fazio, 2000; Herek, 1987; Smith et al., 1956; Watt, Maio, Haddock, & Johnson, 2008) have argued, understanding a person's attitude, influencing his/her attitude to change and/or predicting whether the attitude will be relevant to a person's behavior must be based on an analysis of the function that the attitude serves and the motivation that it fulfills.

How many functions do attitudes serve? Answering that question is a matter of how broadly or narrowly one wishes to construe a motivation. There is nothing sacrosanct about specifying a particular number of functions. If an attitude can fulfill a need or resolve a motivation, then we can see its function in terms of that motivation or need. In general, however, psychologists have focused on a small number of concepts drawn from Katz's and Smith et al.'s conceptions. Because there is considerable overlap in those conceptions, we will organize our discussion around what we consider five basic functions—the four proposed by Katz and the social-adjustive function proposed by Smith, Bruner and White.

THE UTILITARIAN FUNCTION OF ATTITUDES

One of the bedrock assumptions that is generally recognized as underlying people's behaviors is the striving to maximize rewards and minimize punishments. Sometimes put in terms of pleasure and pain, or gains and losses, this assumption is generally consistent with the fundamentals of most theoretical approaches in psychology. We know that there are exceptions to the rule and we can argue about whether the soldier who puts him/herself in harm's way in a Middle Eastern conflict is an exception or whether the personal rewards of helping his/her country outweigh the potential costs of getting shot. For the most part, however, we are not surprised when we hear that people would choose higher pay rather than less pay for a day's work or to suffer less discomfort rather than more discomfort while traveling home from work on a commuter railway.

We learn to approach objects that have **utilitarian** or instrumental value to us. So, too, do we learn to evaluate such objects more highly than objects of lesser value or objects that bring us greater pain. For most people, chocolate brings pleasure and people have positive attitudes toward it. Whether you measure people's evaluation of chocolate by an attitude scale, or by an implicit association test or by the speed with which they approach it at the candy counter, the chocolate-loving community will express markedly positive attitudes toward this product. The opposite is probably true for a bottle filled with vinegar. For most people, the thought of a soft drink with vinegar as its base will evoke attitudes that are demonstrably negative.

Most attitudes take on their utilitarian meaning in a less direct way. For example, a woman may like a political candidate because the candidate is in favor of granting more protection for labor unions. The woman in this illustration is a steel worker from Scranton, PA. She has a favorable attitude toward unions because of their utilitarian value in protecting her job and her income. Her attitude toward the candidate is at least partially determined by the candidate's stance about unions. On the other hand, the manager of the steel plant may feel quite differently. Using the same utilitarian process, she draws the opposite conclusion. Her utilitarian interests may be ill-served by this candidate, and she forms a negative attitude. A store-owner in Scranton who wishes the company and the workers well but who has no personal stake in union-management issues is likely to form an attitude toward the candidate based on completely different considerations, because the candidate's attitude about unions has no utilitarian value for the store-owner.

Reinforcement and the Utilitarian Function

The utilitarian function of attitudes is closely related to the concept of reinforcement in most views of behavioral conditioning. If an attitude toward an object is reinforced by the social environment, then that attitude is likely to strengthen. It may become more extreme, more entrenched and more difficult to change. In a classic study examining the role of reinforcement on people's attitudes, Insko (1965) sought to associate attitudes with positive feedback from others. Specifically, Insko had interviewers phone undergraduates at the University of Hawaii, asking them about their opinions toward the value of adding a Springtime Aloha Week to the existing Fall Aloha Week held annually on the islands. The interviewers asked several questions regarding the festival week and, for half of the respondents, followed every positive statement about Aloha Week with the word "good." For the other half of the participants, the interviewers used the word "good" as a response for every negative statement about Aloha Week. Attitudes were assessed by a questionnaire approximately one week later. Insko (1965) found that students who had been verbally rewarded for their statements in favor of the attitude object (Aloha Week) held significantly more positive attitudes toward creating the Springtime Aloha Week than students who were rewarded following negative statements.

Generating Utilitarian Attitudes: The "BeanFest Paradigm"

Attitude objects that have been associated with reward are seen as more positive, are liked better and are approached more frequently than are neutral objects or objects that imply negative sanctions. Although the utilitarian function of attitudes bears similarities to reinforcement models, the two are not identical. The utilitarian function of attitudes suggests that we categorize objects, issues or other people and then evaluate them in order to navigate through a world filled with positive and negative consequences. It would be important to show that people who have not had experience with attitude objects learn to categorize them and evaluate them in utilitarian ways—that is, to attract positive and avoid negative sanctions.

This is a difficult research question because people's attitudes are multiply determined. We typically have long histories and myriad experiences with an attitude object, some favorable and some less favorable. The voter in our earlier example may have had a variety of experiences with labor unions that he or she brings to the table and may know a lot more about the political candidates than their stand on any one issue. Therefore, while we can make a plausible case that the voter's attitude toward a candidate is based on his/her belonging to a union or being part of management, it is difficult to get direct evidence that the attitude is based solely on utilitarian motives.

A unique contribution to the study of the utilitarian function of attitudes was provided in a study by Fazio, Eiser and Shook (2004). Participants played a computer game in a virtual world of survival. The object of the game was to survive on a virtual planet, accomplished by approaching the objects on the planet—some good and contributing to survival, others bad and blocking survival. The problem for the player was to find out who was good and who was not, i.e., who provided extra energy to the player and who stole energy. Without energy, the player was doomed to destruction.

The playing situation was not a typical one for the players. There was no easy way to determine which inhabitant was good and which was evil. There were no costumes, no insignias, no uniforms to allow a quick determination of good and bad. Instead, the inhabitants were, oddly enough, beans. Players knew only two dimensions on which the beans differed: Their shape and the number of spots on their surfaces. Some examples of the planet's inhabitants are shown in Figure 3.1. The players needed to decide which beans to approach and which to avoid. After approaching a bean, they received immediate feedback about the consequences of the approach. They learned that they either gained or lost the energy needed for survival. So, starting with no knowledge of the strange creatures in Figure 3.1, players needed to categorize which were good and which were bad, which should be approached and which should be avoided.

Players learned the information needed for survival. By trial and error, approach and avoidance, they found that some beans were helpful and some were harmful. Based on what they learned from that experience, they generalized to similar beans based on the configuration of shape and surface spots. When the game was over, participants were shown a set of similar beans and asked to decide if they were good or bad. From their experience with the game, participants had little difficulty

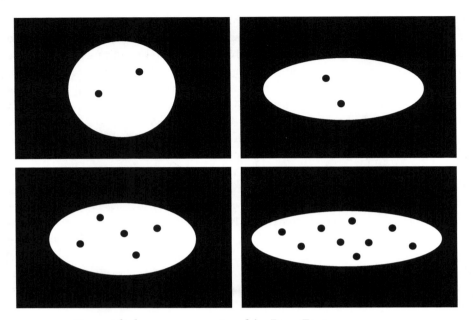

FIGURE 3.1 *Example beans encountered in BeanFest.*

Source: Fazio, R.H., Eiser, J.R., & Shook, N.J. (2004). Attitude formation through exploration: valence asymmetries. *Journal of Personality and Social Psychology*, *87*(3), 293. Reprinted with permission.

expressing an attitude toward the new beans. They had figured out which beans were useful and which were not. Now, with a new set of beans to evaluate, participants used the attitudes that had formed during the initial game to generalize to the new beans on the basis of the extent to which the novel beans visually resembled beans known to be positive versus beans known to be negative. The take-home lesson of the study is that people were able to categorize and evaluate objects on a good-bad dimension as a function of whether those objects were helpful or harmful to surviving in the virtual world. And that is what is meant by the utilitarian function of an attitude.

Fazio et al.'s (2004) studies revealed another fascinating phenomenon. Players were much more likely to learn which beans were harmful than which beans were helpful. This maps well onto a view of the utilitarian function in which it seems more important for survival to avoid harm before seeking gain. When players encountered a harmful bean, they learned to categorize its shape and appearance quickly so that they could avoid such beans as the game progressed. The problem is that sometimes the players were wrong. They over-generalized from the shape or appearance of one bean to what they believed were others in the category, but their generalization was an error. However, because the players deemed the beans to be harmful, they evaluated the beans negatively and avoided contact with those beans. Thus, the players never learned to correct their mistakes. By avoiding contact with beans they believed were negative, they never had the opportunity to find out that, in fact, they had generalized on the wrong dimension and that the beans were not harmful at all.

When players made a mistake in the positive direction—that is, when they decided a bean was helpful to their quest for energy and survival, they approached similar beans in subsequent rounds. If they were mistaken and the bean was actually harmful, they were able to correct their incorrect judgment and form a more useful attitude toward the bean.

If we put these two observations together, we see the formation of a **negativity bias in attitude formation** (see also Ito, Larsen, Smith, & Cacioppo, 1998). People usually form correct judgments of attitude objects on the basis of their utility. However, when incorrect attitudes are formed, only the incorrect positive attitudes are corrected. Incorrect negative attitudes remain negative because people avoid future contact with the object—the kind of contact that could have rectified their judgments.

In summary, then, we can say that people do form at least some of their attitudes based on the utility function of the object. They come to have positive attitudes toward objects that are helpful and negative attitudes toward objects that are harmful, even if they have no prior experience with those objects. Still, those attitudes may be based on objectively incorrect judgments or categorizations. Putting helpful beans in the unhelpful category leads to negative attitudes toward objects that actually have positive utility. Similarly, putting harmful beans in the helpful category leads to positive attitudes toward objects that actually have negative utility. If life gives us more opportunities for interaction (as Fazio et al. did in their virtual reality), the positive attitudes will be corrected; however, because we do not take advantage of such opportunities for interaction on the negative side, the negative will not. People will approach and interact with the objects they erroneously believe have positive utility and discover that they were not positive after all. The same optimism for change cannot be said for erroneous negative attitudes. Once formed, they lead to a lack of contact and a lack of opportunity for correction.

THE VALUE-EXPRESSIVE FUNCTION OF ATTITUDES

Sometimes, attitudes serve to express *values* that a person feels to be an aspect of his or her core personality. Values transcend individual attitudes and behaviors, serving as codes or general principles that guide people's lives. According to Katz (1960), one of the functions of holding and expressing an attitude is that it serves a motivation that *"derives satisfaction from expressing attitudes appropriate to their personal values and self-concept "*(p. 170). For example, some people may support a free trade policy for their nation because support of free trade allows them to express their basic belief in competition as well as their solidarity with people of all nations. Others may oppose the policy because that attitude allows them to express their fundamental support for nationalism. In both cases, expressing an attitude toward free trade facilitates people's ability to give expression to their fundamental values. The attitude may not be utilitarian in any way, but it provides satisfaction as an expression of a core value.

Maio and Olson (1994) conducted research examining the relationship of attitudes and values. They asked participants about their attitudes toward purchasing a ticket for a dance that was organized to support the construction of a smoke-free area at their university. They found that students' attitudes were a function of how strongly they held values that were relevant to the purpose of the dance. Some students had strong values for collective well-being and health. Those students were strongly supportive of the dance and were willing to spend money to support it. Other students had strong values for freedom and individual liberties. They had strongly negative attitudes toward the event, presumably to express their support for their core value of individual freedom. People who rated the relevant values as less important did not show meaningful correlations between their ratings of the values and their attitudes toward the dance. The results demonstrate that people's attitudes are related to their values, to the extent that people's relevant values are strong and important.

People can have their values made important by situational primes. In addition to the differences among individuals in how strongly they hold certain values, environmental stimuli can often serve to make values more or less accessible. In a follow-up study to the one just described, Maio and Olson (1995) systematically varied whether participants' value-expressive or utilitarian motives were made more accessible by a situational prime. Specifically, they read a poster that emphasized value-expressive reasons for donating to cancer research (i.e., helping others) or they read a poster that emphasized the utilitarian value of finding a cure that might help the donor if the donor were ever to contract cancer. Once again, people's values predicted their attitudes, but to a much stronger extent when the poster had made the participants reflect on their helpfulness value rather than their utilitarian value.

Advertising and the Expression of Values

The value-expressive function of attitudes is a particular focus in the field of advertising. Johar and Sirgy (1991) observed that the two fundamental approaches to advertising involve utilitarian and value-expressive attitudes. Advertisers can tell people how useful their product is and how it will make their lives easier. A car, for example, can take you places comfortably, reliably and efficiently. Most people need cars for their daily lives, and advertisers can extol the reasons that their client's car is the most useful one to own.

Alternatively, a person's car can express a value. It can be a social value, such as demonstrating concern for the environment. An electric or hybrid car may save its owner money, but it also expresses its owner's commitment to the environment. Another car may be a fast, glamorous gas-guzzler. It, too, expresses a value of conspicuous consumption. Its owners, like the car, live their lives in the fast lane. In order to persuade potential car-buyers to be attracted to the gas-guzzling automobile, advertisers appeal to the discrepancy between people's current self-image and their desired self-image. Potential customers who would like to think of themselves as living in the world of luxury but know they are not quite the paragons of upper-class society will be most persuaded by a message that shows that their purchasing the luxury automobile will make them the people they ideally want to be.

Another approach to value-expressive persuasion in advertising is to persuade people of the importance of the value in order to bolster their attitude toward the product (Johar & Sirgy, 1991; Ogilvy, 1983). For example, a person may have reasonably positive feelings about being sensitive to environmental protection but does not consider it one of her or his core values. Advertisers may focus a commercial at convincing the consumer to adopt this value rather than focusing the persuasion toward the electric car. Once the value has been raised in importance, attitudes toward objects that enhance that value—in this case, the electric car—can be expected to become more positive as well.

When messages are directed at attitudes that are connected to important values, the messages themselves seem stronger. Hullett (2002) varied the value-relevance of an attitude and then confronted recipients with a message about the attitude. Regardless of whether the messages were pro-attitudinal or counterattitudinal, the more that recipients believed that the attitude issue was related to important values, the more convincing they found the argument. This is yet another reason that advertisers seek value-expressive attitudes to target their persuasive communications.

Self-monitoring: An Individual Difference Approach

A consistent finding in the literature is that people differ in their individual levels of a dispositional trait known as **self-monitoring**. People who are high in self-monitoring are those who are guided by trying to fit into their social circumstances, to be liked and to be approved by others and strive to be the person called for in each situation in which they find themselves (Snyder, 1974; Snyder & Monson, 1975). They are motivated to express attitudes whose major purpose is to accomplish these social functions. At the other end of the continuum are those low in self-monitoring. Such individuals are eager to express their own unique evaluations, whether or not they are accurate or appropriate in the circumstance (Fiske & von Hendy, 1992). Using a sports metaphor, low self-monitors are inclined to call it as they see it rather than express the call that the fans will appreciate.

Snyder and DeBono (1985) used the distinction between high and low self-monitors to examine the interaction between types of persuasion attempts and self-monitoring in the context of commercial advertisements. They reasoned that because people who are low self-monitors seek to form and express attitudes in accord with their true judgment of a situation, they would be most affected by product advertisements that extolled the virtues of the product rather than the image it projects. High self-monitors, on the other hand, would be most affected by advertisements that appealed to images rather than product quality. The researchers presented their participants with advertisements for coffee, whiskey and cigarettes that varied in their appeal to facts or images. They found that high self-monitors were more persuaded to like and to purchase the products that appealed to images. They were also willing to pay a higher price for the products if they were advertised in terms of image. The reverse was true for low self-monitors. They liked and were willing to pay more for brands that were advertised in terms of the quality of the product.

The results of Snyder and DeBono's study add support to the notion that attitudes can serve a variety of functions. As we discussed previously, Maio and Olson (1995) showed that the situational variables can make one of the functions more dominant than the other, causing attitude and behavior change in people who hold those values. People with value-expressive attitudes were more likely to donate to a charity if value-expression had been situationally primed. Snyder and de Bono (1985) took an individual difference approach to the same underlying issue by showing that people's attitudes and behavioral intentions could be influenced by appeals that went directly to the function that a product was likely to serve. If people were systematically low in self-monitoring, then they were influenced by appeals to the functional value of the product.

Attitudes as Possessions. Prentice (1987) reasoned that attitudes may share similar functions to people's most cherished possessions. As an exercise, think of the objects you own that are most important to you. When you examine your list, do you find that your most important possessions serve a useful purpose (like a TV or an iPad) or do they symbolically express your important values (like a wedding ring or family gift)? Our values may well be revealed by our list of cherished possessions (Csikszentmihalyi & Rochberg-Halton, 1981). If our list contains mostly items that are value-expressive, then Prentice argued we may have a tendency to be most responsive to persuasive appeals that feature value-expressive arguments. Conversely, if our possessions reveal a utilitarian purpose, we may be persuaded by arguments that are primarily utilitarian.

In her research, Prentice (1987) asked a group of Yale University students to engage in the exercise above—that is, to list their most cherished possessions. Independent judges determined whether the list of possessions was primarily utilitarian or value-expressive. Several weeks later, the original participants returned to the laboratory for a study on attitudes. They were presented with an attitude issue with which they were relatively unfamiliar and were asked to read a persuasive message that featured (for some participants) an appeal to symbolic values or (for other participants) an appeal to utilitarian values. For example, people who were asked to consider whether there should be a state income tax might have been exposed to a value-expressive argument about the relative fairness of an income tax compared to a sales tax or to a utilitarian argument about how much additional revenue the state would receive from an income tax. When participants were then asked their attitude about the income tax, the results showed partial support for Prentice's hypothesis. People whose possessions were primarily utilitarian were persuaded equally by the value-expressive and utilitarian arguments. However, in support of the hypothesis, people whose cherished possessions were characterized as symbolically expressing their values were more persuaded to support the income tax if the arguments in the message were value-expressive rather than utilitarian.

Value-Expressive Matching and Biased Processing

Ziegler, Dobre and Diehl (2007) proposed that people who are exposed to persuasive appeals are likely to process arguments differently depending on how they coincide with attitude function. Like Snyder and DeBono (1985), Ziegler et al. (2007) focused on differences in self-monitoring to provide a basis for value-expressive attitudes. They asked students at the University of Tübingen in Germany to examine advertisements for a new digital camera. Arguments had been carefully selected to appeal to image or to appeal to the functional utility of the camera. Consistent with Snyder and DeBono's approach, they found that participants had more positive evaluations of the camera to the extent that the arguments matched the functions that attitudes serve for high and low self-monitors. High self-monitors liked the camera better when the argument read, "This digital camera is the optimal lifestyle accessory for any occasion. Show your friends and family what you can do" (p. 274). By contrast, low self-monitors, whose attitudes are not based on the need to present a positive social image, were more influenced by learning about the optical zoom, the focal length and the camera's resolution.

Two other aspects of Ziegler et al.'s experiment were noteworthy. First, the effect of function matching was true only when the persuasive arguments were moderate rather than extremely strong. The experimenters used three versions of messages: One was unambiguously persuasive, one was unambiguously weak and one was moderately persuasive. All participants were persuaded by the unambiguously strong message, regardless of their self-monitoring status, and very few were persuaded by the weak message. Thus, the strength and coherence of the message did make an overall difference in persuasion. It was in the moderate condition that participants were persuaded by arguments specifically geared to social image if they were high self-monitors or to the actual quality of the camera if they were low self-monitors.

The other interesting aspect of this research was the finding that people processed information in a way that specifically supported the functions they needed their attitudes to serve. Asked to rate the persuasiveness of each argument used in the advertisement, high self-monitors found the arguments related to social image to be more effective and persuasive than arguments addressed to the quality of the camera. The opposite was true of low self-monitors. In addition, participants were asked to list the thoughts that had come to mind as they read each of the arguments. Again, participants remembered more arguments that matched their attitude function and remembered them with more positive emotion than arguments that did not match their values.

It seems that matching an argument to the function that attitudes serve for an individual is an effective means of persuasion, particularly when the message is neither so strong as to persuade everyone nor so weak as to be convincing to no one.

An Attitude Object Approach

Another perspective on the value-expressive function of an attitude is to examine the attitude object itself. Attitudes toward objects can be composed of multiple functions. How people feel about their automobile may be partly based on its usefulness in going from one place to another and partly based on how it makes people feel about themselves. Likewise, people's attitudes about their cars can be based on the cost and frequency of repair, but they can also be based on the image it provides to others. Shavitt (1990) proposed that attitudes toward some objects are *primarily* based on functions that are called for by that object. For example, one's judgment about a wedding ring is more a function of the value it expresses—e.g., people's assessment of commitment, love and relationships—and less a matter of the worth of the gold that it contains. A person's air conditioner, on the other hand, is more typically based on its utility in cooling off a room, a car or a house.

In her research, Shavitt (1990) used a coding schedule to identify a set of objects that primarily served a single function. She identified some products as being primarily utilitarian and other products as being primarily the expression of symbolic values. She systematically exposed the participants to advertisements for those products that were based on the product's usefulness (utilitarian advertisements) or symbolic expressions (value-expressive advertisements). She found that persuasion for products that were essentially symbolic (e.g., perfume) was effective if it focused on the appropriate function and not on its utilitarian benefits. Similarly, persuasion directed at products that were essentially utilitarian was effective when it was based on its usefulness rather than the product's symbolic function.

Overall, research has shown that the value-expressive function of attitudes is independent of the utilitarian function. Situational variables, such as priming the accessibility of the value-expressive function, lead to different outcomes than priming the utilitarian function. Moreover, different people are more likely to have their attitudes based on one function over another, and certain attitude objects lend themselves more to either a value-expressive or utilitarian function. Understanding which function pertains to which attitude object in which situation makes an analysis of persuasion more fruitful.

THE SOCIAL-ADJUSTIVE FUNCTION

A different form of attitude expression is one that connects you to others in your environment, particularly to those in your own reference group. Attitudes can be a way of signaling that we fit into our groups. Smith et al. (1956) referred to *the motivation for identifying yourself with your reference group as* **social adjustment**. Imagine a person named Lara who is particularly motivated by social adjustment. When Lara discovers that most others members of a group to which she belongs hold a particular attitude on an issue, she may feel motivated to adopt a similar attitude as a way to be liked by her reference group.

Some people are more like Lara and some less. One personality characteristic that we have already encountered—self-monitoring—predicts the likelihood that people will base their attitudes on the social-adjustive function. As we saw in the previous section, people who are low in self-monitoring typically march to their own drummer—that is, their attitudes reflect their own independent judgment of a situation. High self-monitors, on the other hand, constantly survey their social world, making sure that their judgments and attitudes capture what others expect of them.

De Bono (1987) conducted a study to show that people high in self-monitoring would be more likely to base their attitudes on what they thought others believed whereas people low in self-monitoring would be more likely to be value-expressive, maintaining attitudes that they judged to be correct. After taking an inventory to assess self-monitoring, participants were told that their university was organizing a "mental health awareness" week and, to this end, participants would listen to a recording of a speech given by an expert advocating greater institutionalization of the mentally ill. In the "values" condition, the expert speaker told the audience that attitudes toward institutionalization were related to people's values, including responsibility, kindness and conscientiousness. In the "consensus" condition, the expert recorded the same speech but indicated that he had taken a survey of students at this and other nearby universities and that 70% agreed with his position that institutionalization was the correct course for treating the mentally ill. De Bono found the predicted interaction between self-monitoring and the consensus vs. value information that participants believed. When participants believed that being in favor of institutionalization would be shared by 70% of their fellow students, the high self-monitors (but not the low self-monitors) were convinced to adopt that position. On the other hand, when participants believed that their position on institutionalization was related to their own values, then only the low self-monitors were persuaded. The results revealed that people who habitually care about how they are viewed by others (high self-monitors) are likely to adopt attitude positions based on the attitudes of people in their reference groups.

Murray, Haddock and Zanna (1996) took a different approach to the difference between social-adjustive and value-expressive attitudes by suggesting that attitude function can be primed by events in the social environment. The situations we find ourselves in may make one of those functions more relevant than the other. Murray et al. engineered a social situation in the laboratory designed to make people think of their attitudes as part of a social-adjustive (SA) function or as part of a value-expressive (VE) function. Participants in the experiment engaged in a number of activities that primed one of the two attitude functions. For example, they were asked about their attitudes toward a number of issues. Those assigned to the SA group were asked to explain how other people's opinions and feelings helped them create and maintain their attitudes. Those assigned to the VE condition were asked to explain the personal values that their attitudes reflected.

After either SA or VE motivations were primed, the key attitude measure was introduced. Participants were exposed to a speech similar to the one DeBono (1987) used in the research reported above. All participants listened to an expert advocate institutionalizing the mentally ill. For half of the participants, the speaker justified his position on the basis of a social adjustment appeal: He argued that a vast majority of similar university students favored institutionalization (an SA appeal). The other half of the students heard the position supported as one based on personal values of being a loving and responsible human being (a VE appeal). Murray et al. predicted that, when attitudes about institutionalization were assessed at the end of the experiment, participants for whom SA values had been primed would be more influenced by the SA speech and vice versa for the VE participants. The results shown in Table 3.1 strongly supported Murray et al.'s prediction. Even

TABLE 3.1   *Attitudes Toward Institutionalizing the Mentally Ill by Attitude Function and Communication Type*

FUNCTION	APPEAL	
	VALUES	PEERS
Value-Expressive	70.23	64.69
Social-Adjustive	61.92	75.31

Note: Higher scores indicate more agreement with the communication
Source: Murray, S. L., Haddock, G., & Zanna, M.P. (1996). Creating value-expressive attitudes: An experimental approach. In C. Seligman, J. M. Olson & M. P. Zanna (Eds.), *The Psychology of Values: The Ontario Symposium* (Vol. 8, pp. 107–133). Mahwah, NJ: Lawrence Erlbaum Associates. Reprinted with permission.

though the participants had been randomly assigned to have their social-adjustive or value-expressive function primed, the results mirrored DeBono's self-monitoring individual difference approach.

THE EGO-DEFENSIVE FUNCTION OF ATTITUDES

Some attitudes revolve around the motivation to protect our sense of self and our level of self-esteem. Katz (1960) referred to attitudes that serve this motivation as the **ego-defensive function** of attitudes. Smith, Bruner and White (1956) referred to it as the **externalization function**. In the latter view, *externalized attitudes are unconscious projections of internal threats or conflicts.* Tyrants throughout history may have formed extreme attitudes toward out-groups as ways to compensate for their own inadequacies and failings. Some environmental stimulus most likely served as a subtle reminder of the tyrant's internal failing, resulting in a hostile, negative attack against that person or group.

Katz's view accommodates externalization of internal conflict but includes a broader perspective on the conditions that lead to the protection of the ego. Derogating others does not need to be a projection of an inner conflict. *Attitudes based on the ego-defensive function are designed to bolster a weak and threatened ego*, which we would refer to in the modern era as the protection of self-esteem. Individuals who feel chronically threatened are more inclined to adopt ego-defensive attitudes toward others. Their attitudes are not only characterized as negative against others, but they also tend to be vehement in intensity. Katz considered the behavior of mob leaders or demagogues to be expressions of ego-defensiveness.

Writing during the aftermath of Nazism, the rise of Stalinism and the beginning of the end of Jim Crow in the United States, Katz and other scholars stressed the power of ego-defensive attitudes—i.e., the extremity of the dislike and hatred toward minorities and out-group members. Katz saw three conditions that were facilitative for ego-defensive attitudes to be expressed in a hateful and hurtful form. The first was threat—the real or imagined vulnerability to a person or event. The neo-Nazi imagines that his income or job is being threatened by a Black or a Jew. Second, there must be the possibility of social support, such as revving up a mob or social group to support the ego-defensive position. Third, ego-defensive expression is facilitated by appeals to authority. A strong leader with hateful attitudes provides the comfort and support for the neo-Nazi to express his anti-Semitic or anti-Black attitudes.

Although we seem to live in a safer environment than when the Ku Klux Klan rode herd in much of the United States, and Hitler, Stalin and Mao ruled over much of the globe, the danger of ego-defensive attitudes persists. Prejudice against religious, ethnic and racial minority groups continue to lead to hostile and often lethal behavior in many parts of the world. Prejudice and stereotypes are multi-determined, complex concepts, but such attitudes can properly be conceived as ego-defensive.

The ego-defensive function of prejudiced attitudes was demonstrated in an interesting set of experiments by Fein and Spencer (1997). They reasoned that if attitudes toward other groups served the role of compensating for a threatened sense of self-esteem, then they would find increased prejudice and endorsement of stereotypes when an individual's competence was questioned. In the first part of their study, university students took a series of difficult tests that were alleged to be a high-level test of intelligence. Half of the students had their self-images threatened when they were told that they had done very poorly, whereas the other half were told that they had done very well. In a subsequent portion of the experiment, the participants were asked to evaluate a target person whose characteristics made him seem like a member of a stereotyped minority (gay male) or a member of the majority group. The results showed that, subsequent to the threat posed by their own poor performance on the test of intelligence, students evaluated the stereotyped minority member more negatively and endorsed more negative stereotypes compared to when the participants' self-esteem had not been threatened in the earlier portion of the experiment. Figure 3.2 shows the data on the endorsement of stereotypes following self-esteem threat.

Two additional features of the Fein and Spencer studies add evidence to the notion that negative attitudes toward outgroups can be a function of coping with threats to the ego. In a follow-up study using Jewish women as the minority group, the investigators replicated the finding that self-esteem threats in the form of failure on an intelligence test led participants to endorse more negative stereotypes of the 'Jewish American Princess' and that such endorsement served the function of restoring the participants' self-esteem. Using the negative stereotype to berate Jewish women made the threatened participants feel better about themselves, whereas there was no such increase in self-esteem when the participants had not been threatened. Moreover, if participants were provided with an alternative way to bolster their confidence prior to judging the minority group target, the threatened participants did not resort to using negative stereotypes.

Spencer, Fein, Wolfe, Fong and Dunn (1998) used a similar procedure to examine prejudiced attitudes against African Americans. They found that White participants who felt threatened by their performance on a bogus intelligence task reported significantly more negative stereotypes when they had been subtly primed with photographs of African Americans. In addition, Spencer et al. were interested in whether people needed to engage in a thoughtful, effortful process in order to turn threat into hostile attitudes. They prevented some of their participants from thinking about the intelligence task or stereotypes about African Americans

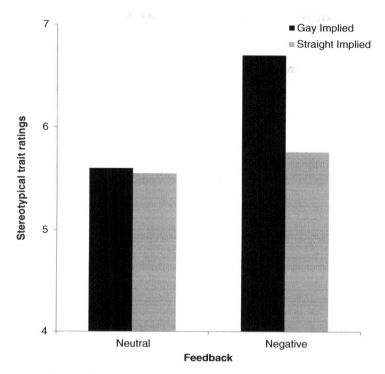

FIGURE 3.2 *Ratings of target on stereotype-relevant traits as a function of feedback and implied sexual orientation of the target. Higher numbers indicate greater stereotyping.*

Source: Fein, S., & Spencer, S. J. (1997). Prejudice as self-image maintenance: Affirming the self through derogating others. *Journal of Personality and Social Psychology, 73*(1), 31. Reprinted with permission.

by having them rehearse and memorize an 8-digit number during the experimental session. It did not matter. The results showed that threats to the ego resulted in negative stereotype use, even when the participants were kept occupied by the memorization task. Apparently, the route from threat to stereotype is relatively automatic.

Thus, negative attitudes toward others, particularly attitudes toward stereotyped minority groups, are facilitated by threats to the ego. This is not to say that all people who harbor hostility toward out-groups are externalizing their own defensive needs for self-esteem. It is to say, however, that attitudes serve many functions and one of the functions served by prejudice, endorsement of negative stereotypes and hostility is an unresolved need to bolster a threatened ego.

THE KNOWLEDGE, OR OBJECT APPRAISAL, FUNCTIONS

There are probably no attitudinal functions more ubiquitous than what Katz (1960) described as the **knowledge function** of attitudes and what Smith et al. (1956) referred to as the **object appraisal function**. The world we live in is filled with an enormous number of objects. Applying meaning to the world around us and meaning to the objects within it is the major task of socialization. Imagine an infant's understanding of its physical and social world: The infant has very little capacity to know which objects co-occur, which to approach and which to avoid. The very crucial goal of the first years of life is devoted to gaining such meaning.

In adult life, the task becomes simultaneously simpler and more complex. It is simpler because it has a foundation of language and concept development to rely on, but more complex due to the interconnectedness and complexity of the people, objects and issues in our lives. Attitudes help us understand and make sense of the endless array of stimuli with which we must cope. Smith et al. (1956) thought the object appraisal function of an attitude was so important that it alone was the most fundamental reason for holding attitudes. They argued that within the need for object appraisal "lies the function served by holding attitudes per se. Without them we should be in the constant throes of determining the relevance of events, of fashioning decisions, and of deciding upon actions—all ab initio" (p.41). Katz concurred, stating that the knowledge function of attitudes "gives meaning to what would otherwise be an unorganized chaotic universe. People need standards or frames of reference for understanding their world, and attitudes help to supply such standards" (p.175).

Research on the object appraisal function of attitudes lay dormant for quite some time, but has been rediscovered as a major concept for research in attitudes. Fazio (2000), for example, argues that the object appraisal function is so fundamental that it should be regarded as special within the list of possible functions served by the attitude. He argues that every attitude serves an object appraisal function. Some attitudes may also serve ego-defensive, value-expressive or utilitarian functions, but all attitudes serve to categorize and classify the objects in our environment (Fazio, 2000; Shavitt, 1990). Moreover, the other functions of attitudes are served by a particular valence of an attitude. For example, in Fein and Spencer's (1997) study, the ego-defensive function was served by the development of a specifically *negative* attitude toward the Jewish American Princess, but the object appraisal function is served by merely having an attitude. Fazio (2000) states, "Regardless of why the individual's attitude took a particular valence, the mere possession of any attitude is useful to the individual in terms of orienting him or her to the object in question. In this sense, the object appraisal function can be considered the primary value of possessing an attitude" (p. 3–4).

Attitude Accessibility as a Key Determinant of Object Appraisal

In order for attitudes to serve the function of guiding us through the world of objects, those attitudes have to be stored in memory and be capable of being used when confronted with the attitude object. As we detailed in our discussion of attitude strength in Chapter 2, this is what is meant by **attitude accessibility**. The more accessible an attitude, the more likely it can help us categorize objects, evaluate them and guide our behavior. Everyone has accessible attitudes that serve the object appraisal or knowledge function, but not every attitude is similarly accessible. Although there is controversy over whether attitudes can be completely inaccessible (Chaiken & Bargh, 1993), there exists a range of accessibility such that some attitudes come more quickly to mind than others.

One source of variability in the magnitude of attitude accessibility stems from a stable difference among people. People vary along a continuum of the degree to which they prefer to evaluate—i.e., prefer to have attitudes about objects. Jarvis and Petty (1996) created a 'need to evaluate' scale that assesses individual differences in people's tendencies to have stable attitudes toward a variety of issues and objects. Research data show that the need to evaluate moderates attitude accessibility. The higher the need to evaluate, the more likely attitudes about a particular attitude object will come to mind (Hermans, De Houwer, & Eelen, 2001).

A second factor that causes variance in the accessibility of people's attitudes is the degree to which they care about particular domains. Some people care very much about politics. They will have an attitude about political parties, newspaper columnists, editorial positions and every piece of legislation working its way through the legislature. Others are relatively disengaged from politics, caring very little about the workings of government. On the other hand, these people may care passionately about sports and carry with them strong attitudes about players, teams and the quality of the officials. People's level of experience with an attitude object also affects attitude accessibility. Those who have had no contact with impressionist art may have no attitude about Monet or Renoir. If they have not had experience with the attitude object, they will be slower to form an evaluation of those artists. Increasing experience with, thinking about, and rehearsing their attitude toward an object all lead to increased accessibility of attitudes (e.g., Powell & Fazio, 1984). The reverse is also true: Under certain conditions, attitudes can be made less accessible. Sanbonmatsu, Posavac, Vanous, Ho and Fazio (2007) showed that repeatedly *decreasing* the relevance of an attitude toward a particular object decreased its accessibility.

Fazio (2000) has labeled the dimension of attitude accessibility the 'attitude-nonattitude continuum.' At one end of the continuum are objects that do not evoke evaluative associations for any of the reasons we have already discussed; these are non-attitudes (Converse, 1970). At the other end is the strong attitude. The more that an object evokes a strong evaluative association in memory, the more useful it can be in orienting us toward or away from the object, to inform our evaluations and to guide our behavior.

Attitudes and Attention

People's attention is drawn to stimuli or objects about which they have strong attitudes. Imagine that you are a tourist in a town that you have not been to before. On Main Street, people are moving about, cars and buses are traversing the avenues and shops are open for business. You survey the scene for a moment. Your cell phone rings and a friend inquires about the town. What did you notice that would inform your friend about the town?

Attitudes affect what people notice. If you are a coffee lover, your first response might be that this town has a lovely coffee shop in the middle where people are relaxing, conversing and sipping their espressos. A health food enthusiast might notice the yogurt shop on the other side of the street. The environmentalist might have been drawn to the use of buses running on natural gas and the bird watcher might have noticed trees that may be just right for spotting bird species. It is not just a preference for describing the things you like or dislike first, but rather it is a phenomenon of attention. We are drawn to attend to objects about which our attitudes are strong and accessible.

Roskos-Ewoldsen and Fazio (1992) conducted an experiment to test the proposition that our attention is drawn to attitudinally relevant objects. They asked participants about their attitudes toward a series of objects. In one version of the procedure, the strength of people's attitudes was manipulated through rehearsal. That is, participants were asked to state their attitude toward the object repeatedly. In a second phase of the experiment, participants were shown an array of line drawings that included the objects characterized by strong, accessible attitudes. They were quicker to notice the objects whose attitudes they had rehearsed, even when the objects were only distracter items and not relevant to the task at hand. Having a strong attitude toward the object led people to notice that object, regardless of its utility. What we see, or pay attention to, is affected by our attitudes.

Smith, Fazio and Cejka (1996) extended this finding by showing that attention to attitude objects is affected not only by attitudes toward the object but also by attitudes toward the category to which the object belongs. Rather than asking participants to rehearse their attitudes toward a specific object, such as a yogurt, they asked people to rehearse their attitude toward an overarching category, such as health foods. After strengthening their attitudes toward the category, Smith et al. (1996) found that participants were more likely to notice and recall the specific attitude object. This is especially interesting when considering that mere exposure to a category without rehearsing their attitudes did not make people more attentive to the attitude object.

Categorization Depends on Attitudes

When encountering other people in our environment, we are often cast into a complex case of categorization. Do you categorize your neighbor by her race, her gender, her age or her occupation? All are possible. Attitudes guide the categorization. Fazio and Dunton (1997) used a priming procedure to assess the strength of people's racial attitudes. They then presented people with pairs of faces and asked them to make similarity judgments. Any number of features could have been used to infer similarity, including race, gender and occupation. Fazio and Dunton found that people for whom race evoked strong attitudes were more likely to use race to categorize the faces and make their similarity judgments on that basis. The valence of the attitude made no difference. To the extent that racial attitudes were strong, in either the positive or negative direction, people used that dimension to categorize the faces.

Young and Fazio (2013) advanced the importance of categorical judgments by suggesting that evaluations of attitude categories affect evaluations of specific attitude objects by affecting their construal. Consider caffeine. How positive or negative is your evaluation of caffeine? The answer to that question might depend on how you categorize the object. If you think of caffeine as the substance that gives you energy for your day's work, you may judge it positively; if you think of it as the substance that prevents you from falling asleep, then you may judge it negatively. Young and Fazio (2013) suggested that the key to understanding the evaluation of a specific object that can be categorized along two evaluatively different dimensions is the strength of your attitude toward the category. Participants in their study repeatedly reported their attitudes toward the positive category, "things that increase energy," or their negative attitudes toward "things that cause me insomnia." After a short delay, they were shown an attitude object (caffeine) that they had not seen earlier in the experiment. When asked to evaluate caffeine, participants who had rehearsed their negative attitude toward the category "things that cause me insomnia" rated caffeine more negatively than participants who had rehearsed their positive attitude toward "things that increase energy." Young and Fazio (2013) concluded that making accessible one's attitude toward the category caused people to construe the object in terms of that category, thereby affecting people's attitudes toward the object. Rehearsing one's positive attitude toward "things that increase energy" made people construe caffeine as one of those "things," and therefore was evaluated positively. In the other condition, repeatedly rehearsing one's positive attitude toward the category caused people to construe caffeine as one of those "things that cause insomnia," leading to a negative attitude.

Attitudes Affect the Quality and Ease of Decisions

The premise of considering such issues as attention and categorization as evidence of the functional nature of attitudes is that they serve the object appraisal or knowledge function of attitudes. They help us to navigate through the complexity of the world by drawing our attention to particular objects and combining those objects into meaningful categories. These functions occur at a relatively primitive level in our consciousness. We do not have to direct high-level resources to attention and categorization, which therefore leaves ample cognitive resources available for higher-level activities, such as making decisions. Decision-making involving objects about which people have strongly accessible attitudes is potentially easier and less stressful than decision-making when people have weak, inaccessible, or in Fazio's (2000) terms, non-attitudes.

A study by Fazio, Blascovitch and Driscoll (1992) provided interesting evidence about the functional nature of decisions based on strongly accessible attitudes. Participants were given the task of making decisions as quickly as possible about which of two abstract paintings they preferred. Some of the participants had rehearsed their attitudes toward the paintings prior to the selection task. The rehearsal process served to make their attitudes more accessible relative to the attitudes of participants who did not rehearse their attitudes. The interesting dependent measure in this study was a physiological assessment of stress. Blood pressure—an indicant of stress—was lower for the participants who had rehearsed their attitudes prior to the rapid selection task.

Rapid decisions are not always quality decisions. The physiological data tell us that the participants whose attitudes were made accessible through rehearsal made their rapid decisions with less stress. But were they judgments that held up under the light of more deliberate reflection? In the same study, Fazio et al. (1992) gave the participants another opportunity to reflect on their decisions, to consider all aspects of the paintings and then rank order their impression of the paintings. The participants who had the more accessible attitudes showed greater correspondence between their rapid pair-wise choices and their more reflective judgments of the paintings than participants whose attitudes were less accessible. Apparently, then, attitudes help people make higher-quality decisions—and with less stress—than people who do not have accessible attitudes.

Attitudes Help Cope with Stress

Attitudes fulfill their object appraisal function by helping us navigate a potentially chaotic world. As we have seen, they help us at basic levels of cognitive processing first by guiding our attention, then helping us group objects into meaningful categories, and finally helping us make less stressful and higher-quality decisions at a sophisticated level of cognitive activity. One implication of this functional utility of attitudes is that they allow us to free up resources to cope with other complex life events. Fazio and Powell (1997) put this implication to the test with incoming freshman students at Indiana University.

Life transitions are notoriously difficult. They often involve opportunity and excitement, but at the same time are accompanied by stress and anxiety. Stressful life events, including those that occur during the college years, lead to compromises in people's mental and physical health (Aneshensel, 1992; Jemmott, Borysenko, Chapman, Borysenko, McClelland, Meyer, & Benson 1983; McClelland & Jemmott, 1980). The transition from high school to college is one of those events that contain a mixture of excitement and anxiety as young people accept new challenges and simultaneously try to understand and evaluate their new surroundings and expectations. From the literature on object appraisal, Fazio and Powell reasoned that transitioning freshmen who had well-formed attitudes about many of the issues they would face at the university would be better able to cope with their new environment than freshmen who were trying to form their attitudes de novo with each passing experience.

The researchers asked freshmen within two weeks of their arrival at college to respond to 54 target issues (i.e., attitude objects) by pressing one of two buttons as quickly as possible to express liking or disliking for the object. 'Objects' in this study were items relevant to the freshman academic experience. They included such items as taking an introductory science course, majoring in a specific field, attending early morning classes, pulling an all-nighter, giving an oral presentation and doing an extra credit assignment. The students also filled out a number of standard assessments of physical and mental health, such as the Beck Depression Inventory and Hopkins Symptom Check List.

The participants returned two months later and filled out the battery of psychological and physical health inventories. The question at issue was whether holding accessible attitudes about academic events made it more possible for students to cope with those events. The functional approach to attitudes suggests that the ability to quickly appraise an object reduces stress (as Fazio, Blascovitch, & Driscoll (1992) had shown with physiological data and that it would also allow students to deal with new events by bringing more of their psychological resources to bear.

Fazio and Powell (1997) made two predictions based on the object appraisal function of attitudes. The first was a main effect of attitude accessibility. The more quickly the students had responded with their affective reactions to the college-based attitude objects, the more healthy they would be two months later. The second was a more nuanced prediction in which the effect of attitude accessibility would be manifest for people who already felt predominantly stressed by the transition. The results of the study strongly supported the latter prediction. People who entered the university with little psychological stress or physical symptoms were not affected in any appreciable way by the degree to which their attitudes were accessible. However, those students who entered feeling stressed were greatly helped through the transition to college by having accessible attitudes. Two months after entering the university, the initially highly stressed students coped considerably better with their stress, reported less anxiety and fewer symptoms as a function of strength of their academic attitudes. It is as though students who entered school without much stress had ample resources to cope with the new experiences of college. Students who entered college with much stress in their lives needed to have accessible attitudes in the academic domain to make resources available for coping with their new stressors. As Fazio and Powell conclude, attitudes serve to structure objects, issues and people along an evaluative dimension, with the consequence of easing decision-making and thereby freeing people from the impinging demands and stresses of the social environment.

THE STATE OF PLAY OF THE FIVE FUNCTIONS

The functional approach to attitudes has focused on five functions introduced into the literature decades ago by Katz (1960) and Smith, Bruner and White (1956). Their research emphases were different, but their conclusions were remarkably similar. Smith et al. focused on understanding the importance of attitudes in the formation of people's total personalities. Katz took more of a social psychological approach to attitudes, focusing on establishing the mechanisms that underlie people's tendencies to hold and to change their attitudes. Nonetheless, their independent emphases suggested that five major functions characterize the reasons that people hold attitudes.

Must it be five? An attitude's function is characterized by the way it fulfills a fundamental human motivation. To the extent that an attitude fulfills additional motivations, it is appropriate to consider whether there are additional functions.

The Need for Affect

Maio, Esses, Arnold and Olson (2004) argue that the functional approach is enhanced by considering people's need for affect. In discussing the definition and structure of attitudes, we considered an attitude to be an overall evaluation of a stimulus object that, in turn, was typically comprised of affect, cognitions and/or behavior. Maio and his colleagues (Maio & Olson, 2000b; Maio & Esses, 2001) suggest that these structural components of an attitude give us reason to consider at least one additional attitude function: The need for affect.

For each of us, our evaluation of an object requires some consideration of how we feel, what we think, and how we have behaved toward the object. These evaluations are usually stored in memory for use when we are confronted with the attitude object. Research has demonstrated that some people are high in the need for cognition—i.e., they rely on careful thought and analysis when they form their attitudes (Cacioppo, Petty, Feinstein, & Jarvis, 1996; Cacioppo & Petty, 1982), while others rely on a need to stimulate their affect (Maio et al., 2004). Maio and colleagues believe that satisfying the need for affect should be considered an entirely separate attitude function. People high in the need for affect seek emotional states. They put themselves into situations in which they are likely to experience emotion, including negative emotions such as fear. One implication of this motivation for affect is that they will be more convinced by persuasive messages that feature emotional appeals rather than fact-based appeals. Similar to the way Snyder and DeBono (1985) and Ziegler et al. (2007) found that people high in self-monitoring were more persuaded by appeals to social status, Maio et al. (2004) found that people high in the need for affect were more persuaded by messages featuring emotions.

In addition, people high in the need for affect tend to adopt attitudes that give expression to their emotion. An implication of this premise is that people high in the need for affect will possess *extreme* attitudes, "because extreme attitudes are particularly likely to be accompanied by strong emotions" (p.19). Maio et al. asked people for their attitudes concerning 30 controversial issues. They found a relationship between the extremity of their attitudes and their need for affect. The higher the participants' scores on the need for affect scale, the more extreme their attitudes on the controversial issues.

SUMMARY AND CONCLUSION

The functional approach asks us to consider *why* people hold attitudes. In the functional view, attitudes serve to satisfy people's important motivations. The number of functions is somewhat arbitrary, depending on the breadth and independence of the motivational categories. Psychologists have generally settled on five broad functions: The utilitarian function of attitudes helps people gain rewards and avoid punishment, the value-expressive function allows people to express important personal values, the ego-defensive function permits people to bolster a threatened ego and protect their self-esteem, the social-adjustive function allows people to fit in with their reference groups, while the object appraisal function enables people to make sense of the myriad conceptual and physical objects in their world. The motivations to which attitudes respond can interact with or stem from individual difference variables, such as self-monitoring, need for cognition, or need for affect. The different functions of attitudes inform other key psychological processes like categorization and attention as well as broad level outcomes such as decision-making and stress reduction.

The key conclusion is that attitudes are not held in a vacuum. They have functional value, allowing us to maximize our rewards, express our values, defend our egos, appraise objects and satisfy our needs. As we shall see, the motivational functions of attitudes are intertwined with many major theories discussed later in this book. The degree to which our attitudes successfully serve these functions helps us to successfully navigate our social world.

CHAPTER 4

Persuasion
Classic Approaches

People are bombarded with a constant stream of communication designed to affect their attitudes. It is estimated that in the United States alone, the average person will see or hear more than 7 million advertisements in a lifetime (Pratkanis & Aronson, 2001). Advertisements are only those persuasive appeals for which the communicator pays a fee. When we consider the millions of other persuasive appeals by candidates for office, leaders of our churches, our friends and our relatives, the volume of persuasion is indeed overwhelming.

Persuasion refers to "an active attempt . . . to change a person's mind" (Petty & Cacioppo, 1981, p. 4), and has been part of the fabric of society since ancient times—with central importance in both ancient Greek and Roman societies. In Greek society, every man (but not woman) was given the responsibility to debate, persuade and decide. The ancient Greeks did not use representatives to make decisions on laws nor lawyers to represent them in court—persuasion about the affairs of society was everyone's responsibility. Plato, one of the great scholars of the day, argued that the study of philosophy was the way to understand truth and wisdom. The truth of a proposition, like the beauty of an object, was understandable by study of its intrinsic philosophical foundations. But Plato was a scholar on one side of a fascinating debate. On the other side were the Sophists, whom we discussed in Chapter 1, who believed that truth lay in the message, not in the object. For the Sophists, what was right was what a person could convince another to believe. It was the argument that mattered, for there was no other truth. The Sophists offered their services (for a fee) to their fellow Athenians, to teach them how to persuade their fellow citizens to believe in whatever position they desired to achieve. This may conjure images of modern advertising agencies whose job is to help clients persuade the public, regardless of the merits of their case. We typically refer to the dissemination of willfully biased ideas and opinions as **propaganda** and, according to Lasswell, Casey and Smith (1935), it is here that the study of persuasion began.

The concept of propaganda had its first use in a papal decree by Pope Gregory XV, when he established the Scara Congregatio de Propaganda Fide in 1622. This office of propaganda was created as a clearinghouse for information that could persuade men and women to understand and accept Roman Catholic doctrine. It was designed to convince and to persuade: Followers of the Roman Catholic Church viewed it as an attempt to educate; followers of the Protestant Reformation probably saw it as propaganda as we currently use the term. Nonetheless, the term propaganda seemed to lie dormant until it was picked up again to disparagingly describe certain "inconvenient news and opinions" (Lasswell et al., 1935, p. 3) put forth by other governments in the run-up to WWI. President Woodrow Wilson created the Committee on Public Information as an independent government agency of the United States, charged with combating the slanted and untrue propaganda of the enemy. In his book *How We Advertised America*, George Creel, the chair of that committee, described the committee's use of the techniques of persuasion that helped persuade America to join the World War (Creel, 1920). He proclaimed, in effect, that he had sold the war to the American public.

SETTING THE RESEARCH AGENDA: ARISTOTLE'S RHETORIC, LASSWELL'S QUESTION AND THE YALE COMMUNICATION AND ATTITUDE CHANGE PROGRAM

The systematic study of the principles of persuasion began in earnest years later. Ironically, it was the needs of another war that energized the scientific study of attitudes. The build-up of Fascist and Nazi regimes in Europe created the need to understand the roots of, and resistance to, propaganda. The Information and Education Division (IED) was created within the War Department and Carl Hovland, a psychologist at Yale University, took leave to direct its program. The IED rejected Creel's approach of 'selling' the war through misinformation and propaganda. Instead, Hovland's group was directed to study the principles of persuasion and to use that understanding to enhance U.S. soldiers' attitudes toward the war. Following the war's conclusion, Hovland returned to Yale University, bringing with him the skills and techniques developed during his wartime research as well as his interest in persuasive communication. It would be with these that he would found the **Yale Communications and Attitude Change Program**.

Hovland was committed to the scientific method. His approach was to systematically manipulate independent variables that he thought would affect persuasion and then measure the outcomes. Prior to Hovland, the longstanding tradition was to seek scientific advance through applied research directly addressing or counteracting rival communication (Delia, 1987). Hovland's contribution—in a move thematic to social psychology as a discipline—was to redistribute the emphasis of communication and propaganda science to basic research. His approach was not wedded to finding out if a particular Nazi or Allied war message was an effective piece of propaganda, but rather to understand the general conditions that rendered messages persuasive.

How can such a program be organized? What factors can be studied systematically to create a mosaic of effective persuasion? The organizational principle that describes the Yale Group's agenda can be ascribed to the Greek philosopher Aristotle, who believed in the importance of persuasion. Aristotle vehemently disagreed with the Sophists that the truth of a proposition is irrelevant to an argument, but he was not as confident as his teacher, Plato, that people trained in philosophy would simply glean the truth of a proposition from study. He believed that it was necessary to use persuasion as a way to teach people the truth.

In *Rhetoric*, Aristotle laid out his understanding of persuasion. In doing so, he also established the agenda for 20th century research in attitude change. Aristotle wrote,

> Of the modes of persuasion furnished by the spoken word, there are three kinds. The first depends on the personal character of the speaker; the second on putting the audience into a certain frame of mind; the third on the proof . . . provided by words of the speech itself.

Aristotle's dictum was later paraphrased by the sociologist Harold Lasswell (1948) as, **"Who says what to whom . . . and with what effect?"** 'With what effect?' was, of course, the dependent variable, and it had become measureable through the pioneering efforts of Thurstone, Likert and Osgood, whose work we considered in the first chapter. Now, with Lasswell's question and Aristotle's insights, the independent variables could be grouped into three discrete categories: (1) the speaker; (2) the communication itself; and (3) the audience. Hovland and his colleagues set out to collect data to examine the many facets of this agenda (e.g., Hovland, Janis, & Kelley, 1953).

Communicator Characteristics and Persuasion

Most prominent in Lasswell's question is the role of the 'who' in the persuasive exchange. That is, *who* is doing the persuading? Much research has looked at these **source characteristics** and what characteristics, regardless of the content of the message, make for a persuasive appeal.

Source Credibility: Expertise

When Aristotle suggested that effective persuasion was a function of the character of the speaker, he signaled the importance of source credibility. One factor influencing credibility is the communicator's **expertise**. Other factors being equal, a physics professor is more believable when trying to convince someone about the possibility of North Korea's building an atomic weapon than is a writer of popular fiction. In this instance, the credibility of the communicator is not endemic to her or his character, but rather resides in the knowledge that the professor has accrued in that position. The writer has greater expertise when discussing literary matters, and she has greater credibility in persuading people what to think about literary agents and publishing companies.

Hovland and Weiss (1951) presented participants with a persuasive communication—identical between conditions—that had ostensibly been written either by a high-expertise source or a low-expertise source. For example, an article about the feasibility of building nuclear submarines was either attributed to J. Robert Oppenheimer, a world-renowned physicist on nuclear submarines, or to *Pravda*, the propaganda magazine of the Communist Party. Similarly, a message about the use of antihistamine drugs was attributed either to *New England Journal of Biology and Medicine*, or to a mass circulation pictorial magazine. After reading the message, the researchers measured changes in attitudes toward each of the topics and found corroborating evidence for the hypothesis: High-expertise sources produced more attitude change (measured as change in attitudes in the direction of the persuasive communication) than low-expertise sources, despite the fact that the messages were precisely the same.

Source Credibility: Trustworthiness
Hovland, Janis and Kelley (1953) separated source credibility into a function of two characteristics: Expertise and **trustworthiness**. They defined expertise as "the extent to which a communicator is perceived to be a source of valid assertions." Trustworthiness, on the other hand is the *"degree of confidence [one places] in the communicator's intent to communicate assertions he considers most valid"* (p. 21). Both expertise and trustworthiness are necessary components of credibility.

One way to instantiate trustworthiness is to have a communicator advocate a position that would seem to be against his or her self-interest. Eagly, Wood, and Chaiken (1978) had participants read a transcript of a politician giving a pro-environmental speech to an influential voting group previously described as either pro-business (and by the nature of the experimental design, anti-environmental) or pro-environmental. They reasoned that participants would expect the source to tailor the message to the audience; however, this expectancy was disconfirmed for the pro-business audience condition as the politician delivered a pro-environmental message. Eagly et al. (1978) predicted that participants in the expectancy disconfirmation condition would be more persuaded (as accessed through attitude change) and believe the source to be more sincere than those in the expectancy confirmation condition. Indeed, this is what they found: Higher reported honesty and sincerity for a disconfirming source, and accompanying increased attitude change—again, in spite of identical messages.

Walster, Aronson and Abrahams (1966) had participants hear a communication from a convicted criminal. The topic of the speech was whether the police should be granted more or less power at the risk of jeopardizing individual liberties. If the convict argued in favor of expanding police power, he was seen as more trustworthy. Similar to Eagly et al.'s (1978) finding, the trustworthy communicator—even a convict—was more successful at persuading the participants than the less trustworthy communicator.

In another study on source trustworthiness, Walster and Festinger (1962) simulated conditions where a persuasive message is inadvertently overheard, rather than explicitly delivered. They had participants listen to a speaker who was trying to persuade another student that the link between cigarette smoking and cancer was a misconception. In the experimental condition, the participants believed that the speaker had no idea the participant was present. In the control condition, the speaker was aware that the participant was listening. Several days later, participants were administered a health survey in their classrooms. The key question on the survey asked participants how certain they were that cigarette smoking leads to lung cancer. The results showed that, for participants who smoked, the link between smoking and cancer was doubted more strongly (i.e., people were more persuaded) when the communication had been overheard rather when it was intended to be heard.

We pause to note that the primary goal of the Yale group was to document the factors that led to increased effectiveness of a communication. The program was less focused on explaining why. Learning theories based on Pavlov's (1927) classical conditioning, Skinner's (1938) operant conditioning and Hull's (1943) drive theory were predominant themes in many branches of psychology during this era and it was a ready assumption that persuasion was a function of learning: Credible sources facilitated learning; non-credible sources inhibited learning. That view has been challenged as being an incomplete or incorrect, leading to more nuanced approaches (Briñol & Petty, 2009; Greenwald, 1968; Petty, Briñol, & Tormala, 2002; Petty, Ostrom, & Brock, 1981). As one illustration, Tormala, Briñol and Petty (2006) suggest that attitudes and persuasion are at the service of self-validity—a feeling of confidence that our reactions to a message are valid. In the view of self-validity theory, we are persuaded by strong arguments from a highly credible source not because we learn the arguments better but because the source provides a sense of confidence, which increases our feeling of self-validity. We will examine more of the current approaches in the chapters that follow.

THE SLEEPER EFFECT

The previously described studies make it clear that source credibility affects the persuasiveness of an appeal. Low credibility acts as a discounting cue, which signals the recipient of a persuasive message to give limited weight, attention or importance to that argument—or to disregard it completely. Discounting cues play a crucial role in the intriguing persuasion phenomenon known as the **sleeper effect**, to which we now turn.

The sleeper effect draws its origin from a study by Hovland, Lumsdaine and Sheffield (1949), who were investigating the endurance of persuasion effects following propaganda films. To study this, the researchers screened the film *The Battle for Britain* to United States servicemen during WWII. As a motivational film, it was designed to increase soldiers' belief in the likelihood of being victorious. The film depicts the Battle for Britain, which pitted the eventually victorious British Royal Air Force against the Nazi Luftwaffe. Five days—and then again nine weeks—after the film, the researchers re-administered the original war attitudes questionnaire to assess attitude change. In general, they found greater attitude change from those participants completing the survey five days after the film compared to those completing the survey after nine weeks. The data demonstrated clear evidence of attitude decay wherein the effects of the film waned over time. The implication—which is consistent with lay intuition—is that attitudes, especially as changed by a persuasive message, tend to decay over time.

However, upon examination of individual items within the scales, the researchers made an intriguing discovery: Some items were rated more favorably at nine weeks, relative to at five days. Additionally, this oddity was strongest for those participants who initially showed lower acceptance of the film's messages. The researchers suspected that some cue embedded in the message may have been the culprit. Cues whose aim was to discount the message—that is, provide recipients a reason not to trust the message or its source—coincided with the delayed attitude change. They referred to this delayed persuasion over time as the sleeper effect.

Recall the study by Hovland and Weiss (1951), described previously, in which people who heard highly credible communicators were more persuaded than people who heard less credible communicators. This effect is depicted on left side of Figure 4.1. Hovland and Weiss's study was also designed to pursue the interesting lead from the Battle of Britain research—examining what would happen over time following successful persuasion. To test this, some participants were asked about their attitudes four weeks following the communications. The results are depicted on the right side of Figure 4.1. We can see that four weeks after exposure to the communication, the persuasion created by the highly credible communicator decayed and the persuasion caused by the less credible communicator increased. By the end of the four weeks, there was no difference between the effectiveness of the highly and less credible communicator. *The sleeper effect refers to the increase in attitude change, following a time interval, resulting from a persuasive appeal from a low credible source.*

The study by Hovland and Weiss provided the first experimental evidence for the sleeper effect, but did not address the process that caused it. One way to think

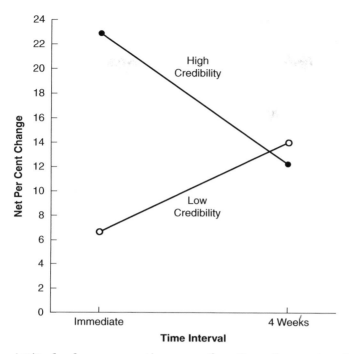

FIGURE 4.1 *Attitude change over time as a function of source credibility.*
Source: Hovland, C. I., & Weiss, W. (1951). The influence of source credibility on communication
effectiveness. *Public opinion quarterly, 15*(4), 635–650. Reprinted with permission.

about the situation is that people tend to dissociate the communication from the
communicator as time goes by. When we hear or read a communication from a
trustworthy expert, we are influenced in part by the words of the message, and in
part by the cue that the communicator is credible. Similarly, when we know the
communicator is not credible, we are influenced by the message minus the effect
due to the low credibility of the communicator. Over time, we dissociate the two
effects. By the term 'dissociation', we mean that people may no longer be consciously aware of the connection between source and message. They may easily
become aware if they are reminded, but time renders the connection less available.

In order to test this idea, Kelman and Hovland (1953) had participants listen
to a communication about the treatment of juvenile delinquents. For one group
of participants, the speaker was a highly credible juvenile court judge while for
another group, it was someone who was recently arrested for peddling narcotics.
Attitude measures were taken before, immediately following and three weeks after
the communication. The top panel of Figure 4.2 shows the replication of the sleeper
effect, as well as the decay that Hovland and Weiss had found. The bottom panel

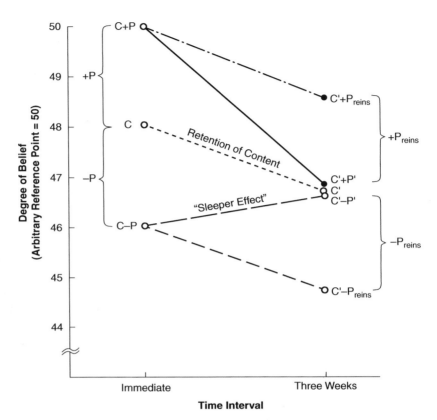

FIGURE 4.2   *Effects of content and prestige factors on degree of belief as a function of time and reinstatement (or not) of the communicator.*
Source: Kelman, H.C., & Hovland, C.I. (1953). "Reinstatement" of the communicator in delayed measurement of opinion change. *The Journal of Abnormal and Social Psychology*, 48(3), 327. Reprinted with permission.

of Figure 4.2 shows what happened when the investigators specifically reminded participants of who the source of the communication was. That is, they *reinstated* the cue that linked the message to its high- or low-credibility source. Under these conditions, attitude decay remained, but the sleeper effect was eliminated. This supports the idea that the dissociation between the message and its source credibility cue is responsible for the sleeper effect.

Revising the Sleeper Effect

An extensive series of studies attempted to verify and then modify the way in which we conceive of the sleeper effect. Gillig and Greenwald (1974) expressed doubt about the sleeper effect, reporting the results of seven experiments that failed to show evidence for what they termed an absolute sleeper effect (i.e., the increase in persuasion over time from a low credible source). They were able to find evidence, however, for a *relative sleeper effect*, which is the tendency for initial persuasion to decrease over time, but decrease less than it does when the message was attributed to a highly credible source. This led to their expressing skepticism about the actual existence of an absolute sleeper effect.

A subsequent series of influential studies was able to delineate the conditions necessary for the absolute sleeper effect. Gruder and his colleagues (Gruder, Cook, Hennigan, Flay, Alessis, & Halmaj, 1978) asked participants to read a message that argued against shortening a normal workweek from five days to four days. Instead of using source credibility as the reason that the audience should discount the message, Gruder et al. (1978) provided a specific statement in the message that warned readers that the communicator's arguments were flawed. They found that the absolute sleeper effect was alive and well, provided the discounting cue followed—rather than preceded—the message. Pratkanis, Greenwald, Leippe and Baumgardner (1988) extended Gruder et al.'s analysis, noting that the sleeper effect was robust when: (1) people pay attention to the content of a message before receiving a discounting cue; (2) the cue is presented immediately following the message; and (3) people attend to the cue. If these three conditions are met, then the absolute sleeper effect will occur. People will show a low degree of persuasion immediately following the message if it has a discounting cue (e.g., a less credible communicator) but show an increase in persuasion over time—i.e., the absolute sleeper effect.

Pratkanis et al. offered a slightly different explanation for the process that underlies the sleeper effect. In their view, the sleeper effect is not based on people dissociating the communicator from the communication. Rather, it is an issue of differential memory decay. From prior work (Miller & Campbell, 1959), we know that when people receive conflicting messages on an issue, they have a difficult time integrating them into a single message. Rather, each is stored separately in memory, and the first message is retained longer than the second. In the case of the sleeper effect, the decay rate for the communicator is more rapid than the decay rate for the message, allowing the content of the message to increase in effectiveness as memory for the source decays.

Kumakale and Albarracín (2004) applied meta-analytic methodology to the sleeper effect by examining 72 individual studies on the topic. Their review reveals two important conclusions about the sleeper effect. First, confirming Pratkanis et al.'s (1988) observation, effect sizes for the sleeper effect were stronger if the discounting cue followed rather than preceded the persuasive message. In other words, reading a message that you soon realize was authored by a disreputable source facilitates a sleeper effect; knowing the compromised credibility of the source prior to reading the message does not. Second, the sleeper effect is most prominent when the initial impact of both the message and the discounting cue are strong and in opposing persuasive directions. If the persuasive message initially overpowers the discounting cue, a sleeper effect does not occur. In sum, the sleeper effect stands—albeit in revised form—as a limiting feature of the effect of source credibility on persuasion. Less expert or untrustworthy sources typically lead to less persuasion; however, under specific conditions, their impact actually increases over time.

Source Attractiveness

Are physically attractive people better able to persuade an audience than are unattractive communicators? Experimental evidence suggests that the answer is yes, but for reasons that are not immediately obvious. Chaiken (1979) employed trained male and female confederates in a field study in which they approached undergraduate students, requesting they complete an opinion survey. Before they gave the survey to the participants, the confederates delivered a brief persuasive message in favor of removing meat from dining halls. Independent judges rated the attractiveness of each confederate. The data showed that attractive sources, relative to unattractive sources, elicited greater agreement with the persuasive message and greater compliance with an attached behavioral measure (signing a petition in favor of the persuasive message).

This does not surprise anyone who has glanced at a magazine advertisement or watched a television commercial. With few exceptions, we expect spokespersons who extol products in advertisements to be attractive. Fashion models sell cars, athletes sell clothes; they do so without the implication that they know more about the products they are selling than we do. Mills and Aronson (1965) had participants listen to a communication given by a beautiful woman. The topic was irrelevant to her beauty, but she was nonetheless more effective than a less attractive communicator in convincing her audience. A later study by Eagly and Chaiken (1975) replicated this effect and added another interesting piece of the puzzle: They found that audiences expected attractive communicators to support more desirable positions.

One potential explanation for these findings is the **halo effect**, which stands as one of the oldest phenomena of social psychology. First described as a 'halo' by Edward Thorndike in 1920, the effect refers to a tendency to apply similar ratings of people's trait indiscriminately. Thorndike (1920a) described a study in which employees of a large company found "very highly correlated and very evenly correlated" (p. 1) trait ratings of other employees in the company. Noting the consistency of such trait ratings in a variety of contexts, Thorndike concluded that people with certain special abilities or qualities are conferred additional advantages by being rated highly on many traits. He concluded that such qualities confer a 'halo' around a person, illuminating all aspects of that person to the level of their unique quality.

In her review on the effects of attractiveness in social influence, Chaiken (1986) found that physical attractiveness indeed conveys certain qualities that impact the persuasiveness of the communicator's message. Highly attractive people are perceived to have qualities of warmth, social emotional competence, expertise and intellectual competence (Chaiken, 1986, p. 150). These are impressive characteristics that people attribute to attractive persons, but they are not the factors that statistically mediate the attractive person's greater persuasiveness. Instead, the factor that appears to cause greater persuasion is liking. Chaiken explains that people show greater liking for others who are physically attractive, and, through this route, are more persuaded by them—a claim supported by considerable research (Chaiken, 1980; Chaiken & Eagly, 1983, Insko, Thompson, Stroebe, Shaud, Pinner, & Layton, 1973; Stroebe, Insko, Thompson, & Layton, 1971; Snyder & Rothbart, 1971). In addition to attractiveness leading to liking, which in turn leads to effectiveness of persuasion, there may also be a kernel of truth in the direct effect of attractiveness on persuasion. Goldman and Lewis (1977) found that physically attractive people have more well-developed social skills, leading Chaiken (1986) to suggest that physically attractive people may actually be more persuasive than less attractive people. The claim suggests a self-fulfilling prophecy wherein attractive people are believed to be more sociable (due to the halo effect), causing people around them to treat them as if they were more sociable, leading to their developing of greater social skills. As a result, attractive people actually come to possess a greater repertoire of tools that help them persuade people—skills such as assertiveness (Dion & Stein, 1978), verbal fluency and self-concepts important for persuasion (Chaiken, 1979). Together, both of these lines of research paint a unified picture of the benefit of having an attractive source deliver a persuasive message. Not only is an attractive source believed to be more credible and to engender more liking, but they may indeed be better able to deliver a persuasive message.

Source Attractiveness: Similarity-Attraction

The **similarity-attraction effect** (Blankenship, Hnat, Hess, & Brown, 1984; Byrne & Griffitt, 1969) refers to the general finding whereby people are attracted to similar others. One of the most robust findings in the similarity-attraction literature is that people feel more attracted to others whose attitudes are similar to their own. Nass and Lee (2001) extended this effect to the persuasion context—with a novel twist: The experimentally manipulated similarity was between a human participant and a computer-generated voice. Thirty-six introverts and 36 extroverts, as determined by their scoring at the extreme ends of an individual difference measure of introversion/extraversion, were asked to listen to a computer-generated speech in the laboratory. The voice for the computer-generated speech was manipulated to be either introverted or extraverted using linguistic vocal cues of speech intensity, mean frequency, frequency range and speech rate. Thus, introverts and extroverts listened to either an introverted or extroverted computer-generated voice read reviews of five books. As they had predicted, Nass and Lee (2001) found that participants who listened to a matching/similar voice extol the value of the books rated the book reviews as higher in quality and indicated a greater likelihood of purchasing the book, relative to participants who listened to a mismatching/dissimilar voice. The authors concluded that the perceived similarity in personality increased attraction, which in turn caused greater persuasion of the same persuasive message.

Gender of the Source

Who are more persuasive, men or women? Goldberg (1968) sought an answer to this question, observing that in traditional Western society, the work of males is typically overvalued relative to identical work of women. He hypothesized that this would carry over to messages delivered by the two genders. To test his hypothesis, he had a group of women rate the persuasiveness of articles across six fields, three stereotypically feminine and three stereotypically masculine. He manipulated whether the article was attributed to a male or a female author. Consistent with his prediction, he found that women rated articles written by men to be more persuasive than when the identical article was attributed to a woman.

However, a replication of the study by Levenson and colleagues (1975), using both male and female participants, found no differences relating to the gender of the author or the participant. A meta-analysis by Swim and her colleagues (1989), examining more than 130 studies conducted using a similar technique, found no support for Goldberg's original conclusion. Most likely, the effect of gender on persuasion is a complex matter that is more related to whether the communication topic is related to gender. In general, despite Goldberg's (1968) original study, there does not appear to be sufficient evidence to support a claim that there is a main effect for either gender in persuasiveness.

THE MESSAGE AND PERSUASION

At the core of any persuasion attempt is an actual persuasive message of one kind or another. Research clarifying what makes for a good persuasive message is grouped under the heading of **message factors**. While there are certain broad classes of messages whose persuasiveness is documented, there is no single prescription for the kind of message that is persuasive in all contexts. To understand message factors is to understand how to persuade a target in a particular persuasive exchange for a particular purpose.

Message Discrepancy

When one receives a persuasive message, there exists a discrepancy between the message and the concurrently held attitude. The traditional framework for understanding this discrepancy between the recipient's attitude and the message is **social judgment theory**, developed by Sherif and Hovland in 1961. Social judgment theory holds that the discrepancy of a message from a recipient's attitude can be understood as falling within one of three latitudes: The latitude of acceptance, the latitude of non-commitment or the latitude of rejection. If we understand attitudes to fall along a continuum from highly negative to highly positive, these latitudes encompass different areas based on where the recipient's actual attitude lies.

Immediately surrounding the recipient's attitude is the latitude of acceptance. These are attitudes that are proximal enough to limit counterargument or disagreement. Such messages, while not precisely matching the recipient's attitude, hold a discrepancy inconsequential enough not to matter. On the far extreme from the latitude of acceptance is the latitude of rejection. This latitude encompasses all areas of the attitude spectrum that the recipient feels are unacceptable. Note that these need not only be on one side of the scale: If someone rejects gun control, it is not to say that she also necessarily believes in open access to firearms for any and all individuals. Such a message, while resting on the same side of the gun control spectrum, may well fall within her latitude of rejection. This area of the attitude spectrum encompasses all positions or attitudes that the recipient rejects forthwith.

Falling between the latitude of acceptance and rejection is the latitude of non-commitment. Within this latitude are attitude positions about which the recipient is undecided; they are neither so similar as to be immediately accepted, nor so dissimilar as to be immediately rejected. Research by Hovland, Harvey and Sherif (1957) suggests that persuasion forms an inverted-U curve around the original attitude, with maximal persuasiveness occurring within the latitude of acceptance, and a gradual tapering off as the position of the persuasive message moves outward (toward and into the latitude of rejection). However, the more extreme the participants' attitudes, the more they judge positions other than their own as occupying the latitude of rejection. The key feature of social judgment theory for persuasion is its guidance for structuring a persuasive message given a recipient's baseline attitude. Attempting to move message recipients into their latitudes of rejection is a very difficult task. On the other hand, persuading recipients to move to positions within their latitudes of acceptance or non-commitment is a task with a considerably greater likelihood of success.

Figure 4.3 illustrates social judgment theory's take on the attitudes of two different individuals. Recipient A, when asked her opinion toward gun control, responds precisely in the middle of the scale. Her latitude of acceptance means that a persuasive message advocating slightly for or slightly against gun control will be have a greater chance of being accepted. On the other hand, due to her neutral position, she will be inclined to reject a message that is either extremely for or extremely against gun control—her latitude of rejection. Between these latitudes

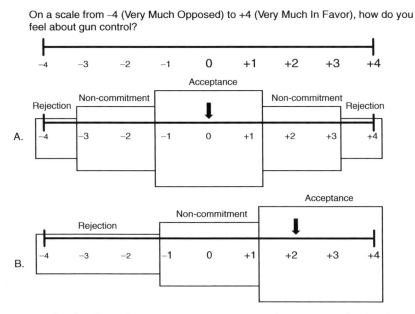

On a scale from –4 (Very Much Opposed) to +4 (Very Much In Favor), how do you feel about gun control?

FIGURE 4.3 *Latitudes of acceptance, non-commitment, and rejection for two message recipients, according to social judgment theory.*

lies her latitude of non-commitment—the moderate positions on both ends of the scale—where persuasion is possible but not automatic.

Recipient B, on the other hand, is considerably more in favor of gun control. Her latitude of acceptance encompasses the extreme end of the scale in favor of gun control; her latitude of rejection encompasses the same extremity but on the opposite side of the scale. According to social judgment theory, Recipient B would be open to persuasion toward the middle of the scale, but would outright reject anything more opposed to gun control than that.

Discrepancy of the Message and Credibility of the Source

Social judgment theory makes it clear that creating messages that are widely discrepant from a recipient's attitude makes persuasion a formidable task. People work hard to resist messages that are in their latitudes of rejection. Convincing Allison, a bona fide dog lover, that cats are preferable as pets will be very difficult, if not impossible. The task of the persuader, however, may not comport well with this resistance. Communicators often wish to create maximal change in people's attitudes. Although they will have more success if the position they are espousing is within the latitude of acceptance, the magnitude of the change can only be small.

The position that is being espoused is, by definition, close to the position that the recipient already holds. In most cases, the optimal change occurs in the latitude of non-commitment where people are willing to entertain a new position. It is in the latitude of non-commitment that factors we discuss in this chapter have the greatest likelihood of being effective.

Nonetheless, there are times when communicators wish to sway people's attitudes toward more extreme positions. Research has shown that when topics are not important to people, then attitude change varies directly with the magnitude of the discrepancy: The greater the discrepancy, the greater the change (Hovland & Pritzker, 1957). On more important attitudes, however, people's latitudes of rejection grow larger and persuasion becomes more difficult. One way to increase persuasion for issues with large discrepancies is to use highly credible communicators. Aronson, Turner and Carlsmith (1963) asked participants to rate the quality of stanzas of poetry. The participants then received feedback from knowledgeable communicators that was either mildly, moderately or extremely discrepant from their own ratings. The communications were attributed either to the famous poet T.S. Eliot or to Miss Agnes Sterns, a teacher at a local state teachers' college. When participants re-rated the stanzas (as a measure of the degree of attitude change), the results showed that for a communicator with only moderate credibility, the message was effective up to a point. However, when the discrepancy increased so as to be extremely discrepant with the participants' ratings, the message was ignored and persuasion vanished. On the other hand, T.S. Eliot's opinion continued to have an effect, even as the discrepancy between the participants' and his message continued to grow.

A study by Bergin (1962) demonstrated a similar phenomenon with regard to important attitudes about the self. Male participants were given information about themselves that differed in varying degrees from their own self-concept. Some were told that they were more feminine than they had initially rated themselves. The message that conveyed their degree of femininity was attributed to a high- or a low-credibility source. At a later rating, participants' own rating of their degree of femininity changed as a direct function of the degree of discrepancy, but only when the source was high in credibility. When highly discrepant information about femininity came from a less credible source, participants were less influenced by it than they were by the mildly discrepant information.

Fear Appeals

This is your brain. This is heroin. This is what happens to your brain after snorting heroine. And this is what your body goes through. . . . It's not over yet! And this is what your family goes through! And your friends! And your money! And your job! And your self-respect! And your future! And your life. . . ! Any questions?

(This Is Your Brain On Drugs, Partnership for a Drug-Free America, 1998)

There is little more motivating than fear. Whether it is fear of losing to cancer, fear of rotten gums from tooth decay or fear of an imminent attack from terrorist factions, persuasive messages often appeal to our fear of some consequence to motivate change. Research on fear appeals traces its roots to an early study by Janis and Feshbach (1953), who exposed high school students to persuasive messages about oral hygiene that relied on fear of varying intensity (high, moderate and low fear). They found that the low-fear appeal was most effective in motivating pro-health behavior, followed closely by moderate levels of fear. The message containing the high degree of fear was the least effective in producing healthy oral hygiene behaviors. The conclusion of this research—that high amounts of fear are counterproductive for persuasion—was adopted as conventional wisdom for many years. Readers may recall that until quite recently, very few advertisements—even those that were designed as public service anti-smoking campaigns—used high levels of fear to motivate change.

The research picture changed slowly, as evidence mounted of a direct relationship between the amount of fear and persuasion. Dabbs and Leventhal (1966) used fear successfully to change people's attitudes on the advisability of taking injections for tetanus. Leventhal and Niles (1965) found a direct relationship between fear and safe driving recommendations, and Evans, Rozelle, Lasater, Dembroski and Allen (1970) showed a similar pattern for upgrading dental hygiene practice. A more recent meta-analysis of the fear appeal literature by Witte and Allen (2000) concluded that "strong fear appeals . . . are more persuasive than low or weak fear appeals" (p. 591). Rogers (1983) provided a theoretical explanation for the role of fear in persuasion. In his **protection motivation theory**, Rogers suggests that the motivation of recipients in response to a fear appeal is protection from negative consequences. How one goes about protecting oneself, however, is contingent upon one's perceived efficacy in the situation. If a person feels he is efficacious in response to a message, a fear appeal is persuasive; but lacking this efficacy, he will not be persuaded (Maddux & Rogers, 1983). This prediction is consistent with Witte and Allen's (2000) meta-analysis, which found that strong fear appeals coupled with high-efficacy messages are best at motivating behavioral changes, and strong fear appeals with low-efficacy messages are worst. In Janis and Feshbach's original 1953 study, participants were not shown an efficacious way to prevent gingivitis and tooth decay. Fear is only persuasive if it provides recipients a route through which they can avoid negative consequences.

Conclusion-Drawing

Some messages are constructed in a way that clearly draws the conclusion that the communicator wishes the audience to remember. More than one debater has been advised to "tell the audience what you intend to say, say it, and then tell the audience what you said." On the other hand, a case can be made to allow the audience to derive their own conclusions from the information presented. Is there an advantage for one type of message over the other? McGuire (1969) observed that early insights about the strengths and weakness of conclusion-drawing stem from the psychoanalytic literature and nondirective therapy (Rogers, 1945) which suggests that patients may be more accepting of conclusions they themselves are led to draw, relative to those explicitly drawn by the therapist. Indeed, in a series of five studies, Slamecka and Graf (1978) found evidence to support this belief in the field of memory. In their studies, participants were presented with pairs of words that were either complete (control condition; rapid—quick) or incomplete (generation condition; rapid—q___). Participants were informed of the rule linking the two words and either memorized the pairs (control) or generated the matching word (generation). All participants were then tested on their memory of the words presented during the stimulus phase. As predicted, the researchers found that recognition and confidence were both higher in the generation condition. This finding suggests there is power in generating information beyond simply encoding.

Conclusion-drawing does not always lead to greater persuasion (Hovland & Mandell, 1952). In order for people to be more persuaded by drawing their own conclusions, they must be motivated to do so. Linder and Worchel (1970) conducted a study to show the importance of motivation on the effect of drawing conclusions. They presented an argument to students in the form of logical syllogisms. Premises were presented which would lead to the conclusion that cigarette smoking is a cause of lung cancer. The investigators varied the number of syllogisms whose conclusions they provided and the number of syllogisms the participants had to solve for themselves. Motivation to arrive at the conclusions was varied by examining the data from those participants who were smokers and those who were nonsmokers. Linder and Worchel reasoned that the issue would be more important, involving and motivating for smokers. The results showed that for participants who smoked, having to do the work of drawing conclusions made the arguments more persuasive than when a high proportion of the conclusions were already drawn. Similarly, Silvera, Kardes, Pfeiffer, Arsena, and Goss (2013) showed participants a persuasive message and then asked some of them to generate their own positive arguments. Other participants were only read the message. Consistent with Linder and Worchel's study, Silvera et al. (2013) found that, for highly motivated participants, being allowed to generate their own arguments was particularly effective—and persuasive.

One-Sided and Two-Sided Communications

Most of us know people who try to persuade us by telling us only their side of an issue and others who tell us both sides. The latter will always conclude that their side of the issue is most accurate, but they do make us aware of the arguments on the other side. The question of whether it is more effective to use one-sided or two-sided communications has had a long history in the field of persuasion, constituting one of the foundational studies of the Yale program (Hovland, Lumsdaine, & Sheffield, 1949). The context of the original study was an attempt by the U.S. government during World War II to convince its troops that it would take at least another two years of hard effort to conclude the war in the Pacific following Germany's surrender in the European theater. Several hundred soldiers were presented with either a one-sided or a two-sided communication that came to the desired conclusion. Initial results showed that both messages were equally effective in persuading the troops. A more interesting pattern emerged when Hovland et al. looked at the data separately from men who were in agreement with the message before they heard it and those who were initially opposed. Those who began in favor of the position were more likely to become even more favorable to the communication's position if it was one-sided. Those who were initially unfavorable were more persuaded when the communication presented both sides of the argument.

Jones and Brehm (1970) extended the understanding of one and two sided communications by suggesting that two-sided communications are more effective to the extent that people realize that there are two legitimate sides of the argument. The researchers devised a courtroom analogue of a persuasion context in which participants were asked to play the role of jurors. They were informed that they would hear the prosecution summary in the case, and half were informed that it was not an open-and-shut case (i.e., there were two sides to the argument). Then, half of the participants were presented with a one-sided prosecution argument and the other half read a two-sided statement. The jurors were then asked how much they were persuaded by the prosecutor's statement. The results indicated an overall advantage for one-sided communications in the courtroom context, but the effect was significantly diminished if the jurors were aware that there was a tenable case to be made on the other side.

The context of an argument also has a bearing on whether one-sided or two-sided communications are most effective in persuasion. In a courtroom, we are unlikely to imagine a prosecutor or attorney making a strong case for the other side. Similarly, we do not expect our presidential candidates to make a two-sided communication as they ask for our support. On the other hand, we might expect a newspaper editorial to acknowledge the other side of an issue as it tries to convince us to believe the position it is advocating. In general, research has taught us that two-sided communications are likely to have advantages when people are initially opposed to the direction of the message or when people are aware that there are tenable arguments to be considered on the other side. To complete the picture, research has also shown that two-sided communications are maximally effective if the 'other side' is presented early, rather than late, in the message (Hass & Linder, 1972).

Audience Distraction

Conventional wisdom suggests that a persuasive message will have the greatest impact if it is clearly stated and recipients can give it their undivided attention. Although there is often truth to conventional wisdom, it is not always so. A message can sometimes have maximal impact if it provides stimuli that distract the audience from the tenets of the message. One such occasion is when the audience is likely to disagree with the position advocated in the message. Festinger and Maccoby (1964) had college students listen to a speech advocating an end to fraternities at their university. Some of the students were fraternity brothers, and therefore highly invested in their pro-fraternity attitudes. Other students were not members of fraternities. While they were listening to the speech, some of the students were distracted by watching *The Day of the Painter*, an amusing Academy Award winning film not at all connected to the issue of fraternities. The non-distracted students only watched a film of the anti-fraternity speech without distraction from the *Day of the Painter* film. Festinger and Maccoby reasoned that an audience strongly invested in the continued existence of fraternities would automatically counterargue a persuasive message levied against their group. Offering the distraction would disrupt them from counterarguing. When students' attitudes were measured following the speech, the results showed that students who were fraternity members were more persuaded by the speech in the distraction condition. Students who already questioned the value of fraternities (i.e., the non-members) were equally persuaded in the two conditions.

In a more directed test of the effects of distraction, Osterhouse and Brock (1970) recruited participants to listen to a persuasive message while being distracted with the task of calling out a series of flashing lights. Distraction was manipulated by varying the frequency of lights, either at moderate or high levels, to be compared with a control condition with no lights. After the task, participants were asked to list counterarguments in response to the message and also to complete an attitude measure about the topic presented in the persuasive message. The researchers found that as distraction increased, counterargument generation decreased, and attitude change toward the message occurred.

One of the domains in which distraction plays a role is in advertising. For many products, finding cogent arguments to present in a brief radio or television commercial can be difficult. Due to the context of the advertisement, such as interrupting a favorite program, or the limitation of finding convincing arguments, persuaders need to find ways to enhance positive responses and combat negative ones. Research has found that distraction can be useful to combat negative associations to a product, particularly if that distraction is humorous. In a novel extension of the distraction effect, Strick, Holland, van Baaren and van Knippenberg (2012) tested the impact of humor on negative responses to persuasive messages in advertising.

They found that humor was an effective strategy precisely because it distracted and disrupted people from forming negative thoughts about the brand being advertised. Rather than increasing positive affect and associations toward the brand, humor enhanced persuasion by inhibiting the formation of negative associations.

Repetition of Messages

Thomas Smith wrote in 1885 that:

> The first time people look at any given ad, they don't even see it.
> The second time, they don't notice it.
> The third time, they are aware that it is there.
> The fourth time, they have a fleeting sense that they've seen it somewhere before.
> The fifth time, they actually read the ad.
> The sixth time they thumb their nose at it.
> The seventh time, they start to get a little irritated with it.
> The eighth time, they start to think, "Here's that confounded ad again."
> The ninth time, they start to wonder if they're missing out on something.
> The tenth time, they ask their friends and neighbors if they've tried it.
> The eleventh time, they wonder how the company is paying for all these ads.
> The twelfth time, they start to think that it must be a good product.
> The thirteenth time, they start to feel the product has value.
> The fourteenth time, they start to remember wanting a product exactly like this for a long time.
> The fifteenth time, they start to yearn for it because they can't afford to buy it.
> The sixteenth time, they accept the fact that they will buy it sometime in the future.
> The seventeenth time, they make a note to buy the product.
> The eighteenth time, they curse their poverty for not allowing them to buy this terrific product.
> The nineteenth time, they count their money very carefully.
> The twentieth time prospects see the ad, they buy what is offering.
>
> (*Successful Advertising*, 7th Edition, 1885)

In a world where one is inundated with advertisements for every conceivable product, repetition of messages is a fact of life. Slogans and talking points for products and candidates are repeated on the airwaves and print media. According to Pratkanis and Aronson (2001), surveys about how people feel about advertisements consistently show that the most common complaint is the repetition of the same ads and slogans. Yet, a product like Ivory soap has been telling consumers that it is 99 and

44/100% pure since Harley Proctor first marketed his soap in 1882. Thomas Smith provides some insight into the processes that lead from the ineffectiveness of a single ad that people barely notice to one that influences consumers to purchase products. Smith was an ad man with good instincts and no research. Nonetheless, his writing suggests a reasonable set of explanations that could serve as a template for research. He first suggests that it requires repeated viewing of an advertisement before the recipient actually reads it. Next, there is a step of irritation at the repetition, but also curiosity. Eventually, the recipient moves toward increased interest, before eventually succumbing to the persuasive advertisement and purchasing the product.

Taking a very different perspective, Robert Zajonc (1968) suggested that there exists in people a non-conscious, automatic reaction to come to like a stimulus object as a result of repeated exposure, independent of any other reason for the greater liking. While not disagreeing about other phenomena that might co-occur with increased exposure, Zajonc's provocative argument was that the mere fact of repeated exposure causes greater liking. No attention, memory or thought processes are necessary.

Zajonc (1968) provided initial evidence in a study in which he told participants that he was studying how people learn non-native languages. English-speaking participants were shown Chinese ideographs once, twice, five times, ten times, twenty-five times or not at all. They were told that each of the characters represented an evaluative adjective and asked participants to guess how positive was each character's evaluative connotation. As predicted, the more often participants had seen a character, the more favorable they estimated its meaning to be. Repeated exposure to the characters led participants to like them significantly more, despite the fact that the procedure did not permit greater knowledge of the characters. The mere fact of repeated exposure led to greater positivity.

Although replicated many times (see Bornstein, 1989), the mere exposure effect is not without its limits. Grush (1976; see also Perlman & Oskamp, 1971) repeatedly exposed participants to positive and negative emotion words. After varying the number of repetitions, he asked participants to rate the valence they associated with the word. In general, he found that the valence of the word polarized as repetitions increased; that is, positive words were rated more positively and negative words more negatively.

Petty and Cacioppo (1979) found evidence consistent with another limitation of mere exposure. As Smith suggested (in his seventh repetition above), repetition can also lead to irritation and annoyance. The researchers presented participants with a persuasive message with 0, 1, 3, or 5 repetitions before assessing their attitudes toward the target. The results formed a quadratic pattern: A single repetition led to attitude change, three repetitions more so, but five repetitions dropped attitudes down to the level found with a single repetition. Similar findings were reported by Appel (1971) and by Calder and Sternthal (1980).

Pechmann and Stewart (1988) suggested that a two-stage model best accounts for the effects of repetition. During the first stage, a persuasive message has little effect until it 'wears in.' Once worn in, each repetition is beneficial. 'Wear-in' best maps onto Smith's 12th through 20th message repetitions, in which each subsequent repetition causes a more favorable attitude to develop. As repetition continues, persuasion enters the second stage of 'wear-out,' where additional repetitions typically produce negative effects (such as message counterargument). However, Pechmann and Stewart found that increased repetition did not always lead to wear-out, finding that under some conditions the effectiveness of repeated messages can be maintained. Gorn and Goldberg (1980) suggest that message variability is important in determining whether message repetition reaches maintenance or wear-out when entering this second stage. In their study, children exposed to many repetitions of the same commercial came to have a negative association with the product advertised; however, this was not so for children exposed to a message with slight variations. Their results, along with similar findings by McCullough and Ostrom (1980) and Mitchell and Olson (1981), suggest that favorable attitudes can be maintained and wear-out avoided by not repeating an identical message. Schumann, Petty and Clemons (1990) extended this work by showing that repetition with slight variation is particularly effective for audiences that are not especially motivated to learn about the product.

In general, the research is supportive of Thomas Smith's recommendations for advertisers. There is a generally positive effect for repeated exposure of a message with the caveat that the message was not evaluated negatively in the first instance and provided that there are slight variations in the message to prevent irritation and wear-out.

THE RECIPIENT AND PERSUASION

Recipients are not merely passive receivers to persuasion attempts. Rather, they embody rich mental experiences before, during and after receiving a persuasive appeal. The ways in which individuals differ is an important topic in all of psychology, and certainly in the area of persuasion. Do the differences among people extend to a personality trait that predicts persuasibility? By a **personality trait**, we mean a characteristic that is manifested across time and situations. The question, then, is whether there is a reliable personality trait that identifies people who are more likely to succumb to persuasion attempts at any time and in any situation. In their book, *Personality and Persuasibility*, Hovland and Janis (1959) conducted a series of investigations on this issue. They were able to identify some personalities who seemed to be more persuasible than others, but the effect was always a weak one. That amount of variance accounted for by trying to find a constellation of persuasible personality traits was far less than that accounted for by more social psychological factors. The search for the answer to the part of Lasswell's question (. . . to whom?) that specified audience characteristics would not be answered by a single personality trait. Rather, research shifted to a question of whether there were differences—certain **recipient factors**—that characterized an individual's response to persuasion in particular circumstances.

Intelligence and Self-esteem

The possibility that intelligence is related to persuasibility is an intriguing one. Are communicators more likely to have success by finding less intelligent people to send a persuasive message . . . or would more intelligent people be more likely to be persuaded? Psychologists have studied the issue but have not found a consistent main effect for intelligence. Crutchfield (1955) found a negative relationship between intelligence and persuasion, whereas Hovland and Janis (1959) found no overall relationship. Hovland, Lumsdaine and Sheffield (1949) examined the relationship between intelligence and the effectiveness of one- or two-sided communications and found none.

There are, however, some interesting and nuanced effects of intelligence on persuasion. McGuire (1969) made an important distinction between the process of **message comprehension** and **message yielding**, which often co-occur. A potential voter may listen to a liberal candidate's speech and decide to support that candidate. A second voter may listen, understand the points that the candidate is trying to make, but decide that she cannot support a candidate who takes a liberal position. A third voter may not pay much attention, or even be confused by, the substance of the candidate's arguments but nonetheless decide to support the candidate. For the first voter, persuasion occurred through both comprehension and yielding; for the second voter, comprehension was high but yielding to the conclusion was not; for the third voter, comprehension was low but the voter nonetheless yielded to the candidate's position. McGuire's (1969) distinction suggests the possibility that intelligence affects the comprehension and yielding processes differently. Intelligence may be positively related to comprehension but negatively related to yielding.

McGuire's distinction was tested empirically by Eagly and Warren (1976), who hypothesized that different levels of intelligence would interact with comprehension and yielding processes to impact persuasion. They asked high school students to listen to persuasive messages that either included arguments (recommendation plus supporting arguments) or did not (recommendation only). The researchers predicted that participants with higher intelligence scores would be more persuaded by messages that included arguments, whereas participants with lower intelligence scores would be more persuaded by messages lacking arguments but drawing to a conclusion. Indeed, this is what they found. Messages that contain genuine arguments require comprehension—which is facilitated by higher intelligence—whereas messages without genuine arguments require yielding to the message—which plays to lower intelligence.

Self-Esteem

Just as people vary in their levels of intelligence, they also vary in their levels of self-esteem. Like differences in intelligence, there is no single main effect for the relationship between self-esteem and persuasion. Research has shown that people who have little confidence or who have feelings of low self-worth are sometimes more easily persuaded than confident people, especially when the message is complex and difficult to comprehend (Gollub & Dittes, 1965). On the other hand, people with low self-esteem feel threatened by messages that challenge their beliefs and are motivated to avoid situations that cause threat (Silverman, 1964). Rhodes and Wood (1992) performed a meta-analysis on the literature linking self-esteem to persuasion. Based on McGuire's (1969) distinction between comprehension and yielding, they predicted a curvilinear relationship between self-esteem and persuasion. At very low levels of self-esteem, they reasoned that participants would avoid the message content, lacking interest or being easily distracted, whereas at high levels of self-esteem participants would comprehend but not yield to a message due to confidence in their own opinions or knowledge. Between these two extremes, however, lies a range within which recipients are maximally persuasible. In their meta-analysis, they analyzed persuasion research that included at least a tertile split of self-esteem, expecting to find an inverted-U curve. The results bore out their predictions: Both high and low self-esteem participants showed significantly less persuasion in response to a persuasive message than did medium self-esteem participants.

Need for Cognition

People differ in their need for cognition. We introduced the concept in Chapter 2, defining **need for cognition** as an individual difference variable that characterizes the degree to which people prefer to use thoughtful information processing. People high in the need for cognition prefer thinking deeply about issues and are more likely to be influenced by message arguments, whereas those low in the need for cognition rely on more fleeting aspects of an issue. As we also noted in Chapter 3, people high in the need for cognition are more likely to hold attitudes for the purpose of satisfying the knowledge function of attitudes (Katz, 1960). We shall re-visit the concept again in Chapter 5 as a variable that distinguishes people's use of different processes of attitude change.

The need for cognition, which is assessed with a validated scale developed by Cacioppo and Petty (1982; see also, Cacioppo, Petty, & Kao, 1986), acts as a recipient factor for persuasion. The greater the need for cognition, the more the recipient peruses the arguments in a persuasive message. Cacioppo, Petty and Morris (1983) provided evidence for this individual difference factor by presenting an argument in favor of raising university tuition to participants who differed in their degree of the need for cognition. Cacioppo et al. found that participants high in the need for cognition reported expending more effort thinking about the arguments contained in the message, recalled the arguments better and were more persuaded by strong arguments compared to people who were low in the need for cognition.

Differences in the need for cognition provide an insight into when people's attitudes become more polarized when thinking about an issue. Tesser (1978) provided evidence for a "mere thought" effect, which is a polarization that occurs when people are asked to think about their attitudes and opinions. Liberals become more liberal following thought; conservatives become more conservative. People who like a particular movie like it more; people who dislike the movie like it less. The link to need for cognition stems from the observation that people high in need for cognition are more likely to think, and, consequently, think about their attitudes.

Smith, Haugtvedt and Petty (1994) found that high need for cognition participants demonstrated greater attitude polarization than low need for cognition participants. However, Leone and Ensley (1986) found the opposite when explicitly instructing participants to consider their attitudes. Lassiter, Apple and Slaw (1996) offered a resolution, suggesting that instructing participants low in need for cognition to consider their attitudes requires them to engage in an activity they usually avoid. In doing so, they behaved like participants chronically high in need for cognition, leading to polarization. Those participants who are chronically high in the need for cognition typically consider their attitudes spontaneously. When Leone and Ensley instructed these participants to consider the arguments, Lassiter et al. (1996) suggested that high need for cognition participants focused on the arguments for the other side of the issue—thus leading to attitude moderation. To test this, the authors systematically varied whether or not participants were explicitly asked to consider their attitudes. As expected, they replicated both sets of findings under the predicted conditions.

Gender of the Recipient

As we noted, the gender of a communicator does not make a systematic difference in the effectiveness of a persuasive communication (Swim et al., 1989). On the other hand, there is a history of research implicating gender differences in the persuasibility of the respondent (Janis & Field, 1959; Knower, 1936). These studies found women to be more persuasible than men. McGuire (1969), in his review of the literature, concluded, "There seems to be a clear main-order effect of sex on influenceability such that females are more susceptible than males" (p. 251). Eagly and Carli (1981) conducted a meta-analysis of the extant literature and arrived at the same conclusion.

One potential explanation for this pattern of gender difference is that much of the material used in early studies of persuasion was of more interest to men than women: For example, a speech on the topic of whether a university football team should be allowed to go to the Rose Bowl. The accumulation of evidence that women are more persuasible than men may have been due to the preponderance of studies that used male-oriented topics. Karabenick (1983), replicating an earlier study by Sistrunk and McDavid (1971), found that women were more influenced by content that lay outside stereotypically female expertise and that men were more influenced by content that lay outside stereotypically male expertise. This suggests that females may not necessarily be more susceptible to influence, but rather researchers have inadvertently created study materials with masculine content, artificially inflating persuasibility. Eagly and Carli (1981) took issue with the interpretation that gender differences in persuasibility are a function of the content of the messages used in the studies. They conducted a meta-analysis of 61 studies that had reported gender differences and confirmed a consistent, although small, difference showing greater susceptibility to persuasion by women compared to men. They also found that studies showing greater female susceptibility to persuasion were more likely to occur when the authors of those studies were male rather than female. However, they found no support for Sistruck and McDavid's suggestion that the basis for the gender difference lay in the content of the materials used in the studies. Eagly and Carli asked a new group of male and female participants to rate their own knowledge and interest in the subject matter of the 61 studies. Men and women showed no reliable differences in their knowledge or interests. The researchers suggested that the basis for believing there is a gender difference in persuasibility may by partly due to male experimenters' eagerness to report gender differences when their findings show that men are less persuadable than women, and female experimenters being similarly eager to report instances that showed no difference.

Other contextual factors may also lead to differences in persuasion as a function of gender. Guadagno and Cialdini (2002) suggested that women and men differ in their goals during face-to-face discussions of persuasion topics. Men show competitive strivings for agency and independence; women strive for cooperation and harmony (Tannen, 1990). This led Guadagno and Cialdini (2002) to predict that women would be more susceptible to persuasion in a face-to-face context in which interpersonal cooperation is desired, but not in a setting in which the interpersonal context is diminished—such as impersonal email exchange. The researchers had male and female dyads discuss whether their university should institute comprehensive exams for students. Participants either had face-to-face discussions with someone of their own gender advocating for the exams, or they had identical discussions with a confederate via e-mail. As predicted, the investigators found that female participants showed more attitude change in the direction of the confeder-ate's remarks than did male participants, but only in the face-to-face, interpersonal context. When the communication was in the more impersonal e-mail format, males and females did not differ in the degree of persuasion.

PERSUASION AS A PROCESS: THE THEORETICAL UNDERPINNINGS OF ATTITUDE CHANGE

Message Learning

What is the process that leads people to change their attitudes when exposed to a communication? In this chapter, we have identified many of the factors that research has shown to facilitate attitude change, but we have not yet considered the process that leads to that change. For decades, the underlying assumption of atti-tude change research was that persuasion was based on *learning* (Hovland & Man-dell, 1952; Kelman & Hovland, 1953). All aspects of the persuasion process were thought to be effective only to the extent that they facilitated **message learning**. Only by attending to, and learning, a message can a recipient then internalize and be persuaded by its content.

This is most clearly the case when considering message-related factors. Well-organized content with logical arguments and conclusions help us learn the con-tent of the message. An instructor who selects a text to teach students the content of social psychology would certainly choose the most well organized and well-written volume, hoping that students would learn and accept its contents. Similarly, some-one trying to persuade a listener of the merits of free pre-school education for the disadvantaged would try to establish her reasoning in a well-constructed logical form. It seems reasonable that people need to learn the message in order to be affected by its contents.

Source characteristics can also be understood in a message learning approach. In Hovland and Weiss' (1951) study on communicator credibility, it was reasonable that an audience would attend more to a communication from a world class physi-cist writing about nuclear submarines than they would to a discredited propaganda magazine. Similarly, in Aronson, Turner and Carlsmith's study (1963), people were more likely to attend to an evaluation of poetry by T.S. Eliot than they were to an evaluation by a non-poet. Greater attention facilitates greater learning.

Another set of studies consistent with message learning as a necessary process for attitude change examined the effect of time delay on persuasion. Imagine that a student prepares diligently for an exam, finishing her studying the night prior to the exam. She is likely to be able to retain what she read and use it well when answering exam questions. However, if the exam were postponed for a week, then some of the content will have been forgotten by the time she needs it. In general, if messages need to be learned and the content retained, then we would expect that the longer the time period between exposure to a persuasive message and the measurement of attitudes, the less attitude change would be found. Miller and Campbell (1959), Insko (1964) and Watts and McGuire (1964) all found that persuasion was greatest when measured immediately following a persuasive message and diminished with the passage of time.

However, problems with message learning as the sole process behind attitude change were accumulating slowly. As Greenwald (1968) pointed out, "the overpowering reasonableness" of message learning allowed investigators to pay scant attention to a number of anomalies in the data. In many of the studies reported by Hovland and his colleagues (Hovland, Janis, & Kelley, 1953; Miller & Campbell, 1959), for example, several of the independent variables that were effective in producing attitude change were not accompanied by evidence of greater message learning. People were influenced by such factors as a highly credible communicator or by a fear-producing argument, but did not show greater memory for the arguments, supposedly a necessary condition for attitude change. As Briñol & Petty (2009) conclude, "The available evidence shows that message learning can occur in the absence of attitude change and that attitudes can change without learning the specific information in the communication" (p.71). A different approach was needed.

Cognitive Response Theory

The new approach was provided by Greenwald (1968) and colleagues in the form of **cognitive response theory** (Greenwald & Albert, 1968; Petty, Ostrom, & Brock, 1981). Let us imagine that you are a student reading a newspaper editorial favoring increases in tuition at your university. As you read the headline, you are probably curious about the arguments that will be raised and, simultaneously, thinking about the hardship that a tuition increase may cause your family. As you begin to read the text of the editorial, you confront the premise that the university is facing budget shortfalls. You may sympathize with the problem of a budget shortfall but your mind races to what you consider wasteful spending on buildings and grounds, not to mention the plethora of assistant deans. As you read on, the persuasive arguments in the editorial continue to activate thoughts and feelings, some of which are in sympathy with the message, and others that run in the opposite direction. All of the thoughts that the communication raised are called 'cognitive responses' to the message.

According to cognitive response theory, we are persuaded not by the words of a message but rather by our thoughts in response to the message. Our cognitive responses can be a complex mix of favorable and unfavorable thoughts. Those thoughts vary not only in their valence (in favor or against the message) but also in their intensity. How much we are persuaded by a message is a function of those thoughts: The greater the number and intensity of positive thoughts about a message, the more we are likely to be persuaded. If the intensity and number of cognitive responses are evenly divided between favorable and unfavorable thoughts, the message will not be effective. And, interestingly, if a message provokes a preponderance of negative thoughts, the persuasion attempt will boomerang, leaving the recipient further against the message after hearing it than before. Note that the strength and direction of the cognitive response is not necessarily based on the strength of the argument. In a communication about raising tuition, for example, a straightforward argument that tuition will increase the pay for the college president may lead one reader to become excited about raising the quality of the administration while another may become infuriated by the extravagance associated with such a step. In this example, the argument is the same but the cognitive responses are diametrically opposed. According to cognitive response theory, the argument will have diametrically opposite effects on the two readers' attitudes.

Cognitive responses can be measured in a number of different ways. Most researchers adopt a procedure outlined by Cacioppo and Petty (1977; 1981b). The persuasive message is generally presented first, followed by an unexpected task that requests the audience to write down, in 150 seconds, all of the thoughts that came to mind when they were listening to the message. The intensity and polarity of the thoughts are then rated as being consistent with the direction of the advocacy or opposed. There seems to be little difference between ratings made by the recipients of the message and ratings made by independent judges, so the participants themselves are usually relied on for those judgments (Petty & Cacioppo, 1981b).

Considerable evidence has supported the role of cognitive responses as mediators of attitude change following a persuasive message (see Petty, Ostrom, & Brock, 1981, for a review). For example, Petty and Cacioppo (1979) had some participants at the University of Missouri listen to an audio tape of an editorial advocating the establishment of comprehensive examinations as a graduation requirement for all University of Missouri undergraduates. Other participants listened to speech arguing against such a proposal. The experiment also varied how strong the arguments were and how involved the participants were in the issue. The results showed the relationship between cognitive responses and persuasion. When the arguments were strong and the participants were highly involved, there were a greater number of cognitive responses and more persuasion. Most importantly, as we would predict from cognitive response theory, the audience's attitudes were correlated strongly with strength and valence of their cognitive responses. Favorable thoughts garnered through the thought-listing procedure correlated highly with persuasion. The more favorable thoughts the audience generated, the greater the persuasion. On the other hand, unfavorable thoughts were negatively correlated with persuasion. The more counterarguments the audience generated spontaneously while listening to the message, the less attitude change there was in the direction of the message.

Cognitive response theory has been, and continues to be, an influential way of conceiving of the process of attitude change. Its active, information-processing approach stimulated considerable research and helped to understand results that message learning could not accommodate. Yet, it became clear that even cognitive response theory was insufficient to explain much of the data on attitude change (Visser & Cooper, 2003). For example, the characteristics of the communicator sometimes had positive, negative or neutral effects on persuasion without entering into people's cognitive responses to the message (Eagly & Chaiken, 1993). In addition, factors that reduced people's cognitive capacity and lowered their ability to engage in cognitive responses sometimes increased, rather than decreased, persuasion. People who were distracted or who were working on a second task that divided their attention were sometimes more persuaded than when their cognitive capacity to respond was not affected. A set of radically new theories suggested that searching for the single, underlying process that accounts for persuasion will continue to produce anomalies because there are actually two processes that lead to change, each one activated under different conditions (Chaiken, 1980; Petty & Cacioppo, 1981). The next chapter is devoted to a consideration of dual-process models of attitude change.

Summary and Conclusion

Ever since the time of early civilization, we have documentation of people trying to effectively persuade others. In modern social psychology, the scientific assessment of how and when attitudes change began with Hovland's rigorous attempt to codify the principles of persuasion. Driven by Lasswell's iconic question of "Who says what to whom . . . and with what effect?" Hovland and his colleagues initiated a program of work to investigate the role of communicator, message and audience effects in persuasion. As we have seen, source credibility, attractiveness, gender, similarity and expertise were foci of research into communicator effects. Many of the findings documented commonsense conclusions but others proved surprising and unexpected. The sleeper effect, which is the tendency for a message attributed to a low credible communicator to increase in effectiveness over time, is one such example that led to extensive work to understand its causes and limitations. In the study of the content of the message itself, research focused on such issues as the magnitude of the message's discrepancy from the communicator's attitude, fear appeals, conclusion drawing, one-sidedness vs. two-sidedness, distraction and repetition. Finally, aspects of the audience, such as gender, intelligence, self-esteem, self-validation and the need for cognition were found to be important for determining the results of a persuasive message.

In studying the process of persuasion itself, researchers have mobilized the message learning approach and cognitive response theory to understand the mechanics underlying attitude change in response to a persuasive message. Although the message learning approach held high face validity, it became difficult to reconcile accumulating inconsistencies in the data. The theoretical impact of cognitive response theory was an important step in integrating the disparate findings for communicator, message and audience effects in persuasion. Ultimately, it too would reveal anomalies and unexplained findings, leading to an explosion of different types of theories—known as dual-process theories—to explain how attitudes change.

CHAPTER 5

Dual-Process Theories of Attitude Change

As we saw in the previous chapter, persuasion research into the 1980s often led to conflicting results trying to codify and categorize the effects of source, message and audience variables. Despite their generative power for new research, reliance on the extant theories of attitude formation and change seemed fraught with inconsistencies. Why should a persuasive communication sometimes be effective even though its arguments were specious? Why should the very same characteristics of a communicator sometimes lead to increased persuasion and sometimes fail to do so? Responding to Lasswell's question, "Who said what to whom with what effect?" seemed to need a more complex answer.

Rather than relying on one process to accommodate the basis for persuasion, a pair of theories, developed simultaneously and independently, suggested that people use two processes when responding to a persuasive message. Whether people are persuaded by the quality of the message, the characteristics of the communicator or other factors depends on the manner that the persuasive message is processed. The Heuristic-Systematic Model (Chaiken, 1980; 1987) and the Elaboration Likelihood Model (Petty & Cacioppo, 1981; 1984) were built upon the observation that variables such as source attractiveness or expertise are effective in some persuasive contexts but almost meaningless in others. The key to unraveling the mystery was tied to the insight that there is variation in the motivation and ability to process incoming persuasive information across both persons and situations. This realization prompted the notion that there are two qualitatively different persuasion processes by which attitudes can change, and that the aforementioned motivation and ability govern which type of persuasive communication is more effective.

THE HEURISTIC-SYSTEMATIC MODEL

The **Heuristic-Systematic Model** (HSM) of attitude change is one of the two prominent dual-process theories in the field of persuasion. Like the Elaboration

Likelihood Model (ELM), which we shall describe below, the HSM provided a new, overarching framework in which to consider the existing data on persuasion and make predictions about the effects of previously unstudied persuasion variables. The HSM derives its name from the two distinctive ways that persuasive information can be processed in the model: Information can either be processed heuristically—in a fast, low-effort mode of processing where people execute simple decision rules to make evaluations based upon certain cues in the persuasion context—or systematically, in which one must possess both the motivation and ability to process effortfully and to consider the substance of the incoming persuasive information.

This basic distinction between systematic vs. heuristic processing resembles the larger structure of dual-process theories in other areas of psychology such as memory (Craik & Lockhart, 1972) and attention (Shiffrin & Schneider, 1977; Schneider & Shiffrin, 1977). In general, dual-process theories involve two distinct processing systems: An intuitive, unconscious system that is fast, automatic and has a large capacity (System 1) and a deliberative, conscious system that is slow, effortful, intentional and capacity-limited (System 2; e.g., Kahneman, 2003, 2011; for an expansive review of dual-process theories in social psychology, see Chaiken & Trope, 1999). While System 1 is ostensibly influenced by affect and/or experience and operates continuously, System 2 can override System 1 and is influenced through more cognitive information, such as logic or evidence. **Heuristics**, or cognitive "shortcuts," *generally refer to unconscious System 1 processes that are efficient and usually effective but occasionally bias judgment in predictable ways* (cf. Kahneman & Tversky, 1973, 1996; Tversky & Kahneman, 1974). For instance, the ease with which we can recall horrible plane crashes appearing in the news may bias us to overestimate the frequency of plane crashes relative to car crashes (the availability heuristic; Tversky & Kahneman, 1973). While the System 1 and System 2 dichotomy has been popular for separating complex psychological processes into component parts, other researchers have continued to advocate for using a unified single-process approach (e.g., Kruglanski & Gigerenzer, 2011).

Heuristic and Systematic Processing

To illustrate the difference between systematic and heuristic processing, imagine that you are in the market for a new car. Let us also imagine that you care about a car's environmental impact, its safety features and its responsiveness. One day, on an airplane trip, you thumb through the magazine in your seat pocket and come across an advertisement for a new car. It contains considerable information about the car and also features your favorite movie star proclaiming that she owns this type of car. How will you use the information in this advertisement and will it help you decide to purchase the car?

One possible use of this hypothetical advertisement is to cull through all of the information very carefully. The EPA estimates that the car will likely provide more than 30 miles per gallon of fuel. A chart shows you the probable re-sale value over a ten-year period, and the results of testing by *Car and Driver* magazine proclaim the car to be particularly responsive. These are persuasive arguments for seriously considering this car as the one you will purchase. You have paid attention to the substance of the advertisement, considered the arguments and were favorably impressed. You have engaged in systematic processing.

On the other hand, you may have noticed that a very talented, attractive and well-liked movie star owns the car. "Good person, good car," you may think, and you flip to the next page of the magazine. This is an example of heuristic processing. You did not do the work of considering the substance of the argument. You did notice the advertisement, paid some attention, but found that your time on the airplane could be spent more effectively by reading the next article in the magazine. In this illustration, the advertisement still affected your attitude toward the car, but by an entirely different mechanism. You made the quick association between the car and the attractive, well-liked owner and came away with a favorable evaluation of the car.

Formally, **systematic processing** is defined as *processing information in order to thoroughly understand any and all available information through careful attention, deep thinking and intensive reasoning* (Chaiken & Ledgerwood, 2012, p. 247). It is an effortful process, requiring thought and consideration of the arguments. When using systematic processing, attitude change will be mediated by a person's understanding and acceptance of the information supplied in the message. **Heuristic processing** is different; it is much less demanding of cognitive resources. It relies on a relatively automatic application of easily understood decision rules to process information. Heuristic decision rules are a bit like mini-theories, but their veracity is rarely scrutinized. They have been learned from experience or from the advice of others. When exposed to a communication, a person using heuristic processing may rely on simple rule-of-thumb cognitive shortcuts to form their evaluation. For instance, one may rely on heuristic properties of the communicator and believe, for example, that experts must be credible or that likable communicators (as a result of their physical attractiveness, charisma or any other quality) are trustworthy. Alternatively, one may be influenced by surface properties of the communication itself, surmising that the arguments in a communication are strong from the mere length or the sheer number of arguments presented, being easily convinced by statistics without skepticism with the assumption that they are credible, or accepting an argument because it is familiar or easy to understand and process. Contextual factors may also exert a heuristic influence, for example, as one may infer the strength or correctness of a communication from any apparent consensus about the issue. While this is by no means an exhaustive list of the types of heuristic information possibly contained in a message, it illustrates how aspects of persuasive communication can be influential regardless of the actual content of the message.

Although the distinction between heuristic and systematic processing routes suggests a mutually exclusive dichotomy, this is potentially misleading. In the HSM, both heuristic and systematic processing of information can operate at the same time and have additive or subtractive effects. In cases of a "disagreement," where the evaluations made based on heuristic and systematic processing are opposite in valence, the influence of the systematic route generally attenuates or overrides any potential effects that heuristic processing might have had (e.g., Bator & Cialdini, 2000; Chaiken & Maheswaran, 1994; Maheswaran & Chaiken, 1991). If the heuristic and systematic routes lead to the same positive or negative evaluation, however, the result can instead be an increase (or decrease) in persuasion relative to the influence that either of the processing modes would have had when acting alone.

Driving Goals and Principles

Accuracy Motivation. Perhaps the most distinctive feature of the HSM is the emphasis it places on the goals and principles that drive processing of persuasive information. The first and most basic goal postulated in the HSM is that people seek to hold *valid* evaluations of attitude objects (Chaiken, 1980). This validity-seeking goal is accompanied by **accuracy motivation**, that is, a *motivation to hold correct attitudes and process incoming attitude-relevant information objectively* (Chaiken, Lieberman & Eagly, 1989). It is quite likely that, with a bit of introspection, you may discover that you possess this goal even on an explicit, consciously recognizable level. Indeed, there is considerable evidence that people often believe they are objective (cf. Griffin & Ross, 1991; Robinson, Keltner, Ward, & Ross, 1995; Ross & Ward, 1996), even when clearly exhibiting biases (Pronin, Lin, & Ross, 2002). The motivation to hold accurate attitudes varies across persons and situations: When accuracy motivation is low, we are particularly susceptible to the influence of heuristic cues and processing when considering a persuasive communication.

Limitations to Accuracy: Effort and Sufficiency. Despite the power of accuracy motivation in the service of validity-seeking goals, processing of persuasive information is not explained by this motivation alone. Instead, the HSM makes use of two cognitive principles that specify and constrain the amount of processing done by the recipient of persuasive information. The first of these two principles is the **least effort principle**: *In any given persuasive context, evaluators generally try to conserve cognitive resources whenever possible.* It is not that people are lazy; it is that the potential demands on people's cognitive capacity are excessive, so we have learned to be economy-minded in our expenditure of effort (e.g., see Fiske, 1992). We bring our full cognitive capacity to bear when we must; otherwise, we seek economical ways to accomplish our mental tasks. Using heuristic processing to arrive at conclusions from persuasive information is one such opportunity to conserve mental effort.

The accuracy motive pushes us to use the full resources of our mental energy when responding to a persuasive message. The least effort principle tells us that we cannot expend that kind of effort on every persuasion task. The reconciliation of these competing motives is the **sufficiency principle**: *If recipients of attitude-relevant information seek to hold correct attitudes and process information objectively while expending the least amount of effort, then there exists some optimal balance between correctness and effort expenditure.* According to the HSM, for any judgment that we might make there exists a level of confidence that we require to be satisfied with that judgment. In essence, we seek a sufficiency compromise—one that enables us to be as confident as necessary while expending effort in the most efficient way (see Figure 5.1).

Imagine, for a moment, that you are visiting a new amusement park. On first entering the park, it is unlikely that you would form an impression of the entire amusement park after going on only one ride. If you, like other people, are motivated to obtain an accurate assessment of the park's quality (perhaps so you can tell your friends or relatives about it, for instance), you would hardly be satisfied with generalizing an evaluation of the bumper cars to all of the other rides across the park. Instead, you might ride a sufficient number of attractions in order to have a "good enough" idea of the park's general quality before feeling confident about recommending it to a friend. One can imagine how the number of rides sufficient to form an evaluation might vary across dispositional factors (e.g., whether a person suffers from vertigo or motion sickness) or situational factors (e.g., how long the lines for the rides are, how hot it is outside, etc.). If you are feeling especially tired because you barely slept the previous night and it happens to be 110 degrees (*F*) outside while the park is very crowded, you might be able to imagine being satisfied with forming a general impression of the park based on how impressive the sign on the entrance looked, or how big and scary the roller coasters looked from a distance, before turning back and going back to your air-conditioned room.

Figure 5.1 illustrates the psychological schematic that relates confidence to information processing in the HSM. In the top panel, people hold an evaluation of an attitude object with a degree of confidence that is very close to their desired level. They do not need much new information to raise their confidence level. When confronted with a persuasive communication, they can minimize cognitive energy by applying simple decision rules to process any new information. Panels B and C in Figure 5.1 show larger confidence gaps. What these individuals can glean from simple heuristic processing is not likely to convince them that they have reached their accuracy goals, so systematic processing of the information is called for.

Typically, there are two types of factors that prompt us to expend the additional cognitive effort to form an evaluation of an attitude object. First, if the judgment is personally relevant to us, we are typically motivated to increase our desired level of

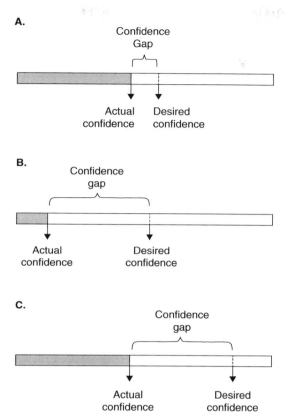

FIGURE 5.1 *Illustration of the sufficiency principle.*

Source: Chaiken, S., & Ledgerwood, A. (2012). A theory of heuristic and systematic information processing. In P.A.M. van Lange, A.W. Kruglanski, & E.T. Higgins (Eds.), *Handbook of theories of social psychology* (pp. 246–266). Thousand Oaks, CA: Sage. Reprinted with permissions.

confidence. Second, if our expectancies (based on previous judgments or attitudes) are disconfirmed, this may decrease our current level of confidence, prompting us to collect more information and subsequently revise our judgment (Maheswaran & Chaiken, 1991).

Empirical Evidence for Dual Processes

A series of experiments by Chaiken (1980) demonstrates how accuracy motivation and the sufficiency principle interact to drive attitude change through heuristic or systematic means. In the first study, participants considered a persuasive attempt that contained either two or six strong arguments on one of two topics. Participants' motivation to form valid evaluations was varied by manipulating the degree to which they were involved in the topic. In the high issue-involvement condition, participants expected to discuss the very same topic that they were exposed to in a previous experimental session. In the low motivation condition, participants thought they would be discussing a different attitude topic. In addition, the communication was from a likable or unlikable source. Participants who were highly involved with the issue were influenced to change their attitude as a function of the strong arguments to which they were exposed. More strong arguments produced more persuasion than just a few, and attitudes of the highly involved participants were unaffected by source likability. By contrast, participants with low involvement showed the reverse pattern and were persuaded significantly more by a likable vs. unlikable communicator, while being unaffected by variation in the strength of the arguments in the message. This experiment demonstrated that issue involvement plays a major role in determining the amount of influence that different aspects of a persuasive message exert on participants' attitudes towards the issue. With low issue involvement, participants did not feel the need to consider and evaluate the arguments. "Likeable people have correct opinions" was apparently a sufficient heuristic to close the confidence gap. With high involvement, participants were only satisfied by attending to the quality of the arguments in the message.

The operation of heuristic and systematic processing is not necessarily mutually exclusive. An experiment by Darke, Chaiken, Bohner, Einwiller, Erb and Hazlewood (1998) clarifies the simultaneous processing of both heuristic and systematic information under conditions of varying issue involvement. In this experiment, participants read about the results of a fictional poll of students' opinions towards the institution of senior comprehensive exams as a requirement for graduation. While this poll did not include any actual arguments for or against the exams, it experimentally manipulated information about how many students had been polled (10 or 1,000) and what percentage of students agreed vs. disagreed with the proposal to institute the exams (80% in favor vs. 80% opposed). In addition, participants' accuracy motivation was manipulated through varying personal relevance, where participants believed the policy would either be instituted next year (high relevance condition) or in ten years (low relevance condition). As predicted from the HSM, when the issue was of low personal relevance, participants relied on consensus as a heuristic cue implying correctness (Axsom, Yates, & Chaiken, 1987), showing increased favorability towards the issue when consensus was high vs. low regardless of the sample size of the poll. When the issue was highly relevant to participants, however, participants only showed increased favorability towards the issue when consensus was high *and* when the sample size of the poll was large enough to be convincing according to the Law of Large Numbers (Nisbett, Krantz, Jepson, & Kunda, 1983). Although participants had high accuracy motivation and therefore processed the information systematically, they were still influenced by heuristic information about consensus, but *only* when it made sense to actually consider that information. In other words, in this study *both* heuristic information (consensus) and systematic information (i.e., the reliability of the poll based on sample size) combined to influence participants' evaluation of the issue.

This study illustrates a number of important points. First, it shows how situational differences in accuracy motivation can determine the weight with which heuristic information is considered. Second, it shows how heuristic information can impact evaluation even when accuracy motivation is high, since consensus information influenced participants' judgments when they were processing systematically and the information about consensus was reliable. Finally, this study suggests the conclusion that, during systematic processing, the influence of heuristic cues may depend on their perceived reliability in providing evidence for an evaluative conclusion, an idea that reappears later in this chapter in our discussion of the unimodel.

Beyond Objective Processing

The operation of heuristic and systematic processing under varying levels of involvement just described are fairly straightforward and hold for cases where we are, in accordance with the validity-seeking goal, attempting to hold correct attitudes while satisfying the sufficiency and least-effort principles. The HSM acknowledges, however, that we are not *always* motivated to engage in objective processing. One way biased processing can occur is as a result of directed-thought techniques that tilt one's cognitive responses in a particular direction when processing systematically (Killeya & Johnson, 1998). Alternatively, it can arise spontaneously, as a result of aspects of the persuasion context or from one's own motivations and goals. This is especially true when the persuasive message is ambiguous, and where heuristic cues can guide the direction of systematic processing (see Bohner, Chaiken, & Hunyadi, 1994; Chaiken, Giner-Sorolla, & Chen, 1996; Mackie, 1987). Consistent with the work on attitude functions that we surveyed in Chapter 3, people hold a variety of motivational goals other than validity-seeking. Satisfying these motivational goals may bias the accuracy of our evaluations. Two illustrative examples of such biasing motivational goals are defense motivation and impression management. **Impression management motivation** refers to *the motivation to have others see oneself in a positive light.* In a study by Tetlock (1983), participants engaged in effortful, systematic processing in order to adopt confident attitude positions that they thought would be acceptable to a group of people whose attitudes they did not know. **Defense motivation**, on the other hand, is *the drive to defend or maintain a particular attitude*, for example, through confirmation bias (cf. Wason, 1960). As you can see, the goals implied by these motivations—defense of one's positive image and defense of a particular attitude—can easily come into conflict with the goal of arriving at attitudes and beliefs that are objectively correct.

Often, defense motivation occurs as a result of our prior knowledge either positively or negatively biasing the processing of incoming information (e.g., Wood, 1982; Wood, Kallgren, & Preisler, 1985; see also Giner-Sorolila & Chaiken, 1997), but occasionally mere involvement through increased personal relevance can be enough to induce bias. In an experiment by Jonas, Schulz-Hardt and Frey (2005), participants were presented with a choice between two different gifts and had to make a decision in one of three different contexts. They either were asked to choose the gift for themselves, or act as an advisor to provide advice to their "clients" (other participants) about which present to receive, or act as an advisor and make the actual decision on behalf of their clients. After their preliminary decision, participants were allowed to conduct a brief information search about other previous participants' reactions to the two presents. As expected, Jonas et al. found that making a decision for themselves led to the presence of a confirmation bias in the subsequent information search (i.e., selecting choice-congruent reactions to read about), whereas making a recommendation to someone else eliminated this bias. This experiment showed that we are more likely to engage in biased processing when we have a motivational stake in the outcome. Rather than striving for accuracy, we seek to defend an attitude that we already have.

But what about the advisors who made decisions on behalf of their clients instead of simply giving them advice? They showed even greater confirmation bias than did the participants who chose for themselves. The authors observed that this result only occurred, however, when the advisors expected to meet the clients again and justify their choice but not when they had to justify their recommendation impersonally. This is a clear instance of impression-management goals at work: instead of serving in the defense of a desirable pre-existing attitude or belief, impression management has to do with the desire to show socially acceptable and appropriate attitudes to others. In this case, participants did not set out with a particular attitude in mind that needed defending. Instead, having made a choice, and forced to justify it to their peers, the advisors engaged in biased processing in their information search so they could present to their client that they had made the most socially desirable judgment.

THE ELABORATION LIKELIHOOD MODEL

Developed independently from and simultaneously with the HSM, the **Elaboration Likelihood Model** (Petty & Cacioppo, 1981; 1984; see also Petty & Briñol, 2012, and Sherman, Gawronski, & Trope, 2013, for recent reviews) presents a dual-process approach to understanding persuasion. The ELM was designed to understand with greater precision some of the complex contradictions that had characterized earlier work in attitude change (see Chapter 4). Similar to the HSM, the Elaboration

Likelihood Model outlines two paths to attitude change: The "quick-and-easy" (System 1) **peripheral route** and the more deliberate, effortful (System 2) **central route** to persuasion. These two routes echo the difference in processing style highlighted by the heuristic-systematic dichotomy, but their distinctiveness revolves around the crucial concept of **elaboration**. The use of the term "elaboration" in daily life lends insight into the way in which the term is discussed in the literature on persuasion: Much like the lay phrase "to elaborate on an argument," the psychological meaning of elaboration indicates a departure beyond mere encoding or learning of a persuasive message. In the ELM, elaboration implies that the recipient of the persuasive message has not only committed cognitive resources to processing the message, but has also added their own thoughts and opinions about the arguments being presented as well as evaluating issue-relevant information that may not even be contained in the message itself. Since elaboration is conceptualized by the subjective cognitive responses of the recipient to a persuasive message, it follows that research into the ELM frequently makes use of thought-listing procedures (Brock, 1967; Greenwald, 1968) that we considered in Chapter 3 to assess participants' reactions to persuasion attempts (e.g., Cacioppo & Petty, 1981a; Cacioppo, Harkins, & Petty, 1981). Research confirms that the valence of these cognitive responses (positive or negative) in thought-listing procedures—specifically the ratio of positive to negative thoughts—correlates highly with subsequent attitude change (Cacioppo & Petty, 1979, 1981a; Cacioppo, Harkins, & Petty, 1981; Osterhouse & Brock, 1970; Petty & Cacioppo, 1977; Rucker, Petty & Briñol, 2008). This relationship between the valence of cognitive responses and the outcome (i.e., attitude change) of central-route processing, as well as the pathways through which central and peripheral processing mediate the influence of persuasive information on one's attitudes, is illustrated in Figure 5.2.

When we elaborate a message using the central route to persuasion, the effectiveness of the message is determined by the evaluation of the strengths and weaknesses of the arguments either stated or implied by that message (Petty & Cacioppo, 1981, 1984; Petty et al., 1983). This effortful process attempts to evaluate the objective merit of the arguments under scrutiny: It might involve thinking about logical conclusions following from the arguments, attempting to connect or reconcile the current arguments with other information, or imagining counterfactuals. Under conditions of low elaboration, however, our evaluation of persuasive information is largely driven by our interpretation of basic cues in the message context or environment, or by our use of automatic, non-conscious rules-of-thumb that influence decision-making. For instance, a message relayed to us by a very attractive source (regardless of the message's actual content or persuasive merit) might be highly persuasive under the peripheral route, or, similarly, we might find an objectively unpersuasive message very persuasive if we are happily eating ice cream at the time of its reception (ostensibly a positive mood cue). These cues are processed as part of the peripheral route to persuasion.

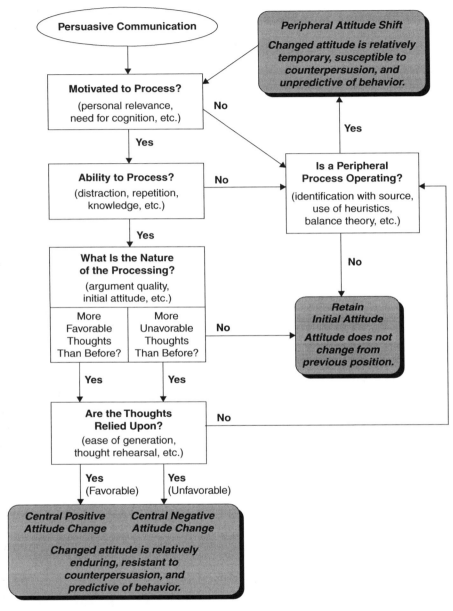

FIGURE 5.2 *The Elaboration Likelihood Model.*

Source: Petty, R.E. & Briñol, P. (2012). The Elaboration Likelihood Model. In P.A.M. Van Lange, A. Kruglanski, & E.T. Higgins (Eds.), *Handbook of theories of social psychology* (Vol.1, pp. 224–245). London, England: Sage. Reprinted with permission.

While many variables can act as persuasive arguments to influence attitudes under conditions of high elaboration, there is also a large list of variables that can act as peripheral cues to persuasion under conditions of low elaboration. Many traditional source factors in persuasion, such as attractiveness, credibility and expertise—as well as one's identification with the source of the message (e.g., Kelman, 1958)—can influence attitudes when processed peripherally. As alluded to above, specific properties of the message can also act as peripheral cues, such as the speed with which a message is spoken (Miller et al., 1976), the number of arguments it contains (where more is better; Petty & Cacioppo, 1981), the order of argument presentation (where earlier arguments are weighted more heavily; Petty, 1997) or the misattribution of positive affect to the message (Petty & Cacioppo, 1983; Schwarz & Clore, 1983). In addition, more basic processes can, in turn, influence attitudes through the peripheral route, such as in classical conditioning (Staats & Staats, 1958; Cacioppo et al., 1992), reinforcement learning (e.g., with food; Janis, Kaye, & Kirschner, 1965), and through punishment (e.g., electric shock; Zanna, Kiesler, & Pilkonis, 1970) or mere exposure effects (Bornstein, 1989; Zajonc, 1968). The number of factors that can serve as peripheral cues is enormous.

Two Key Determinants of Central Processing: Motivation and Ability

What determines how much we elaborate? As the first two steps in the flowchart depicted in Figure 5.2 show, the two factors in the ELM that control the extent of elaboration are **motivation** and **ability**: One must have the capacity as well as the desire to process persuasive information centrally to do so. An advertisement for children's cough medicine, for example, might be processed peripherally if the recipient is not actually a parent (and therefore isn't motivated to process the message). It likewise might be processed peripherally if the recipient is actually a parent but is busy changing their child's diaper and therefore is unable to devote the proper attentional resources required to process the message centrally—after all, what good are strong, convincing arguments if they fall on deaf ears? If either motivation or ability to elaborate is absent, then persuasive information is processed peripherally. To the extent that *both* motivation and ability to elaborate are present, then the message will be processed centrally and evaluated based upon the merits of its persuasive arguments.

Motivation. The relationship between the central and peripheral routes to persuasion is illustrated by a classic study by Petty & Cacioppo (1984). Similar to Chaiken (1980), the authors manipulated elaboration likelihood through the degree of personal involvement the participants had with the issue. In this instance, participants heard a communication advocating introducing a comprehensive examination as a graduation requirement for all undergraduate students. High-involvement participants were led to believe that the implementation of the comprehensive exam would occur while they were still in school; participants in the low-involvement condition thought it would be implemented many years into the future. The communication that the participants heard was either long (containing nine arguments) or short (containing three arguments). For half of the participants, all of the arguments were strong and cogent; for the other half, they were weak and specious.

High motivation caused participants to process the arguments centrally. Strong arguments were more effective—i.e., they produced greater favorability towards the issue—than weak arguments. Moreover, nine strong arguments were more effective than three strong arguments. When the ideas were weak and specious, however, nine arguments were actually *less* effective than three such arguments. This is consistent with the idea of elaboration: when people elaborate a message, they counterargue and form conclusions that might be quite different from the direction in which the arguments were intended to persuade. When argument after argument continued to be weak, participants who were using central processing became less and less convinced. These persuasion results stood in contrast to those of participants who were not motivated to process the arguments centrally. For people for whom the issue was not personally involving, the strength of the arguments made virtually no difference. Instead, more arguments were more persuasive than few arguments, regardless of whether they were strong or specious.

Petty, Cacioppo and Schumann (1983) demonstrated the basic difference between central and peripheral processing in the context of a mock consumer advertisement. They had participants evaluate a bogus advertisement for Edge disposable razors under high or low involvement: under high involvement, participants were offered the opportunity to choose a brand of disposable razor at the conclusion of the experiment, increasing their motivation to pay attention to the message. The experimenters also manipulated argument quality, such that the arguments endorsing the razor were either convincing or specious. Similar to Chaiken's (1980) study, Petty et al. (1983) manipulated the likability of the message source (a peripheral cue), this time by varying whether the source was a well-known and well-liked celebrity vs. an average-looking, unknown person. Once again, under conditions of high elaboration (i.e., high involvement) participants exhibited greater central-route argument differentiation (i.e., greater favorability towards the razors when seeing strong vs. weak arguments) relative to the low-elaboration condition. That is, highly involved participants were more persuaded by strong arguments than by weak arguments and the celebrity status of the endorser made no difference whatsoever. Under conditions of low elaboration, however, it was the peripheral cue that exerted a much stronger influence on final attitudes. For participants in the low-involvement condition, endorsement by the famous celebrity led to more positive attitudes toward the razor than an endorsement by an unknown consumer. What about people's intentions to purchase Edge razors? In the high-involvement

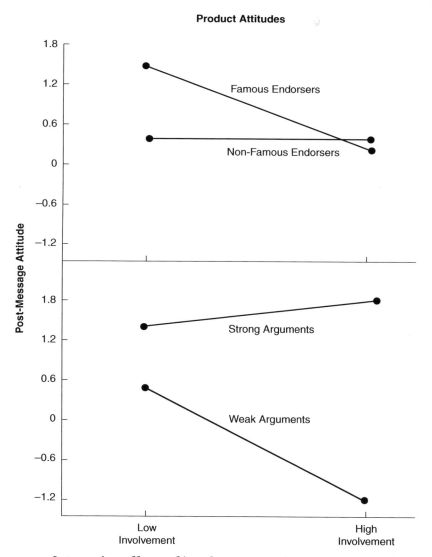

FIGURE 5.3 *Interactive effects of involvement and source likability (top) or argument strength (bottom) on post-message attitudes.*

Source: Petty, R. E., Cacioppo, J. T., & Schumann, D. (1983). Central and peripheral routes to advertising effectiveness: The moderating role of involvement. *Journal of Consumer Research*, 135–146. Reprinted with permission.

condition, intentions to purchase the razor mirrored people's attitudes. They were more likely to intend to purchase the razor following strong arguments than weak ones. In the low-involvement condition, attitudes did not mirror intended behavior. Although their attitudes were influenced by the peripheral cue, their attitudes did not lead to an increase in purchasing intentions. Together, these two studies illustrate the differential operation of the central and peripheral routes to persuasion and the canonical relationship that they have to elaboration.

Ability. Central processing requires the ability to elaborate a message. If their attention is overloaded, if they are under severe time pressure (Mackie & Worth, 1989) or if the message is too complex (Eagly, 1974; Ratneshwar & Chaiken, 1991), people may lack the capacity to engage in central processing. Cooper, Bennett and Sukel (1996; see also Cooper & Neuhaus, 2000) suggested that the ability to process information affects persuasion in an important area of civic life: The courtroom. Trials typically include all of the elements of persuasion: The communicators (i.e., the witnesses and attorneys) and the communication (i.e., the testimony) are designed to convince an audience (i.e., the jurors) to believe in one side of the argument. Cooper et al. reasoned that in the persuasion context of the courtroom, jurors are typically motivated to process the arguments so that they can make a proper decision. What jurors may lack in some cases is the ability to do so. This is especially problematic in civil trials, where plaintiffs sue for damages, and the communicators are often expert witnesses who are called upon to convey their special knowledge. If expert testimony is too complex or specialized for jurors to understand, then the jurors cannot use central processing to elaborate the arguments. Despite their motivation to process the arguments, their lack of ability will cause jurors to engage in peripheral processing, using an irrelevant aspect of the situation to render their final verdicts.

To investigate this hypothesis, Cooper et al. (1996) asked mock jurors to consider the case of a plaintiff who had contracted cancer from exposure to PCBs at his work place. There was only one issue for the jurors to decide: Does exposure to PCBs cause cancer? The plaintiff's expert was a biologist who testified that PCBs cause cancer. Two factors were varied in this study. The first was the complexity of the expert's testimony. For half of the mock jurors, the testimony was presented with maximum complexity, making it very difficult to understand. For the other half, the same substantive testimony was presented, but in easy-to-understand language. The characteristics of the expert were also varied in order to provide a mechanism for peripheral route processing. Half of the time, the expert graduated from an internationally prestigious college, held an internationally prestigious Ph.D. and worked at a similarly prestigious institution. The other half of the time, the expert held his degrees from less prestigious institutions. Although their credentials differed, both had been qualified by the court to provide expert testimony.

In the end, the jurors were asked how much they were persuaded by the expert's testimony. The results showed that when the testimony was complex, such that the jurors lacked the ability to process it, then they engaged in peripheral processing: The credentials of the expert made all of the difference in the jury's decisions. Jurors indicated that they believed the testimony more when the source was a highly prestigious expert and they found in favor of the plaintiff. When the testimony was comprehensible, however, such that the jurors had the ability to process it, they made no use of the expert's credentials. Instead, they engaged in central processing, making their decisions based on the substance of the testimony.

On the Malleability of Persuasive Information

The ELM does not make a formal distinction between arguments that influence the recipient through the persuasive message itself (message variables) and non-message information that can act as an argument in its own right (e.g., source variables). Instead, the ELM conceptually separates argument content (e.g., source and message variables) from process (elaboration of arguments) (Petty & Briñol, 2008; Petty, Wheeler, & Bizer, 1999). Even though many studies use source vs. message variables to operationalize the central vs. peripheral routes of persuasion in the ELM (e.g., Petty, Cacioppo, & Goldman, 1981), there is no conceptual reason to prevent source variables to act as persuasive arguments under conditions of high elaboration likelihood (Petty & Cacioppo, 1981; 1984) or message variables to act as peripheral cues (Petty & Cacioppo, 1984).

Furthermore, not only does the ELM reject traditional classification of persuasive information into categories such as source vs. message variables, but it also embraces the flexibility of persuasive information with respect to whether it can be processed centrally or peripherally. "Central" and "peripheral" are not properties of types of persuasive information but rather refer to the *process* in which those pieces of information are used to create an attitude or evaluation (or modify an existing one). It is possible for the same variable to serve as a persuasive argument in the central route when elaboration likelihood is high, and to serve as a peripheral cue to persuasion when elaboration likelihood is low.

A study by Petty and Cacioppo (1980) illustrates this flexibility. Participants were exposed to a persuasive message that either advertised a beauty product or a roofing contractor. The attractiveness of the communicator was also manipulated. When participants considered the message under conditions of high elaboration likelihood, they showed more positive attitudes towards the beauty product vs. the roofing contractor, suggesting that they viewed the source's attractiveness as a relevant argument for the beauty product but not for the roofing contractor. Under conditions of low elaboration likelihood, however, attractiveness of the source was effective for both the beauty product and the roofing contractor. It acted as a peripheral cue, changing attitudes in the positive direction as a function of the attractiveness of the endorser. As suggested by the results of this experiment, source attractiveness—along with many other variables typically associated with the peripheral route—can function both as a peripheral cue and as a message-relevant persuasive argument, depending on the context (Kahle & Homer, 1985; Petty & Cacioppo, 1981; Heesacker et al., 1983; Puckett et al., 1983).

Central vs. Peripheral Processing and the Elaboration Continuum

One observation about the Petty et al. (1983) data mentioned earlier in this chapter is that even though participants in the high-elaboration condition showed significantly greater argument differentiation than participants in the low-elaboration condition, participants with low involvement were still more persuaded by strong arguments than by weak ones. In other words, even in a situation hypothesized to maximize the influence of peripheral cues, participants were still showing *some* amount of argument differentiation—just not as much as in the high-elaboration condition. An essential part of the ELM—and a part that is frequently underappreciated—is that the central and peripheral "routes" to persuasion actually represent endpoints of an **elaboration continuum**. Just as our motivation and ability to attend to persuasive information vary continuously instead of dichotomously, the extent to which we elaborate—which depends upon these constraints—is not simply on or off, active or inactive, present or absent. As a consequence, it is very rarely the case that persuasive information is influencing one's attitude exclusively through the central or peripheral route.

Like the two types of processing in the HSM, these two endpoints are distinguished by the ability and motivation of a recipient to process and elaborate incoming persuasive information. Circumstances that engender high elaboration likelihood—where the recipient is fully able and highly motivated to process a message—lie on one end of the elaboration continuum and lead to the use of the central route to persuasion, whereas circumstances in which a recipient is either completely unwilling or unable to process persuasive information lie on the other end and foster the use of the peripheral route to persuasion.

While the elaboration continuum highlights this *quantitative* distinction between the two routes of the ELM—the extent to which one is willing and able to elaborate a message—the processes used to evaluate persuasive information are also *qualitatively* different (Petty & Wegener, 1999; Petty et al., 1999). Central and peripheral processing may reflect different sides of the same elaboration continuum, but they are not the same process. This is illustrated visually in the different pathways for central and peripheral processing in Figure 5.2. If the two routes were only quantitatively distinct, for example, there would be no need for their current labels. If a certain variable's effect on persuasion can be directly defined in terms of the amount (and not type) of influence it has, then the concept of the elaboration continuum would be sufficient to explain attitude change through the ELM.

However, variables in the ELM differ by *how* they affect processing at different ends of the continuum and not just by *how much*.

To support this argument, recall our previous example examining the relationship between argument strength and argument quality under different elaboration conditions (Petty & Cacioppo, 1984). Recall that the investigators in that study provided participants with a persuasive message that either contained three weak arguments or nine weak arguments. These arguments were presented with either high personal relevance (high elaboration) or low personal relevance (low elaboration). As one would expect, in conditions of high elaboration it was more persuasive to have only three weak arguments instead of nine, as each argument was individually scrutinized for validity and (probably for the most part) found lacking. Adding more arguments only hurt the message's persuasiveness when participants were motivated to process them. In the low elaboration conditions, however, participants found the nine weak arguments more persuasive than the three weak arguments, indicating that they were using the number of arguments to evaluate the message's validity instead of argument strength. If the only factor that varied across elaboration conditions was how much they processed each argument, we would expect participants to process only some messages or to process every message only partially in conditions of low elaboration likelihood. If that were true, then nine weak arguments would still be less persuasive (or at least equally so) than three weak arguments. The results of the study, however, showed the reverse, implying that there was something else (i.e., quantity of arguments as a peripheral cue) guiding judgments apart from the degree of argument scrutiny.

An important consequence follows from the idea that the central and peripheral routes are qualitatively as well as quantitatively different: In the ELM, when what is thought of as a peripheral cue increases persuasion under high elaboration, it is because the cue is being processed differently (i.e., being treated as an argument) and not because of an additive effect of the cue on the arguments as sometimes observed in the HSM (Petty & Wegener, 1999; see Maheswaran & Chaiken, 1991). Furthermore, this implies that peripheral processes can still operate under high-elaboration conditions but will be scrutinized as arguments and, if found lacking in validity, will be discounted (Petty & Cacioppo, 1986; Petty, 1994). Ultimately, these conclusions provide evidence that the elaboration continuum, as well as the two conceptually distinct routes to persuasion, is a necessary construct. The influence of persuasive information in the ELM is computed by determining the relative weights placed upon the results of the different routes to persuasion at any point in the elaboration continuum, and not by just a simple matter of "which one, when." Indeed, at most points along the elaboration continuum, both central and peripheral processes co-occur and jointly influence attitudes, depending upon the extent of elaboration (Petty, Kasmer, et al., 1987, Petty, Cacioppo et al., 1987).

Causes and Consequences of Increased Elaboration

We have already seen how a variable such as source attractiveness can sometimes serve as a persuasive message and at other times serve as a peripheral cue, depending on the context. In addition to being simple inputs into the central or peripheral processes of persuasion, certain situational or dispositional factors can affect the process of persuasion by influencing the extent of elaboration that occurs, thereby changing the weight placed on central vs. peripheral information in the message. As evidenced by our earlier examples, one of the most frequently manipulated variables that affects elaboration is personal relevance, with increased relevance motivating increased elaboration because of the greater motivation to be correct (similar to the HSM; Petty & Cacioppo, 1979).

The presence or absence of distraction also affects elaboration likelihood by decreasing the ability (instead of motivation) to discriminate between strong and weak arguments. Increasing distraction reduces counterargument for weak (but not strong) arguments while reducing the number of favorable thoughts for strong (but not weak) arguments (Petty, Wells, & Brock, 1976; Petty & Brock, 1981). As a consequence, weak arguments are more persuasive in circumstances of distraction and strong arguments are less persuasive in such circumstances because the weaknesses and strengths of each (respectively) are less readily apparent. Extensive research has identified many other variables that affect elaboration in addition to distraction, such as prior knowledge (Wood et al., 1995), expectation of discussion (Chaiken, 1980; Leippe & Elkin, 1987), physiological arousal (Sanbonmatsu & Kardes, 1988), time pressure (e.g., Ratneshwar & Chaiken, 1991), speed of speech (Smith & Shaffer, 1991), number of message sources (Harkins & Petty, 1987; Moore & Reardon, 1987), ambivalence about the topic (Maio et al., 1996), recipient posture (Petty et al., 1983; but see Briñol, Wagner & Petty, 2011), deprivation of control (Pittman, 1993), personal responsibility (Petty, Harkins, & Williams, 1980) and recipient mood (Worth & Mackie, 1987; Bless et al., 1990). As a general rule, anything that affects one's motivation or ability to process persuasive information effortfully is potentially a factor that could affect elaboration. Individual differences, such as need for cognition (Cohen, Stotland, & Wolfe, 1955; Cacioppo et al., 1983; Haugtvedt & Petty, 1992; see also Fleischauer, Enge, Brocke, Ullrich, Strobel, & Strobel, 2010, and See, Petty, & Evans, 2009) and self-monitoring (Petty & Cacioppo, 1986), can similarly play a role in affecting the degree to which one is motivated and able to process incoming persuasive information.

It is important to note that the impact of a particular variable on elaboration likelihood is not always a main effect, i.e., an increase or decrease in elaboration. A particular variable may not always simply produce more or less elaboration but may interact with other persuasion variables to produce increased elaboration at one level and decreased elaboration at another. For instance, framing persuasive arguments as rhetorical questions increases elaboration when the questions are not personally relevant to the recipient (i.e., when they are already at low levels of elaboration likelihood) but decreases elaboration under conditions of high personal relevance because the rhetorical form is distracting when the recipient is already motivated to scrutinize the arguments (Petty, Cacioppo, & Heesacker, 1981). In addition, as we noted in Chapter 4, moderate repetition of a message's arguments can increase elaboration, as it provides greater opportunity to consider the implications of a message's contents, but excessive repetition can reduce elaboration through inducing tedium or reactance (and serving as an additional negative affect cue; Cacioppo & Petty, 1979, 1980, 1985).

Besides simply determining the weight ascribed to central vs. peripheral processing (i.e., the "input") during persuasion, the level of elaboration when processing persuasive information can also have a direct effect on the outcome of persuasion (i.e., the "output"). In addition to causing greater weight to be assigned to central route vs. peripheral route arguments in evaluation, greater elaboration leads to greater attitude accessibility (see Chapter 2), increased argument rehearsal and more extensive modification of existing attitude schema. These, in turn, cause attitudes changed through central route processing to be more internally consistent, accessible, enduring and resistant to change (Petty & Cacioppo, 1986).

Under conditions of high elaboration, there exist many possible factors that may enhance the permanence of attitudes changed through the central route to persuasion. It has been shown, for example, that attitudes are more enduring when the persuasive messages are about more interesting or involving issues (e.g., Ronis et al., 1977), when there is more time to consider a message (Mitinick & McGinnies, 1958), when potential distractions are removed (Watts & Holt, 1979), when a message is repeated (Johnson & Watkins, 1971) or when people believe that they are about to be interviewed about their opinions (Chaiken, 1980). In addition to being more persistent, attitudes changed under conditions of high elaboration also typically display more internal consistency. They exhibit greater correlations between the cognitive responses generated in response to a message, one's final attitude after encountering the message and one's subsequent behavior or behavioral intentions (e.g., Petty et al., 1983; Chaiken, 1980; Petty & Cacioppo, 1979).

As a final caveat, it is important to note that when the ELM refers to attitudes being changed through the central route being more persistent, accessible, consistent and resistant than those changed through the peripheral route, it refers to attitudes that have changed *to the same degree* (Petty & Wegener, 1999). It is not accurate to say that *any* change created by central route processing is more stable than attitudes changed through peripheral route processing but that—all else being equal—attitudes that change under conditions of greater elaboration will be more persistent, consistent and resistant than attitudes that change due to heuristic cues or peripheral processing.

Objective vs. Biased Processing in the ELM

Normally, when processing centrally in the ELM, one carefully weighs the merits and weaknesses of the arguments at hand in order to form an evaluation. Naturally, one interprets strong arguments as convincing and weak arguments as specious. This is what is referred to as **objective processing**, involving *the formation of a global evaluation from the interpretation of the strength of the various arguments for and/or against the issue at hand*. As we have seen, many factors can affect the objective functioning of central-route processing by serving as persuasive arguments in and of themselves (given the right context) or through affecting the amount of elaboration undergone to arrive at an evaluation. In addition to variables affecting elaboration in an objective way, however, certain variables can convert normal, objective, data-driven, bottom-up message processing into **biased processing**, or *top-down interference in objective processing that motivates or enables the message recipient to generate or inhibit particular thoughts in the service of maintaining pre-existing attitudes or goals*. In other words, in biased processing, one might conveniently overlook the weaknesses of a specious argument or disparage an otherwise strong argument in favor of satisfying some motivational goal with an evaluation of a particular valence or intensity. For instance, one might overlook the specious arguments of a television advertisement advocating for a cozy, comfy sleeved blanket if one happened to already own one. The motivation to feel good about one's prior purchase might bias processing of the persuasive message and result in even more positive attitudes towards what some people might view as a ridiculous garment.

As in the HSM, biased processing is more likely to take place when the information in the message is ambiguous or mixed instead of strong or weak (Chaiken & Maheswaran, 1994). Biases can occur in both central and peripheral processes. Typically, biases in conditions of high elaboration change the directionality of processing for all relevant incoming information (i.e., through changing the valence of cognitive responses in reaction to that information) and/or remove motivation to scrutinize or correct for the influence of peripheral cues. Biased peripheral route processing, on the other hand, can impact evaluations directly or may affect the most accessible or salient peripheral cues (Petty & Wegener, 1999). For example, one might view a source as lacking credibility or likability if one is already motivated to dislike the product they are advertising. One common biasing factor that arises when encountering persuasive information is the presence of prior issue-relevant knowledge: Having prior issue-relevant knowledge will typically aid in the production of counterarguments and reduce the influence of peripheral cues, resulting in fewer favorable thoughts and less attitude change regardless of elaboration likelihood (Wood, 1982). In addition to the recipient's prior knowledge, the recipient's motives can also bias processing in the direction of a specific goal, such as the motivation to protect one's freedoms (Brehm, 1966), the motivation to achieve psychological balance (Heider, 1958), the motivation to see oneself in a good light (e.g., impression management; Tedeschi et al., 1971), the motivation to affirm positive aspects of the self (Steele, 1988) or in the defense of one's ego in cases where the issue is very high in personal relevance (e.g., Greenwald, 1980, 1981).

Persuasion variables, contexts or goals that induce bias can also potentially exhibit differential effects across the elaboration continuum: They may encourage objective processing of a message at one level of elaboration while instigating biased processing at another level of elaboration. When a threat accompanies a personally relevant persuasive message, for instance, it may bias the processing of the normally objective central route to process the message in an ego-protective fashion instead, with the goal of arriving at a conclusion that avoids or buffers against the threat. This effect is less likely to occur, however, when the message is not personally relevant (Petty & Cacioppo, 1986). Although it may be very difficult to detect the operation of bias in our judgments (see Pronin, 2007, 2009; Pronin & Kugler, 2007; Pronin, Lin, & Ross, 2002), when we do detect the presence of bias in our evaluations, it conflicts directly with our motivation to hold correct, accurate attitudes. The next section details the reconciliation between the biases we detect in our judgment and our motivation to be objective.

Awareness of Biases and Flexible Correction

Since there are so many ways that biased processing can be instantiated, one can imagine at least some circumstances in which we could be aware of our own biased judgment. While much of biased processing certainly slips under the metacognitive radar, when we detect our own biased processing we often take steps to correct it. The Flexible Correction model (Petty & Wegener, 1993; Wegener & Petty, 1995, 1997) attempts to explain the process of correcting biases in judgment and elucidating the circumstances under which this correction occurs. The Flexible Correction model was originally designed to address corrections for two contextual biases, assimilation effects and contrast effects, that positively and negatively (respectively) bias judgments when the attitude object is examined in a positive context. As a brief example, you might recall the halcyon days of taking an Honors or Advanced Placement (AP) class vs. a regular class back in high school. Generally, being enrolled in an Honors or AP class is considered a positive thing—after all, the class is exclusive, rigorous and desirable for the prestige it brings to your college applications. If you perform slightly above average in the class, you might expect an outside observer to be more impressed with your grades and evaluate you more positively than if you had scored higher in a regular class. This is an example of assimilation: The positive context (the Honors/AP class) might bias people's evaluations of your intelligence when, in reality, your intelligence would be the same regardless of which class you were taking. If you performed slightly below average, a contrast effect might occur instead: You could be evaluated even *worse* as a result of that performance. Even though you were in the more prestigious class, people's evaluation of your intelligence might suffer due to the contrast effect with the achievements of others in the Honors/AP class.

The Flexible Correction model (Wegener & Petty, 1997) acknowledges that there is variation in one's initial impressions and evaluations, and that frequently these impressions and evaluations are in the service of some motivation or goal (and thus susceptible to bias). The first step in correcting bias is to realize that one is being biased in the first place. As in the dual-process theories we have been considering, the motivation and ability to detect biased processing vary across persons and situations. If evaluators are not motivated or able to detect any biasing factors (either internal or external in origin), they will retain their initial biased judgment. If biasing factors are found, however, there is another motivation/ability check to see if they will actually be corrected using the evaluators' lay theories of how the bias is affecting them. Any correction induced by these theories will be opposite in direction of the bias' influence and will correspond in magnitude to the subjective perception of the magnitude of the bias. These corrections can vary in effort expenditure, and the model acknowledges that corrections, in general, take more effort than relying on one's uncorrected initial reaction.

Use of these theories in how to correct for bias (and how much) can be disrupted, however, when the theory about how one is being influenced (and how one should correct for it) is not perceived to be applicable to the target attitude or context, does not seem to be in line with the goals of the evaluation or is not cognitively accessible. Finally, in a similar fashion to attitudes that were created through the effortful process of elaboration, evaluations that have been corrected with a greater amount of effort are more temporally persistent, resistant to change and more likely to guide further judgments than those that took little effort to correct. One method to correct for potential bias is to create awareness of the biasing factor. Petty, Wegener and White (1998) showed that instructing an audience to remove bias from their judgments decreased reliance on the likeability of a communicator (a peripheral cue) without affecting processing (elaboration) of the message, and these corrections can take place effectively in conditions of low and high elaboration likelihood. If that bias had not actually influenced us, however (i.e., for the case of source likability, under central route processing), attempts to correct for the bias can actually lead to *overcorrection* in the opposite direction (Petty et al., 1998).

Metacognitive Persuasion

As we noted earlier (see Chapters 2 and 4), recent research has taken notice of another aspect of human cognition: The thoughts we have *about* our own cognitions. Petty & Briñol (2008; 2009; Petty, Briñol, & Tormala, 2002) have used the term

metacognition to refer to these second order cognitions. These metacognitions (see Alter & Oppenheimer, 2009a, for a thorough review) can exert a powerful influence on our judgments even outside the context of persuasion: our perceived ease of processing a stimulus—a persuasive appeal or otherwise—can serve as a cue indicating risk (Alter & Oppenheimer, 2009b), intelligence of a communicator (Oppenheimer, 2006), category membership (Oppenheimer & Frank, 2008), credibility (Reber & Schwarz, 1999), attractiveness (e.g., Reber, Winkielman, & Schwarz, 1998; Winkielman & Cacioppo, 2001), confidence (e.g., Alter, Oppenheimer, Epley, & Eyre, 2007; Schwartz & Metcalfe, 1992) or familiarity (e.g., Tversky & Kahneman, 1973; Whittlesea & Williams, 2000).

Imagine that two people receive a message about a topic such as limiting government surveillance of private communications. Each person may find the argument compelling, but one is more certain of the value of the argument. We can say that the person's certainty is a cognition about his or her cognition. As she thinks about and processes the message, the greater her confidence in her reaction to the message, the greater the message's impact on her attitudes toward surveillance. The impact of confidence can work in either direction. A strong argument about limiting surveillance may generate a positive reaction and, if the recipient is confident in her reaction, will lead to more change in the direction of limiting surveillance. A weak argument may generate negative reactions and, if the recipient is confident about her thoughts, will lead to more negative reactions to placing limits on surveillance. The greater the confidence, the more impact the argument will have on the person's ultimate evaluation of the issue in either direction (Petty & Briñol, 2009).

Confidence in one's thoughts can occur for any number of reasons. Some people may habitually feel confident, believing that they can discern strong arguments from weak ones. The truth of this self-belief is not important, but the feeling of confidence that they have about their thoughts renders those thoughts influential. Alternatively, variations in the social environment can induce different levels of confidence. Petty et al. (2002) asked university students to consider a persuasive message on instituting comprehensive final examinations prior to graduation. Some students listened to arguments that were of high quality (e.g., it would positively impact students' starting salaries after graduation) and other students listened to low quality arguments (e.g., student anxiety would lead to better performance.) As we have seen previously in this chapter (e.g., Petty, Cacioppo, & Schumann, 1983), participants are likely to adopt a more favorable attitude toward an issue if exposed to a high-quality rather than low-quality argument, especially if they are engaging in a high degree of elaboration. However, the metacognitive approach suggests that people's *thoughts about their thoughts*—that is, their degree of metacognitive confidence—would make a crucial difference in how argument strength affects attitudes. The data from Petty et al.'s (2002) study were consistent with their predictions: For participants who experienced greater positive than negative thoughts in response to the message, increasing confidence increased persuasion; however, for participants who experienced more negative than positive thoughts, increasing confidence decreased persuasion. The researchers concluded that confidence in one's thoughts caused those thoughts to be more heavily relied upon when evaluating a persuasive message.

Similarly, Briñol, Petty and Tormala (2004) examined the metacognitive hypothesis with respect to product advertisements. They created two sets of advertisements for Ginex, a (fictitious) cellular phone. One contained strong arguments for the phone, such as "Ginex is waterproof and shock-resistant." The other contained weak arguments, such as "Ginex's password has only 3 digits." Participants read the messages, listed their positive and/or negative reactions to the arguments and rated the degree of confidence they had in each of those judgments. As in the Petty et al. (2002) study, the audience's degree of confidence was critical to determine the effectiveness of the advertisements. Individuals who generated primarily positive thoughts (i.e., those who had seen the strong ad) showed more favorable attitudes toward Ginex as thought-confidence increased. Those who read the weak ad and who had consequently generated primarily negative thoughts showed the opposite pattern: Less favorable attitudes toward the product as confidence in their thoughts increased.

Taking a slightly different approach, Petty et al. (2002; study 3) systematically manipulated students' confidence in their thoughts using a priming technique. They asked half of their participants to think about previous occasions in which they had thought about an issue and experienced high confidence in their thoughts. The other half was asked to think about occasions in which they had felt considerable doubt about their thoughts. Petty et al. (2002) found that students' attitudes toward comprehensive exams was a joint function of the degree of elaboration, the strength of the arguments and the confidence that participants had in their own thoughts. As the ELM would predict, high elaboration of the arguments led people who heard high-quality arguments to believe in the value of comprehensive exams and for those who heard specious arguments to have negative attitudes toward the exam. However, as further predicted by the metacognitive approach, this relationship only held for those who had confidence in their own thoughts. As Figure 5.4 shows, participants primed to think confidently about their thoughts showed the effect of attitude quality, whereas those who were led to doubt their own thoughts showed no effect.

Other metacognitions besides confidence can similarly affect persuasion. Changing *how* one thinks about one's thoughts, for example, or what aspects of them are made accessible through framing effects produces changes in the effectiveness of persuasion (Rucker, Petty, & Briñol, 2008). Additionally, as we saw in the previous chapter, more traditional persuasion variables—such as source characteristics—have been found to have second-order effects through metacognition (see Briñol & Petty,

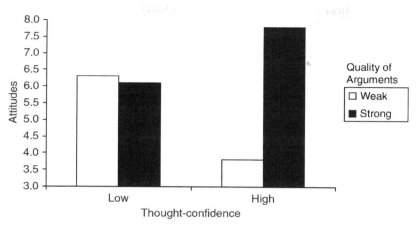

FIGURE 5.4 *Attitudes as a function of argument quality and participants' confidence in their thoughts.*
Source: Adapted from Briñol and Petty (2003, Experiment 1).

2009; Horcajo, Petty, & Briñol, 2010). Even the mere *perception* of elaboration can exert similar effects to actual elaboration, producing more certain attitudes when perceived elaboration is high vs. low (Barden & Petty, 2008). These perceptions of mental effort (and how they compare to actual effort required to persuade) play a key role in the effectiveness of self-persuasion processes (Briñol, McCaslin, & Petty, 2012). These sweeping effects of metacognition suggest that the impact of people's second-order cognitions on persuasion will continue to be a fertile avenue for further study.

Reconciling the HSM and ELM

Despite the Elaboration Likelihood Model and the Heuristic-Systematic Model's two distinct research traditions, they share much in common that bears revisiting. First, both theories postulate that a desire to hold correct attitudes is an important "default" mode of operating and that, while we may try to be correct in our beliefs, there are other motivations, biases and constraints that can also affect our processing. Second, both specify two qualitatively (and not just quantitatively) different routes to persuasion, through the central/systematic route and the peripheral/heuristic route. In both theories, the more effortful route results in attitudes that are more persistent over time, resistant to counter-persuasion and predictive of behavior in comparison to the low-effort mode. Finally, both theories acknowledge that these two processing modes can co-occur: While the ELM uses the concept of an elaboration continuum to govern the activation and relative weight of the two modes, in the HSM these two processing modes are orthogonal and can be additive or subtractive in their cumulative effect.

The theories are not without their notable differences, however. First, they differ slightly in their treatment of how people go about seeking correctness. Generally, the ELM acknowledges that people, in the absence of other motivations, desire to possess correct attitudes. While this resembles the validity-seeking goals of the HSM (Chaiken, 1980, 1987), the HSM posits a general desire to be objective. The ELM, on the other hand, emphasizes the subjective nature of the assessment of one's own correctness. In the ELM, people may arrive at the "correct" attitude based solely on their own independent evaluation of relevant information, or they may expand their set of information to include the (potentially biasing) implications of their evaluations, others' opinions, or explicit strategies (Petty & Cacioppo, 1986). Furthermore, when utterly convinced of a pre-existing attitude's validity, the ELM affirms that people can believe that being biased helps them to be correct (Petty & Wegener, 1999)—or, if they believe a certain bias is causing them to come to incorrect conclusions, they may attempt to correct for it (Wegener & Petty, 1997), even overcorrecting in some situations (Petty, Wegener, & White, 1998).

Second, although the HSM allows for the combination of heuristic and systematic processing across differing levels of motivation and ability, the HSM and ELM make divergent predictions about the postulated net influence from the combination of heuristic/peripheral and systematic/central processing at different levels of elaboration. At high levels of motivation and ability to process the message, the ELM predicts that central route processing will be the predominate mode of processing and that peripheral cues will factor but little into the impact of the persuasive attempt. The HSM makes the same prediction when those heuristic cues *disagree* with the results of systematic processing, postulating that the results of systematic processing will override the effects of the heuristic cues (Chaiken & Maheswaran, 1994; Maheswaran & Chaiken, 1991). When those heuristic cues *agree* with the results of systematic processing, however, the HSM—in contrast to the ELM—predicts an additive effect on persuasion. As the extent of elaboration predicts the relative weighting of central route arguments and peripheral cues in the ELM, the valence of the resultant cognitive responses is not relevant to the weighting of information processed centrally or peripherally. In other words, one of the ways the ELM departs from the HSM is that it predicts the discounting of the influence of peripheral cues when (a) elaboration is high and (b) the valence of the peripheral cues is congruent with the valence of the cognitive responses generated through central-route processing.

The Elaboration Likelihood Model—and dual-process models of attitude change in general—have not gone without criticism. These criticisms often take issue with how dual-process theories of attitude change "lump" or "split" variables or processes (Petty et al., 1999)—for instance, how the ELM separates persuasion processes into central and peripheral routes but collapses across certain persuasion variables instead of identifying qualitative differences. Another avenue of criticism deals with the way in which the ELM treats issue involvement: Some researchers (Johnson & Eagly, 1989) contend that the ELM inappropriately combines together two separate types of involvement, value-relevant involvement (VRI) and outcome-relevant involvement (ORI), which may have significantly different effects on persuasion. The general form of the criticism is that certain persuasion variables, such as involvement, may be more complex and multifaceted than the ELM currently specifies. Finally, recent evidence has challenged the hypothesized simultaneous operation of the central and the peripheral route by demonstrating differential processing of validity information that depended on the timing of the information received (Peters & Gawronski, 2011).

The Parametric Unimodel

Although most criticisms of dual-process models concern nuances of the two systems of information processing, a far more radical critique questions whether we need two processes at all. Every course featuring the scientific method teaches students the desirability of parsimony. All else being equal, an appropriate scientific theory should not contain more principles than necessary to predict and explain data. Is it necessary to have two processes to account for persuasion data, or would one process suffice? Kruglanski and Thompson's (1999) parametric unimodel is an attempt to account for existing attitude change data and predict new phenomena through a single process built upon a number of fundamental parameters. With its roots in Kruglanski's (1989) earlier Lay Epistemic Theory (LET; see also Kruglanski, 2012; Kruglanski, Dechesne, Orehek, & Pierro, 2009), the unimodel represents a significant conceptual departure from dual-process theories.

Unlike dual-process theories of attitude change, the unimodel seeks to avoid specifying specific aspects of the cognitive workings of persuasion or particular heuristic or peripheral cues that guide evaluation under some circumstances but not others. Instead, persuasion in the unimodel is treated as merely a special case of judgment formation where a perceiver analyzes evidence and produces an evaluation. In the ELM (and, to a lesser extent, the HSM), there are a great many persuasion variables that are allowed to interact with one another to affect the process and outcome of persuasion in different ways. The unimodel, on the other hand, attempts to specify a general method for arriving at a judgment and a small number of parameters that sufficiently account for variance in the process of arriving at a judgment. In this way, the unimodel is an attempt at a more parsimonious and simple explanation for the process of evaluation.

Like every scientist, recipients of persuasive information in the unimodel are hypothesis-testers with their own motivations, goals, pre-existing knowledge and potential biases. People use evidence to arrive at a conclusion. Similar to syllogistic models of attitudes discussed in Chapter 2, the unimodel uses major and minor premises to specify how people arrive at evaluations. In the unimodel (and Lay Epistemic Theory more broadly), evidence is referred to as a minor premise (i.e., *a belief statement*): It could be an observation that "my neighbor drives a BMW" or a fact such as "Coca-cola contains high-fructose corn syrup." This minor premise, then, is evaluated in tandem with another piece of information—a major premise (i.e., *a value statement*)—to draw a conclusion. Major premises that match our previous examples of minor premises could be "BMWs are very expensive" and "high-fructose corn syrup is unhealthy when consumed in large quantities." Generally, the major premise used in an evaluation is an inference rule taken from a person's prior knowledge or beliefs, whether this is attitudinally relevant knowledge, stereotypes or metacognitive beliefs about oneself, the attitude object or the way the world works. From the combination of these major and minor premises we might draw the conclusions "my neighbor is very rich" or "it is unhealthy to drink a lot of Coca-cola." If our knowledge or beliefs are different, however, we would draw completely different conclusions or be unable to draw conclusions at all: Neither a native of a remote island village (who lacks any knowledge of BMWs) nor Donald Trump (who doesn't consider BMWs to be expensive relative to other potential cars) would come to the conclusion that their neighbor is very rich.

The unimodel elaborates several parameters that constrain and specify how people arrive at evaluations using major and minor premises. The first and most important parameter of the unimodel is that of subjective relevance, or *"the degree to which the individual believes in a linkage between the antecedent and the consequent terms in a major premise"* (Kruglanski et al., 2004; emphasis added). To illustrate this, consider our previous example of Coca-cola: In this example, the major premise of "high fructose corn syrup (HFCS) is unhealthy when consumed in large quantities" links the presence of the HFCS in Coca-cola to the conclusion that Coca-cola is unhealthy when drunk in large quantities. If we believe that HFCS is indeed unhealthy when a lot of it is ingested, then the link between the evidence and the conclusion is valid. If we *do not* believe that HFCS is unhealthy, however, then the fact that it is an ingredient in Coca-cola should have no bearing (no subjective relevance) on whether or not it is healthy to consume large quantities of Coke. This element of judgment is of prime importance to the judgment being made: If one perceives the link between the evidence given in a persuasive message (the arguments) and the conclusion being offered by the message (i.e., attitude change) to be absent, then regardless of any other factors, attitude change will not occur. Of course, subjective relevance is not a belief-disbelief dichotomy. Like elaboration in the ELM, subjective relevance in the unimodel lies along a continuum that determines the weight we lend to the inference rule (major premise) being used to reach the conclusion. In contrast to subjective relevance—which lies at the heart of judgment in the unimodel—all of the other parameters are more akin to conditions that enable or facilitate the judgment's occurrence.

Although the unimodel departs in many ways from previous dual-process theories, it, like the HSM and ELM, incorporates motivation and ability into its parameters. In the unimodel, the amount of motivation to process information in order to reach a conclusion is determined by the evaluator's situationally salient processing goals. As in the dual-process models, these processing goals may depend on an individual's need for cognition (e.g., Cacioppo & Petty, 1982) or desire to be accurate in his or her judgments (Chaiken et al., 1989; Petty & Cacioppo, 1986). Processing goals may also depend on the desirability of any pre-existing attitudes, echoing the defense motivation goal in the HSM (Chaiken, 1980, 1987). In addition, processing goals can vary by the degree of accountability for the judgment the individual feels (Tetlock, 1985) or by an individual's own need to evaluate (Jarvis & Petty, 1996) or need for cognitive closure (Kruglanski & Webster, 1996; Webster & Kruglanski, 1998). Frequently, when evaluators have some motive for ceasing processing (e.g., they are tired, or convinced they are already correct or just do not enjoy thinking about the issue), information that appears earlier has an increased effect relative to late-appearing information, regardless of whether the information has to do with the source or the message (Erb et al., 2002). As in previous models of persuasion, one's ability, in addition to one's motivation, matters in forming an evaluation. In a similar way to the concept of elaboration (and need for cognition), the unimodel acknowledges that lower levels of cognitive capacity (either through dispositional or situational constraints) favor highly accessible, simple decision rules while impairing ability to utilize complex information in judgments.

Summary and Conclusion

In this chapter, we have seen how both the Heuristic-Systematic Model and the Elaboration Likelihood Model integrate findings from past research in the classical study of persuasion and generate new evidence to bolster their theoretical framework. The HSM introduced us to thinking about persuasion through the interaction between a basic set of principles and the changing motivations and goals of the person making the judgment, a theme woven into the ELM and the parametric unimodel. In the HSM, reconciliation of accuracy motivation and the least effort principle drives the extent of heuristic and systematic processing and, ultimately, the amount of persuasion effected by a message. In the ELM, situational and dispositional motivation and ability determine the extent of elaboration of a message, which in turn determines the weight applied to the result of information processed through the central and peripheral routes. Although motivations and goals are still important in the unimodel, it poses a significant theoretical departure from dual-process theories of persuasion in that it treats persuasion as merely another case of judgment and persuasive information as simply evidence in support of a conclusion that can be evaluated.

Despite their differences, the HSM and ELM together emphasize the usefulness of using two distinct processes to parse and make sense of the seemingly contextually dependent, ever-changing influence of variables encountered in persuasive communication. The dual-process models have contributed a great deal in this way by expanding and classifying our knowledge of how (and when) different variables act as persuasive arguments, peripheral cues, factors affecting elaboration or factors that bias processing. Persuasion research has been enriched by challenges to dual-process theories in the form of the unimodel, which attempts to explain persuasion parsimoniously through a broader architecture underlying judgment formation in general. Both single- and dual-process theories of persuasion continue to receive empirical support, and the distinction between single and dual processes has permeated other fields of intellectual inquiry, including the emerging field of social neuroscience (See Chapter 10).

CHAPTER 6

Predicting Behavior from Attitudes

As actors in a social world, we seek to understand our fellow actors. We seek information to help us navigate the social world, including understanding the behavior of other people. Knowing others' attitudes is an important step in understanding and predicting their behavior. In this chapter, we will focus on the proposition that people's behavior can be predicted from their attitudes.

It seems so intuitively appealing that attitudes and behavior should be related that many attitude theorists interleafed evaluations and behaviors in the very definition of attitudes. Attitudes have been referred to as "implicit behaviors" (Hovland et al., 1957), "implicit responses" (Doob, 1947) and "acquired behavioral dispositions" (Campbell, 1963). Gordon Allport considered the relationship between attitudes and behavior to be so intrinsic that he argued "without attitudes, it is impossible to account satisfactorily either for the consistency of any individual's behavior or for the stability of any society" (Allport, 1935, p. 798).

A strong correspondence between attitudes and behavior is the cornerstone of advertising and campaigning. Consider the enterprise of electing candidates to public office. The industry that has grown up to help candidates and parties succeed in elections gears its efforts toward influencing the electorate's attitudes. And those efforts come at a substantial cost. According to the British Broadcasting Company, more than $49 million (U.S.) was spent on the 2010 general election in Great Britain. Although a hefty price tag, it was relatively inexpensive compared to the $6 billion that was spent on the presidential election in the United States in 2012. Advertisements and personal appeals by candidates are typically measured by the degree to which they raise a candidate's 'favorability' ratings and lower the candidate's 'unfavorability' in the polls. These influence attempts are directed at people's attitudes—i.e., their evaluations of the candidates. However, that is not what the candidates are ultimately interested in. Their ultimate goal is to influence voting behavior, not attitudes. The prize for all political campaigns is the actual ballot-casting behavior of the electorate. The assumption that favorable evaluations of the candidates lead to votes at the ballot box is, nonetheless, a palpable expectation.

THEORETICAL CONSIDERATIONS: CONSISTENCY

In addition to intuition, a family of theories based on the principle of cognitive consistency buttresses the notion that people's behaviors will be consistent with their attitudes (Abelson et al., 1968; Heider, 1958; Newcomb, 1957). One of the original theories of consistency was known as **balance theory** (Heider, 1946; 1958). Fritz Heider was a psychologist in the gestalt tradition, which had its roots in the field of visual perception. In the gestalt view, the brain is seen as wired to perceive certain patterns in the environment. For example, someone perceiving a curved line on a

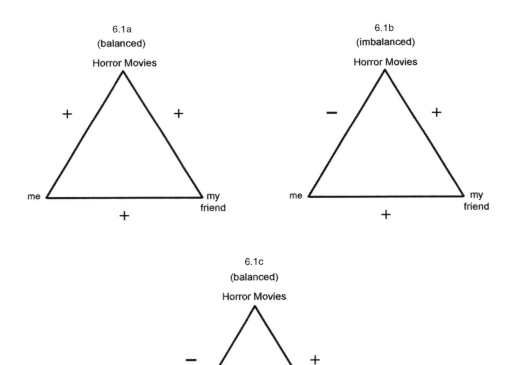

Note: + refers to a positive sentiment; - refers to a negative sentiment

FIGURE 6.1 *Balanced and imbalanced triangles representing attitudes towards one's friend and horror movies.*

paper will continue to see the line as curved, even if it is broken at various points. The mind prefers 'continuation' and 'good form' and will naturally perceive stimuli that way. In the field of social relations, Heider believed that the human perceiver is wired to prefer balanced relationships in their evaluations of people and objects. Consider a basic set of positive and negative evaluations (that Heider referred to as "sentiments") that you have about a friend of yours and an object (e.g., horror movies). If you have a favorable attitude toward your friend and you both share favorable attitudes toward horror films, then the relationship is balanced (see Figure 6.1a). If you and your friend disagree about horror movies, then there is a state of imbalance. You will experience what Heider called a "strain" to restore balance. Figure 6.1 shows both of those relationships. In Figure 6.1b, the imbalance causes a strain, which exerts pressure on you to revert to the pattern shown in Figure 6.1a. In that case, you would change your attitude toward horror films; you and your friend could then go to the movies together. Alternatively, you could try to persuade your friend to dislike horror films (Figure 6.1c). In that case, you could go to the movies together to watch the latest comedy.

In consistency theories, behaviors are similar to attitudes in that they express positive or negative relationships between a person and an attitude object. A positive evaluation of a movie and the behavior of attending the movie are both expressions of positive sentiments toward the movie (Collins, 1969). When your liking for the movie and your behavior toward the movie are similarly positive—or similarly negative—then a balanced state is achieved. People prefer balanced states, rating them as significantly more pleasant than unbalanced ones (Jordan, 1953). If there is a lack of balance, people experience pressure to change either their attitude or behavior in order to restore balance. Thus, consistency theories provide a basis for understanding why people are motivated to achieve concordance between their attitudes and their behaviors. In fact, we label people who "say one thing but do another" as hypocrites, finding them far less pleasant than people whose attitudes and behaviors are consistent.

EVIDENCE OF INCONSISTENCY: AN AUTOMOBILE TRIP LEADS TO QUESTIONING THE ATTITUDE-BEHAVIOR LINK

In Chapter 1, we briefly introduced you to a study by the sociologist, Richard LaPiere. In 1934, he reported research that revealed a dramatic disparity between what people report and what they actually do. According to Smith and Terry (2012), LaPiere's research was inspired by a family automobile trip that he and his wife had taken across the United States accompanied by a Chinese friend. Anti-Chinese prejudice was strong at that time and the LaPieres worried about whether they would be able to receive service and accommodations. In fact, they had no difficulty being served.

Two months later, the group was headed to one of the same regions to which they had travelled previously. Concerned about possible embarrassment, LaPiere contacted the hotel at which they had previously stayed and inquired if the proprietor would offer accommodations to a gentleman of Chinese origin. The proprietor told the group that he absolutely would not serve Chinese, which precisely contradicted the behavior of the proprietor during the earlier visit.

LaPiere decided to conduct a larger study to see if there was widespread discordance between people's reports and their actual behavior, at least in the general area of racial prejudice. He recruited a young Chinese couple and set out on an automobile trip, stopping at 251 hotels and restaurants, covering the gamut from the luxurious to the basic. The group was denied service only once. At the other 250 establishments, the group had no problem receiving courteous service. After the trip, LaPiere mailed a survey to all of the businesses that they had visited, asking them if they would accept "members of the Chinese race" in their establishment. Although he included a "depends on the circumstances" response in addition to the standard "yes" and "no," LaPiere found that 92% of the venues they had visited replied that they would *not* accept ethnic Chinese people on their premises. In their actual behavior toward the Chinese couple, however, less than one-half of one percent had actually behaved in a discriminatory manner.

META-ANALYTIC REVIEWS: ADDITIONAL QUESTIONS ABOUT ATTITUDES AND BEHAVIORS

LaPiere's study was a curious reminder that people do not always do what they say they would do. What remained unclear was whether the study implied a disjunction between attitudes and behaviors. One criticism of LaPiere's study is that it did not truly assess attitudes. Instead of measuring proprietors' evaluations of Chinese Americans or their evaluations of discriminatory behavior, LaPiere only asked proprietors what they would do when confronted with a request for service. Proprietors' behavior did not correspond to what they said they would do, but it is not clear that attitudes were part of the equation. LaPiere's study was well-cited but did not dampen the enthusiasm of researchers for conceiving of attitudes as a predictor of people's behavior (Kraus, 1995).

Decades later, Wicker (1969) took on the challenge of assessing the cumulative impact of attitudes on behavior across more than 45 studies published in the three decades following LaPiere's report. In research areas that included attitudes toward minority groups, academic cheating and job satisfaction, Wicker could find only a few studies in which attitudes correlated more than $r = .30$ with behavior. In many studies, there was no correlation at all. The average correlation across all of the studies was a rather small $r = .17$. One way of thinking about the magnitude of this correlation is that, when behavior and attitudes are assessed in the same study, less than 3% of the behavioral variance can be said to be reliably due to people's attitudes.

WHEN DO ATTITUDES PREDICT BEHAVIORS?

Readers of this volume should not be surprised that attitudes do not always predict behavior. We have already encountered several issues that are critically important in the attitudes-to-behavior relationship. In Chapter 2, we saw that attitude strength matters when it comes to determining behaviors: Strong attitudes are more likely to have behavioral consequences than weak attitudes. In Chapter 3, we saw that attitudes that serve particular functions are more likely to influence behaviors for those people who find those functions important. People with strong needs to present themselves in a positive light, for example, are more likely to act in accordance with attitudes that serve that particular function and less inclined to act consistently with attitudes that are not relevant to that function. Conversely, people with a strong knowledge function will act on attitudes that fulfill that function rather than attitudes that fulfill symbolic functions. This is to say that the relationship between attitudes and behaviors is moderated by other variables. We expect attitudes to strongly predict behavior under certain conditions, and less so under other conditions. The overall correlation of people's attitudes and behaviors might not be high, but we would expect it to be high in theoretically relevant conditions.

More than 25 years after Wicker's analysis was published, Kraus (1995) conducted a more extensive and statistically sophisticated analysis of 88 studies that measured attitudes and behaviors. The meta-analysis revealed a highly significant impact of attitudes on behaviors across the studies. In Kraus' terms, the levels of predictability implied a "substantial and practically important relationship" (p. 69) between the two concepts. More importantly, the results showed that there were certain conditions that increased the relationship and others that decreased it. For example, consistent with evidence we discussed in Chapter 2, participants who reported being more certain about their attitudes showed greater attitude-behavior consistency than those who were less certain. Attitudes formed by direct experience with the attitude object led to more consistent behaviors than attitudes developed without direct experience. More accessible attitudes were more likely to lead to behaviors consistent with the attitude than attitudes that were not accessible, and attitudes that were measured at the same level of specificity as the behaviors were more likely to be consistent. This concept is known as the principle of compatibility and is a particularly important issue in the study of attitude-behavior correspondence.

Principle of Compatibility

Attitudes, it turns out, are useful predictors of behavior if there is high correspondence between the measure of the attitude and the measure of the behavior (Fishbein & Ajzen, 2010; see also Ajzen, 1987; Fishbein & Ajzen, 1974). Suppose that we wanted to predict a person's beer-drinking behavior from a measure of his attitudes toward beer. The response to the attitude scale will predict his behavior more fully to the extent that the attitude question is specific to the behavior we wish to predict. Attitudes will predict behavior to the extent that it is specific to the time, social context, target object and particular type of behavior. If a person is asked about his attitudes toward having a premium beer in the company of friends in the evening, we should not be surprised if the attitude measure fails to predict whether he guzzles a Bud Light alone in his pajamas at 7 A.M. The observation that *matching the level of specificity of an attitude measure to a specific behavior produces a high level of attitude-behavior correspondence* is known as the **principle of compatibility** (Ajzen, 1988; Ajzen & Fishbein, 1980). In a review of 124 datasets, Ajzen and Fishbein (1977) found that attitude-behavior correspondence was positively and significantly related to the extent to which the attitude and behavior measures satisfied the principle of compatibility ($r = .83$).

Subsequent directed, empirical tests of this hypothesis corroborated their findings. In one study, Davidson and Jaccard (1979) used multiple attitude measures that varied in the degree of compatibility. They found that the specificity of the attitude measure mattered greatly for the magnitude of the attitude-behavior correlation, where general attitude measures were almost unrelated to behavior ($r = .08$), slightly specific attitude measures were weakly correlated with behavior ($r = .32$) and specific attitude measures were more strongly related to behavior ($r = .57$). The increase in measured attitude-behavior correlation in meta-analyses (Kraus, 1995; Wicker, 1969) is therefore likely to be at least in part a function of increased specificity of the attitude measures employed by researchers over the years. Indeed, in the eight studies that manipulated the level of attitude-behavior correspondence (i.e., the match between specificity of the attitude measure and the behavior measure) in Kraus' (1995) meta-analysis, the correlation between attitude and behavior measures was a robust $r = .54$ when attitudes toward specific behaviors were compared to actual behaviors. In other words, it is difficult to predict frequency of drinking a premium beer on a particular day from attitudes toward beer in general, whereas predicting the amount of premium beer consumed on a given day from a person's measured attitude toward drinking the premium beer that day is much more reliable. There is some evidence, however, that global attitude measures are not completely misleading or unrepresentative of behavior. While specific attitude measures are best for predicting their specified behaviors, global attitudes may be useful in predicting aggregations of multiple behaviors across the domain covered by the global attitude, or repeated behaviors such as recycling (Fishbein & Ajzen, 1974; see also Werner, 1978; Weigel & Newman, 1976).

The conclusions from research exploring attitude-behavior correspondence grow a little more complex, however, when one considers the role of implicit attitudes as well as explicit attitudes. As we shall see later in Chapter 9, measures of explicit and implicit attitudes may not necessarily correlate with each other (Fazio & Olson, 2003; Payne, Burkley, & Stokes, 2008), posing a challenge for attitudes researchers in determining which behaviors are differentially predicted by implicit vs. explicit attitude measurement. Some research has suggested that implicit attitude measures more strongly predict spontaneous or nonverbal behavior, whereas explicit attitude measures better predict deliberate, effortful behavior (Fazio & Olson, 2003; Gawronski & Bodenhausen, 2006; Strack & Deutsch, 2004), although many instances exist where implicit attitudes predict deliberate behaviors and vice versa (e.g., Agerstrom & Rooth, 2011; Olson & Fazio, 2007; Payne, Krosnick, Pasek, Lelkes, Akhtar, & Tompson, 2010; von Hippel, Brener, & von Hippel, 2008; Widman & Olson, 2013). Clearer examples of this distinction come from the literature on stereotyping and prejudice, where implicit measures often predict nonverbal friendliness and perceived bias in interaction and explicit measures predict prejudicial bias in verbal behavior as well as subjective friendliness ratings (Dovidio, Kawakami, & Gaertner, 2002; see also Dovidio et al., 1997). This distinction between the relative effects of implicit and explicit attitudes on behavior will be discussed in more detail in relation to the MODE model (Fazio, 1990; see also Fazio, 1986; Fazio & Towles-Schwen, 1999) later in this chapter.

Structural Components of Consistency

In addition to being affected by measurement issues, attitude-behavior consistency is also partly determined by the functional and structural properties of the attitudes themselves (see Chapters 2 and 3). Typically, attitudes that serve a value-expressive function are highly related to behavior. In one study (Fazio & Williams, 1986), political attitudes were found to be highly predictive of behavior, with attitude measures correlated with voting behavior at $r = .78$ and $r = .63$, depending on the specific candidate in the 1984 United States presidential election, Ronald Reagan or Walter Mondale. Attitudes towards other social behaviors that are less value-expressive, such as donating blood, are comparatively less ($r = .24$) predictive of behavior (Chang et al., 1988). The importance of value-expressiveness has been replicated in other domains as well, for example in studies of memory (e.g., Eagly et al., 1999).

As we discussed in Chapter 2, attitude structure is also related to its success in predicting behavior. Attitudes that are more stable (Doll & Ajzen, 1992) and accessible (Glasman & Albarracín, 2006) increase the strength of the attitude-behavior relationship, serving as a moderator of the relationship between attitudes and behaviors (see Cooke & Sheeran, 2004, for a review). Internal consistency between the various components of the attitude is also crucial for predicting attitude-behavior correspondence. Whether it be consistency between overall favorability and the valenced cognitions about the attitude object (evaluative vs. cognitive consistency; Norman, 1975) or affective and behavioral consistency (Chaiken, Pomerantz, & Giner-Sorolla, 1995), consistency between the different attitude sub-components generally strengthens the attitude-behavior relationship.

Not only do specific aspects of the attitude increase attitude-behavior correspondence, but our knowledge *about* our attitude can also affect the extent to which our attitudes predict behavior. Analyzing the reasons that we hold our attitudes can cause those attitudes to change temporarily, especially when our knowledge about the attitude object is low (Wilson, Dunn, Kraft, & Lisle, 1989; Wilson, Kraft, & Dunn, 1989; see also Wilson, Lisle, Schooler, Hodges, Klaaren, & LaFleur, 1993). To illustrate Wilson et al.'s point, consider your attitude toward ketchup. Let us assume that you like ketchup, put it on your hamburger and hot dog, but rarely give it much thought. If someone asks you why you like ketchup, you might conjure some reasons. It is made from tomatoes, a healthy vegetable. The U.S. Food and Drug Administration has, from time to time, considered it a vegetable. It lasts forever in the refrigerator. By the time you think of the reasons for liking this attitude object to which you usually give scant thought, you really like ketchup. The attitude you report has become temporarily more positive, but it is a distortion of your real attitude. If asked immediately after this exercise whether you intend to put ketchup on your omelet and extra ketchup on your hamburger, you may think you will. But the distortion created by thinking about your attitude actually has actually made it less predictive of your future use of ketchup (Wilson et al., 1989). This is especially the case when attitudes are affectively rather than cognitively based (Millar & Tesser, 1986; see also Maio & Olson, 1998).

Dispositional vs. Situational Influences on Consistency

Individual difference factors can be a powerful predictor of the attitude-behavior relation. As mentioned in Chapter 5, need for cognition is a powerful individual difference factor that changes how (or what aspects of) incoming information influence our attitudes. It is no surprise, then, that need for cognition has also been shown to affect the translation of attitudes into behavior with the attitude-behavior correlation being larger for those with high ($r = .86$) vs. low ($r = .41$) needs for cognition (Cacioppo & Petty, 1982; Cacioppo, Petty, Kao, & Rodriguez, 1986). Depending on the distribution of individual differences in a population, certain populations can also show higher or lower attitude-behavior correlations than average. The extent to which one's attitudes are **crystallized** (i.e., stable, non-ambiguous and non-ambivalent) has been shown to affect the attitude-behavior correlation (Sears,

1986; Visser & Krosnick, 1998)—since one's attitudes become more crystallized with age, we would expect that age would increase attitude-behavior correspondence. Non-student populations, for example, show more attitude-behavior correspondence ($r = .48$) than student populations ($r = .34$; Kraus, 1995), possibly because non-student populations are typically older and possess crystallized attitudes. Finally, personality characteristics such as self-monitoring have also been shown to affect the degree to which attitudes predict behavior, with individuals lower in self-monitoring exhibiting a stronger attitude-behavior relationship (Snyder, 1974, 1987; Snyder & Kendzierski, 1982).

As with most research in social psychology, situational factors also play a large part in determining attitude-behavior correspondence. The above-cited relationship between self-monitoring and the attitude-behavioral correlation, for example, is partly constrained by situational factors, such as time pressure, that increase attitude-behavior correspondence for people low in self-monitoring but not for those high in self-monitoring (Jamieson & Zanna, 1989). Objective self-awareness, which is the focusing of one's attention on oneself (e.g., Carver & Scheier, 1981; Froming et al., 1982; Gibbons, 1978), also has been shown to affect the attitude-behavior relation. Objective self-awareness has often been instantiated by having people look at themselves in a mirror while performing a given task. In one study on self-awareness, Diener and Wallbom (1976) had students solve anagrams with an opportunity to cheat by taking extra time on the difficult task. Students in general express anti-cheating attitudes. When students were left to their own devices, however, Diener and Wallbom found that a whopping 71% of students took extra time despite the experimenter's explicit instructions against doing so. When students were made self-aware by sitting in front of a mirror and listening to a recording of their own voices, the proportion of students cheating by taking extra time dropped precipitously to 7%. Although students typically have strong attitudes against cheating, these data demonstrate that their actual cheating behavior can vary significantly as a function of self-awareness. Further research by Froming, Walker and Lopyan (1982), assessing the role of situational self-awareness in moderating the attitude-behavior relationship, elaborated on these findings, showing that one's behavior is more likely to correspond to one's attitude when seeing oneself in a mirror but more likely to correspond to norms or beliefs *about* the attitude when speaking to an audience. Although there are no doubt many more idiosyncratic situational factors that affect the attitude-behavior relation, these examples illustrate that situational as well as dispositional factors can directly affect attitude-behavior correspondence *and* indirectly affect the attitude-behavior link through their influence on other individual or structural variables.

As we have seen, research has identified a number of situational and individual difference variables that affect attitude-behavior consistency. Although the search for factors that moderate the link between attitudes and behaviors has been productive, two integrative theories have been particularly useful guides for understanding when and why attitudes predict behaviors. The MODE model (Fazio, 1990; 2007) and the Reasoned Action Approach (Fishbein & Ajzen, 2010) have provided conceptual clarity to the relationship and it is to those theories that we now turn.

THE REASONED ACTION APPROACH

Perhaps the broadest empirical and conceptual approach to addressing the attitude-behavior link has been Fishbein and Ajzen's (2010) Reasoned Action Approach. This perspective took its original form as the theory of reasoned action (Fishbein & Ajzen, 1975), which spawned more than a thousand empirical investigations and several theoretical modifications. The theory of reasoned action took the position that the most direct predictor of people's behavior is their intention toward a behavior. If we want to predict whether people will go to the polls to vote in an upcoming election, the best indicator of whether they will vote is their stated intention to vote or stay home. The more nuanced theoretical question is what predicts their intentions. In the theory of reasoned action, intentions were thought to be based on two factors: people's beliefs about the positive and negative consequences of the behavior and their beliefs about what other relevant people in their environment would want them to do. That is, behavior intentions were based on their attitudes about the behavior and by their judgment of the subjective norms for behaving. Subsequently, the model was adjusted to consider additional variables that contributed to the attitude-behavior link. The Integrative Model (Fishbein, 2000) added the importance of descriptive norms (i.e., what other people *actually* do in similar circumstances). The theory of planned behavior (Ajzen, 1985) added a consideration of people's beliefs about their ability to control the behavior in question. Recent theorizing has integrated the earlier approaches into the more comprehensive *reasoned action approach* (Fishbein & Ajzen, 2010) that we shall now consider in more detail.

The Role of Attitudes in the Reasoned Action Approach

Attitudes play a key role in the reasoned action approach, which is depicted in Figure 6.2. An attitude toward a behavior is based on **behavioral beliefs**, i.e., *beliefs about the consequences a certain behavior and the value attached to each of those consequences*. In Chapter 2, we described Fishbein's (1967) expectancy-value model of attitudes in which he theorized that attitudes can be described by the sum of all the values attached to the possible consequences of performing that behavior weighted by the expected probability of each of those consequences occurring. For example, imagine that you are considering purchasing a used car. If the car isn't a dud, it will make transportation much more convenient for you. However, there is also a small chance that the car you purchased could be a lemon, in

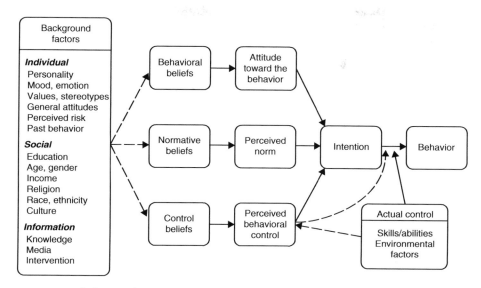

FIGURE 6.2 *Schematic presentation of the reasoned action approach.*
Source: Fishbein, M. & Ajzen, I. (2010). *Predicting and changing behavior.* New York: Psychology Press.
Reprinted with permission.

which case you would be out a great deal of money—a very undesirable outcome. Your attitude toward purchasing the used car in the reasoned action approach, then, would be the positive value you ascribe to the convenient transportation afforded by the car measured against the large (negative) cost that you would incur if the car doesn't work, with each outcome weighted by your assessment of its probability.

The process of summing the gain or loss of each possible outcome weighted by its subjective probability produces an **expectancy-value index** of that behavior. As an example, people's attitudes towards promoting or preventing various societal changes depend upon their beliefs about whether those changes would produce desirable or undesirable outcomes (Bain, Hornsey, Bongiorno, Kashima, & Crimston, 2013). Empirical research has indicated that the mean correlation across studies between this expectancy-value index and direct measures of attitudes towards certain behaviors is $r = .50$ (Armitage & Conner, 2001), at least partially validating the theoretical claim about the important role behavioral beliefs play in the creation of attitudes towards certain behaviors. Mean correlations between measured attitudes and behavioral intentions, for comparison, can typically range from $r = .45$ to $r = .60$ (Albarracín et al., 2001; Armitage & Conner, 2001; Hagger et al., 2002; Sheeran & Taylor, 1999), indicating that behavioral beliefs are indeed instrumental in understanding the structure of attitudes towards specific behaviors.

Normative Influences on Behavior

Although attitudes are directly linked to behavioral intentions, they are not the only influence. The decision to purchase a used car in the previous example will be affected not only by your attitude toward the car but also by what relevant other people would think about your purchase. Perhaps your friends believe that used cars are for wimps and your closest cousins have bought brand new cars. These beliefs about how other people might view your behavior are relevant to what car you ultimately intend to purchase. Note that there are two types of beliefs that form your judgment of the norm. One is a belief in whether important individuals or groups would approve or disapprove of your behavior. The other is a belief in what those individuals and groups actually do when confronted with a similar behavioral choice. The former belief is considered an *injunctive norm*, addressing your concern for doing what important others think you should do in the situation. The latter is considered a *descriptive norm*, addressing what you think people really do in the situation. Taken together, your assessment of the injunctive and descriptive norms form the *perceived norm*, which is directly related to your behavioral intention.

How important is the perceived norm in affecting people's behavior? Research has shown that people's assessment of the perceived norm is quite important (Armitage & Conner, 2001), but the weighting depends on factors intrinsic to the social situation. Suppose, for example, that you wanted to have a four-week holiday. Your request is within the rules of your company, but your supervisor had made it clear that four successive weeks off was against the norm. The impact of this normative belief could vary situationally and would affect your behavior more if you were just starting a career in the company than it would if you had already made a decision to search for a new position. Typically, research has found perceived norms to be less predictive of behavior than attitudes (Albarracín et al., 2001; Armitage & Connor, 2001: Hagger et al., 2002; Sheeran & Taylor, 1999), but this depends on the weight ascribed to the perceived norm. This weight may depend on individual characteristics such as self-monitoring (Snyder, 1974)—i.e., with low self-monitors being less susceptible to outside situational or normative influence (Ajzen, Timko, & White, 1982)—or it may exhibit considerable variation depending on circumstance and culture (Trafimow & Finlay, 1996). In one study, Ybarra and Trafimow (1998) suggested that whether attitudes or norms were more predictive of behavioral intentions depends on whether individualistic or collectivist thoughts were more accessible in people's memories. By priming collectivist thoughts, Ybarra and Trafimow found that norms were more influential than attitudes but priming individualistic thoughts resulted in greater weight attributed to attitudes.

Perceived and Actual Behavioral Control

Ajzen (1985) introduced the concept of behavioral control to the reasoned action approach. He argued that neither attitudes nor norms would predict behavior in the absence of people feeling confident that they could actually perform the behavior. A person considering using condoms in a romantic relationship may evaluate the behavior positively and believe that his friends would approve of his using condoms. However, if he worries about where to purchase them or whether he will be able to use them, then the probability of his actually using them will be low. The person seeking a used car in our previous example may have positive attitudes toward used cars and believe that her friends and relatives would approve. If she does not believe she can successfully locate a reliable dealer and/or know how to negotiate for the car, then the probability that her behavior will match her attitude or her perception of the norm will be diminished. Control beliefs, closely related to Bandura's (1977) concept of self-efficacy, translate into confidence in one's ability to enact the behavior that, in turn, influences behavioral intention.

In the depiction of the reasoned action approach in Figure 6.2, note that there is a separate role played by *actual control*. Perceived behavioral control is a psychological variable that influences people's intention to behave. By contrast, actual control refers to limiting or facilitating conditions that permit or prevent the behavior in question. The car purchaser cannot carry through on her intention to purchase a used car if she cannot get to the dealership or has no money in her bank account. The potential condom user may evaluate the use of condoms highly, know how to use them, feel his friends would approve, but if he does not have them at the moment, he cannot use them. Actual control may have a role in influencing perceived behavioral control (as indicated by the broken line at the bottom of Figure 6.2), but it has a moderating role on the relationship of behavioral intention to behavior. Without actual control to perform the behavior, then intention will not predict behavior.

In Fishbein and Ajzen's (2010) view, behavior is a function of just a small number of variables. Shown by the solid arrows in Figure 6.2, these variables are expected to predict behavioral intentions and behavior regardless of circumstance or issue. The reasoned action approach recognizes that individual and social circumstances are complex and that any number of background factors, including income, race, religion and personality, may play a role in how people behave. However, such background factors do not play a direct role in predicting people's behavior. Rather, they exert their influence by affecting how people construe their beliefs about behavior, norms and control.

EMPIRICAL EVIDENCE FOR THE REASONED ACTION APPROACH

In more than 1,000 studies using over 300,000 participants, the reasoned action approach has been able to predict intended and actual behavior from specific attitudes (Armitage & Conner, 2001; Myers, 2010; Six & Eckes, 1996; Wallace et al., 2005). Generally, empirical reviews and meta-analyses have validated the robustness of the reasoned action approach across a wide variety of paradigms, attitudes, and behaviors (Albarracín, Johnson, Fishbein, & Meullerleile, 2001; Ajzen, 1991, 2005; Armitage & Conner, 2001; Downs & Hausenblas, 2005; Godin & Kok, 1996; Hagger, Chatzisarantis, & Biddle, 2002). When the three elements of the reasoned action framework are used together to predict behavior, multiple correlations predicting behavioral intentions range from $r = .63$ to $r = .71$ (Albarracín et al., 2001; Armitage & Conner, 2001; Hagger et al., 2002; Sheeran & Taylor, 1999). Even for behaviors that one might surmise are largely automatic (such as use of an addictive recreational drug such as ecstasy), studies have shown a clear relationship between attitudes, subjective norms and perceived behavioral control to both behavioral intentions and actual behavior (Conner, Sherlock, & Orbell, 1998). As would be expected given the research on attitude-behavior correspondence preceding the theory of reasoned action, prediction of behavioral intentions and actual behavior is even more accurate when specific attitudes are used to predict specific behavior. For instance, one study found that while attitudes towards environmental issues are not predictive of participation in recycling programs, attitudes towards recycling itself significantly predict recycling behavior (Oskamp, Harrington, Edwards, Sherwood, Okuda, & Swanson, 1991).

Mapping Behavioral Intentions to Behavior

Most of the research conducted in the reasoned action framework uses attitudes, subjective norms and perceived behavioral control to predict behavioral intentions instead of actual behavior. It is a natural question, then, to ask whether or not behavioral intentions are a valid proxy for behavior, since behavior is the true variable of interest. On average, research has shown that behavioral intentions are indeed related to behavior: On the most aggregate level, a review of meta-analyses presented a mean correlation of $r = .53$ between behavioral intentions and behavior, strongly suggesting that there is a robust link between the two (Sheeran, 2002). A meta-analysis involving 185 studies in various domains whose dependent variable was actual behavior demonstrated strong support of the three theoretical components of the reasoned action framework for predicting behavior (Armitage & Conner, 2001). Experimental evidence manipulating behavioral intentions and measuring effects on behavior further solidify this link: Experimentally inducing new intentions often induces new behavior (Webb & Sheeran, 2006). Even the act of merely asking about behavioral intentions increases the likelihood of the behavior being enacted (Levav & Fitzsimons, 2006).

Implementation intentions leverage automatic processing through linking anticipated critical situations to specific goal-directed responses in an attempt to increase the link between behavioral intentions and behavior (Gollwitzer, 1999). Forming implementation intentions—regardless of whether they are general or specific

(Ajzen, Czasch, & Flood, 2009)—further increases the chance of behavioral intentions producing the actual behavior (e.g., Orbell, Hodgkins, & Sheeran, 1997; for a review, see Sheeran, Milne, Webb, & Gollwitzer, 2005). This appears to be true in laboratory studies as well as in large-scale field studies (see Gollwitzer & Sheeran, 2006). The reinforcement of the intention-behavior link can also operate through automating the initiation of the behavior in question by transferring behavioral control to situational cues that trigger the planned implementation (Gollwitzer, 1999). When implementation intentions compete against other automatic influences on behavior, such as habits (Adriaanse, Gollwitzer, de Ridder, de Wit, & Kroese, 2011) or chronic anxiety (Webb, Ononaiye, Sheeran, Reidy, & Lavda, 2010), the accessibility of the behavioral intentions does not appear to replace the automatic activation of the undesired behavior but does allow flexibility of choosing which behavior to enact, given the person's goals. These competing implementation intentions can backfire, however, if they take the form of a negation (i.e., to *not* enact a habitual behavior) as they may ironically increase the accessibility of the habitual response, especially if it is strong (Adriaanse, van Oosten, de Ridder, de Wit, & Evers, 2011). Despite their effectiveness, it has been called into question whether or not implementation intentions actually reinforce the intention-behavior link more so than explicit commitment (Ajzen, Czasch, & Flood, 2009). Regardless of the specific mechanism driving the effectiveness of implementation intentions, a great deal of empirical evidence suggests that it is reliable to extend results found for predicting behavioral intentions under the reasoned action framework to actual behavior, as we shall report in the following section.

Applications of the Reasoned Action Approach

The reasoned action approach been applied extensively outside the domain of the social psychology laboratory. One domain in which the reasoned action framework has frequently been applied is in attempting to use attitudes towards sexual health to predict various preventative behaviors (Ajzen, Albarracín & Hornik, 2007). In one typical study, Albarracín, Johnson, Fishbein and Meullerleile (2001) showed that behavioral beliefs ($r = .56$) and normative beliefs ($r = .46$) about condom use significantly predicted explicitly measured attitudes and subjective norms, which in turn predicted behavioral intentions ($r = .58$ and $r = .39$, respectively). In addition, actual condom use behavior was significantly related to behavioral intentions ($r = .45$). By validating the reasoned action framework in a diverse array of domains and for a wide variety of attitudes, applied studies such as this one not only point to the robustness of the theory's predictions but also indicate key determinants of actual health behavior that can be targeted by interventions. Perhaps more importantly, they also indicate the strength of the relationship between behavior and the three predictor variables, facilitating interventions that target the factor that predicts the most variance in behavior and therefore yields the most behavioral change.

Research on health behaviors has not been limited to condom use, but also has been extended to predicting birth control use (e.g., Reinecke, Schmidt, & Ajzen, 1996, 1997), abortions (Petkova, Ajzen, & Driver, 1995), drug use (e.g., Conner, Sherlock, & Orbell, 1998), and other general health behaviors (Ajzen & Manstead, 2007). Finally, the reasoned action framework has also been extended into the domains of consumer research (e.g., Sheppard, Hartwick, & Warshaw, 1988) as well as predicting education attainment behavior, such as high school completion rates by African American students (Davis, Ajzen, Saunders, & Williams, 2002). Although this is by no means an exhaustive list, it illustrates the diversity of possible areas in which predictions from the reasoned action approach can be applied with robust results.

Challenges to the Reasoned Action Approach

One criticism of the reasoned action approach is that it is not psychologically realistic as a process model. Although it often does a good job of predicting behavior when one has all the relevant information about behavioral beliefs, subjective norms and perceived behavioral control, the model is heavily cognitive in nature and de-emphasizes the affective predictors and moderators of attitude-behavior correspondence. This can be problematic for practical prediction for health behaviors, for example, where affective aspects of an attitude can often have disproportionate weight in influencing behavior (Dutta-Bergman, 2005). Researchers have proposed additional moderating variables that attempt to explain observed differences in the strength of the attitude-behavior relationship. Some of these potential variables are the valence of the attitude in question (i.e., whether it is positive, negative, or ambivalent; Conner & Sparks, 2002), whether the specific behavior involves acting or refraining to act (Richetin, Conner, & Perugini, 2011) and whether the attitude and linked behavior would result in instrumental vs. emotional outcomes (Crites, Fabrigar, & Petty, 1994; Trafimow & Sheeran, 1998; van der Pligt, Zeelenberg, van Dijk, de Vries, & Richard, 1997).

The last of these potential moderating variables is especially important for research applying the reasoned action framework to various commonly studied health and sexual behaviors, as emotional reactions during decision-making under risk or uncertainty are especially powerful drivers of behavior (the "risk as feeling" hypothesis; Loewenstein, Weber, Hsee, & Welch, 2001). In this vein, research has demonstrated that positive and negative behavioral beliefs about the emotional outcomes of a behavior are significantly better at predicting risky behavior than are beliefs about the behavior's instrumental benefits or drawbacks (Lawton, Conner, & McEachan, 2009). Negative affective beliefs in particular seem to be the most powerful predictor for various health behaviors when compared to positive affective beliefs and instrumental beliefs, regardless of valence (Lawton, Conner, & Parker, 2007).

More generally, research suggests that whether the behavioral belief concerns instrumental or emotional outcomes determines how predictive it is of behavior, with instrumental aspects of one's attitude being a better predictor of cognitively driven instrumental behaviors (e.g., voting) and emotional aspects of one's attitude better predicting affect-driven emotional behaviors (e.g., contraceptive use; Glasman & Albarracín, 2006). Similarly, when analyzing reasons for one's attitude prior to behavior, reconsidering the instrumentality or emotionality of the attitude increases attitude-behavior correspondence for behaviors in the same domain, but not in the opposite domain (Millar & Tesser, 1986; see also Wilson, Dunn, Kraft, & Lisle, 1989). In other words, increasing the salience of instrumental aspects of an attitude leads to higher attitude-behavior correspondence when the behavior is cognitively driven but not affectively driven (and vice versa).

Another controversy in the reasoned action approach concerns the potentially special status of moral beliefs. Consistent with the reasoned action approach, our belief in moral issues of right and wrong may be subsumed under the concept of an injunctive norm, which we described earlier. However, some researchers have suggested that moral beliefs are discriminable from subjective norms (Conner, Lawton, Parker, Chorlton, Marstead, & Stradling, 2007; Maio & Olson, 1995) and have a different impact on behavior. Research supporting this suggestion has found that the importance of moral beliefs in attitude-behavior correspondence is greater for some types of behaviors—notably ones with a moral component—than for others (Godin, Conner, & Sheeran, 2005; Maio & Olson, 2000a; Sparks & Manstead, 2006). In particular, linking moral values to a specific action seems to increase behavioral intentions towards that action, even making others' actions and motivations more easily understood when they are linked to a moral value (Effron & Miller, 2012). Other proposed factors that have been shown to affect behavior are individual differences in personal need for satisfaction (Hagger, Chatzisarantis, & Harris, 2006), situationally anticipated negative self-conscious emotion (Hynie, MacDonald, & Marques, 2006), and individual differences in self-efficacy beliefs (Manstead & van Eekelen, 1998; see Bandura, 1997). While the simple but effective reasoned action approach continues to be a very useful tool for understanding how attitudes translate into behavior and structuring interventions, empirical evidence has repeatedly pointed to the importance of additional moderating variables not included in the canonical reasoned action model.

THE MODE MODEL

Historically, the **MODE** (Motivation and Opportunity as Determinants of behavior) **model** (Fazio, 1990; see also Fazio, 1986; Fazio & Towles-Schwen, 1999) developed as a set of propositions designed to delineate some of the limits of the reasoned action approach. As the name of the theory suggests, the reasoned action approach stresses cognitive elements of one's attitudes that predict behavioral intentions and subsequent behavior. The MODE model, in contrast, serves as a counterpoint in that it considers two qualitatively different ways—the deliberate and the spontaneous—in which our attitudes influence our behavior. Unlike the reasoned action approach, which grew out of a structural attempt to predict behavioral intentions from attitude measures, the MODE model's approach to attitude structure incorporates a more flexible definition of an attitude as an association in memory between an object and one's evaluation of it, and proceeds to delineate precisely how this association influences subsequent behavior (Fazio, 2007). As we shall see, the emphasis on memory in this definition underscores the critical role of attitude accessibility in predicting behavior.

Deliberative Attitude-Behavior Correspondence

According to the MODE model, our attitudes can influence our behavior in two qualitatively different ways, either exerting their effects deliberately or spontaneously, depending on whether or not *both* motivation and opportunity to consider one's prior attitudes are present in the situation. In this way, the MODE model bears much resemblance to other dual-process theories of attitude change that we explored in the last chapter (Petty & Cacioppo, 1981, 1984, 1986; Chaiken, 1980, 1987), which considered one's motivation and ability to carefully consider persuasive information.

The **deliberative** pathway in the MODE model is qualitatively similar to the process outlined in the theory of reasoned action/planned behavior in that it is characterized by the exertion of cognitive effort (Olson & Fazio, 2009). When motivation and opportunity to make a deliberative decision are present, we consciously consider the various decision alternatives, weigh the costs and benefits of each behavior and consciously reflect upon our pre-existing attitudes relevant to the situation before creating a plan for behavior that may be enacted (Fazio & Towles-Schwen, 1999). The motivation necessary to make a deliberative decision can come from a variety of sources. Paralleling models of attitude change, one of the most fundamental of these motivations is the presupposed motivation for accuracy, such as making correct decisions and holding correct attitudes (e.g., Chaiken, Lieberman, & Eagly, 1989). Other motivations can also help motivate deliberation, however, such as the need for positive self-esteem (e.g., Sedikides & Strube, 1997) or the need to belong (e.g., Baumeister & Leary, 1995). While holding accurate attitudes may be a part of our self-esteem or may serve belongingness goals, these motivations often steer us to deliberate in the service of a desired end state or consequence (Olson & Fazio, 2009). In addition to possessing some motivation to consider our attitudes deliberately, we also require the opportunity to do so. Opportunity is a broad criterion for one's ability to consider one's prior attitude, whether it be a time constraint or a more physical barrier such as in retrograde amnesia—if we are under time pressure, for example, we are unlikely to consciously recall our pre-existing attitudes from memory (Jamieson & Zanna, 1989). Importantly, *both* motivation and opportunity are crucial for deliberative decision-making and for making use of specific, situationally (and behaviorally) relevant attitudes: If either motivation or opportunity is lacking, we instead are more likely to rely on general or global attitudes and make use of the information from those attitudes in a spontaneous fashion (Sanbonmatsu & Fazio, 1990; see also Fabrigar, Petty, Smith, & Crites, 2006).

Spontaneous Attitude-Behavior Correspondence

Unlike the reasoned action approach, a large amount of research and applications of the MODE model has been directed towards investigating the **spontaneous**, rather than deliberative, mode of decision-making in order to identify the circumstances under which we forgo deliberative processing. When we lack the motivation or opportunity to engage in deliberative decision-making, spontaneously retrieved attitudinal information may then guide our decisions without conscious consideration of our attitudes or even conscious awareness of their influence (Petty, Fazio, & Briñol, 2009). The canonical example of how attitudes may influence our behavior under the spontaneous route is when we encounter an extremely aversive stimulus in our environment, such as the appearance of a cockroach in our kitchen: It doesn't take much scrutinizing of our previous attitude to know our intended plan of action, whether it is to crush it with our boot or leap up on a chair. The key to attitude-behavior correspondence when attitudes are considered spontaneously, then, is the degree to which the attitude is accessible in memory (see Chapter 2)— our attitudes towards cockroaches are *extremely* accessible, for example, coming to mind instantly upon presentation of the attitude object and subsequently guiding behavior without conscious reflection.

This accessibility is determined by a strong association between an evaluation (attitude) and the mental representation of the attitude object (Fazio, 1990), often created through repeated pairing of the stimulus and its evaluation. Recall our example of Powell and Fazio (1984) from Chapter 2, where repeated expression of an attitude increased its accessibility (although bounded by diminishing returns). Beyond increasing attitude accessibility, repeated rehearsal of an attitude towards an object can also affect subsequent construal of related objects. For example, if you rehearse your (negative) attitude towards an "injection" vs. your (positive) attitude towards an "immunization," you are likely to construe and evaluate "flu shots" in a negative vs. positive way (Young & Fazio, 2013). Accessibility can even be strengthened in cases when the evaluations are non-conscious. Repeated pairing of an object and an evaluation, for instance, has been shown to "create" implicit attitudes through covariation of two stimuli in a classical conditioning paradigm, demonstrating the ability of experience to affect attitude accessibility at the implicit level as well (Olson & Fazio, 2001). In other words, the mere repeated association through simultaneous presentation of novel attitude objects with other positive or negative objects creates corresponding positive or negative attitudes both on the explicit *and* implicit level.

Whether through repeated pairing with the attitude object or some other mechanism, attitude accessibility—often operationalized through reaction time measures to attitudinal questions (see also, e.g., Fazio & Williams, 1986)—is extremely important for predicting behavior in the spontaneous route. As we saw in Chapter 2, highly accessible, or "strong," attitudes, such as those typically formed through direct experience (see Regan & Fazio, 1977), are in general more stable, more resistant to persuasion and more predictive of behavior than "weak" attitudes low in accessibility (Fazio & Williams, 1986; Petty & Krosnick, 1995). There have been numerous studies that have illustrated the link between attitude accessibility and predictive validity through directly comparing attitude-behavior correspondence for attitudes with low vs. high response latencies (Berger & Mitchell, 1989; Fazio, Powell, & Williams, 1989; Fazio & Williams, 1986; Kokkinaki & Lunt, 1997). At the far end of the spectrum, attitudes that are extremely weak or inaccessible are typically non-attitudes (e.g., one's attitude towards door frames), where encountering an attitude object for which we possess an extremely strong attitude—such as a cockroach or, for someone addicted to smoking, a cigarette—may elicit automatic evaluative responses (Fazio, Sanbonmatsu, Powell, & Kardes, 1986). This automatic activation may then have a number of downstream consequences for spontaneous behavior (Glasman & Albarracín, 2006; see Fazio, 2001).

When spontaneously activated attitudes guide behavior, they typically do so either through producing an immediate evaluative impression or through indirectly influencing our cognition in a variety of ways (Petty, Fazio, & Briñol, 2009). In terms of evaluation, our spontaneously activated negative attitudes towards certain racial groups, for example, can negatively impact impression formation in interracial interactions in the absence of motivation to control prejudice (Olson & Fazio, 2004). When motivation to control prejudice is present, however, spontaneously activated attitudes (as assessed through implicit measures) are less predictive of behavior because of motivated correction for both negative and positive racial attitudes. Indeed, we shall see in Chapter 9 that the impressions formed by these spontaneously activated racial attitudes have real consequences for interaction outcomes and perceived interaction quality.

Our attitudes can spontaneously impact our cognition (and therefore subsequent behavior) by acting as a biasing cue in our judgments or biasing our information processing to assimilate new information in an attitudinally congruent manner (e.g., Fazio & Williams, 1986; Houston & Fazio, 1989). In one illustrative study

(Schuette & Fazio, 1995), participants who evaluated two studies with ambiguous evidence and conflicting conclusions when their attitudes were highly accessible (and their accuracy motivation was low) produced judgments that were more in line with their initial attitudes than did participants whose attitudes were either less accessible or who were more motivated to be accurate (and thus engage in deliberative judgment). Echoing earlier work on biased scanning (Janis, 1968; Janis & Gilmore, 1965) and confirmation bias (Johnson & Eagly, 1989; Wason, 1960), highly accessible attitudes can bias the conclusions we draw from ambiguous information if we are not motivated and able to be objective or careful in our judgments so as to override such biases. In addition to biasing information processing, our accessible attitudes have also been shown to automatically orient visual attention towards corresponding attitude objects (Roskos-Ewoldsen & Fazio, 1992) and influence our categorizations of attitude objects (Smith, Fazio, & Cejka, 1996; Fazio & Dunton, 1997). Highly accessible attitudes can even exert influence at a very basic level through biasing visual perception of objects, such that it is more difficult to distinguish very similar but novel images from prior attitudinally relevant vs. attitudinally irrelevant stimuli (Fazio, Ledbetter, & Towles-Schwen, 2000).

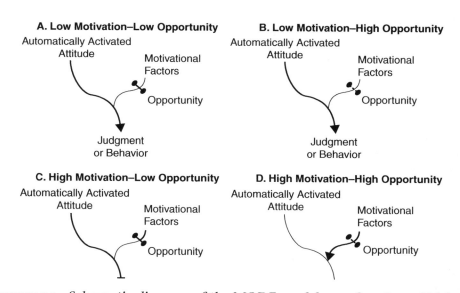

FIGURE 6.3 *Schematic diagram of the MODE model as a function of high vs. low motivation and opportunity. Highlighted paths indicate strong vs. weak influences on behavior, with opportunity acting as a gating mechanism.*

Source: Olson, M.A., & Fazio, R.H. (2009). Implicit and explicit measures of attitudes: The perspective of the MODE model. R.E. Petty, R.H. Fazio & P. Brinol (Eds.) *Attitudes: Insights from the new implicit measures*, (pp. 19–63). New York: Psychology Press.

Similar to other dual-process models, the MODE model recognizes that deliberate and spontaneous processing are not necessarily mutually exclusive or even zero-sum (See Figure 6.3). Olson and Fazio (2009) describe the *parallel activation of spontaneous and deliberate processing* as **mixed processes** that possess both spontaneous and deliberate components, with the caveat that all deliberative components must possess the necessary motivation and opportunity to function—as before, if these elements are not fully present, the influence of one's original, automatically activated attitudes predominates (e.g., Schuette & Fazio, 1995). Typically, these mixed processes commence with a spontaneous element "starting point" that may have downstream consequences for other deliberative elements (Olson & Fazio, 2009).

Applications of the MODE Model

Research has been conducted applying the principles of the MODE model to a number of important topics including clinical research (e.g., Conklin, Strunk, & Fazio, 2009), but the majority of the MODE model's application (and the area in which it finds a great deal of empirical support) is in the domain of racial prejudice and discrimination. Typically, these studies utilize a priming procedure adapted from Fazio et al. (1986). In this procedure, on each trial participants are first exposed to an attitude object of interest for a very brief period of time and then presented with an evaluative adjective with the task of classifying the adjective as either "good" or "bad." The comparison of interest, then, is the extent to which the valence judgment is facilitated or hindered (measured in reaction time) by presentation of the prime (the attitude object) before the judgment (see Fazio, 2001 for a review). Negative implicit attitudes toward African Americans, assessed in this fashion, predict a multitude of both conscious and nonverbal phenomena: Participants harboring negative implicit attitudes appear less friendly and interested to African American experimenters (Fazio et al., 1995), are less likely to select African American candidates for competitive positions (Olson & Fazio, 2007) and judge essays as being of lower quality when written by an African American author (Jackson, 1997). These spontaneously activated negative attitudes also predict a host of negative nonverbal behaviors (e.g., Dovidio, Kawakami, Johnson, Johnson, & Howard, 1997; Dovidio, Kawakami, & Gaertner, 2002).

To apply the principles of the MODE model to racial prejudice, however, we must also consider the role that deliberative processes play in regulating or controlling the spontaneous expression of negative implicit attitudes. To that end, Dunton & Fazio (1997) created the Motivation to Control Prejudiced Reactions (MCPR) scale to assess participants' concerns with acting prejudiced and restraint exercised to promote positive interactions and avoid disputes. Recall that in our discussion of prior attitudes' influence on evaluation in spontaneous processing, participants high in motivation to control prejudice (and who therefore engaged in deliberative processing) showed less racial bias than participants who felt little to no motivation to control prejudice (Olson & Fazio, 2004). Similarly, opportunity to engage in deliberative processing also plays a role in the extent to which spontaneously activated attitudes influence behavior. Some elements—nonverbal behavior, for example—do not allow as much opportunity for conscious control (DePaulo & Friedman, 1998) and may therefore be more susceptible to influence from automatically activated negativity (Dovidio et al., 1997). Finally, even when both motivation to control prejudice and the opportunity to do so are present, deliberative downstream control of prejudiced behaviors only occurs if people realize that prejudice is the attribute under scrutiny. Without this awareness, the motivation to control prejudice and other similar variables is not relevant (see Jackson, 1997; Olson & Fazio, 2007).

Criticisms of the MODE Model

Over the years, the MODE model has accumulated quite a bit of empirical evidence (see Petty, Fazio, & Briñol, 2009, for a review) but has met with criticism as well. One criticism of the empirical support for the MODE model is that experiments testing the MODE model's predictions for the role of attitude accessibility only manipulate or measure the variable of interest (accessibility) and its effects on the attitude-behavior relation (Eagly & Chaiken, 1993). If other structural aspects of attitudes that covary with attitude strength, such as certainty/ambivalence, amount or degree of knowledge, or temporal stability also produce high attitude-behavior correspondence, then it is problematic to infer that attitude accessibility is the primary predictor of behavior in spontaneous processing. Some studies, for example, have shown that stable attitudes better predict behavior in some circumstances than do accessible attitudes (e.g., Doll & Ajzen, 1992).

Some researchers have also called into question MODE's assumption that attitude accessibility is necessary for evaluation (Bargh, Chaiken, Govender, & Pratto, 1992). Automatic attitude activation, they argue, is not solely a function of attitude accessibility because people automatically evaluate stimuli with which they have had no prior experience and therefore could not have a prior attitude (Bargh, Chaiken, Raymond, & Hymes, 1996; Chaiken & Bargh, 1993; Duckworth, Bargh, Garcia, & Chaiken, 2002). Although the empirical support for the criticism is still contested (see Fazio, 2001), MODE advocates and critics nonetheless agree that greater attitude accessibility leads to greater attitude strength. The greater the accessibility, the more rapid is the evaluation of the attitude object (See Fazio, 2001, for a comprehensive review).

SUMMARY AND CONCLUSION

One of the original assumptions about the importance of studying attitudes was that attitudes predict behavior. That assumption was challenged in the 1960s by meta-analytic reviews of the evidence, questioning the reliability of the attitude-behavior link. The research we presented in this chapter shows the results of the subsequent scrutiny. The relevant question changed from *do* attitudes predict behavior to *when* do attitudes predict behavior. Understanding the compatibility of the attitude and behavior helped to resolve some of the discrepancies. In addition, the attitude-behavior relationship is moderated by a number of important situational and dispositional factors, such as people's need for cognition or level of self-monitoring. Overall, research has demonstrated that attitudes are not the only determinant of behavior, but they are substantially predictive of behavior in a variety of domains.

Two dominant theories of attitude-behavior relations sprang from the literature, identifying variables that affect attitude-behavior consistency: The reasoned action approach and the MODE model. The reasoned action approach takes a controlled cognitive view of predicting behavior from a combination of attitudes, perceived norms, and control beliefs. The dual-process MODE model explains how attitude-behavior consistency depends on whether one engages in deliberate or spontaneous processing. Both of these approaches have contributed a great deal to research on the attitude-behavior relation, providing much-needed theoretical scaffolding under the field's diverse research findings and enabling researchers to design effective interventions attempting to promote positive behaviors and curb negative or harmful ones.

This chapter has discussed the myriad reasons that we act (or fail to act) in accordance with our personal opinions, beliefs and attitudes. We know, however, that occasionally we leap *before* we look—in other words, sometimes our behavior can determine our attitudes just as much as our attitudes may determine our behavior. The next chapter explores this reciprocal attitude-behavior relationship in depth, along with the ways in which our behavior shapes and changes our attitudes in a variety of domains.

CHAPTER 7

Predicting Attitudes from Behaviors

From the time that LaPiere (1934) pointed out discrepancies between people's behaviors and attitudes, social psychology has had an abiding interest in the relationship between the two concepts. In previous chapters, we discussed factors that strengthen the relationship of attitudes and behaviors. In most instances, we asked how attitudes shape behavior. Political and commercial advertising spend large amounts of currency affecting attitudes in the expectation that attitudes foretell people's behavior. As psychologists, we have learned to ask not whether attitudes affect behavior, but rather under what conditions do attitudes lead to behaviors? Under what set of circumstances can we expect people to purchase a product that they evaluate highly or vote for a candidate toward whom they have a positive attitude?

In this chapter, we will turn the relationship around and consider the occasions in which behaviors influence and predict attitudes. Some of our behavior precedes our attitudes and influences or determines how we evaluate objects. We will begin by paraphrasing an example used by Daryl Bem (1972) to illustrate his influential theory of self-perception. You are in a grocery store and a friend asks you if you like the new organic brown bread that a company has been marketing. You have very little idea what a slice of such bread would taste like. Then you recall that you had been at a dinner in which you selected a similar slice of bread from the bread basket. You do not recall how it tasted but you do recall having selected it. Your friend has asked for your attitude toward organic brown bread and you now have an answer. You state confidently that you like it. Why? It is not because you have a well-formed attitude about the bread that has been stored in memory. What you remember is your behavior. You previously selected the brown bread. That implies that you like such food and you answer positively. In this instance, your behavior preceded the formation of your attitude. You used your recollection of how you acted to infer how you must feel about the object.

IMPLICIT BEHAVIORS AFFECT ATTITUDES: THE PSYCHOLOGY OF EMBODIED PERSUASION

The most subtle behaviors can affect attitudes. In the preceding section, we considered a hypothetical situation in which an explicitly chosen behavioral act of selecting a piece of bread produced the evidence that a person could use to deduce his attitude. At the other end of the continuum is the effect of subtle and implicit behavioral acts caused by feedback from physiological and implicit body movements. We refer to these responses as *implicit* because they are committed non-consciously and/or because people are not aware of their connection to a particular attitude.

Imagine a person who is about to celebrate his 21st birthday. His friends have reserved a table at an upscale pub and he anticipates receiving some gag gifts on the occasion. On his friends' guest list are some people he knows and others whom he does not know. What is his attitude about the party? Despite some reasons to be apprehensive, he notices a spring to his step, a smile on his face and a heart that is pounding away in excitement. His body has provided information about his evaluation of the party. He did not consciously intend to have his heart race or move his face into a smile. Nonetheless, these implicit behaviors tell him that he is happy and he evaluates the upcoming event positively. In fact, we are so accustomed to our implicit bodily reactions being consonant with our attitudes that we are likely to use them as an indicant of our own attitudes—even when they are not.

In a research study that captures much from our hypothetical birthday party, Valins (1966) provided male participants with feedback from physiological measures after they saw pictures of women. The feedback was bogus and not at all related to the participants' actual heart rate. Nonetheless, the men who thought their heart rate increased in response to some of the pictures rated those pictures as more attractive than they rated pictures not accompanied by heart rate change. Several weeks later, when the same participants re-rated the photos, the ones that had been accompanied by bogus heart rate information continued to be more highly evaluated. Similarly, Taylor (1975) had women rate pictures of men accompanied by bogus feedback about their physiological responses. If they did not expect any subsequent interaction with the men, then their evaluation of the men's attractiveness was based on their impression of their own physiological responses—even though the feedback about their responses was false.

How Do Body Responses Lead to Evaluation? Information and Mere Association

Briñol and Petty (2008) suggest several reasons that information about implicit bodily responses might lead to persuasion. One is based on information that the body provides, even though it may sometimes lead to false conclusions. Taylor's (1975) and Valins' (1966) studies made use of people's knowledge that increased physiological response in the context of a heterosexual stimulus signals attraction. People use the implicit response that their bodies provide to help deduce their attitudes. The studies by Taylor (1975) and Valins (1966) are particularly interesting because they show people relied on what they believed their bodies told them, even though that information was wrong.

Another basis for the impact of bodily responses on attitudes is the *mere association* of an attitude object with a bodily response. Cacioppo, Priester and Bernstson (1993) paired an evaluation of an object with a body movement usually perceived as either positive or negative. Typically, people associate bringing items toward themselves (approach behavior) as positive and moving them away (avoidance) as negative. Cacioppo et al. (1993) had participants evaluate stimuli toward which they had no prior attitude (novel Chinese ideographs) at the same time that they either flexed (approach) or extended (avoidance) their arm. Results showed that participants had more positive evaluations of the ideographs presented during flexion than ideographs presented during extension. Similarly, Tom, Pettersen, Lau, Burton and Cook (1991) asked people to evaluate a new pen while simultaneously shaking their head up and down (a typical sign of agreement) or from side to side (a typical disagreement). Participants in the Tom et al. (1991) study had more positive attitudes toward the pen if they nodded up and down rather than side to side (see also, Förster, 2004).

The difference between the Taylor (1975) and Valins (1966) studies, on the one hand, and the Tom et al. (1991) and Cacioppo et al. (1993) studies, on the other, is that in the latter studies, participants did not think that nodding or flexing were related to their evaluations of the attitude objects. Participants were merely led to engage in these behaviors at the same time as exposure to the attitude object. Attitudes were formed by the mere association between the object and the embodied responses.

Strack, Martin and Stepper (1988) devised a particularly interesting demonstration of mere association. They had people smile or frown while evaluating a cartoon. In most circumstances, smiling and frowning are bits of helpful information. If it makes people smile, the cartoon must have been good; if it makes them frown, it was not so good. What was unique about Strack et al.'s procedure is that their participants did not realize they were smiling or frowning. The investigators had participants hold a pen in their mouths under one of two different sets of instructions. In the first, they were instructed to hold the pen between their lips without the pen touching their teeth. If you try this yourself, you will notice that your face is drawn into a frown position. In the other condition, participants were asked to hold the pen in their teeth without touching it to their lips. Again, you can try this with your own pen and you will notice that your face assumes a smiling position. Although participants did not realize consciously that they were frowning

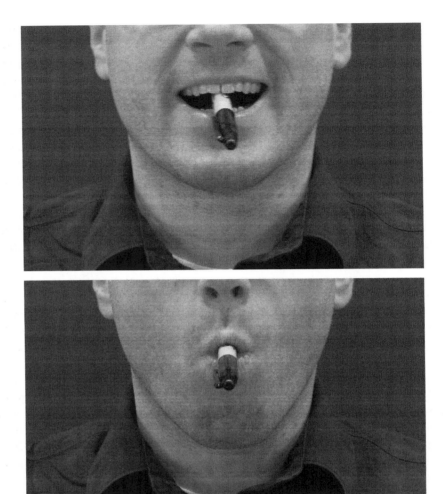

FIGURE 7.1   *Illustration of the technique used to contract the different facial muscles; top, smile condition; bottom, frown condition.*

or smiling, the juxtaposition of the cartoon with the smile position affected their attitudes such that they rated the cartoon as funnier than participants whose faces were in the frown position.

Embodied Responses and Thought Confidence

In Chapter 5, we discussed the metagcognitive approach to persuasion in which people's confidence in their own reactions to a message affected how much their attitudes changed. Petty and Briñol (2003; 2008) suggested that embodied responses can impact persuasion by affecting people's confidence in their own reactions to a persuasive message. Imagine that you are listening to a speech on an important topic, but one that you have not thought much about in the past. If you hear a speech filled with strong arguments, there is a good chance that you will have positive cognitive responses (see Chapters 4 and 5) to the message. If you hear a speech with specious arguments, it is likely that you will respond negatively, conjuring many counterarguments against the message. The chances are that you will be more persuaded by the speech with strong arguments than weak arguments, especially if you were motivated to process the arguments through the central route to persuasion. But suppose your body makes you question your reactions. Will you still be persuaded?

Briñol & Petty (2003) conducted a study to examine the influence of such an embodied response to a persuasive message. University students were asked to consider a proposal to require all students to carry official identification cards while on campus. As in the hypothetical example above, half of the students were given a message in which the arguments were strong and half were given a message in which the arguments were specious. The embodied cognition came in the form of head movements. Half of the students in each group were asked to nod their heads up and down while reading the arguments; the other half were asked to shake their heads from side to side.

Briñol and Petty reasoned that nodding one's head up and down is an implicit behavior associated with confidence—confidence in one's own reaction to the message. If a student had heard a strong argument and had a positive reaction, then head nodding would provide confidence in that reaction. If a student had heard a specious argument, then head nodding would provide confidence that the negative reaction was warranted. On the other hand, shaking the head from side to side is a marker of no-confidence. Briñol & Petty predicted that students who shook their heads would have diminished confidence in their reactions to the strong or weak messages. In contrast to the students who nodded up and down, the student who shook their head should be less persuaded by the strong arguments and less skeptical of the weak arguments.

How persuaded were the students about carrying identification cards? As predicted, people who were nodding their head up and down were more persuaded by the strong arguments and less persuaded by the weak arguments. People who shook their heads from side to side (forming the "no" response) held positions that were not greatly influenced by any of the arguments. Moreover, people in the head nod and head shake conditions did not differ in the number or valence of their thoughts but, as predicted, did vary in the degree of confidence that they held about those thoughts. The subtle movement of the head either validated their thoughts or attacked their confidence, depending on the direction they moved their heads. The impact of the head movement manipulation on the participants' attitudes is depicted in Figure 7.2.

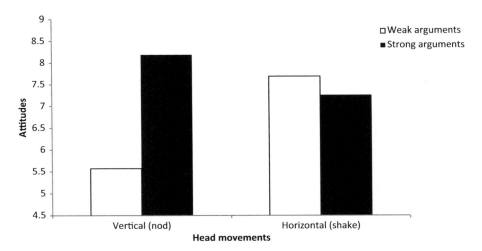

FIGURE 7.2 *Attitudes as a function of argument quality and head movement.*
Source: Binol & Petty (2009). Persuasion: Insights from the self-validation hypothesis. In M.P. Zanna (Ed)
Advances in experimental social psychology, (Vol 41, pp 69–118) San Diego, CA: Academic Press.

EXPLICIT BEHAVIORS AFFECT ATTITUDES: COGNITIVE DISSONANCE

Leon Festinger had been an influential social psychologist before he authored the **theory of cognitive dissonance** in 1957 (Festinger, 1957). In his earlier work on **social comparison processes**, Festinger (1954) proposed that people are intrinsically driven to compare their opinions and abilities with the opinions and abilities of others. In the attitude field, this implied that people had strong motivations to have attitudes that were consistent with the attitudes of other people. This conclusion is consistent with balance theory approaches that we considered in Chapter 6. It did not take long for Festinger to expand the concept of interpersonal consistency to address the intra-individual consistency between a person's own attitudes and behaviors.

Festinger's (1957) view was that people mentally represent aspects of their lives in terms of cognitive elements. These elements or cognitions can represent how a person feels, how a person behaves or how a person views the environment. Because our feelings, thoughts, behaviors and perceptions must all be represented in the mind in terms of cognitions, Festinger suggested that people are affected by the relationship among those cognitions. Some pieces of knowledge psychologically follow from one another, even though one may be knowledge about a feeling and another about a behavior, while other pieces of knowledge are inconsistent. For example, if someone likes a Jaguar better than a Camry but purchases the Camry, those elements do not follow from one another. The behavioral cognition (purchasing the Camry) does not follow from the evaluative cognition (liking the Jaguar). In Festinger's terms, if a person has a pair of cognitions such that one follows from the obverse of the other, then they are in a dissonant relationship. By contrast, if one cognition does follow from another, then the pair is in a consonant relationship.

Festinger considered people to be motivated or driven to avoid dissonant cognitions. When we perceive that we have cognitions such that one follows from the obverse of the other, we find ourselves in an aversive, uncomfortable state of arousal that Festinger called *cognitive dissonance*. Just as we need to reduce other aversive drive states like hunger and thirst, people are driven to reduce their cognitive dissonance. We drink to reduce our thirst; we eat to reduce our hunger; we alter our cognitions to reduce our dissonance. It follows that we would avoid such states—and we try—but a few examples make clear that we experience dissonance on more than a few occasions.

Attitudes Follow Behavioral Choices

We are confronted with making decisions in our lives every day. We choose between breakfast cereals, lunch locations and dessert choices. We choose which college to attend and from which graduate school we will try to earn a Ph.D. We choose between Republicans and Democrats, conservatives and liberals, to lead our nations into the future. One of the ubiquitous features of almost any choice is that we have to relinquish something in order to gain our selected alternative.

Consider the following fanciful dilemma about the Camry and Jaguar: Your own car has come to the end of its useful days and you need to purchase a new one. You enter the decision phase of your search for a new car with very positive attitudes about two of them: The Jaguar and the Camry. You love the Jaguar, except you know it is expensive and has a terrible record for reliability. On the other hand, it's gorgeous. You also love the Camry. Its reliability record is superb; its price is good. You just do not feel it is as sexy as the Jaguar. For different reasons, your attitudes about both automobiles are strong and salient. Nonetheless, you can buy one, not two. You would choose one car for its looks or the other for its reliability. The choice is a close one, but you have to make it. You act; you behave; you put down the money for the Jaguar. Research has shown that your action will set off a process that will result in a change in your attitudes to bring them in line with your behavior. Your attitude toward that car you chose will become more positive. You will extol its good features and minimize the bad ones. As a mirror image, your attitudes toward the rejected car will become more negative following your decision.

The choice to buy a Jaguar came at a cost, not only for the amount of money you spent but also because of all of the excellent features of the Camry that you have relinquished. The reliability and the modest fuel cost of the Camry are no longer possible once the Jaguar is selected. These desirable features of the Camry are inconsistent with a decision to purchase the Jaguar. And there is more. Selecting the Jaguar brought with it all of the unwanted features of that alternative. You made your choice and drove your Jaguar out of the showroom with the knowledge that you had wiped out your bank account and were facing the likelihood of months of loaner cars and repairs. These cognitions are also inconsistent with your choice.

Driven by the unpleasant state of cognitive dissonance, the inconsistency must be reduced. People can be quite creative about diverse ways to accomplish this goal, but they will reduce their dissonance by coming to like the Jaguar much more than they did prior to their choice and liking the Camry a lot less.

Consider the number of ways we can go about reducing the overall inconsistency between the negative features of the Jaguar and the fact that we just purchased one. We can *add cognitive elements that are consistent with our choice behavior*. For example, we can suddenly remember that Jaguar is a fast car that can cruise the Autobahn at thrilling speeds. We can remember that Camry's brakes were seriously implicated in recent product recalls. These elements support our choice and add consistency to our set of cognitions. A second, not mutually exclusive, approach is to *change the importance of cognitive elements*. For example, we can decide that our image is overwhelmingly important to us, so any automobile that adds to that image is especially appealing whereas any vehicle that threatens that image is especially unappealing. A third possibility is that we can *change the valuation we put on cognitive elements* such that what we used to think of as an attractive element of the Camry is now considered an unattractive one. For example, a consumer from North America may have considered the Japanese origin of Camry a positive feature of that car prior to the choice, but now believes that purchasing a car made by a British company is better for the North American economy.

What is important to emphasize is that people had attitudes toward both alternatives prior to their selection. Then they behaved: They bought one of the two cars. From that point on, people experienced cognitive dissonance because of the discrepancy between their behavior and the evaluative features of the two alternatives. They were motivated—by the very fact of their behavior—to alter their cognitions until they confirmed that their chosen alternative was far better than the rejected one. The evaluative summaries that we refer to as attitudes had changed. The motivation for the change was the reduction of cognitive dissonance.

Empirical Research on the Spreading of Alternatives

There are several predictions that we can infer from this example. One is that, following a behavioral choice between two alternatives, the chosen alternative will become more attractive and/or the rejected alternative will become less attractive.

This pair of hypotheses can be described as the **spreading of alternatives** following a choice. A second hypothesis is that the closer the two items are in their evaluation prior to a choice, the more cognitive dissonance will ensue and the more we will see a spreading of the alternatives. A third hypothesis is that the more important the decision, the more the evaluation of the alternatives will spread. All of these changes of attitudes are motivated by needing to reduce cognitive dissonance. The Jaguar and Camry are only hypothetical examples. The results of numerous studies, however, support the prediction, beginning with an experiment by Jack Brehm (1956), the first experiment ever published on the topic of cognitive dissonance.

Brehm asked volunteer participants to rank a series of home appliances (e.g., toasters, blenders, irons) in terms of their evaluation of the items. As a token of appreciation, Brehm reported that the company sponsoring the research was pleased to present one of the items to each participant. The participant was allowed to choose one of two items that were available to take home. At this point, the instructions varied as a function of experimental condition. In the condition that was thought to arouse a high degree of dissonance, Brehm brought out items that had been ranked quite high on the list (the #2 and #3 choice for each participant). In the low-dissonance condition, the participants were given a choice between a highly attractive item (#2 on the list) and a less attractive item (#7 on the list).

From our prior example of the Camry and Jaguar, we can see the basis for the high dissonance and low dissonance distinction. When the two items are almost equal in attractiveness, relinquishing the positive features of the unchosen alternative is difficult and arouses considerable dissonance. In the low-dissonance condition, the choice is a relatively straightforward one. One item was highly ranked because the participant saw many positive features in that item relative to one ranked near the bottom of the list. Relinquishing the inferior item presents very few cognitive elements that are inconsistent with the choice, thus cognitive dissonance will be low. The prediction from dissonance theory is that, once they make their choice, participants in the difficult choice condition will be motivated to spread the alternatives they had been provided. As a way of reducing their dissonance, they will derogate the unchosen item and come to like the chosen alternative even more than they had before the choice. Brehm also included a control condition in which he gave one of the items to the participants as a gift. The item was always an attractive one (the #2 item), but there was no choice.

Following the choice or the gift, participants were asked for a new rating of all of the items. The dependent measure was the new rating of the participants' attitudes toward the chosen and unchosen items, relative to their attitudes prior to the choice. The results are shown in Table 7.1. This seminal dissonance study showed that attitudes change following behavior. Once making the behavioral choice, attitudes toward the chosen alternative became more positive and attitudes toward the

TABLE 7.1 *Change in Evaluation of Alternatives*

CONDITION	CHANGE FROM FIRST TO SECOND RATING FOR:		
	CHOSEN ITEM	NONCHOSEN ITEM	NET CHANGE
Low dissonance (items of disparate value)	+0.11	0.00	+0.11
High dissonance (items of close value)	+0.38	−0.41	+0.79
Gift (control)	0.00		

Source: Brehm, J. W. (1956). Postdecision changes in the desirability of alternatives. *The Journal of Abnormal and Social Psychology, 52*(3), 384. Reprinted with permission.

unchosen alternative became more negative *provided that* the choice was a difficult one. An easy choice evokes no dissonance and no need to change attitudes.

Another important aspect of the data presented in Table 7.1 is shown in the control (gift) condition. Merely being presented with an item to keep, without having chosen it, did not lead to any distortion of attitudes toward the item. The #2 item was attractive before it became a gift and it was just as attractive after it became a gift. Attitude change toward an item occurred only if it had been chosen freely and only if it had been chosen over an alternative that made the decision sufficiently difficult to create a high degree of cognitive dissonance.

A large program of research continued to support this basic finding. Dissonance created by behavioral choices occurs regardless of the type of choice (e.g., gifts or college courses), and increases with choice difficulty and importance (see Cooper, 2007; Stone & Fernandez, 2008; Wicklund & Brehm, 1976, for reviews). The change in attitudes toward chosen items has been shown in young children as well as adults. Egan, Santos and Bloom (2007; see also Egan, Bloom, & Santos, 2010) conducted a study in which preschool children were asked to choose among equally valued candies. After rating three colors of M&Ms relatively equally, they were shown two of the M&Ms and asked to make a choice between them. The children were then given a second opportunity to make a choice—this time, between the M&M they had rejected in the initial choice and the third M&M that had not entered into the initial choice. This method allowed the investigators to examine the derogation of the unchosen item without having to use attitude scales that might have been difficult for the preschoolers. If the dissonance involved in the first choice led to derogation of the unchosen candy, then the children would overwhelmingly choose the third M&M on the subsequent choice. This is precisely what they found. Despite the fact that the candies were all rated equal in attractiveness prior to the initial choice, the lowered evaluation of the rejected candy caused it to become less favorable than the third candy.

Festinger (1964) believed that the arousal of dissonance occurred only after a choice had been made. In the period preceding a choice, people were thought to be committed to making unbiased evaluations of the object or objects involved in the choice. The discomfort of dissonance followed the act of choosing but only when the choice was irreversible. However, data confirming the timing of dissonance arousal has been difficult to obtain. Consistent with recent work by Nordgren, van Harreveld and van der Plight (2006), it may well be that people experience dissonance simply by anticipating that they must make a choice. Anticipating giving up desirable aspects of a chosen item and accepting undesirable aspects may be sufficient to facilitate the unpleasant drive state of dissonance.

On Timing and Culture

There are also cultural differences in attitude change, with research showing that residents of Western cultures (i.e., Europe, North America, Australia and New Zealand) manifest attitude change following a choice more than residents of East Asia (Heine & Lehman, 1997; Hoshino-Browne et al., 2005). The differences have been attributed to the different degrees of orientation that the cultures have toward independence and interdependence (Hoshino-Browne, 2012; Kimel, Grossmann, & Kitayama, 2012; Kitayama & Uchida, 2005; Markus & Kitayama, 1991). Western cultures stress independence and autonomy. In Western cultures, people are expected to make rational decisions for themselves. In Asian and other interdependent countries, there is a greater emphasis on maintaining harmonious social interactions and fitting in. People's choices are expected to bring harmony and avoid inconsiderateness.

Hoshino-Browne, Zanna, Spencer, Zanna, Kitayama and Lackenbauer (2005) compared attitude change in interdependent and independent cultures in Japan and Canada. They found that when asked to make choices solely for themselves, people from independent rather than interdependent cultures showed more dissonance reduction and changed their attitudes to justify their choices. When asked to make choices that would affect other people rather than themselves, then it was people from interdependent cultures that showed more dissonance. In both cultures, the dissonance process motivated people to change their attitudes. However, the choice must be interpersonal for it to motivate people raised in interdependent cultures, while it must be personal for people raised in independent cultures (Imada & Kitayama, 2010; Na & Kitayama, 2012).

Attitudes Change Following Attitude-Discrepant Behavior

Have you ever said anything you did not fully believe or found yourself arguing for a position that did not completely conform to your attitudes? Perhaps you expressed attitudes that were more positive to a romantic partner than you actually believed or expressed an extreme political attitude that did not truly conform to your more moderate belief. These instances produce cognitive dissonance. A behavioral expression that contradicts an attitude creates the unpleasant tension state of dissonance and drives a person toward reducing it. Cognitive dissonance theory holds that the cognition that will change is the cognition that is least resistant to change. In a predicament in which you made a public statement that contradicts your attitude, the cognition that is least resistant to change is the attitude. The behavior was public and only a delusional form of denial can change it. The attitude, by contrast, is typically private and can be changed to conform to the behavior. Myriad studies have shown this to be true, but none more clearly than the original experiment conducted to test this proposition (Festinger & Carlsmith, 1959).

Festinger and Carlsmith (1959) designed a laboratory task in which participants performed an exceedingly dull, boring and tedious set of activities. For example, they were asked to rotate pegs on a peg board, rotate them back, and continue doing it for an excruciatingly long period of time. A control group that was simply asked how interesting the activities were confirmed that the experimenters had created a truly boring set of experiences. In the two experimental groups, the experimenter began an elaborate cover story designed to make it credible for the participants to make a public statement that the activities were fun, interesting and exciting—a position that would clearly be discrepant from their true attitudes toward the activity.

The experimenter explained that what the study was *really* about was an examination of the role of expectation on how well participants performed the activities. He explained to each participant that he had been in a control condition in which there had been no explicit explanation. Had the participant been in the experimental condition, the experimenter continued, a confederate whom he had hired would have joined the participant in the waiting room and carried on about how much fun the experiment was. The experimenter then "realized" that the confederate was late and that the next participant was already in the waiting room. What to do? The experimenter had an idea. Addressing the participant, he exclaimed, "Hey, I have an idea: I can hire you." He asked the participant if he or she could serve as the confederate for the person waiting in the next room. All participants agreed and entered the waiting room where the next participant (actually a true confederate of the experimenter) was waiting. The participant then tried to convince the waiting student that the task was fun, interesting and exciting. In this manner, Festinger and Carlsmith created the conditions for dissonance. The task was constructed such that anyone performing it would have a negative evaluation or attitude about the task, yet participants found themselves delivering a speech proclaiming precisely the opposite. The prediction based on dissonance theory was clear: Making a statement that the task was interesting should produce attitude change in that direction. When subsequently asked to evaluate the task, participants who had made the attitude discrepant speech should evaluate the task more positively than participants in the control condition.

There was one important addition to the experiment that made this study a controversial addition to the literature and set dissonance theory apart from other theories of consistency that we discussed in the prior chapter. Unlike the concepts developed in other consistency theories (for example, balance theory, see Chapter 6), dissonance has a *magnitude*. People can experience more or less of the drive state. According to dissonance theory, the magnitude of dissonance increases as the discrepancy between an attitude and behavior increases in magnitude or importance, but is reduced by cognitions that are consistent with the behavior. As consonant cognitions increase, the magnitude of dissonance decreases. As the importance of the consonant cognitions increase, the magnitude of the dissonance decreases.

Recall that Festinger and Carlmsith had offered to hire the participant to make the attitude discrepant statement. In one condition, they offered the participant $20; in the other condition, they offered only $1. The hypothesis derived from dissonance theory is that the financial inducement would serve as a cognition consistent with the decision to make the attitude discrepant speech. Because $20 is a larger, more important cognition supporting making the speech, it was expected to lower the dissonance. By contrast, the knowledge that someone received only a dollar for his or her behavior would hardly serve as a reason (i.e., consistent cognition) to make the statement. The prediction was that the low inducement would lead to greater dissonance and the greater dissonance would result in more attitude change toward the task. A $20 inducement would serve to reduce the magnitude of dissonance and eliminate the need for attitude change.

Subsequently, a secretary in the psychology department gave all participants a rating scale asking them to evaluate how much they liked the performance tasks. Figure 7.3 shows that the results were in line with the dissonance theory prediction. Those participants who made the statement that was contrary to their attitudes and who had only been offered a small amount of money for doing so found the task far more enjoyable than either the control condition or than the participants who had a $20 justification.

Festinger and Carlsmith (1959) deliberately created an attitude in the laboratory. In some ways, this was an artificial attitude that had no antecedents in the participants' lives. It had little to do with their prior history of liberalism or conservatism, their prior history with the attitude object and so forth. For experimental control, it was ideal. But would attitude-discrepant behavior affect other attitudes that mattered in participants' lives? The answer to that question was a resounding yes. Research has shown that attitude discrepant behavior leads to attitude change across a variety of broad and local issues. In some studies, it affected attitudes on a national scale, such as the right to free speech (Linder et al., 1967), and in others, it

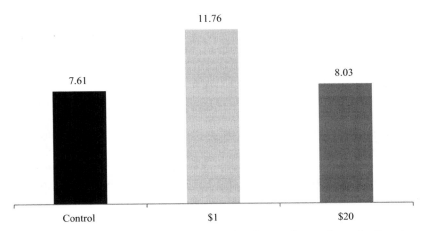

FIGURE 7.3   *Evaluation of boring tasks after being interviewed about the experimental tasks (control) or convincing a confederate of their enjoyment of the experiment after being paid $1 or $20. Higher means indicate greater favorability.*

Source: Festinger, L., & Carlsmith, J. M. (1959). Cognitive consequences of forced compliance. *The Journal of Abnormal and Social Psychology, 58*(2), 203. Reprinted with permission.

affected people's attitudes toward more local issues in the city in which they lived (Cohen, 1962) or the campus that they attended (Scher & Cooper, 1989; Wakslak, 2012). Changing attitudes following discrepant behavior has been found to be a robust phenomenon.

Changing Attitudes by Not Behaving

In the numerous studies conducted on the influence of behavior on attitudes, people have been induced to behave in particular ways and the consequences on their attitudes were measured (see Cooper, 2007, for a review). Aronson and Carlsmith (1963) asked a slightly different question. What if you are motivated to behave but are induced to refrain? Can that also have an impact on your attitudes? The answer is yes, and for the same reason. If you have an attitude that makes you want to behave toward an attitude object (e.g., eating your favorite flavor of ice cream) but you refrain from doing so, this similarly creates a state of dissonance. You did not actually do anything, but the inconsistency nonetheless exists. This should have a consequence on your attitude toward the ice cream. It also follows that the less significant a reason you had for refraining from purchasing the ice cream, the greater the dissonance.

Aronson and Carlsmith (1963) allowed young children to play with a set of toys. The experimenter explained to the children that he needed to leave the room for a few moments. He selected the most attractive toy and told the children that he did not want them to play with it while he was gone. Some children were told that he would be very angry with them if they disobeyed—in fact, he would collect all of his toys and go home. For other children, the admonition was quite mild as the experimenter told them he would be annoyed if they played with the toy. None of the children played with the toy in the experimenter's absence.

Refraining from playing with an attractive toy created cognitive inconsistency. A child may have thought, "I like the toy but I am not playing with it." Children who had been given the more severe threat had a big, important cognition that was consistent with the decision not to play with the toy. "He will pick up all of his toys and go home." The children in the mild threat did not have this consonant cognition. Aronson and Carlsmith predicted that the low threat condition would lead to genuine devaluation of the attractive toy, such that children would cease to play with it even when subsequently permitted and would rank it lower on an evaluative measure. That is precisely what the investigators found. Mild threat led to greater internalization and attitude change. In a replication of this study, Freedman (1965) found that when children were invited to return to the toy room a month and half later, those who had been in the mild threat condition continued to refrain from playing with the toy.

Attitudes and Effort: The Psychology of Effort Justification

Imagine that you want to be a member of a group but it requires a considerable amount of effort to join. Fraternities and sororities are examples of groups that many students seek to join. Those groups often require some effortful or difficult form of initiation in order to become a member. Sometimes, a particular fraternity or sorority may not be as spectacular as you hoped it would be. Aronson and Mills (1959) argued that such a situation would be a fertile ground for the arousal of cognitive dissonance. Engaging in effortful, unpleasant activities in order to join a group only to find that the group was not worth the effort causes dissonance that can be reduced by adopting a more positive attitude toward the group. Why did you work hard in order to join the group? The dissonance-reducing answer is that the group is truly wonderful, thus justifying the effort you expended.

Aronson and Mills (1959) conducted a now-classic experiment to test the dissonance theory prediction. They asked University of Minnesota students if they would like to join a discussion group about sex. Participants were students who indicated that they were interested in joining. The experimenter told the students that, in his experience, not everyone was suitable to join a discussion about sex.

Therefore, if they wished to proceed, they would need to pass a "screening test." The amount of effort was instantiated by the level of embarrassment that the test included. In the high effort condition, students had to read a list of explicitly sexual words describing body parts and actions as well as a lurid paragraph from a sexual novel. In the low effort condition, students only had to read a list of mildly sexually tinged words, like 'kissing' and 'petting.'

After passing the screening test, the participants were told that the group had already begun their discussion for the day's meeting. Students were told that they could listen to the meeting as it was unfolding and they could actually join the group at its next session. Participants put on earphones so they could overhear the conversation. In truth, there was no discussion group and what the participants thought they were overhearing was a tape recording of a very boring conversation about the secondary sexual characteristics of animals. Participants were asked to evaluate the conversation and evaluate the group members. The results are depicted in Figure 7.4. As predicted, high-effort participants evaluated the discussion and the group members more positively than the low-effort participants or than a control group that was not asked to pass a screening test. Having suffered considerable effort and embarrassment to join a group caused high effort participants to adopt a positive attitude toward a group that was not objectively warranted by the quality of the group or its discussion.

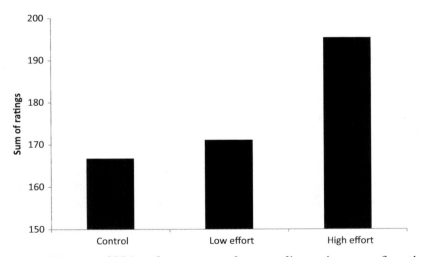

FIGURE 7.4: *Degree of liking for group and group discussion as a function of magnitude of effort.*

Source: Aronson, E., & Mills, J. (1959). The effect of severity of initiation on liking for a group. *The Journal of Abnormal and Social Psychology, 59*(2), 177–181.

The hypothesis that expending effort leads to dissonance arousal and attitude change has been supported in a variety of contexts including attitudes toward video games (Wann & Chiou, 2010), political issues (Wicklund, Cooper, & Linder, 1967) and psychotherapeutic self-improvement (Axsom, 1989; Axsom & Cooper, 1985).

Explaining the Effect of Behavior on Attitudes: The Search for Mechanisms

Much of the research examining the process by which attitude discrepant behavior affects attitudes has followed the research paradigm that Festinger and Carlsmith (1959) created. The notion that people strive for consistency was not especially controversial, but the prediction that behaving contrary to attitudes for a small incentive leads to more attitude change than for a high incentive certainly was. This latter finding created a maelstrom of controversy in social psychology. In the heyday of learning theory as a basic tenet in psychology, it was almost heretical that behavior elicited for a small incentive would lead to more change than a behavior induced for a high incentive. That seemed to strike at the heart of reinforcement and learning approaches to psychology. Whether it really did or not, it provoked a number of social psychologists to offer different reasons for the findings, mostly based on criticisms of the methodology (Chapanis & Chapanis, 1964; Janis & Gilmore, 1965; Rosenberg, 1965). Decades of research, however, have confirmed the basic finding (see Cooper, 2007, for a review).

Nonetheless, the intellectual debate that ensued showed some limits to the pervasiveness of the impact of behavior on attitudes. For example, a behavior inconsistent with attitudes does not produce dissonance if people believe they can "take it back." If a student makes a speech arguing for an increase in tuition fees at her university but also believes that she can tell people later that she did not really mean it, it produces no attitude change (Carlsmith, Collins, & Helmreich, 1966; Davis & Jones, 1960). The apparent **commitment** to the counterattitudinal behavior is important.

Another limiting condition is the **freedom** that a person perceives to act—or decline to act—in a counterattitudinal fashion. Festinger and Carlsmith's participants were asked if they would be willing to serve as the confederate who extolled the virtues of the performance tasks. What if it had been a required part of the experiment? Linder, Cooper and Jones (1967) conducted a conceptual replication of Festinger and Carlsmith's experiment but systematically varied the participants' freedom to make the attitude-discrepant speech. The issue was whether students should have the right to hear speakers from the Communist Party of America—something that the government of North Carolina had banned from state universities. Students were nearly unanimous in their opposition to the ban. Participants in Linder et al.'s study were either required to write an essay in support of the unpopular ban or were given the freedom to decide whether they were willing to write it. In addition, like the conditions in Festinger and Carlsmith's (1959) experiment, participants were offered either a small amount or a large amount of money to write their pro-ban essays. The results of the study replicated those of Festinger and Carlsmith's—i.e., significant attitude change when people wrote essays contrary to their attitudes for small incentives rather than large incentives—*but only* when participants were given the freedom to turn down the request. There was no dissonance in the absence of decision freedom.

A third interesting limitation to the impact of behavior on attitudes is whether the behavior seems to matter—i.e., whether it produces any **unwanted or undesirable consequences**. Similar to the issue of commitment discussed earlier, the question is whether *any* attitude discrepant behavior causes dissonance and therefore leads to attitude change, or whether something unwanted needs to occur. For example, in Festinger and Carlsmith's paradigmatic study, the participant convinced the next student that the task was going to be interesting. The "next student" (actually the confederate) politely thanked the participant for telling her because she had always found psychology studies to be dull and she was now looking forward to this one. Cooper and Worchel (1970) argued that this was just the kind of unwanted event that is important for dissonance-produced attitude change. Someone who you believe is a fellow student has now been duped (by you!) into believing something that is not true. What if she had not been convinced? The participant's statement would still be discrepant with his or her attitudes, but would have produced no unwanted consequence. Would participants avoid feeling dissonance because of a "no harm, no foul" judgment, or does dissonance occur whenever a behavioral statement and an attitude are discrepant?

Cooper and Worchel (1970) conducted a study nearly identical to Festinger and Carlsmith's, in which participants were asked to convince the next participant that the dull peg-turning task was interesting. Some were offered a small incentive and others were offered a large incentive. The new variable was whether the waiting student was convinced, as in the Festinger and Carlsmith study, or remained unconvinced. In the latter case, the confederate politely thanked the participant for his opinion, but indicated that he did not think he would enjoy the experiment. The results presented in Figure 7.5 showed precisely the same effect found by Festinger and Carlsmith—i.e., more attitude change when the incentive was low rather than high, but showed no attitude change for either incentive condition when the confederate was unconvinced. Apparently, the mere logical inconsistency between attitude and behavior is not sufficient to produce dissonance and lead to attitude change. From this and similar studies, it appears that bringing about an unwanted consequence is important (See Harmon-Jones, 2000, for a different perspective). Without the consequence, no dissonance occurred.

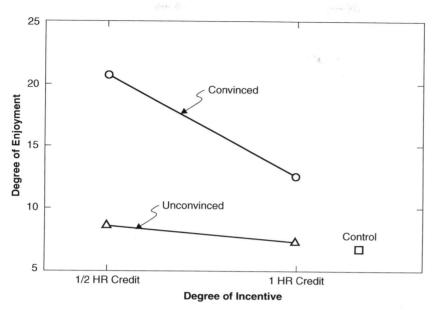

FIGURE 7.5 *Attitude towards experiment after attempting to convince a confederate of their enjoyment where the confederate was convinced or remained unconvinced and the participant was given a small vs. large incentive.*

Source: Cooper, J., & Worchel, S. (1970). Role of undesired consequences in arousing cognitive dissonance. *Journal of Personality and Social Psychology,* 16(2), 199. Reprinted with permission.

New Insights and Theoretical Mechanisms

At the 30th anniversary of the publication of the original theory of cognitive dissonance, Festinger (1987) remarked that no good theory goes unchallenged and unchanged, and so it was with dissonance theory. A number of alternate approaches have been proposed that do not question the basic assumption we have made in the current chapter, but dispute or modify the mechanism. The alternative approaches embrace the notion that attitudes are affected by behavior and that they change to become consistent with the way a person has acted. The issue is why.

The New Look. Cooper and Fazio (1984) suggested that the impact of behavior on attitudes needed a new perspective as a way to deal with the limiting conditions that had been found in the literature. Why did inconsistent behaviors only lead to dissonance if the behavior was freely chosen, for example? Didn't unchosen behavior also qualify as being inconsistent with attitudes? Why did attitude-discrepant behavior need to be accompanied by the possibility of an aversive consequence? Why is behavior that is inconsistent with attitudes not sufficient to produce attitude change? Cooper and Fazio (1984) took the position that the fundamental conditions for the arousal of dissonance needed modification. They argued that dissonance occurs when a person accepts responsibility for bringing about an aversive, unwanted event. Inconsistency between attitudes and behaviors usually brings about an unwanted event and that is why it typically arouses dissonance. However, if circumstances make it apparent that no aversive event will occur, then no dissonance will ensue. That is consistent with the result of numerous studies in which attitude change did not follow from inconsistent behavior if there was no possibility of an unwanted consequence (Cooper & Worchel, 1970; Cooper, Zanna, & Goethals, 1974; Nel, Helmreich and Aronson, 1969; Scher & Cooper, 1989).

The New Look model also proposes that not every behavior that produces an unwanted consequence leads to dissonance or attitude change. People need to feel that they are personally responsible for bringing about the unwanted event. The consequence not only needs to be unwanted, but it also must be foreseeable (Goethals, Cooper, & Naficy, 1979) and the behavior that led to the consequence needs to have been chosen freely (Linder et al., 1967). In Cooper and Fazio's (1984) view, it is when, and only when, people take *responsibility for the unwanted consequences of their behavior* that dissonance is aroused and attitude change occurs.

Action Based Model. Harmon-Jones and his colleagues offered a functional approach to the motivation behind cognitive dissonance (Harmon-Jones, 1999; Harmon-Jones & Harmon-Jones, 2002). They proposed that attitude change occurs following behavior for both proximal and distal reasons. Similar to the original theory, the *proximal motivation* is to reduce the negative arousal caused by inconsistent cognitions. The *distal motivation*, however, is to prepare the organism for unequivocal action. When people experience conflict between two courses of action, they face a potential dilemma and threat of inaction. A decision between two attractive automobiles has the potential to immobilize people unless they can move quickly from the conflict to action. Changing cognitions facilitates a clear and positive evaluation of the chosen automobile and therefore facilitates unequivocal action to purchase it. Attitude change serves the immediate function of reducing arousal but the arousal is functionally related to serving the distal purpose of an orientation to unconflicted action.

As an illustration of their research, Harmon-Jones & Harmon-Jones ((2002); Harmon-Jones et al., 2008) showed that increasing a person's action orientation leads to increases in attitude change following a free choice. In their research, participants were asked to choose between two exercise programs. If participants were primed to think about actions needed to complete a goal, they were more likely to change their attitude to become more positive about the exercise program they selected. Interestingly, this occurred whether or not the goal was related to exercise. Merely thinking about the steps needed to approach and accomplish a goal resulted in greater attitude change toward the chosen alternative.

Self-Esteem. One of the pioneers of dissonance theory, Elliot Aronson, offered a modification of the mechanism for dissonance arousal. Aronson (1969; 1992) suggested that not just any inconsistent cognitions lead to cognitive dissonance. Fundamental to the arousal of dissonance, he suggested, was the implication of the self. When people act in a way that is at odds with what they think of themselves, then dissonance is aroused. Here are two examples. You can observe that the sun is shining in a cloudless sky and that it is not casting a shadow on the ground. Based on past experience and your knowledge of physics, these cognitions are inconsistent. Whereas Festinger would have expected this inconsistency to result in dissonance arousal, Aronson's self-esteem position would not. On the other hand, if you write an essay contrary to your belief, that inconsistency does cause dissonance because it directly implicates your self-concept. Are you the kind of person who would say something that you do not believe? As Aronson colorfully explained it, only "schnooks" would do such a thing, and you would not like to think of yourself as a schnook. The easiest way to convince yourself that you are a proper person and not a schnook is to convince yourself that you favored this position all along.

In the self-esteem view, dissonance is aroused when people engage in behaviors that violate their expectations of the kind of people they are. Most people have reasonably high self-esteem and feel that they are good and moral people. If they find that they have done something that violates that view, dissonance ensues. Of course, it is also possible that some people take a dim view of themselves and will experience dissonance if they do something good. In an intriguing demonstration of this view, Aronson and Carlsmith (1962) led people to create an expectation of their ability at a novel task. Through false feedback, some people were systematically led to believe they were particularly good at a social sensitivity task in which they had to choose the picture of a schizophrenic from an array of photographs (in actuality, all photographs were of Harvard undergraduates). Others were led to believe they were bad at the task. On a final trial, performance feedback was manipulated so that people either did well or poorly. For some people, the feedback on the final trial was consistent with their self-expectations. People who thought they were good found that they performed well on the final trial; people who thought they were bad found that they performed poorly on the final trial. For others—i.e., those who thought they were good but performed poorly and those who thought they were bad but performed well—the feedback was inconsistent.

As a measure of dissonance, all of the participants were told that the experimenter had accidentally failed to record the data on the last trial. The participants were asked to pick the schizophrenics again. This ruse enabled participants to stay with the answers they had previously given or change them in the hope of changing their score. Here is what Aronson and Carlsmith found: People who had received feedback that their final performance was consistent with their expectations stayed with their prior answers. There was also no surprise that people who expected to perform well but were told that they had performed poorly changed their answers on the final trial and improved their scores. This could be due to dissonance or it could have been due to a simple desire to score well. The key condition was the group who had expected to do poorly but found they had done well on the final trial. The investigators found that people in this group actually changed their responses to the final trial in order to fail. They altered their performance in order to meet the negative expectation that they held of their own ability.

Self-Affirmation theory. Claude Steele (1988) and his colleagues argued that what appears to be evidence for cognitive dissonance arousal may actually be part of a broader concern with establishing the goodness of one's self-concept. When the self-concept is threatened, people take action to restore its integrity. In a manner similar to Aronson's self-esteem view, Steele (1988) suggested that people who behave in ways that are inconsistent with their attitudes are not only acting inconsistently, but are also compromising their self-integrity. What drives them is not the restoration of consistency but re-establishing their overall self-worth. Like dissonance theory, self-affirmation concurs that behavior can motivate attitude change. The difference is the perspective on what motivates the change.

Self-affirmation theory holds that people will use any means available to restore the integrity of a self that has been threatened. Writing an essay or making a speech that one does not believe threatens self-integrity. Making a behavioral choice between alternatives when the choice is not crystal clear threatens self-integrity. According to self-affirmation, people change their attitudes to restore self-integrity because that is the avenue that is open to them in a typical experiment. The theory maintains that if other avenues had provided a way for participants to feel good about themselves, they would not have needed to do the difficult work of changing their attitudes.

A study by Steele and Liu (1983) provides an example of their approach. Participants were asked to perform a behavior that was inconsistent with their attitudes. Specifically, they were asked to write an essay favoring a rise in tuition rates. Some of the participants were given a way to remind themselves of some of their personal values, while others were not. When asked for their attitudes toward tuition following their writing an essay advocating higher tuition, participants who had not expressed their personal values changed their attitudes, becoming convinced that tuition hikes were good. Those who had expressed their personal values did not change their attitudes. Steele and Liu interpreted these data to mean that inconsistent behavior leads to attitude change, but only when attitude change is the exclusive way to restore self-integrity. If people have alternative ways to express their values and self-integrity—such as thinking about the quality of their personal values—they will adopt those methods instead.

The alternate viewpoints about the motivation for attitude change following inconsistent behavior have led to lively debate and research. The four views of dissonance we have discussed (inconsistency, action orientation, the New Look and self-esteem; see also Beauvois & Joule, 1999, for an alternate approach) often lead to different predictions, as does the self-affirmation viewpoint. For example, Steele, Spencer and Lynch (1993) systematically varied self-esteem by providing false feedback on a personality test. They found that people with high self-esteem seemed to have more resources available to buttress their overall self-systems and changed their attitudes less than people with low self-esteem. On the other hand, other studies found little support for that position (Stone, 1999). When Blanton and Cooper (1995) and Blanton et al. (1997) gave people a choice between changing their attitudes following counterattitudinal behavior or bolstering their self-systems, participants preferred to change their attitudes to resolve their dissonance.

The Self-Standards Approach. A more recent model of the relationship between behaviors and attitudes through cognitive dissonance is the self-standard model proposed by Stone and Cooper (2001). Stone and Cooper argued that the self may sometimes be significant in the dissonance process because there are occasions in which our expectations for ourselves constitute the standard of judgment that we use to determine if an event is unwanted. Sometimes it is not. Like the New Look (Cooper & Fazio, 1984), the self-standards model holds that dissonance is created by behavior whose consequences are judged to be unwanted. When people behave, they compare the outcomes of their behavior against a relevant standard of judgment. If that comparison shows the consequence to be unwanted and aversive, then dissonance is aroused and attitudes change.

Stone and Cooper proposed that the arousal of dissonance depends on the standard of judgment that is adopted. The standard can be either *normative or personal*. Different circumstances may lead to the use of one standard or another and different people may chronically use different standards. In order to visualize the difference between the standards, consider a casual runner out for a Sunday run. He checks his wristwatch and finds that he ran his first mile in 5 minutes and 30 seconds. Is this a good time or a bad time? It absolutely depends on the standard of judgment our runner uses. If he uses a normative standard, then he will base his judgment on what most people in his reference group would use. For most casual runners, 5:30 is a wonderful run. However, our runner may have set his hopes on a five-minute mile. Whether realistic or not, the runner compares his time to his own personal standard of judgment and it comes up short. For this runner, his assessment of the consequence of his behavior is that it is disappointing.

When people behave in ways that are contrary to their attitudes, the self-standard model proposes that a similar assessment of standards takes place, as it did for our runner. If a person makes a counterattitudinal statement that will dupe and disappoint a fellow student, that consequence will be compared against a standard of judgment to determine whether it is deemed unwanted and aversive. When compared against a normative standard, it will most likely be considered aversive. Most people in our culture would think it not acceptable to dupe a fellow student. The person's judgment using the normative standard of judgment is that the consequence is unwanted and that should lead to the arousal of dissonance and attitude change (Voisin & Fointiat, 2013). However, if a person uses a personal standard of judgment, then whether or not the consequence is aversive depends on what he expects of his own behavior. As Aronson and Steele suggested, most people have a positive impression of themselves and would probably conclude that the consequence of their behavior (duping the fellow student) did not measure up to their high self-standards. However, someone with a negative sense of self or even a perverse sense of humor may decide that duping a fellow student by convincing him that a dull task was interesting did not fall short of his or her personal self-standard. For this person, there will be no attitude change because there will be no dissonance.

Stone and Cooper (2003) showed that the standard of judgment that people use to assess the consequence of their behavior can be altered by situational interventions. Before writing a statement with which they disagreed, participants had their self-esteem measured on a standard scale (Rosenberg, 1965) and then engaged in an unrelated puzzle task. They were asked to unscramble letters in order to create English words. For half of the participants, the letters could be unscrambled to create words that primed normative concepts such as "society," "culture," "us," whereas the other half had letters that could be unscrambled to create a personal prime such as "myself." After engaging in the subsequent speech-writing task, participants were asked for their attitudes. Those participants who were primed with normative words showed dissonance. They apparently compared their behavior against the normative standard and changed their attitudes accordingly. Participants primed with personal words, however, used a different standard of judgment. Those people with measured high self-esteem changed their attitudes, whereas those with low self-esteem did not. Apparently, when the prime caused them to think about themselves, participants who thought highly of themselves found their behavior wanting and experienced dissonance. Those who had low self-esteem found that their behavior met their (low) expectations of themselves and did not change their attitudes. In the normative prime condition, self-esteem made no difference. As predicted, the behavioral consequence was assessed against the standard of what most people would find wanting and people of low and high self-esteem changed their attitudes.

Self-Perception Theory

In the early days of research on dissonance theory, Daryl Bem (1972) presented an entirely different theoretical approach to understanding the impact of behavior on attitudes. Self-perception theory accepted the data that dissonance researchers had gathered. Yes, behaviors predict attitudes and behaviors inconsistent with attitudes lead to new attitudes. Yes, people who perform attitude-inconsistent behaviors for small incentives change their attitudes more than those who perform inconsistent behaviors for large incentives. Yes, people who freely engage in attitude discrepant behavior manifest more attitude change than those who are forced to do so by an authority. Bem's provocative approach was that we do not need to invent theoretical accounts of internal states to understand why it happens.

Self-perception theory argues that in most circumstances, people have very poor insight into their internal states. Attitudes, for example, are not immediately accessible. At the beginning of the current chapter, we provided an example of a person assessing his attitude about organic brown bread. Does he like it or not? Rather than having an evaluative summary jump into mind, he is clueless about his attitude until he assesses his past behavior. When he realizes he has chosen to eat this bread on a previous occasion, he infers that he must like it. Bem argued that the same principle occurs whenever we are asked to assess our attitudes. We act as perceivers of our own behaviors—just as though we were asked the question about someone else. When asked if a friend is a liberal or conservative, for example, we cannot have direct access to our friend's internal state. But we do have memory of her behavior. We recall that she spoke in favor of expanding health care and that she was in favor of free pre-school education for the poor. We infer she is a liberal.

Self-perception theory contends that people who are asked about their attitude toward a peg-turning task do not immediately know how much they liked it. Rather, they function like the person who was asked about brown bread in our earlier example, or as they would reason if asked how a friend of theirs liked the peg-turning task. They would assess their friend's behavior for clues to their friend's attitude. When asked about their own attitude, they similarly recall that they made a statement to another person extolling its excitement and interest. Their conclusion is that they must have liked it.

Importantly, there are times that you would not be able to infer your attitude from your behavior, just as you would not be able to infer your friend's attitude. If your friend had been paid a great deal of money to say the peg-turning task was interesting, you would realize that your friend's statement was controlled by the situation (in this case, the money) rather than its being a statement descriptive of his attitude. Similarly, if an experimenter ordered your friend to write a speech favoring a ban on controversial speakers, you would not be able to infer your friend's attitude. That behavior, too, was under the control of situation demand. Bem reasoned that if we consider people to be perceivers of their own behaviors, we come to the same conclusion as dissonance theory: People change their attitudes to match their behaviors when the situational demands do not appear to be controlling the behavior—e.g., when incentives are low and choice is high.

Like cognitive dissonance, the self-perception process leads to the prediction that behaviors can be the source of an attitude. One major difference is that self-perception does not claim that attitudes have *changed* (Bem and McConnell,

1970). In the self-perception approach, people are simply inferring what their attitudes must be, based on their behavior. In the dissonance approach, people are driven to change their attitudes because the internal tension state must be reduced. The question, then, is whether attitude-behavior inconsistency does indeed cause arousal and, secondly, whether the arousal is what motivates attitude change.

Arousal Following Behavior-Attitude Discrepancy

Evidence points to the conclusion that, as Festinger predicted, the discrepancy between behavior and attitudes leads to physiological arousal and psychological discomfort. Zanna and Cooper (1974) used a technique called the **misattribution procedure** to find some of the first evidence. In their study, participants were asked to take what they believed was a vitamin supplement, presented as part of a study on visual perception. The pill, which was actually just a placebo capsule filled with milk powder, was said to have arousing properties that would cause people to feel a bit tense and uncomfortable. In a second condition, the pill was said to have no physiological impact. While waiting for the vitamin pill to take effect, participants were asked (or told) to write a statement extolling the value of raising tuition at their university. The experimenters reasoned that in the condition in which the pill had no side effect, participants would show attitude change, just as dissonance theory and self-perception theory would predict. However, if attitude change is based on the need to deal with unpleasant arousal, then (mistakenly) attributing your arousal to the side effect of a pill rather than to an inconsistent essay you have just written would make attitude change moot as a way to reduce the arousal. The results of the study showed that attitude change was eliminated when people thought their arousal was due to the pill's side effects. These results contradict self-perception theory's provocative assumption that people are not driven by internal states but rather are simply perceivers of their own behavior.

Further research continued to show support for the occurrence of arousal following counterattitudinal behavior. Cooper, Zanna and Taves (1978) showed that if people were given a stimulant (an amphetamine) that they believed was a placebo, the increased arousal resulted in more attitude change following counterattitudinal behavior. Apparently, the increased arousal was attributed to writing the counterattitudinal essay and resulted in people showing a greater urgency to change their attitudes. Similarly, reducing physiological arousal with the use of a sedative reduced the amount of attitude change following attitude discrepant behavior.

Croyle and Cooper (1983), Elkin and Leippe (1986) and Losch and Cacioppo (1990) found physiological evidence for the assumption that attitude-discrepant behavior leads to arousal. They found increased skin conductance (SCR) following counterattitudinal behavior, which is an indicant of an aroused autonomic nervous system. Similarly, Martinie, Olive, Milland, Joule and Capa (2013) found evidence for arousal using electromyograph recordings. Harmon-Jones and his colleagues (Harmon-Jones, Harmon-Jones, Fearn, Sigelman, & Johnson, 2008) as well as Kitayama, Chua, Tompson and Han (2012) found specific neural correlates of dissonance in the relative left cortical region of the anterior circulate cortex (ACC) of the brain. There is also evidence that the psychological discomfort that accompanies the physiological arousal is the prime motivator of attitude change following counterattitudinal behavior (Elliot & Devine, 1994; Losch & Cacioppo, 1990; Rydell, McConnell, & Mackie, 2008).

The fact that attitude inconsistent behavior leads to arousal supports the role played by cognitive dissonance. Is there a role for self-perception? There are probably at least two instances in which people infer their attitudes from their behaviors without experiencing cognitive dissonance. One is in the realm of what we have called "non-attitudes" (Converse, 1970; Fazio, 1989; see Chapter 3). There is a class of objects about which people have very little pre-formed evaluations and it is most likely that, when asked, people must use any behavior toward those objects as a clue to their evaluation. For most people, brown bread may be one of those objects. The other instance is when the behavior is only mildly inconsistent with one's attitudes. Fazio, Zanna and Cooper (1977) asked people to write essays that were discrepant from their attitude on an important issue. They found that when the essays were widely discrepant from their own attitudes, in what is termed their latitude of rejection (Sherif & Hovland, 1961; see Chapter 4), people changed their attitudes in the direction of the essay, accompanied by the arousal and discomfort expected when dissonance is present. However, when people were asked to write essays that were only mildly discrepant (in their latitude of acceptance), attitudes also changed in the direction of their essays, but were not accompanied by arousal or discomfort. Apparently, people writing within their latitude of acceptance changed their attitudes as a function of self-perception.

Behavior and Attitudes in Groups

You spend much of your social life in groups. The impact of your group memberships has a profound bearing on your self-concept, your behaviors and your attitudes. Finding that you disagree with members of a group to which you belong creates dissonance and leads to attitude change to reduce the unpleasant dissonance state (Matz & Wood, 2005). Group membership can also prescribe and proscribe appropriate avenues for dissonance reduction. Sometimes, group membership makes it impossible to change attitudes because to do so would strike at the very heart of that which defines the group. In one study, Cooper and Mackie (1983) asked members of a Young Republican club at a university in the United States to write an essay favoring the Democratic candidate for president. They complied, but how would they resolve their dissonance? With their group made salient, it would be impossible to change attitudes about a hotly contested presidential race in which such attitudes served as the core of group membership. The authors predicted and found that the Republican participants would resolve their unpleasant tension state by becoming more hostile toward Democrats rather than by changing their attitudes toward the presidential race.

Group membership also offers people the opportunity to compare their own inconsistent behavior with the behavior of others in their group. McKimmie, Terry and Hogg (2009) found that people could use their group membership to apply a principle of **metaconsistency** to their behavior-attitude link. To the extent that other people in one's important social group also behave in an inconsistent manner, it can reduce an individual group member's need to resolve his or her dissonance. On the other hand, to the extent that one stands alone in attitude behavior inconsistency, the more the inconsistent behavior can influence the group member's attitudes.

Groups can also behave. Members of a society frequently learn that a spokesperson has expressed the group's position. Sometimes individual members agree with that position and sometimes they do not. Sometimes, a group takes action, such as a nation going to war or a labor union negotiating a deal with management that individuals oppose. Glasford, Dovidio and Pratto (2009) have shown that discrepancies between behaviors of groups and the attitudes of individual members arouses cognitive dissonance and results in attitude change strategies that are either directed toward the issue on which the group took action or are directed against the group itself.

Vicarious Dissonance: Dissonance Aroused by the Behavior of a Group Member

One recent venue in which groups have played a role in the relationship between behaviors and attitudes has been the identification of the vicarious process of cognitive dissonance (Cooper & Hogg, 2007). When people are in groups, especially those groups that they care about, bonds form among members. It is a basic fact of social life that people derive much of their sense of self from the groups to which they belong (Hogg, 2007; Tajfel & Turner, 1986; Turner, 1982). We quickly categorize the world into those who share our group memberships (ingroups) and those who do not (outgroups). Social identity and social categorization theories hold that people not only favor their ingroups over outgroups, but also form bonds of attraction and empathy with other members of their ingroup. William Jefferson Clinton, while a candidate for President of the United States in 1994, scored substantial points in his debate with President George H. W. Bush when he responded to an audience member by saying, "I feel your pain." This is the quintessential statement of common group membership. It is as though Clinton said, "We are all Americans. We share common bonds and feelings. We feel each other's pain."

If it is true that common ingroup membership causes empathic bonds in which members feel each other's pain, then is it possible that group members can feel each other's dissonance? Norton, Monin, Cooper and Hogg (2003) argued that they could. In a series of studies (Monin, Norton, Cooper, & Hogg, 2004; Norton et al., 2003), they had participants observe another person behaving in a way that contradicted his or her attitude. The investigators predicted that counterattitudinal behavior by another person would create dissonance in the observer, provided the actor and observer shared a common group membership and the observer felt highly attracted to his group.

Norton et al. (2003) created a situation in which a student listened to a fellow student deliver a speech advocating higher tuition rates at the university. It was made clear that the fellow student did not agree with the position he was asked to espouse in his speech. We know from research in individual dissonance discussed in this chapter that this situation would normally result in dissonance arousal for the speaker and would cause the speaker to change his or her attitude. The key question for Norton et al. was whether the speaker's behavior would also cause the observer to change his or her attitude. The results showed that if the speaker was from the observer's social group and the observer felt highly identified with his group, then the observer shared the actor's discomfort. The observer experienced dissonance vicariously, changing his or her attitude to express a more positive evaluation of tuition hikes.

Cooper and Hogg (2007) and Stone and Focella (2011) presented evidence that vicarious dissonance processes can lead to the promotion of healthy behaviors. Female students in Brisbane, Australia, and Tucson, Arizona witnessed fellow group members publically endorse the position that people should always use sun protection when going outdoors. This is a popular position, especially in parts of the world in which the rate of skin cancer is high. However, the participants also witnessed the speaker acknowledge that, in truth, she did *not always* apply sunscreen. This admission was dissonant with the speaker's professed attitude about the universal use of sunscreen. If (and only if) the witness was in the same social group as the speaker, she experienced dissonance vicariously. When asked about their own attitudes toward sunscreen, participants who were in the speaker's group became even more favorable to using sunscreen and took action to obtain more sunscreen when given the opportunity.

Summary and Conclusion

In this and the previous chapters, we have shown that attitudes and behaviors are linked in reciprocal ways. Attitudes predict and influence behaviors (Chapter 6), and behaviors predict and influence attitudes (current chapter). None of this happens all of the time. Social psychology is a discipline directed toward determining the social circumstances in which relationships hold. In the current chapter, we have seen that implicit behaviors such as smiling and nodding one's head influence attitudes, sometimes by providing information and sometimes by altering people's confidence in their reactions. We have also seen that explicit behaviors affect attitudes and attitude change. This is particularly likely for behaviors that are freely chosen, that result in unwanted events and that are engaged in without much apparent inducement. Looking inwards, observing our own behavior and attempting to rationalize, justify or explain it motivates us to do so in a way that maintains consistency between our attitudes, our actions and the self (even when those attitudes did not exist beforehand). Similarly, when observing our own attitudes and behavior and looking outwards, we are motivated to preserve consistency with the attitudes and behavior of important others, whether they be specific others or members of a valued ingroup.

Cognitive dissonance theory has had a major impact on research linking behaviors to attitudes. Debate continues over the precise mechanisms that account for attitude change as a result of behavior. Some argue that the drive to achieve consistency motivates behaviors, while others contend that the desire to achieve a high level of self-esteem is the underlying mechanism. Other models suggest that dissonance is aroused when taking responsibility for aversive consequences, whereas alternatives suggest that is an orientation for action that is paramount. The debate has produced an impressive amalgam of data revealing the circumstances in which behavior influences attitudes. As researchers continue to synthesize a robust history of decades of research with new theoretical frameworks, the state of knowledge of the reciprocal attitude-behavior relationship continues to evolve even as methodological innovations shed new light on the processes of rationalization, evaluation and the reduction of dissonance.

CHAPTER 8

Resistance to Persuasion

In the course of marketing a product, millions of dollars are spent to sway an audience to sample the product or to switch allegiance from a competitor's product. General Mills, for example, spends millions of dollars to sway its audience to eat Wheaties rather than Corn Flakes. Marketers develop major campaigns using all forms of media, create appealing packages for their products and arrange special sales. Their campaigns are often based on the principles that we have discussed throughout this book. Nonetheless, despite their best effort, only a small percentage of people are convinced to try the new cereal or to switch their allegiance from Corn Flakes to Wheaties. This is not to feel sorry for cereal manufacturers. U.S. residents alone spend nearly 7 billion dollars annually on their breakfast choices. A shift of only a few percentage points toward the advertised product is a gain of millions of dollars for the manufacturer. However, it does reveal an important point about the ease of changing people's attitudes. People are remarkably good at resisting persuasion—that is the issue we will examine in the current chapter.

THE CONCEPT OF RESISTANCE

William McGuire was a pioneer in the study of resistance to persuasion. He counseled that **resistance to persuasion** is not simply the inverse of persuasion itself (McGuire, 1964). It is true that some persuasion attempts are ineffective because the arguments used in the message are weak and specious. Others are ineffective because people are uninvolved. Others are ineffective because the source of the information is so unreliable as not to be taken seriously and still others are ineffective because the intended recipient paid no attention. However, these are not what McGuire and subsequent attitude theorists consider to be prototypical of resistance.

Rather, *resistance is an active process by which one defends one's beliefs against attack.* Strong arguments can be counterargued, sources can be derogated, ulterior motives can be attributed, new facts can be brought to bear, all in an attempt to defend one's existing attitudes. In this chapter, we will examine some of the factors that motivate people to resist persuasion, and we will consider some of the processes we use to accomplish the resistance. We will also examine the cost and consequences of our struggles to resist persuasion.

MOTIVATION TO RESIST PERSUASION

Consistency as a Motive for Resistance

Throughout this book, we have discussed the myriad ways that attitudes are formed and changed. Once formed, however, attitudes enter a network of cognitive and evaluative structures. Each of these structures has implications for other structures in the network. For example, imagine that a person named Scott has an attitude about crime that makes him oppose capital punishment. This attitude sits comfortably in a network of attitudes and assumptions that is consistent with his attitude about capital punishment. For example, he believes that juries occasionally make mistakes. He is aware of the large number of convictions that have been overturned by modern DNA evidence. He also has religious attitudes that make him endorse forgiveness as a response to transgression, and he attends a church in which opposition to the death penalty is nearly unanimous. He has attitudes about other issues that are consistent with his attitude toward the death penalty. He believes in some government control over the possession of handguns because of the potential for violence, and he supports efforts to negotiate international conflicts before they erupt into the horrors of war.

Scott opens a magazine and finds an article on the death penalty. It presents a cogent argument that the death penalty is a deterrent to crime and should be supported. This is an issue that piques Scott's interest. However, it is not an argument that shares an even playing field with the attitude Scott already has. If Scott were to change his attitude about capital punishment, how could he reconcile it with his religious conviction? How could he reconcile it with his knowledge that people are erroneously convicted of crimes they did not commit? How would he explain it to his friends?

We can recognize Scott's problem in terms of consistency theories of attitudes (see Chapter 6). Heider (1958) stressed a strain toward balance in people's attitudes and relationships. If we examine some of the cognitive elements that Scott has to consider, we can see his current capital punishment attitude is consistent with the evaluative summaries (i.e., attitudes) toward a number of issues and people.

In Figure 8.1a, we see that a balanced state exists between Scott's attitudes toward capital punishment, his belief that juries make mistakes, his evaluation of his friends and church colleagues and their evaluation of capital punishment. Even his knowledge that Rush Limbaugh, the conservative radio commentator, is in favor

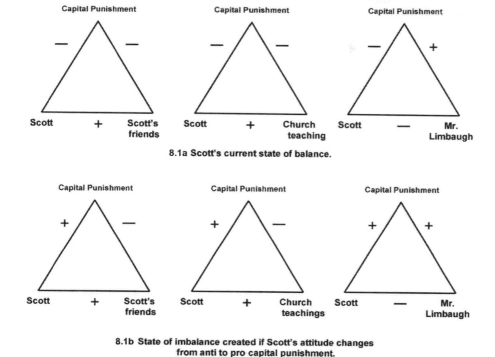

8.1a Scott's current state of balance.

8.1b State of imbalance created if Scott's attitude changes
from anti to pro capital punishment.

FIGURE 8.1   *Some of the elements in Scott's current state of balance.*

of capital punishment is balanced because Scott holds a negative attitude toward
Mr. Limbaugh. In Figure 8.1b, we can see the imbalance that would be created by
a change of attitude toward capital punishment. The relationship with his friends
and their attitudes toward capital punishment would become strained (imbalanced)
if he were to change his attitude. His concurrence with Rush Limbaugh would similarly cause imbalance.

Scott would not find it impossible to change his attitude, but a change would
have consequences. He could try to persuade his friends to hold the same new attitude that he developed, he could change the church he attends, he could find new
friends or he could come to embrace Rush Limbaugh. All of these are possible, but
they are difficult and uncomfortable. Changing an attitude causes havoc to one's
psychological balance. A long line of research in consistency demonstrates that people prefer to maintain consistency by persuading others to change rather than to
undergo change themselves (Festinger, 1950; Schachter, 1951).

Psychological Reactance and Resistance to Persuasion

People appreciate and value their freedoms—including the freedom to make their own choices, the freedom to express their opinions, the freedom to hold attitudes and the freedom to behave as they wish. The consequence of perceived restrictions to these freedoms gives rise to the state of **psychological reactance** (Brehm, 1966; Brehm & Brehm, 1981) and results in motivation to restore those freedoms. This motivation to restore freedom has implications for resistance to persuasion.

One of Brehm's (1966) illustrations to help explain the impact of reactance focused on a man named John Smith who enjoyed playing golf on Sunday afternoon. He occasionally did other things on Sunday, such as watch television or work on projects. One Sunday, his wife insisted that he play golf. This should have been wonderful news for a man whose passion for golf was palpable. On the other hand, prior to this Sunday, he had been free to play golf or not, to watch television or not, or to engage in myriad activities of his choosing. Now his freedom to choose one of those other activities has been threatened, creating the state of psychological reactance. In response to that restriction, Smith decidedly declared he did not wish to play golf, preferring instead to take a drive in the country. By lowering his evaluation of golf and choosing an alternative action, Smith regained his freedom for that Sunday and, by implication, for the many Sundays to come.

Reactance theory holds that people experience reactance when a behavior that they consider to be a **free behavior** is eliminated or threatened with elimination. Not every behavior falls into this category. People do not believe that they are free to walk in space or to breathe underwater without the aid of oxygen. In order for a behavior to be considered free, it must be something a person has the physical or psychological means to accomplish and the person must know by experience, general custom or formal agreement that these behaviors may be engaged in. Restricting people's freedom to engage in actions that they never considered to be "free" does not result in reactance. However, when custom, past experience or formal agreement confers that freedom on people, any restriction leads to reactance and an attempt to restore that freedom.

One of the earliest empirical studies that addressed the question of how people's preferences can change as a function of reactance was conducted by Brehm, Stires, Sensenig and Shaban (1966). They asked participants to evaluate four music albums, allegedly as part of a consumer preference test being conducted by a music company. In return, the music company would allow the participants to choose one of the albums as a free gift. After participants expressed their opinions of the four albums on an attitude scale, the experimenter proceeded to offer the gift. However, participants in the reactance condition were told that the company had apparently forgotten to send samples of one of the albums. The missing album was always the one that the participants had ranked third out of the four albums. In a control condition, all four items were available for choosing.

Participants were asked to re-rate the albums. Even though their most liked record was available for a free gift, and even though their second-ranked album was also available, participants in the reactance condition suddenly felt more favorable to the album that had been eliminated. Seventy percent of the participants raised their evaluation of the eliminated record, whereas there was no significant increase in the control condition. People's evaluation increased because their freedom to have (what they really did not want anyway) had been taken away.

Reactance also works to make a desired alternative less attractive if people think their freedom to have something else is being threatened. Consistent with the example of Mr. Smith and his golf game, Brehm (1966) reported a study in which children were asked to express their preference for an array of seven toys. At a later session, the children were allowed to choose any of the toys for themselves. Prior to the choice, a second child told the first child that he or she *must* choose Toy X, with X manipulated so that it was always the toy that the first child really wanted. The child then had the opportunity to select the toy that he or she wanted. In a control condition, in which the children were not offered the freedom-restricting advice from their peers, the children's choice at the second session remained relatively stable, and they tended to choose the item that they liked best during the first session. However, when the children were told what they must choose, they decided that they did not like the first-ranked toy as much after all. On average, the toy dropped into second or third place after their peer told them they must choose it.

Reactance is especially high when the **importance of the threatened freedom** is high. A study by Brehm and Cole (1966) addressed this point. Participants came to a study whose purported purpose was to evaluate partners based on their answers to a few questions during a lab session. Some participants were led to believe that evaluating their partner was an important task and others were led to believe that it was a trivial exercise. The partner was actually a confederate of the experimenter who had the opportunity to meet the participant prior to the evaluation task. The experimenter explained that she was running late and the two students needed to wait in a reception area. The confederate excused herself from the waiting room for a moment and returned with a soft drink that she gave to the participant. She refused any money for the gift. The reader can well imagine the potential quandary for participants as they contemplated the experimental task. The confederate's "favor" could be construed as a not-so-subtle demand to be evaluated positively in the upcoming evaluation task. This is a restriction of the individual's freedom to evaluate the partner however she pleased. Especially when the task was important, the implied threat to the participant's freedom was predicted to arouse reactance.

One way to regain freedom without distorting one's ratings of the partner was to demonstrate independence. The partner was afforded this opportunity by a

TABLE 8.1 *Number of Persons Who Performed the Favor*

	LOW IMPORTANCE	HIGH IMPORTANCE
No favor		
Helped	9	7
Did not help	6	8
Favor		
Helped	14	2
Did not help	1	13

Source: Brehm, J.W. (1966). A theory of psychological reactance. *New York*.
Reprinted with permission.

clever ruse. While waiting for the evaluation task to begin, the experimenter put a pile of papers on the confederate's table and asked her to sort the papers into piles, certainly a tedious task. The participant could volunteer to help if she liked. Indeed, in a no-reactance control condition in which the confederate had not brought the soft drink, half of all participants offered help with the tedious task. However, in the favor condition, the threat to freedom had very different consequences depending on the importance of the freedom that had been usurped. In the condition in which the evaluative task was trivial, the freedom to evaluate the confederate positively or negatively was not terribly important and participants were led to return the favor that the confederate had done for the participant. Indeed, 87% of the participants offered help. But when the freedom to evaluate the confederate was important, only 1 participant out of 14 participants agreed to help. In reactance terms, when they perceived a threat to their freedom, participants in the high importance condition experienced reactance and acted to restore their freedom by establishing their independence on the paper-sorting task.

Reactance and the Expression of Attitudes

In the research we have considered thus far, people's behavior changed as a function of threats to their freedom. The behavior was typically based on their evaluations of objects such as music albums for adults and toys for children. We now consider the role of psychological reactance on people's attitudes toward a persuasive message. Measuring the effect of reactance following a persuasive message can be complex because the persuasive message carries content that can be cogent and convincing. Yet, if people believe that their freedom to adopt whatever attitude they wish has been threatened, then reactance will work against the intended effect of the persuasive message.

Worchel and Brehm (1970) asked people about their attitudes toward the Communist Party of the United States and to indicate whether they thought it should be treated like any other political party. Participants were about equally divided in their initial attitude toward this issue. They were then asked to listen to a message that either advocated treating the Party as any other or banning it as an agent of a foreign government. Thus, some participants listened to a well-constructed, cogent speech advocating the position that they already favored and some listened to a similarly effective speech taking the opposite position. In the high threat condition, reactance was aroused by liberally sprinkling the speech with remarks such as "You cannot believe otherwise," or "You have no choice but to believe this." In the low threat condition, participants heard precisely the same speech but without the threatening comments.

Worchel and Brehm predicted that reactance would be experienced in the pro-attitudinal condition only. In the counterattitudinal condition, where the direction of the speech was contrary to the opinion that they had just expressed on a questionnaire, the investigators reasoned that the participants would feel they had already declared their freedom to take the opposite position. This can be considered a "prior declaration of freedom" (Brehm & Brehm, 1981). The interesting reactance theory prediction was for people who were being urged to believe what they already believed—i.e., those who were exposed to a pro-attitudinal communication. In the low threat condition, the pro-attitudinal speech effectively persuaded 56% of the participants to become even more ardent in their original position. However, when the threat to the freedom to hold a different position was high, only 20% became more convinced of their position while 65% moved in the direction *opposite* to the speech they heard. As predicted, the level of threat did not affect participants in the counterattitudinal condition.

These results, supported in several additional investigations in both Western and Asian cultures (Imajo, 1996; Snyder and Wicklund, 1976; Wicklund, 1974) reinforce the point that reactance is a motivation designed to restore freedom. In some cases, it can cause resistance to a strong message and in other cases can lead to boomerang changes opposite to the position advocated in the message. The boomerang effect will occur if the audience feels that it is the primary way to restore their freedom to hold whatever attitude they wish. If freedom has already been declared, then reactance does not motivate resistance.

Censorship of Communications and Attitude Change

Sometimes, people in authority decide that a communication is so undesirable that they forbid people to hear it. In totalitarian societies, the ruling military may censor a pro-democracy treatise or may forbid any criticism of the authorities. Even in democratic countries where the freedom to express views is fundamental to the fabric of society, reports are classified, thus becoming unavailable to the public, and information is "redacted" from testimony or reports, rendering them uninformative. University administrators may refuse to invite some speakers to college campuses because their views are considered too radical, dangerous, or insulting. Whether or not a particular act of censorship is wise, the process of psychological reactance makes a clear prediction about censorship's consequences. Restricting access to particular points of view threatens people's freedom. The consequent reactance should lead people to want to hear the communication even more than they did prior to the censorship and to adopt the position advocated in the censored speech.

Several studies confirm this prediction. Ashmore, Ramchandra and Jones (1971) told participants they would hear a speech taking one of two positions: police should be allowed on university campuses, or they should not. Some participants were told that the dean had censored the speech and they would not hear the communication. Attitudes of the participants were then measured and showed that censorship led participants to change their attitudes in the direction of the communication that had been censored. In a subsequent study, Worchel and Arnold (1973) replicated and extended this finding. In their study, the characteristics of the censor were varied (positive or negative). Like Ashmore et al., Worchel and Arnold (1973) found that the censorship of a communication created attitude change in the direction of the communication and that this occurred regardless of the participants' liking for the censor. In addition to creating attitude change, censoring a communication increased participants' desire to obtain the communication.

We conclude by noting the power of the motivation to restore freedom. In the studies that we have examined in this section (see also Worchel, Arnold, & Baker, 1975), people clamored to hear or read a persuasive message when they were denied the freedom to do so. They changed their attitudes toward the message, even though they never had the opportunity to elaborate its content, purely as a motivation to restore their behavioral freedoms. Although these studies show us that reactance can sometimes exaggerate persuasion, reactance more generally operates as a motivation to resist persuasion. The notion that a communicator wants you to act in a certain way or believe in a certain position can be a threat to freedom. Children resisted a toy that they liked, adults downgraded what they thought of a music album and people showed boomerang attitude change as ways to restore their behavioral freedom.

STRENGTHENING RESISTANCE: INOCULATION FROM PERSUASION

What do we need to help us resist persuasion? One requirement is information. We can resist a message best if we have information to refute the content of the message. Surprisingly, some of our most trusted attitudes are backed by a paucity of information and are subject to attack. McGuire's (1961; 1964) classic work on resistance to persuasion pursued this line of reasoning. There are a number of attitudes we hold whose bases we rarely think about. Is democracy the best system of government? Why is marriage between a brother and sister bad? Should people brush their teeth after every meal? Not only do we have attitudes about these issues, but most of us also hold them with great certainty. As we know from our discussion in Chapter 2, attitude certainty is a component of attitude strength, which generally predicts stability over time. McGuire reasoned that even attitudes that we hold with great certainty are vulnerable to attack if we rarely consider the basis for those attitudes or the reasons that can be marshaled to refute likely counterarguments.

Using a biological metaphor, McGuire coined the term **inoculation theory** to describe an attitude's vulnerability to attack and the strategic process we can use for building resistance. He likened our mental apparatus to our body's physical resistance to disease. Our physical systems operate in an environment in which viruses and bacteria attack constantly. However, our bodies become vigilant to extant viruses and bacteria, forming antibodies to fight the many germs. If we fail to have appropriate antibodies, then the germs successfully attack and we fall ill.

Consider the following example to illustrate McGuire's point. When Hawaii was a separate nation, it kept itself apart from trade, commerce or interaction with Western nations. In 1824, King Kamehameha II decided to become the first of its monarchs to travel abroad. The king and his wife traveled to London, where they quickly came in contact with the measles virus. They died within weeks. The royal family, who had never been in contact with the measles because it had never existed on the islands, was unable to withstand the virus' effects. McGuire's analogy is clear. To the extent that attitudes exist in a "germ-proof" environment, they are subject to attack. To resist the attack, we need to find ways to build the mental equivalent of physical antibodies.

McGuire suggested that we can build resistance to persuasion by allowing ourselves exposure to small doses of counterarguments in much the same way that our resistance to viruses is enhanced by small doses of live virus. Empirical research focused on attitudes that McGuire considered "cultural truisms:" that is, attitudes that we hold because they are generally agreed upon in the culture but we rarely consider the basis for our beliefs. What is your attitude toward brushing your teeth after every meal? How about every day? Most of us hold positive attitudes toward tooth brushing at least on a daily basis. Moreover, our degree of certainty is probably quite high. Are we sure that tooth brushing does not cause an erosion of enamel? Are we sure that the sugar content of our toothpaste doesn't outweigh the positive consequences? Most of us have rarely thought about the various aspects of tooth brushing and would be hard pressed to argue convincingly for our positions.

By analogy to the virus model, we can imagine at least two ways to protect against attacks to our attitudes. One way would be to strengthen the already existing attitude by providing further reasons for holding it. We can add information in a way that is analogous to taking a vitamin supplement to protect our physical health. Alternatively, we could become acquainted with a weak form of a potential attitude attack. It would allow us to begin to develop our own counterarguments that can be used against a subsequent persuasive message. Just as the body builds resistances to a weak form of a virus that it receives in an inoculation, we can build defenses against the substance of a counterattitudinal message that we may be exposed to in an attack.

In the first study to test the effectiveness of inoculation on resistance to persuasion, McGuire and Papageorgis (1961) collected a set of cultural truisms, such as mental illness is not contagious, brushing our teeth is good, and penicillin has been a great benefit to society. Participants indicated their attitudes about the truisms and then were placed in one of three experimental conditions. Two of the conditions were designed to provide inoculation against attack. In the *refutation condition*, participants were shown a brief, one-sentence argument that contradicted their attitudes (e.g., that frequent tooth brushing wipes the enamel from your teeth) and were asked to write a few sentences refuting that argument. In the *supportive condition*, participants were shown one brief attitude-consistent argument (e.g., that tooth brushing kills germs that grow in the mouth) and were then asked to write a few sentences to elaborate on that argument. In the third condition, referred to as *counterarguments only*, there was no indication that their opinions would be attacked during a subsequent session and there was neither a supportive nor a refutation inoculation.

Two days later, the participants returned for a second session. During this session, they were exposed to a strong, three-paragraph statement that attacked the truisms, after which their attitudes were assessed. A *control* condition was also run in which attitudes toward the truism were assessed without intervention or attack. The results are presented in Table 8.2. The control group shows how much consensus there was about the truisms, with participants averaging 12.62 out of a maximum of 15 across all of the issues used in the study. Table 8.2 shows the vulnerability of the attitudes to attack, with the mean (6.64) dropping below the mid-point of the scale.

McGuire and Papageorgis found that the refutation conditions allowed participants to resist the attack. The refutation defense was significantly more effective at producing resistance to persuasion than the supportive defense. It is as though protecting one's attitudes with a small dose of virus (i.e., considering the counterargument) produced greater resistance than a dose of vitamins (i.e., further consideration of the arguments you already knew).

Subsequent research added to McGuire & Papageorgis' (1961) findings. In one study, Papageorgis and McGuire (1961) examined the effectiveness of refuting the

TABLE 8.2 *Beliefs After Immunization and Exposure to the Strong Counterarguments*

ISSUES	STRONG COUNTERARGUMENTS ONLY (NO IMMUNIZATION)	IMMUNIZATION CONDITION								CONTROL (NO IMMUNIZATION OR COUNTERARGUMENTS)
		READING				WRITING				
		SUPPORTIVE		REFUTATIONAL		SUPPORTIVE		REFUTATIONAL		
		PASSIVE	UNDERLINE	PASSIVE	UNDERLINE	OUTLINE	NO OUTLINE	OUTLINE	NO OUTLINE	
D	4.74	8.25	9.50	12.70	10.00	9.00	9.17	7.57	7.57	12.88
M	7.06	6.17	5.33	11.14	10.86	8.75	4.89	8.71	7.33	11.50
P	8.62	8.78	11.62	11.10	13.86	7.67	7.56	9.71	10.89	13.44
T	6.42	6.33	5.11	11.00	10.29	5.67	5.25	10.30	11.40	12.69
Weighted mean	6.64	7.47	11.51	11.51	11.13	7.94	6.53	9.19	9.46	12.62
Total *N*	130	32	32	35	31	32	32	31	35	130

Note. Higher scores indicate higher agreement (1–15).

Source: Papageorgis, D., & McGuire, W. J. (1961). The generality of immunity to persuasion produced by pre-exposure to weakened counterarguments. *The Journal of Abnormal and Social Psychology, 62*(3), 475. Reprinted with permission.

very *same* argument that would later be used to attack your position or whether refuting a *different* argument would suffice. The strong arguments that participants received in the second session were either expansions of the one-sentence attack they had refuted in the first session or were completely different attacks. The results showed that counterarguing a weak form of an attack during the first session buttressed people from the effect of the second message, even if the arguments were different. Both types of refutation defenses increased people's resistance to the strong counterarguments.

Another issue that McGuire and his collaborators considered was whether active or passive defenses better prepare people to protect their attitudes from attack. Is the ability to resist a persuasive message greater if people actively construct the arguments that refute the message relative to reading prepared arguments that refute the message? After receiving the weak form of the argument in the first session, participants in a *passive refutation defense* condition read the experimenter's prepared reasons to disbelieve the initial attacking arguments, whereas those in the *active refutation defense* condition constructed their own arguments. The results showed that both defenses were effective but the active defense was both more effective and longer-lasting than the passive defense.

If anyone ever told you to take your vitamins *and* become inoculated against bacterial diseases, then you know the answer to the question of which defense, or set of defenses, is the most powerful and effective at facilitating resistance to persuasion. It is a combination of supportive and refutation defenses that provides the greatest defense against attack and allows people to maintain their initial attitudes.

THE EFFECT OF FOREWARNING ON RESISTANCE TO PERSUASION

Some of the most effective messages that produce attitude change are those whose persuasive purposes are disguised. Imagine a commercial on television that begins with a popular songwriter singing a song. Only as the music proceeds do we realize that the words of the song are actually a political message in favor of increasing exploration for fossil fuels. At the other end of the spectrum, we can imagine a commercial that begins, "In ten seconds, we will try to convince you to support exploration for fossil fuel," and then counts down the seconds until the message begins. Our intuition would probably tell us that the forewarning of the persuasive intent of a message will cause resistance to that message.

Ample research supports this intuition (Allyn & Festinger, 1961; Festinger & Maccoby, 1964; Freedman & Sears, 1965; Hass & Grady, 1975; Petty & Cacioppo, 1977; Tormala, 2008). Freedman and Sears (1965) designed a study to assess the role of forewarning. High school students were told that they were going to hear a talk entitled, "Why Teenagers Should Not Be Allowed to Drive," an unpopular position among the under-18 set. Some of the students knew of the position to be adopted approximately ten minutes in advance of the talk. Other students were not told until immediately prior to the message. When attitudes were measured after the message, Freedman and Sears found that students who had a warning period prior to the talk resisted the substance of the message far better than those for whom the message was virtually a surprise.

Why does forewarning lead to resistance? One of the activities that forewarning provokes is the production of cognitive responses. As we developed in Chapter 4, recipients of a persuasive message engage in cognitive responses to those messages, especially to the degree that they are involved with or care about the topic of the message. Given knowledge of the topic and direction of a forthcoming message, the recipient has ample time to respond to the topic, even in the absence of specific knowledge of the arguments contained in the message. By the time recipients are exposed to the message, they may have already formed cognitive responses in opposition to the message and/or generated responses in support of their original opinions (Blankenship, Wegener, & Murray, 2012; Petty & Cacioppo, 1977; Tormala, 2008).

Persuasion by Fiction. The idea that forewarning increases resistance to persuasion helps us understand a fascinating phenomenon in persuasion. Often, we are persuaded to believe in a particular position, and we wonder what it was that convinced us to hold this attitude. We did not read about it in the newspaper and were not exposed to a message in the media. Then we realize that the source of our attitude was a work of fiction. We may not have had an attitude about a topic before reading the fiction, or we may have been convinced to change from one position to another. However, we are somewhat surprised to realize that our only contact with this issue or attitude object was through a novel we read or a movie we saw, neither of which was based on facts or true events. Dal Cin, Zanna and Fong (2004) argue that narratives have the power to persuade us precisely because they lower forewarning, which in turn lowers counterarguing (see also Moyer-Gusé & Nabi, 2010). Reading a newspaper editorial entitled "Preserving our Prairies from Big Oil Greed" may not persuade those who believe in increased oil exploration. The title alone is a forewarning, which, in turn, leads to cognitive responses in defense of one's pro-oil position. However, reading a chapter of *Little House on the Prairie* in which Mary is forced off her land because of the greed of an oil magnate may have a persuasive effect on the reader's attitude. According to Dal Cin et al. (2004), the reason for the persuasive effect of the narrative is that the reader has not been forewarned and offers little resistance. Moreover, identification with the protagonist may allow the reader to view the world the way the protagonist viewed it, again causing lowered resistance.

Fiction generally allows us to become transported into a story, as though the events were real and the reader is a witness. Green and Brock (2000) define the concept of **transportation** as "a convergent process where all mental systems and capacities become focused on events in the narrative" (p. 701). Engaging in such transportation makes us particularly vulnerable to persuasion. In one of their studies, participants read a fiction narrative, *Murder at the Mall*. In that story, a mentally ill man is given leave from his hospital for a day out in the city. At the mall, the protagonist commits a murder. To the extent that readers felt transported into the story, they failed to notice that they were being persuaded to take an attitudinal position with which they had formerly disagreed, namely that mentally ill patients should be kept incarcerated rather than given freedoms. They also failed to notice flaws in the logic of the story and, in the end, changed their attitudes to become more in favor of incarcerating the mentally ill. The lack of forewarning and the transportation into the flow of the narrative reduced resistance.

VALUE LINKAGE: INVOKING DEPTH OF PROCESSING

Values are overarching guides to evaluations. They are maintained at a high level of abstraction and serve as guides to people's attitudes and behaviors (Maio & Olson, 1998; Rokeach, 1973). In Chapter 3, we noted that one of the functions that attitudes serve is to allow people to express their basic values. It is not surprising, then, that when attitudes are linked to values, resistance to persuasion is activated.

Imagine you are a person who believes that the minimum wage paid to workers should increase. There are any number of reasons that may have caused you to arrive at his conclusion. Some may be based on economic reasoning—e.g., a wealthier work force will add more tax revenue to the community. Some may be based on value considerations, such as compassion. You may believe that a substantial minimum wage is important because it is the more compassionate approach and compassion is one of the overarching values by which you lead your life. Research shows that the extent to which attitudes are linked to overarching values predicts how resistant they are to attack, with more strongly linked attitudes being more resistant (Blankenship & Wegener, 2008; Rokeach, 1968).

What is it about a value that causes attitudes linked with it to resist persuasion? Blankenship and Wegener (2008) suggested that the value-attitude linkage leads to increased resistance by creating greater depth of processing of the arguments that are linked to the value. If compassion is a value that is important to you, you are likely to be attentive to information about attitude objects that are linked to that value. You will have paid more attention to arguments about the plight of the working poor and their need for better living conditions rather than to economic or political arguments relative to the minimum wage issue.

In a series of experiments, Blankenship and Wegener (2008) demonstrated the critical role played by information processing in the chain of events that link important values to resistance. The investigators presented university participants with arguments about why Tashkentistan should be granted admission to the European Union. (The country, Tashkentistan, does not exist, but its name was sufficiently plausible to be believable.) They specifically linked the arguments to values. For half the participants, the arguments were linked to values that participants thought were important (e.g., freedom and self-respect), whereas for the other half, the values were less important (social power and wealth). The arguments that linked Tashkentistan's admission to the EU were manipulated so that for some participants the arguments were strong and for others they were weak. Blankenship and Wegener found that when the arguments were strong and were linked to important values, participants elaborated the message—that is, they processed the arguments carefully and were more persuaded than when the arguments were linked to unimportant values.

The investigators then subjected participants' new attitudes toward Tashkentistan to counterattack. As predicted, they found that attitudes formed by strong arguments were resistant to counterattack if they had been linked to important values. If the arguments—whether weak or strong—had been linked to unimportant values, then people did not resist the counterattack. Crucial to Blankenship and Wegener's theoretical interest is that the linkage to important values was caused by differences in elaboration, and they found evidence consistent with this logic. People's resistance to the counterattack was based on the factors they varied in their experiment (i.e., strong arguments linked to important values) and was mediated by the degree to which they elaborated (i.e., paid attention and responded to) the arguments in the initial message. In Blankenship and Wegener's view, having an attitude based on important values makes people feel involved in the issue and makes them process the arguments that were used to create their attitudes more deeply, and the increase in the depth of processing results in attitudes that are resistant to change.

THE IRONY OF VALUES

Despite their importance and centrality, there is an ironic element to values. The very fact that values are widely shared, held with a high level of certainty and confidence and rarely questioned makes them vulnerable to attack. Much like the truisms that McGuire and his colleagues studied, people often lack an arsenal of support for their overarching values. As Maio and Olson (1998) point out, people rarely question their basic values and fail to build arguments supporting their views. Maio and Olson (1998) found that merely asking people to analyze the basis for some of their most cherished values caused a weakening in support of those values.

Bernard, Maio and Olson (2003) asked people to focus on a specific important value, namely their support for equality. Bernard et al. showed that when participants were exposed to an essay attacking the virtue of equality, their support for equality eroded significantly. However, akin to McGuire and Papageorgis' (1961) work on simple truisms, when the experimenters provided other participants with arguments that could inoculate them against the attack, resistance was facilitated. This was true whether the inoculation was passive (i.e., having participants read information) or active (i.e., having participants generate their own arguments). The most effective resistance to an attack on their value of equality was a combination of passive and active inoculations.

The notion that we hold our values as truisms implies that our attitudes are more resistant to change than our values. Consider your attitude toward a policy such as affirmative action in hiring. You may support affirmative action in part because it follows from a highly cherished value such as "equality." As Bernard et al. (2003) and Maio and Olson (1998) showed, you rarely question your support for equality. On the other hand, affirmative action is controversial. As a policy in hiring, it has been supported and questioned by any number of articles in the media and may well have been a topic of discussion among your friends, relatives and classmates. The likelihood is that you are better prepared to resist attack on the specific attitude than you are to the basic value of equality. Blankenship, Wegener and Murray (2012) raised the fascinating possibility that resistance to changing a specific attitude—such as support for affirmative action—is best overcome by attacking the more vulnerable value that generated it. Under the guise of a study about evaluating reading material, Blankenship et al. (2012) had students read an editorial supposedly written by a professor. Half of the students were told that the editorial questioned the use of affirmative action, while the other half were told that the editorial questioned equality as a guiding principle in society. In fact, the ambiguously worded editorial was the same in both conditions. Blankenship et al. (2012) found that people resisted any attack on their specific attitude toward affirmative action when the editorial was alleged to be written for the purpose of attacking that position. However, they were more persuaded to change their attitude about affirmative action when they believed that the editorial questioned the value of equality. The results also showed that when the editorial attacked the specific attitude of affirmative action, people were able to resist the attack by generating numerous counterarguments. However, when the editorial was believed to be attacking the value of equality, attitudes toward affirmative action changed due to people's reduced *confidence* in the importance of that value.

STRATEGIES OF RESISTANCE: HOW DO WE DO IT?

We have defined resistance as an active process by which we defend our attitudes from attack. It is not merely the absence of persuasion but rather an active resistance that results in maintaining one's attitudes. We can be 'not persuaded' for any number of reasons that are only tangentially related to the act of resistance (e.g., we were not paying attention and/or the argument was poorly constructed). According to Wegener, Petty, Smoak and Fabrigar (2004), the difference between active resistance and the lack of persuasion resides in the degree of personal involvement people have in a given issue. The more the issue is personally relevant to them, the greater the probability that people will have thought about the issue and the more likely they are to engage in the active process of resistance.

What are the strategies that people can use to help them actively resist a message? Jacks and Cameron (2003) asked a number of students at the University of North Carolina to consider the following question: "When someone or something challenges your opinion, how do you respond?" The students' answers fell into seven categories:

1. *Attitude bolstering.* People reassure themselves of the basis for their opinions and the facts that support it. The more important people believe the issue to be and the more knowledgeable they are, the more likely they are to endorse attitude bolstering as the way in which they resist persuasion.

2. *Counterarguing.* People argue against specific assertions made in the content of the persuasive message. As with attitude bolstering, people believe that they would counterargue more as a function of the importance of the issue and their knowledge of the facts surrounding the issue.

3. *Assertions of confidence.* In this approach, people do not counterargue specific points of the message but rather assert that nothing could possibly change their minds.

4. *Source derogation.* The act of resistance is accomplished by casting doubt on the credibility of the communicator. We have seen this approach used in situations like those established by Hovland and his colleagues in their studies of communicator credibility (e.g., Hovland & Weiss, 1951; see Chapter 4). Curiously, in Jacks and Cameron's (2003) study, respondents reported that they would rarely use source derogation and that it was the least socially desirable method of combating persuasion. As we will see shortly, respondents' protestations that they would not use source derogation were probably overstated.

5. *Selective exposure and biased processing.* People actively seek arguments and sources that support their points of view. This is consistent with the results of research by Brannon, Tagler and Eagly (2007). In their study, participants were presented with information that supported and refuted their attitude. Their resistance motivation led them to selectively read only those arguments that supported their attitude and ignore the information that refuted it. People are also likely to interpret evidence as supporting their own beliefs, even when

it does not. Lord, Lepper and Ross (1979) showed that people who received a message that contained arguments that contradicted their attitude processed the message in such a way that they believed it actually supported their position.

6. *Negative affect.* People become angry or irritated with the message and communicator, countering the attack by focusing on the emotional experience that the message created.

7. *Social validation.* People focus on amount and quality of the social support they receive for their current opinions. This approach is consistent with social comparison theory (Festinger, 1954), which holds that people strive to hold attitudes that are consistent with the attitudes of similar people, and consistent with Heider's balance theory, described earlier in this chapter.

The seven resistance strategies represent people's thoughts about how they believe they would respond to a persuasive attack on their attitudes. It was based on a hypothetical: People were asked what they thought they would do if their attitudes were attacked. What do people *really* do? In a subsequent study, Jacks and Cameron (2003) selected a group of students who were in favor of the use of the death penalty in cases of first-degree murder and asked them to listen to a 4-minute speech arguing against the death penalty. The investigators used a thought-listing technique (Petty & Cacioppo, 1986, described in Chapter 4), in which participants wrote down precisely what they were thinking as they listened to the message. The results of the experiment showed that the most common responses to resist the persuasive message were counterarguing and attitude bolstering. Source derogation was also high on the list of responses, despite the fact that in the hypothetical scenarios, respondents had rated source derogation as unacceptable and as unlikely to be used. In reality, it was one of the most likely ways students reacted to persuasion.

It is also interesting to see which strategies were most effective at resisting persuasion. Jacks and Cameron (2003) assessed attitudes prior to and subsequent to listening to the speech. They found that counterarguing was the most effective: People who counterargued the points made in the speech were least persuaded to change their opinions. Source derogation, although frequently used, was among the least successful means of resistance. People who used source derogation to counter the message were among the most persuaded. So, too, were people who merely asserted their confidence in their initial opinion and those who responded by expressing irritation at the speech.

Resisting persuasion is multi-faceted (Wegener et al., 2004) with several techniques at people's disposal to actively combat persuasive messages. The greater people's involvement and knowledge, the more likely they are to counterargue the content of the message and this, in turn, seems to be the most effective resistance strategy available.

Resistance as a Difference among Individuals

Although a social psychological analysis of resistance focuses mainly on the situational variables that people are exposed to, we should also note that some people are more resistant to persuasion than others. One of the earliest measures of individual differences in persuasion was Rokeach's research on dogmatism (Rokeach, 1954). People high in dogmatism are more resistant to persuasive communications. So, too, are people who score high on measures of authoritarian personality (Altemeyer, 1981). Dowd, Milne and Wise (1991) constructed a scale to assess people's inclination to experience reactance, which, as we have seen, is an important motivator of resistance to persuasion. Other individual difference measures have assessed people's belief in how persuadable they believe themselves to be (Briñol, Rucker, Tormala, & Petty, 2004).

Sometimes, the belief in how persuadable one is can have ironic consequences. Rather than being correlated with resistance, it can lead to greater yielding to an attacking communication. Alberracin and Mitchell (2004) measured individuals' levels of "defensive confidence," defined as the degree to which people believe they can defend their positions against attack. Alberracin and Mitchell (2004) noted that people high in defensive confidence were more willing to put themselves in a position to receive attacking messages. Confident that they could defend their attitudes, they did not engage in selective exposure or biased processing but rather were willing to be exposed to messages that adopted contrary opinions to their own. This confidence may have been misplaced because Alberracin & Mitchell found that people high in defensive confidence were more, rather than less, persuaded by persuasive arguments against their original attitudes.

A more recent measure of individual differences to resist persuasion was developed by Saucier and Webster (2010). They defined the concept of **social vigilantism** (SV), an enduring disposition characterized by believing that one's attitudes are superior and more accurate than attitudes held by others and also a felt responsibility to assert their superior beliefs to others. A sample item of the social vigilantism scale is "I feel as if it is my duty to enlighten other people." The 14-item SV scale successfully predicted people's resistance to a persuasive attack. The higher the SV scores, the more likely people were to raise counterarguments against a message and to derogate the communicator of the message. As predicted, high SV individuals were resistant to persuasion, regardless of the strength of the arguments used or the credibility of the communicator.

CONSEQUENCES OF RESISTANCE

Reciprocal Relationship of Resistance and Self-Control

Resistance to a persuasive message requires cognitive resources. It is an active process that helps to keep attitudes stable in the face of countervailing messages.

Generally, as we have seen, counterarguing is the most frequently used and most effective way of combating counterattitudinal messages (Jacks & Cameron, 2003; Petty & Cacioppo, 1979). As an active, motivated process, counterarguing requires vigilance, skill and willpower to engage in the work required to resist persuasion. It also requires a certain amount of ability (Wood, Rhodes, & Biek, 1995), concentration and self-control (Burkley, 2008). To the extent that people's self-control is limited, their ability to resist a persuasive attack is also limited (Muraven, Tice, & Baumeister, 1998).

What do social psychologists mean by self-control and how is it related to resistance? Baumeister and Vohs (2005) refer to **self-control** as the active inhibition of unwanted responses that might interfere with the achievement of a desired goal. Confronted by a strong persuasive message that attacks your attitude, you must garner the resources to resist, which usually includes generating counterarguments to those being presented. If you allow yourself exposure to new arguments without defending your current ones, then resistance is less likely. Resistance requires self-control.

Baumeister and his colleagues have made a convincing case that self-control is a limited resource. Once used, there is a period in which control is depleted and cannot be used efficiently. It is like a muscle that requires use but that can be temporarily depleted from too much exercise. Imagine that you are exercising in the gym and that you are capable of doing 20 push-ups. When you have completed the 20, it is quite difficult to do another 20. You have the strength to do that number of push-ups, but the strain on your muscles from the original set depletes the muscle strength for any task that requires the use of those muscles immediately following their original use.

So, too, with self-control. If people use their self-control to regulate their activities, they will experience self-regulatory depletion (Baumeister, Vohs, & Tice, 2007). They will be less prepared to engage in any activity that requires self-control, including the activity of generating counterarguments to fend off persuasive attacks on their attitudes. Robert J. Lifton (1961) studied brainwashing during the Korean War. He cited one victim as saying, "You are annihilated, exhausted, you can't control yourself. . . . You accept anything the (brainwasher) says" (p. 23).

The ability to self-regulate and exercise self-control transcends the particular situation in which the self-control was used. Anything that depletes one's self-regulatory ability has implications for subsequent attempts at self-control. If you are a dieter who needs to use self-control to refrain from eating a piece of luscious cake, you will be less likely to have sufficient self-control leftover for tasks that you normally could accomplish. Imagine that you are asked to accomplish a task that requires vigilance and self-control: To transcribe a composition as quickly as possible but to omit the letter *e* every time it occurs. This may not require great ability at transcription or a high degree of intelligence, but it does require concentration and self-control. According to the depleted resource model of self-control, refraining from eating the piece of cake will make your performance on the transcription task less successful. Similarly, if you were asked to do the transcription task before coming face to face with the cake, you would be less successful at refraining from eating the cake. Although the two tasks are not related substantively, they both require self-control. Using self-regulation on the first task depletes the resource and diminishes its use on the second task.

Wheeler, Briñol and Hermann (2007) conducted a study in which people engaged in a self-regulatory depletion task that had been developed by Baumeister, Bratslavsky, Muraven and Tice (1998). In the first part of the procedure, participants engaged in the task we just described. They were instructed to cross out every *e* they could locate in a written passage. However, for some of the participants, the second part of the task was designed to strain their cognitive and attentional resources even further. In the high self-regulatory depletion condition, the participants were instructed to cross out each *e*, *except* when another vowel appeared in the same word (e.g., heal) or when a vowel was one letter removed from the *e* (e.g., fore). This high depletion task required a great deal of concentration to abide by the new rules, especially as it violated the rule learned in the first part of the task. In a low self-regulatory depletion condition, the participants engaged in the same activity, using the same rule about the letter *e* that they had practiced in the first part.

Following the high or low level of self-depletion, Wheeler et al. (2007) exposed participants to a counterattitudinal message advocating mandatory comprehensive examinations for all students. They found that the depletion manipulation affected students' ability to form counterarguments against the message, particularly when the pro-exam arguments were weak. That is, what was normally an easy task—generating counterarguments against a weak message—became an undoable task. The depletion of self-control caused by concentrating on the vowels before and after *e* led to weaker counterarguments. Persuasion was also affected by the self-regulatory depletion. Participants who had been depleted could not resist either the strong or weak arguments, showing persuasion for both of them.

Burkley (2008) used a very different ego depletion mechanism to assess a similar hypothesis. He used a physical task in which he asked participants in a *high depletion* condition to squeeze a handgrip for as long as they could. He was not interested in the amount of force the participants could use, but he was interested in the degree of persistence they could muster to keep the grip in the squeezed position. It requires concentration and effort. Participants in a *control condition* were not asked to squeeze the grip. Following the hand grip (or control) session, the participants were shown an essay in support of a policy that their university was allegedly considering shortening the summer vacation. A pilot test had shown that this position was highly counterattitudinal. Could students offer resistance to this communication? The answer was no if they had been in the *high depletion* condition.

Participants who had squeezed the hand grip were persuaded by the arguments in favor of the new policy more than were participants in the control condition.

Note that the argument that prior self-control depletion affects one's ability to resist persuasion is not based on effort or fatigue. It is about the act of control. In another experiment, Burkley (2008) compared resistance to a persuasive message from people who had engaged in a self-control task versus another mental task. As an example of the former, Burkley adopted a thought suppression task from research conducted by Wegner (1992). Participants were told *not* to think about a white bear. This task has repeatedly been shown to require a great deal of self-control to accomplish. As an example of a low self-control task, Burkley had participants complete difficult math problems. The math task was tedious and cognitively difficult but did not rely on self-control. When participants were then shown an essay favoring the shortening of the summer break, it was only the participants in the thought suppression task that failed to resist the arguments. The results support the notion that people need self-control in order to resist persuasion effectively. The depletion of self-control makes resistance difficult.

The Consequence of Resistance on Self-Control

Just as self-control is an antecedent of resistance, it is also a consequence. In the chain of reasoning we examined in the last section, the use of self-control regulation makes it less available for use on something else. In the studies we described, people who depleted their self-control regulation on another task were less able to resist persuasion. The reverse is also true. Resisting a persuasive attack makes us vulnerable to diminished ability to perform other tasks that rely on self-control.

One of Burkley's (2008) studies addressed this point. Instead of working on a depletion task and then being exposed to a persuasive message, participants performed the tasks in the reverse order. As in Burkley's previous studies, the attitude-discrepant message that people were exposed to was the shortening of the summer break. Some of the students were particularly motivated to resist this persuasion because the issue was relevant to them (i.e., it would be implemented while they were still students), while the other participants were less motivated to resist because they would never be affected by the proposed change. After reading the message, all participants were asked to solve a list of anagrams. They were asked to work as long as they possibly could and to signal the experimenter when they wished to leave. To persist on this task took self-control rather than ability at anagrams because, unbeknownst to the participants, the anagrams were not solvable. The results showed that, as predicted, participants who were personally involved in the summer schedule issue successfully resisted the arguments in the message. However, also as predicted, they were not able to persist as long at the anagrams task. The resistance to persuasion took its toll on subsequent ability to exercise self-control.

SELF-CONTROL AND THE SEQUENCE OF RESISTANCE

Have you ever been bombarded by several persuasive messages in close proximity? During the political election season in many democratic countries, you may wait patiently for a television show to begin, only to see an advertisement for a political candidate. If you agree with the message, you may nod with a smile. If you disagree, you may marshal the resources to counterargue and resist. But the evening has just begun. With the election looming, there is yet another advertisement, perhaps for the same candidate or perhaps for an issue that a candidate supports. It is possible that this sequence will continue for some more moments until the program actually begins.

Knowles, Brennan and Linn (2002) examined the consequences to resistance based on the sequence of political messages. They showed participants seven political messages and measured participants' yielding or resistance to these messages. Of particular interest was the comparison of the first message with the last. The work that we have described in this chapter makes a prediction: Because resisting depletes, but nonetheless requires self-control, whichever message is presented first will be resisted more than the message presented last. Indeed, that is what Knowles et al. (2002) found. Regardless of the content of the message, people were able to resist less if the message was at the end of the sequence than if it was at the beginning. Moreover, if the experimenters allowed people time to replenish their reserve of self-regulatory resources, then people were able to resist the final message as effectively as they resisted the first.

RESISTANCE AND CERTAINTY: ANOTHER RECIPROCAL RELATIONSHIP

When people are certain about their attitudes, they are generally more likely to resist a persuasive message. As we saw in Chapter 2, when we discussed the structure of attitudes, certainty is a component of attitude strength. A long tradition of research in persuasion has shown that the stronger one's attitude, the more long lasting it is and the more resistant it is to attack (e.g., Babad, Ariav, Rosen, & Solomon, 1987; Bassili, 1996; Krosnick & Abelson, 1992; see Petty & Krosnick, 1995 for a review). For example, Bassili (1966) contacted people by phone to inquire about their position on three political issues and the certainty with which they held those attitudes. He challenged their attitudes with persuasive communications and, as predicted, found that the respondents resisted persuasion to the degree to which they expressed certainty about their positions. He also found that certainty was related to stability. The more certain people were about their attitudes, the less they changed over time.

Just as certainty promotes resistance to attitude change, resistance also has an effect on attitude certainty. The relationship is a complex and interesting one. At first glance, it would seem that if you successfully resist a persuasive message, you would maintain confidence in your attitude. However, the real impact of resistance on confidence depends on how you interpret your resistance. Tormala and Petty (2004) refer to this as a *metacognitive* approach (see Chapter 2) because the impact depends on your cognitions (i.e., interpretations) about your cognitions. Those latter cognitions include the strength of the persuasive message, the stability of your opinion and the basis for your resistance.

To put the metacognitive approach in a broader framework, it is compatible with the logic of attribution theory (Kelley, 1972). Kelley reasoned that people make attributions about other people's mental states by analyzing their behavior and the situation in which the behavior was embedded. If a target person gives money to a charity, an observer uses the behavior to conclude that the target person has a charitable disposition. However, the attribution to that particular disposition would be *discounted* if we knew that the target was wealthy, that his boss gives special perks to people who contribute to charity and that the contribution is deducted automatically from the target's paycheck. In such circumstances, an observer would be less confident about deciding that the target is a charitable person. On the other hand, if it is difficult for the target to make the contribution—perhaps he already lives at the poverty line and he must travel a good distance in order to drop off his contribution each week—then our attribution of charitableness would be *augmented* by this knowledge. We would most likely conclude that the target must be highly devoted to charity and we would be more confident in that attribution. According to Kelley, people use similar attribution logic in inferring their own internal states that they use when inferring the internal states of others. Our behavior gives us a clue about the strength of our own attitudes, but these inferences can be augmented or discounted depending on other factors.

Resisting persuasion can be a signal of attitude certainty, but it can be augmented or discounted and lead to different conclusions. Tormala and Petty (2002) asked students to read a persuasive, counterattitudinal message advocating comprehensive exams at their university. The investigators systematically manipulated the perception of the *strength* of the attacking message. Some participants were told that they were being subjected to the strongest arguments the university had to offer; others were told that they were reading weak arguments because the researchers wanted to see students' reactions to all points of view. In fact, the messages were the same in both conditions, but the ruse allowed the investigators to examine the consequences of resistance based solely on people's perception of the strength of the arguments they resisted. A control group was also run, in which participants were only asked about their attitudes toward comprehensive exams.

After reading the message advocating comprehensive exams, participants in all conditions were asked about their attitudes and the certainty with which they held them. Control participants and the experimental participants expressed attitudes opposed to instituting comprehensive exams. Figure 8.2 shows the results of how certain the participants were about those attitudes. The figure shows that people who resisted an argument they believed was strong became more certain of their original opinion than the control group and more certain than people who believed the arguments were weak.

In a subsequent research study, Tormala and Petty (2004) exposed people to a counterattitudinal message and asked them to write down any counterarguments that came to their minds as they read the message. The experimenters told some of the participants that their counterarguments were very strong compared to the arguments generated by most students. The other half of the participants was told that their arguments were quite weak. The results showed no attitude change as a function of the message. Students in both groups resisted persuasion from the essay. However, when students were led to believe that they had generated only weak counterarguments in response to the attacking message, they became *less* certain of their initial opinion. The observation that they could only generate weak responses to the attack caused participants to discount the confidence with which they held their initial opinion.

Another reason to discount how certain we are about our attitudes is our conclusion about why we resisted a persuasive message. Earlier in this chapter, we mentioned that people have a loose hierarchy of resistance strategies. At the low end

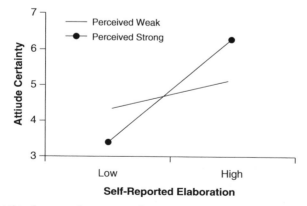

FIGURE 8.2 *Attitude certainty as a function of perceived message strength and self-reported elaboration.*

Source: Tormala, Z. L., & Petty, R. E. (2004). Source credibility and attitude certainty: A metacognitive analysis of resistance to persuasion. *Journal of Consumer Psychology, 14*(4), 427–442. Reprinted with permission.

of the hierarchy is source derogation—i.e., resisting a communication by assassinating the source's character or knowledge, and at the high end is actively counterarguing the substance of the message. Tormala, DeSensi and Petty (2007) had students read a message with which they disagreed. They led some of their participants to believe that only a minority of students supported the policy and led the other participants to believe that a majority supported the policy. When participants were led to believe that they had resisted the communication because only a minority of students held that position and that ignoring the minority was an illegitimate strategy to resist persuasion, the participants showed lower confidence in their initial position. Although they had resisted an influence attempt, their metacognitive interpretation led them to discount their resistance. They decided that their reliance on an illegitimate resistance strategy implied less confidence in their original opinion.

Like the relationship of resistance to self-control, the relationship between resistance and attitude certainty is reciprocal and interestingly complex. Certainty about one's attitude leads to greater resistance through its impact on attitude strength. On the other hand, resisting persuasion generally causes increases in certainty, but that conclusion can be tempered in fascinating ways by how the resistance is interpreted.

SUMMARY AND CONCLUSION

There is ample reason for people to try to maintain their attitudes in the face of the myriad influences to which we are exposed. From friendly conversations to political and commercial advertisements, we are buffeted by an array of persuasion, propaganda and influence attempts. The stability of the way we view the world makes it important for us to resist persuasion. And we do.

Resistance is defined as an active process by which one defends one's belief against attack. Resistance is motivated by processes that include cognitive consistency, which is the notion that people prefer their attitudes to fit with each other. Being persuaded to change one's attitude has the potential to create inconsistencies with other attitudes and behaviors. Resistance is also motivated by reactance, which has the ironic effect of increasing or decreasing persuasion, depending on the freedom that is threatened. Resisting the effects of censorship, for example, is interpretable in terms of reactance.

While there are many techniques to enact resistance, including strategies to buffer against it in advance through inoculation and forewarning, research has identified counterarguing as the most effective strategy to resist persuasion and derogating the source is one of the least effective.

Resistance requires the expenditure of psychological resources and self-regulation. If those resources are diminished due to prior effort or individual differences, resistance becomes difficult. Similarly, resistance comes at a cost to self-regulation. The act of resisting persuasion uses a person's self-regulatory resources, diminishing the ability to use those resources on other tasks. As we have seen throughout this book, our attitudes serve important functions and help guide our ultimate behavior. Knowledge of how to deal with information that helps us to secure and modify our attitudes while nonetheless protecting them from inappropriate influences may be among the most important lessons from research on attitudes.

CHAPTER 9

Implicit Measurement of Attitudes

In Chapter 1, we noted that attitude research began in earnest when L. L. Thurstone declared that "attitudes can be measured" and then proceeded to describe a method for doing so. We referred to Thurstone's method as an example of an explicit assessment of an attitude. Although assessed meticulously with carefully designed opinion items, his scale—like the Likert and Semantic Differential scales—ultimately requires a person to select a response that accords with his or her attitude. Thurstone was aware that situations might exist that make people hesitant to state their attitudes. His remedy was twofold: the first is to phrase items in a way that would avoid the appearance of there being a correct or socially approved answer and the second was to administer the scale in a social context that assured anonymity.

Social life does not always comport with Thurstone's prescription as the way to secure truthful evaluations of objects. Why might people use attitude scales in ways that do not accurately reflect their underlying evaluations? We briefly pointed to some of the reasons in Chapter 1. A person might believe that her attitude is socially unacceptable or undesirable (Edwards, 1957). One individual may feel negatively toward a law to help new immigrants become citizens but may not want to admit it on an attitude scale. Guaranteeing anonymity may help to allay her concern, but she may also be hesitant to admit the attitude even to herself. Another individual may be willing to express an anti-immigrant attitude in the context of a conservative political meeting but less willing to do so in the context of a university forum. Motivations to distort private evaluations in public contexts include altering behaviors within experimental contexts to match predicted experimenter expectations (demand characteristics; Orne, 1962), worrying about how one is being evaluated by the researcher—i.e., "evaluation apprehension" (Rosenberg, 1965)—or managing one's impression in front of the researcher (Tedeschi et al., 1971).

"BOGUS PIPELINE" MEASUREMENTS: OVERCOMING RESISTANCE TO REPORT

People's reluctance to report an attitude can be overcome if they believe that the researcher already knows their true evaluation of an attitude object. Imagine the person who is reluctant to report her attitude about an immigration law for fear that it will be taken as a sign of prejudice or closed-mindedness. As she considers her options on a Likert scale, she quickly balances her initial, negative response to the law with considerations of the appearance of prejudice. She assesses a number of social factors, including the researcher's ability to see the mark she is about to place on the scale and a number of personal factors such as her own desire to be a consistently fair-minded person. She balances all considerations and chooses a number. There is every likelihood that it will be a different number than the one that initially came to mind when thinking about the immigration law.

One way to overcome the effect of social desirability and self-presentation concerns when assessing attitudes on sensitive issues is to use indirect measures that are difficult to for people to control. In Chapter 1, we considered a number of possible indicants of physiological approaches to measuring people's attitudes, including the dilation of their pupils (Hess, 1965), and the movement of their facial muscles into smiles and frowns (Cacioppo & Petty, 1981c; Vanman, Paul, Ito, & Miller, 1997). Other research has examined amygdala responses in the brain using functional magnetic resonance imaging (fMRI; Phelps et al., 2000; for more detail, see Chapter 10), and cardiovascular reactivity (Blascovich, Mendes, Hunter, Lickel, & Kowai-Bel, 2001). As we shall discuss in Chapter 10, obtaining such data is important, but it has been difficult to provide a metric with which the physiological data can serve as a reliable and general measure of attitudes.

A different approach to bypass the social desirability issue is to use a physiological device that is bogus rather than real. Jones and Sigall (1971) used the term "bogus pipeline" to refer to a series of measures that purport to be able to measure attitudes with the use of a machine that taps into people's physiological responses. Cooper (1971) used such a machine to assess participants' liking for another person. He told participants about a "differentiated galvanic skin response machine" that was much like a lie detector, but could be used to assess the direction and intensity of people's true responses. Participants were connected to the DGSR, and were asked to predict what the machine was already telling the investigator about their true attitude toward the target person. Of course, there is no such machine, but people's belief in its validity resulted in relatively honest assessments.

Sigall and Page (1971) used a bogus pipeline procedure to assess participants' attitudes toward stigmatized others. Their study focused on people's evaluations of the physically handicapped. They arranged an experimental situation in which a confederate of the experimenter, posing as another participant in the study, acted obnoxiously toward the participant. For half of the participants, the confederate was physically handicapped; for the other half, the confederate was not. The experimenter then introduced what he described as an "adapted electromyograph" machine which, like the DGSR of Cooper's (1971) study, was capable of reading people's true reaction toward a stimulus object. In order to convince people of the machine's ability to read their attitudes, the experimenter asked the participants a series of attitude questions. Rather than ask the participants to respond, the experimenter allegedly read the responses that the adapted EMG machine provided. To the participants' amazement, the machine accurately read the participants responses to a wide variety of items. What the participants did not know was that the experimenter had access to a questionnaire that the participants had filled out earlier, and the attitudes the machine allegedly read via EMG output were simply the experimenter's reading of the participants' explicit attitudes as measured by the earlier questionnaire.

At the conclusion of the experiment, participants were asked about their attitudes toward the obnoxious confederate. The researchers had two predictions. First, people would be reluctant to admit that they did not like a fellow student, even if he had been unnecessarily obnoxious during the experiment. A control group of participants had been in the same experiment without the bogus pipeline procedure and were asked to report their attitudes on an explicit Likert-type measure. Sigall and Page found that participants were reluctant to report negative attitudes about the confederate on the explicit measure, especially when the confederate was handicapped. However, when 'predicting' what they thought the EMG machine could directly measure, people reported their negative attitudes toward the handicapped. A second study reported by Sigall and Page (1971) showed similar results regarding White American students' attitudes toward Black Americans. The bogus pipeline studies reveal that people report different attitudes in sensitive situations, presumably because their belief in the validity of the measure allows people to bypass their social desirability concerns.

Implicit Attitude Measurement

We typically think we know what our attitudes are, but do we? Nisbett and Wilson (1977) have shown that we are remarkably poor at knowing the causes of our own behavior. We believe that our introspections reveal the process that leads us to behave, to think and to evaluate, but our introspections are more flawed than accurate. This raises the intriguing possibility that flawed introspection not only fails to reveal causal processes in our thinking, but also fails to show us our true evaluations of stimulus objects in our environment. That is, we may err when reporting our attitudes because we do not always have total access to those attitudes. Measures such as the bogus pipeline can help alleviate our unwillingness to report socially sensitive attitudes, but would not help assess attitudes to which people have only limited access.

The possibility that we do not always have total access to our attitudes is supported by well-established phenomena in other areas of psychology, such as research in the field of memory. As seen in many cognitive psychology experiments, people can see a list of words, report no recollection of the words on the list at a later time, but still show faster reaction times for word strings that are related to the words they had seen. Although memory for the word affects subsequent judgments, when asked explicitly, people report no memory trace for the words whatsoever. Such memories are referred to as *implicit memories* (Roediger, 1990). The parallel to attitudes is the possibility that people may have evaluations of objects stored in memory but have no conscious awareness of those evaluations. If the attitude is stored without awareness, it is unlikely to be measured accurately on a Likert, Thurstone, or Semantic Differential scale, which ask respondents for their explicit evaluations, nor will they be revealed on bogus pipeline measures that rely on the assumption that people are aware of their true attitudes. The development of techniques known as *implicit measures* provided a new way to examine attitudes that people are either unwilling or unable to report accurately on conventional explicit attitude scales.

Implicit Measures and Automaticity

Implicit measures of attitudes take advantage of the psychology of automaticity, which Bargh (1994) characterizes as a group of processes that function outside of conscious awareness, require little cognitive resources, and cannot be consciously controlled (started or stopped). For example, a substantial program of research on spontaneous trait inferences (Uleman, Newman, & Moskowitz, 1996) has shown that people automatically make inferences about others' traits and characteristics after simply observing their behaviors. These trait inferences occur without observers intending to make them, and without necessarily being aware that they are occurring. As Uleman et al. (1994) note, we are "inveterate" in our "scanning (of) the world around us . . . reading its meaning" (p.212)—our practiced mind cannot help but to automatically infer meaning into our environments.

The fact that there are conditions that facilitate our making judgments about ourselves and others implicitly and automatically raises the possibility that our attitudes can also be expressed automatically. A pioneering study by Gaertner and McLaughlin (1983) made use of automatic attitude expression to study White American students' attitudes toward stereotypes of Black Americans. A series of studies using explicit attitude measurements had shown the presence (Katz & Braly, 1933) and later reduction (Karlins, Coffman, & Walters, 1969) in negative stereotypes over the decades. As we have seen, explicit measurements of sensitive issues may reveal a combination of attitudes and other downstream processes, such as social desirability and self-presentation. Gaertner and McLaughlin (1983) sought an alternate measure that avoided those downstream consequences. They adopted a finding from a study in people's cognitive ability to recognize word patterns. Meyer and Schvaneveldt (1971) had asked participants to decide, as quickly as possible, whether a string of letters constituted a real English language word or whether they were just nonsense letters that did not comprise a word. Participants were shown two strings simultaneously. For example, in one condition, the string of letters APPLE and the string KUPOD appeared together and participants needed to judge that at least one of the strings did not constitute a word. In two other conditions, both strings did constitute real words. In one of those conditions, the words were related semantically (i.e., BREAD/BUTTER) while in a second condition, the words were real but not highly associated with each other (DOCTOR/BUTTER). Meyer and Schvaneveldt found that participants were much faster at the task when the words were real, but even faster when the words were semantically related (BREAD/BUTTER) than when they were not. The researchers concluded that people's quick reaction time was a result of their accessing words from memory and that the semantic association between the words implicitly facilitated the memory search.

Gaertner and McLaughlin reasoned that *evaluative* associations would create faster word recognitions in the same way that semantic associations created faster recognition in Meyer and Schvaneveldt's study. Moreover, just as people did not have to think consciously about the association between bread and butter, so too would the evaluative associations facilitate responding speed without conscious thought or control—i.e., automatically. Adapting the methodology from the recognition study to the study of stereotypes, Gaertner and McLaughlin paired evaluatively positive and negative words (e.g., 'lazy' or 'smart') with the social groups 'White' and 'Black.' They reasoned that if people generally associated the word 'smart' more with Whites than with Blacks, the smart/White combination would be recognized as real words more rapidly than the smart/Black pairing. Similarly, negative stereotypes toward Blacks might be revealed by faster recognition of lazy/Black than lazy/White. Overall, the results showed that White participants were more likely to associate positive evaluations with Whites, but were not more likely to pair negative evaluations with Blacks. The results of the study indicated that Whites' stereotypes of Blacks were indeed changing, but only subtly. Whites were ascribing less stereotypically negative traits to Blacks but, importantly, were withholding ascribing positive characteristics. They reserved positive evaluations for their own group. Their findings supported a growing body of work (e.g., Crosby et al., 1980; Gaertner, 1976; Gaertner & Dovidio, 1981; Katz, 1970) suggesting that a subtler form of racism, based on affective and associative components, underlies contemporary stereotyping and prejudice.

The Evaluative Priming Measure

Methodologically, Gaertner and McLaughlin's study showed that evaluatively consistent concepts facilitated response speed. Pairing a positive trait with a positively evaluated group made the trait word easier to recognize; a mismatched evaluation made the word more difficult to recognize. The facilitation and interference were automatic in the sense that they did not occur consciously nor did people intend for their evaluation of social groups to affect their recognition of the trait words. In a study discussed in Chapter 2, Fazio, Sanbonmatsu, Powell and Kardes (1986) went a step beyond Gaertner and McLaughlin's approach by showing that stronger attitudes facilitated recognition of an adjective that was evaluatively paired with an object. The stronger the attitude, the more rapidly people can categorize an evaluatively similar adjective into categories of good or bad. If a person has a positive attitude toward chocolate and then is shown a positive adjective such as 'smart,' the person is quicker at categorizing 'smart' as a positive adjective than he or she would be to categorize an evaluatively discordant adjective, such as 'hostile,' as negative. Moreover, the stronger the attitude is toward the object (i.e., if the person *really* likes chocolate), the more it facilitates categorization.

Fazio, Jackson, Dunton and Williams (1995c) converted these findings to one of the most well-known implicit measures to assess sensitive attitudes. The *evaluative priming measure* (EPM), originally introduced into the literature as a "bona fide pipeline," uses the automatic facilitation created by a primed attitude object (e.g., Blacks vs. Whites) to assess people's attitudes toward those groups. The dependent measure in the EPM is the latency with which an adjective is categorized as evaluatively good or bad, following presentation of the primed attitude object. The more rapid the recognition, the more indicative it is of the participant's attitude toward the prime. Because of its importance as an implicit measure, we will describe the experimental phases that comprise the EPM in the context of racial attitudes.

The procedure is generally described to participants as a series of tasks designed to study word meaning as an automatic skill. In the first phase, participant's response latencies are measured as they categorize a series of adjectives (e.g., 'likeable,' 'awful') as good or bad. The second phase is presented as a face-learning task: participants are shown a series of headshots on a computer screen and asked to study them. In the third phase, they are presented with a face and asked to recognize whether or not they had seen the face in the prior phase. The fourth phase contains the measure that will serve as the implicit assessment of racial attitudes. Participants are told that the previous tasks will now be combined in order to study the degree to which word-meaning skills are truly automatic. To the extent that word-learning skills are automatic, they should not be affected by doing multiple tasks simultaneously.

The simultaneous tasks are the word learning (i.e., categorizing the adjectives as good or bad) and face learning. To this end, participants are presented with a Black or White face, which is followed by an evaluative adjective. The latency of response to whether the adjective is good or bad is presumed to be affected by the evaluation of the face. To the extent that people have more positive evaluations of Whites than Blacks, then their categorizing positive adjectives as positive should be quicker following a White prime than a Black prime, measured as a change in their response latencies from the first phase of the procedure. Similarly, negative evaluations of White faces should lead to quicker categorization of negative adjectives as bad and slower categorization of positive adjectives as good. A score that considers the effect size of the response latencies is then calculated, with greater negativity toward Blacks and positivity toward Whites yielding a negative attitude score, and the opposite pattern of positivity toward Blacks and negativity toward Whites yielding a positive score.

The scores that people obtain on the evaluative priming measure are not produced consciously from memory and are not affected by what people believe they should say about sensitive race-related attitudes. It remains to ask how we know that the scores reflect attitudes—i.e., evaluations of attitude objects. One way to assess the validity of implicit measures is to ascertain whether they accomplish what explicit measures accomplish. In Chapter 2 and Chapter 5, we noted that, with certain caveats, strong attitudes typically predict people's behavior. Considerable research has shown that people's scores on race-related EPMs do indeed predict their racial behavior and judgments. For example, in the Fazio et al. (1995) study in which the EPM was developed, participants were debriefed by a Black experimenter. After chatting for several minutes, the experimenter provided ratings of her impressions of each participant's interest, friendliness, eye contact and physical distance. The results showed that the experimenter's perceptions of the participants' friendliness were predicted by the participants' scores on the EPM (see Table 9.1). The more the EPM indicated negative evaluations of Black people, the more unfriendly they seemed to the experimenter.

Olson and Fazio (2007) administered the EPM to participants in a study on committee selection procedures. They were asked to serve as members of a committee evaluating job applicants for the Peace Corps. They reviewed school transcripts, an interview summary, work history and a personal statement. In the comparison of interest, two dossiers were created to instantiate a moderately qualified Black candidate and a moderately qualified White candidate. Participants rated each applicant on a number of dimensions, including their likeability, level of their credential and their suitability for the job. The data revealed that the EPM scores predicted people's preference for the White applicant over the similarly credentialed Black applicant: The more prejudiced the participant's index of automatic attitudes was, the more likely he or she was to evaluate the White candidate's dossier more favorably and to choose the White candidate for the job.

In a direct test of the predictive validity of EPM-derived measures, Towles-Schwen and Fazio (2006) recruited White college freshman who had been randomly paired

TABLE 9.1   *Correlation Matrix of Variables*

VARIABLE	1	2	3	4	5	6
1. Unobtrusive estimate	—					
2. Modern racism level	.15	—				
3. Interaction rating	.31**	−.09	—			
4. Rodney King verdict	−.06	−.53***	.02	—		
5. Responsibility	.32*	−.41***	.26*	.52***	—	
6. Attractiveness	.18	−.35***	.07	.39***	.20	—

Note. Higher scores on the unobtrusive estimate, the interaction rating, the verdict, and the responsibility and attractiveness measures reflect a more favorable response to Blacks. Higher scores on the modern racism level variable reflect a more negative response.
*p<.10. **p<.05. ***p<.0l.
Source: Fazio, R. H., Jackson, J. R., Dunton, B. C., & Williams, C. J. (1995). Variability in automatic activation as an unobtrusive measure of racial attitudes: A bona fide pipeline? *Journal of Personality and Social Psychology, 69*(6), 1013. Reprinted with permission.

with a Black roommate. The researchers collected two measures over the course of the semester: an EPM measuring implicit racial attitudes toward Blacks at the beginning of the semester, and a series of self-report measures after 15 weeks. At the end of the academic year, the researchers collected information from the university housing office as to if—and if so, when—the roommate pair stopped being roommates. Whereas neither concern for acting prejudiced (r(54) = .09), nor restraint to avoid dispute (r(54) = .03), significantly predicted splitting up, EPM implicit racial attitudes did, r(55) = .30, p < .03. These data show that, while explicit motivations to control prejudice and maintain relationships did not predict actual relationship maintenance, implicit racial attitudes—as measured by the EPM—did.

The Implicit Association Test

Although there are many contemporary measures of implicit attitudes—including the Go/No-Go Association Task (Nosek & Banaji, 2001), the Extrinsic Affective Simon Task (De Houwer, 2003), and the Affective/Evaluative Priming Task (Fazio, Jackson, Dunton, & Williams, 1995)—no single measure has gained the same level of proliferation and debate as the Implicit Association Test (IAT; Greenwald, McGhee & Schwarz, 1998; Greenwald, Nosek, & Banaji, 2003; Nosek, Greenwald, & Banaji, 2005; Greenwald, Poehlman, Uhlmann, & Banaji, 2009). At the time of writing, a search of the scholarly sources finds over 6,000 citations of Greenwald, McGhee and Schwartz's (1998) original article. Its use extends into many different and divergent areas of social psychology, including, but not limited to, prejudice and stereotyping (Baron & Banaji, 2006), self-esteem (Greenwald & Farnham, 2000), voting behaviors (Greenwald et al., 2009), identity (Knowles & Peng, 2005) and attitude-behavior discrepancies (Dovidio et al., 1997). This last area of study, in particular, represents relevant questions not only to the broader social problems addressed by studies using the IAT, but also to the study of implicit attitudes as well.

The best way to understand the IAT is to actually take the test, offered online through Harvard's Project Implicit (implicit.harvard.edu). Theoretically, the IAT's basic premise is to measure the difficulty a respondent experiences in pairing two psychological constructs—such as 'male' and 'science,' or 'male' and 'liberal arts'—to a single behavioral response (a keyboard press). See Figure 9.1 below for an example trial from a Project Implicit race IAT.

Experientially, the IAT ties in directly to the automatic evaluative reaction structure of implicit attitudes. Imagine two individuals experiencing a set of formative experiences in early childhood: Going to a petting zoo and watching a movie. The first individual has a wonderful time feeding the goats at the petting zoo, but

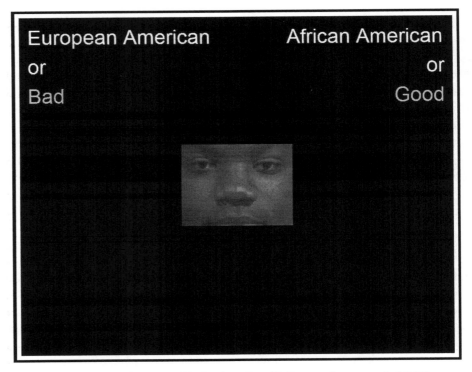

FIGURE 9.1 *Image of Harvard's Project Implicit running a racial IAT.*

a terrible time watching the movie *Arachnophobia*. The second individual has quite the opposite experience, enjoying a viewing of *Charlotte's Web*, but having a terrible time at the petting zoo due to a particularly aggressive and hungry goat. If you were to ask both individuals to respond, as quickly as they can, with an animal with which they have a positive and a negative evaluation, this will likely net responses of "goats and spiders" and "spiders and goats," respectively, from the individuals. That is to say, the first individual has an easier time associating goats with positivity and spiders with negativity, whereas the second individual has an easier time with the opposite.

Now imagine bringing both individuals into an experiment where the experimenter will show pictures of goats, spiders, positive words ('happy,' 'joy') and negative words ('sullen,' 'sad'), and ask the respondents to raise either their left or right hand depending on the stimuli. For the first block of trials, the individuals must raise their right hand if they see pictures of goats or positive words, and their left hand if they see pictures of spiders or negative words. Doing so requires the individuals to associate the response categories of 'goats' and 'positivity' to one distinct behavior, and 'spiders' and 'negativity' to another distinct behavior. For the first individual, there is no issue: Goats already hold a positive association from the earlier formative experience. The second individual, however, finds issue making this association due to the pre-existing association between goats and a negative formative experience. When the first stimulus, a picture of a goat, is presented, the second individual finds greater difficulty in making a correct behavior, whereas the first individual finds no such difficulty. As each stimulus is presented, the second individual must fight the pre-existing association between goats and negativity, and spiders and positivity, which are incongruent with the behaviors required for the experiment.

After several trials, the next block begins, with goats and negative words requiring raising one's left hand, and spiders and positive words requiring raising one's right hand. This time, the pattern is reversed, with the first individual struggling to perform the same behavior when two concepts, unrelated in her mind, are paired to the same behavior—on the other hand, the second individual performs quick, accurate responses due to her pre-existing association consistent with the experiment's instructions.

At the end of the experiment, the reaction time and error rate for each individual is compared between the two different blocks—that is, participants are compared against themselves. The first individual responded quicker and more accurately on the first block relative to the second, whereas the second individual responded quicker and more accurately on the second block relative to the first. Such a pattern of data would support the conclusion that the first individual has a stronger association between goats and positivity and spiders and negativity, as compared to goats and negativity and spiders and positivity; the second individual, on the other hand, shows the reverse pattern. Each individual's ability to respond to one set of pairings versus the other is facilitated by the closeness, or inhibited by the distance, of their implicit associations. The IAT measures precisely this difference, using keyboard response times instead of hand-raising.

In its current incarnation (Greenwald, Nosek, & Banaji, 2003), the IAT uses seven blocks of trials (see Table 9.2), covering the different combinations of stimuli pairing and including several practice blocks. Much in the same way as our spiders and goats example above, participants are asked to categorize stimuli presented on a computer screen, based on provided labels, using one of two keyboard responses indicating either the left or right side of the screen.

Take, for example, a classic race IAT measuring implicit associations of valance (positive and negative words) toward different races (Black and White faces). In the first block of trials, which provides practice for categorizing the face stimuli, participants are presented Black and White faces, which, as per Table 9.2, they must categorize a left- or right-key response, respectively. The second block of trials serves the same purpose and proceeds in the same manner, except that the face stimuli are replaced with pleasant and unpleasant words. The third block, which serves as an identical practice for the critical test block 4, pairs two sets of stimuli, such as Black

TABLE 9.2 *Breakdown of Blocks for the Implicit Association Test Using the Adaptations from Greenwald, Nosek, & Banaji, 2003*

BLOCK	NO. OF TRIALS	FUNCTION	ITEM(S) ASSIGNED TO LEFT-KEY RESPONSE	ITEM(S) ASSIGNED TO RIGHT-KEY RESPONSE
1	20	Practice	Faces of Blacks	Faces of Whites
2	20	Practice	Pleasant words	Unpleasant words
3	20	Practice	Faces of Blacks + Pleasant words	Faces of Whites + Unpleasant words
4	40	Test	Faces of Blacks + Pleasant words	Faces of Whites + Unpleasant words
5	20	Practice	Faces of Whites	Faces of Blacks
6	20	Practice	Faces of Whites + Pleasant words	Faces of Blacks + Unpleasant words
7	40	Test	Faces of Whites + Pleasant words	Faces of Blacks + Unpleasant words

Source: Adapted from Greenwald, A.G., Nosek, B.A., & Banaji, M.R. (2003). Understanding and using the implicit association test: I. An improved scoring algorithm. *Journal of Personality and Social Psychology, 85*(2), 197. Reprinted with permission.

faces and pleasant words, to a single behavioral response—a left-key response. The right-key response, on the other hand, is tied to both White faces and unpleasant words. In such blocks, participants are shown both faces and words throughout the trials and asked to categorize them as quickly and accurately as possible. Block 5 serves as a replication of block 1 but with the response keys flipped—White faces on a left-key response and Black faces on a right-key response. Block 6, which again serves as an identical practice for block 7, flips the pairings of faces and words. White faces and pleasant words are tied to one key press, while Black faces and unpleasant words are tied to the other key press.

The scoring algorithm (Greenwald, Nosek, & Banaji, 2003) used for the IAT compares the response latency between the critical test blocks (blocks 4 and 7 above), after a series of calculations. Excessively slow (> 10 seconds) or fast (<300 milliseconds) responses are excluded based on the reasoning that they do not reflect a conscious, timely response that would be informative to implicit associations existing in one's memory. Error trials have their times replaced with the mean response latency for correct trials in that block. Finally, the critical blocks are compared directly, after taking into account performance on the practice trials. At its core, the IAT score compares a participant's reaction times in blocks 4 and 7—that is, the two blocks featuring both sets of stimuli with counterbalanced pairings. Faster reaction times (and fewer errors) are taken to indicate stronger implicit association in one's memory of those sets of pairings (typically White/good and Black/bad). The stronger the implicit association, the researchers argue, the stronger the attitude—such as a pro-White or anti-Black implicit bias.

In addition to the standard IAT and the IAT's many theoretical variants, which we will discuss later, there is also a procedure for a **brief IAT** developed by Sriram and Greenwald (2009). Like many psychological tools, the IAT was developed to be robust and thorough in measuring its psychological attribute; also like many such tools, research and practice has informed researchers that a full incarnation is not necessary for achieving valid results. Sriram and Greenwald proposed a variant of the IAT in large part designed to cut down on the number of blocks and trials (from 7 blocks and 180 trials to 2 blocks and 80 trials) required of participants. Although not without its criticisms (Friese & Fiedler, 2010; Rothermund & Wentura, 2010), the brief IAT is a viable alternative to the full IAT when assessing attitudes implicitly.

Validity of the IAT

How valid an assessment is an IAT score? One indicator is whether the IAT aligns with cultural expectations about how groups are evaluated. Race-related IATs comport with the observation that prejudice and racism are alive in subtle forms. IAT scores of White participants show that that Whites are considerably faster at responding to the pairing of Black with unpleasant than with the pairing of Black and pleasant (Greenwald et al., 1998). Additional research using what may be called the known-group paradigm provides data showing that people have more implicit negative attitudes toward outgroups relative to their own ingroups. Jewish and Christian participants showed more positive evaluations of their own religious ingroup compared to the outgroup (Rudman, Greenwald, Mellott, & Schwartz, 1999) and Japanese Americans and Korean Americans showed more positive IAT scores for their own group relative to the outgroup (Greenwald et al., 1998). Agerström and Rooth (2009) found IAT-based bias for Swedish men over Arab-Muslim men, and the difference correlated with a decreased probability of inviting the latter as actual job interviewees. Swanson, Rudman and Greenwald (2001) used the IAT to reveal negative attitudes about vegetarians. Ashburn-Nado, Voils and Montith (2001) found anti-outgroup bias on the IAT directed against arbitrarily created minimal groups—groups ostensibly based on some criterion such as shared artistic preference, but, in actuality, assigned randomly.

Considerably less research has examined differences in behavior as a function of differences in IAT scores. In other words, in addition to showing that certain known groups are favored or disfavored on the IAT, do differences in individual IAT scores predict differences in relevant behavior? An intriguing study by McConnell and Leibold (2001) provided such data. The study was designed to test the IAT's ability to predict behaviors in social interactions, while also comparing it to several other metrics. Participants arrived at the lab, ostensibly for a study on word perception, and were greeted by a White female experimenter. Covertly, they were both video and audio recorded throughout the experiment. The experimenter asked participants to pull up a chair, after which she asked several interview questions and told a scripted joke before instructing participants to fill out a questionnaire booklet. Following completion of the questionnaires, participants completed a standard Black/White IAT. Then a new experimenter—this time a Black female—was introduced after completion. The new experimenter repeated steps similar to the first (chair ➔ questions ➔ joke) and the experiment ended.

Afterward, the various materials collected during the study were compiled to form several measures. The two experimenters rated their interactions with each participant on overall measures of the ease and friendliness of the interactions. They also rated their recollections of specific behaviors such as the participants' eye contact, speech errors and smiles. Judges observed the video and audio recordings of the interactions and made similar molar and micro judgments of the participants' behavior. The correlations between the IAT scores and the ratings are presented in Table 9.3. The data showed a strong relationship between pro-White IAT bias and Black/White discrepancy on several behavioral markers of discrimination. In particular, those participants with greater pro-White IAT bias demonstrated greater smiling, fewer speech errors and less speech hesitation when interacting with the White, as compared to the Black, experimenter. The IAT scores also showed a strong

TABLE 9.3 *Correlations between IAT, Explicit Measures of Prejudice, Experimenters' Ratings, and Judges' Molar Ratings and Assessments of Biased Participant Social Behavior*

	PREJUDICE MEASURES		SOCIAL INTERACTION BIAS RATINGS	
	IAT	EXPLICIT	EXPERIMENTERS'	MOLAR
Explicit measure of prejudice	.42**			
Experimenters' ratings	.39*	.33*		
Judges' molar ratings	.34*	.26	.41**	
Biased participant social behaviors				
Forward leaning (.64***)	−.26	.12	.05	−.08
Facing experimenter (.77***)	−.03	−.08	.31*	−.03
Body openness (.47**)	.17	.02	.20	.43**
Expressiveness (.60***)	.09	−.20	.00	.25
Eye contact (.35*)	.25	.20	.20	.55***
Seating distance (.69***)	.26	.14	.31*	.15
Speaking time (.85***)	.51**	.18	.41**	.30
Smiling (.71***)	.39*	.21	.15	.28
Speech errors (.53***)	.42*	.05	.14	−.03
Speech hesitation (.53***)	.35*	.13	−.07	.11
Fidgeting (.42**)	−.06	−.15	.00	.02
Laughter at joke (.56***)	.19	.03	.27	.35*
Social comments (.46**)	.32*	.02	.12	.44**

Note. All measures are coded such that larger, positive values reflect relatively more positive attitudes and behaviors toward Whites in comparison to Blacks. Values in parentheses indicate interjudge correlations. $N = 41$.
*$p < .05$.
**$p < .01$.
***$p < .001$.
Source: McConnell, A.R., & Leibold, J.M. (2001). Relations among the Implicit Association Test, discriminatory behavior, and explicit measures of racial attitudes. *Journal of Experimental Social Psychology, 37*(5), 435–442. Reprinted with permission.

relationship with the molar ratings of both the judges and the experimenters. In addition, the participants had filled out a number of explicit measures of prejudice. Although the explicit measures correlated significantly with the IAT scores, only the IAT scores—and not the explicit prejudice scores—predicted the specific and the molar behavioral responses. It is also interesting to note that the behaviors the judges and experimenters noted were substantially those that one might call 'spontaneous,' insofar as they are behaviors which people rarely (if ever) deliberately control. One hardly intends to make speech errors or avoid eye contact when talking with someone—instead, they happen spontaneously, beyond our intention or control.

The major results of McConnell and Leibold's study have been replicated conceptually in a number of domains in addition to racial prejudice. For example, Asendorpf, Banse and Mücke (2002) had participants complete both an explicit measure of shyness, as well as a shyness IAT (with anchors on shy/nonshy and me/other) after being observed in a shyness-inducing situation. They found behavioral prediction in line with previously reported results, such that explicit self-reports of shyness uniquely predicted only controlled shyness behavior and the implicit IAT scores uniquely predicted spontaneous shyness behavior. Perugini (2005) added additional evidence in a study measuring preferences of snacks versus fruits, finding that explicit attitudes predicted self-reports of past behavioral choices (controlled), and IAT scores predicted in-the-moment choices between actually receiving snacks or fruit (spontaneous). Rudolph, Schroder-Abe, Riketta and Schutz (2010) found a similar pattern when examining the predictive validity of implicit and explicit self-esteem measures.

This pattern of behavior has been described as a **double dissociation** between implicit and explicit measures (Asendorpf, Banse, & Mücke, 2002; Perugini, 2005; Greenwald & Nosek, 2009). Although much of the research examining this double dissociation uses the IAT in demonstrating its implicit components, it is not unique to the IAT in any way. For processes or constructs to be doubly dissociated is to say that neither affects the others' functioning or downstream influence. As shown in the research described above, attitudes measured explicitly are more likely to predict or determine controlled behaviors while attitudes measured implicitly are more likely to predict or determine spontaneous behaviors.

Evidence supporting this conclusion comes from a 2009 meta-analytic review by Greenwald, Poehlman, Uhlmann and Banaji that reviewed 122 studies encompassing nearly 15,000 participants. They found, on average, a moderate correlation between IAT scores and behavior (.27), but a slightly higher average correlation between behaviors and self-report measures (.36). However, for socially sensitive topics, self-report measures demonstrated a significant decrease in correlation not mirrored by IAT scores. IAT scores further demonstrated greater predictive validity for instances of interracial interaction behaviors. From Greenwald et al.'s (2009) analysis, both IAT scores and self-report measures provide a unique contribution with respect to predictive validity, but IAT measures are more robust to self-presentational concerns on the part of the participant.

CONCERNS ABOUT THE IAT

The IAT has been one of the most commonly employed technique for measuring attitudes implicitly—and arguably the most controversial. It has provided a window into people's automatic evaluations of categories relative to other categories (i.e., Black vs. White; straights vs. gays; men vs. women). Although widely used, it has not escaped criticism conceptually and methodologically. We will briefly sketch some of those criticisms.

Predictive Validity

As we have already seen, the IAT has been successful finding evaluative differences between known groups and between ingroups and outgroups. It has been more controversial in its ability to predict behaviors on the basis of *differences* in IAT scores. The McConnell and Leibold (2001) study is an example of successful prediction (see also Ziegert & Hanges, 2005). On the other hand, studies using a similar approach have failed to find differences (Karpinski & Hilton, 2001). Fazio and Olson (2002) point to the possibility that the measurement sequence used in studies such as McConnell & Leibold's may have facilitated the strong correlations between the IAT measurement and behaviors. That is, administering the IAT immediately prior to the interaction with a Black experimenter may have resulted in the conscious activation of racial attitudes.

Blanton and his colleagues have been skeptical of the data analyses that have been offered as support for the predictive validity of the IAT (Blanton & Jaccard, 2008; Blanton, Jaccard, Gonzales, & Christie, 2006). Blanton, Jaccard, Klick, Mellers, Mitchell and Tetlock (2009) re-analyzed McConnell and Leibold's data (as well as the data for Ziegert & Hanges, 2005) and disputed the conclusions—and, importantly, the implications about predictive validity—of the original researchers. In a meta-analytic review of the IAT literature, Oswald, Mitchell, Blanton, Jaccard and Tetlock (2013) assessed the predictive validity of the IAT across 46 reports, which used 86 different samples. Their targets were six different criterion categories typically used when examining the IAT's predictive validity: Interpersonal behaviors, person perception, policy preferences, microbehaviors, response times (such as seen in the shooter bias experiments) and brain activity. Their analysis found that the IAT was only a significant predictor of brain activity, and that the measure tended to fare no better than explicit measures (such as feeling thermometers or the Modern Racism Scale). Oswald et al. (2013) concluded that the IAT does not embody the field's goal of an unobtrusive predictor of bias.

The questioning of the predictive validity of the IAT should not lead us to dismiss the IAT as irrelevant to behavior. Rather, it points out the widespread use of this measure that is less than two decades old and the scrutiny that such a measure bears in the field of research. In their review of the literature in 2002, Fazio and Olson concluded that, "more research on the predictive validity of the IAT is needed" (p. 310). That call for scrutiny continues to be relevant.

Personal Attitudes or Cultural Stereotypes?

The IAT assumes that when people respond to stimulus objects, they are responding with their own automatically activated attitudes. Some observers (e.g., Arkes & Tetlock, 2004; Olson & Fazio, 2004) have noted another possibility—i.e., that people are responding to categories through the vantage point of cultural stereotypes. This will be more true of some categories than others, but may be especially a problem when attitudes toward socially sensitive topics are assessed. A respondent may have her or his own response to the category 'Muslim,' but is also aware of the way the culture-at-large views Muslims. Is it a person's view of the cultural stereotype that affects the speed of categorization or is it her or his personal view?

Arkes and Tetlock (2004) argue that the IAT assesses knowledge of cultural stereotypes rather than an implicit endorsement of those stereotypes. They note a parallel in Correll, Park, Judd and Wittenbrink's (2002) research on shooter bias, which found both Black and White participants shoot at unarmed Black targets in a computer game more quickly than unarmed white targets. Correll et al. (2002) report that these results did not vary in magnitude with explicit self-reports of bias, but did vary with perceptions of cultural stereotypes—measured as estimates of prevalence of violence and dangerousness that White Americans would perceive among African Americans. Drawing on studies by Brauer and colleagues (2000) showing modest correlations between implicit and explicit measures, Arkes and Tetlock suggest that implicit associations as measured through the IAT may simply demonstrate perceived cultural endorsement of stereotypes rather personal endorsement. Once again, there are arguments on both sides of the issue (see Nosek & Hansen, 2008), but the question of the impact of cultural stereotypes on the traditional IAT is an important consideration.

Olson and Fazio (2004) argued that the cultural stereotypes are only one type of extrapersonal information that can influence IAT scores. Extrapersonal information refers to any information associated with an attitude that does not contribute to a person's summary evaluation of the attitude object. We may be cognizant of information about how others feel about an attitude object and thus respond to categorical judgments with that knowledge. The information may be broad, such as a cultural stereotype, or idiosyncratic, such as knowledge that Aunt Helen strongly dislikes a particular stimulus category. I know how others feel, but if that knowledge does not enter into my own summary evaluation of the object, it is thought of as an extrapersonal consideration. Olson and Fazio's criticism of the IAT as traditionally administered is that it allows for multiple plausible meanings of the response categories ranging from cultural stereotypes to knowledge of other people's attitudes, as well as one's own summary evaluation.

In one study, Han, Olson and Fazio (2006) showed that participants took into consideration clearly inaccurate, counterattitudinal attitudes of others (an extrapersonal consideration) when responding to an IAT, but were not influenced by those considerations in any other report of their true attitude. Han, Czellar, Olson and Fazio (2010) showed that when people were primed with normative constructs, they responded to the IAT very differently than if they were primed with idiographic constructs. Before taking a Black/White race IAT, half of their participants used a rating scale to respond to how 'most people' liked a series of non-racial attitude objects such as apples, sports and teachers. Others responded idiographically by indicating their own unique attitudes toward the issue. In a later part of the procedure, participants took the IAT. The results showed that those who were primed to think normatively were indeed influenced by cultural and racial stereotypes relative to participants in the idiographic condition. One solution proposed to remedy the issue of extrapersonal associations is the use of the personalized IAT (Olson and Fazio, 2004), which we shall address later in this chapter.

The Meaning of the Comparison

Unlike other measures that examine attitudes implicitly, the IAT relies on a comparison of two known categories. The IAT is designed to assess the liking for one category *relative* to the liking of another category. If White participants receive a racial prejudice score from the IAT, it means that there was a preference for the category White over the category Black—i.e., there was less response interference combining Whites with good than Blacks with good and less response interference combining Blacks with bad than Whites with bad. These relative associations should be interpreted with caution. Showing that individuals' IAT scores are favorable to Whites does not necessarily mean that Whites dislike Blacks (Blanton et al., 2009). It shows greater favorability to Whites than Blacks, which is a different shade of meaning than concluding that the IAT score means that Whites dislike Blacks. Nosek, Banaji and Greenwald (2002) have also reported that more than half of Black participants show effects in the same direction as White participants—i.e., a relatively favorable evaluation of Whites versus Blacks when responding to the IAT. This finding has since been replicated among Blacks, with similar levels of outgroup favoritism, by Spicer and Monteith (2001, between 50%-65%) and Ashburn-Nardo, Knowles and Monteith (2003; 60%+). Furthermore, the effect has been extended to low-status versus high-status residential colleges (Lane, Mitchell, & Banaji, 2003), rich versus poor and thin versus fat (Rudman, Feinberg, & Fairchild, 2002), and academics (San Jose State University versus Stanford University; Jost, Pelham, & Carvallo, 2002). In all these cases, lower status group members showed a degree of outgroup favoritism, demonstrating that participants have an easier time matching positivity to a high status outgroup than to their own group.

Arkes and Tetlock (2004) question meaning of the comparative judgments made with the IAT somewhat differently, as misrepresenting the multi-dimensionality of the construct. Drawing on the contrasting images of Jesse Jackson—famed Black civil rights activist—and Jesse Helms—five-term Republican Senator aggressively opposed to civil rights and affirmative action—the authors draw attention to the fact that both individuals agree that Blacks are in trouble, despite disagreeing on the cause (historic oppression and exploitation versus abdication of personal responsibility, respectively). They question whether differential reaction time measures such as the IAT can reliably distinguish between these two very different associations with Blacks, despite both associating similar levels of blanket 'negativity.' While Arkes and Tetlock are more concerned with which grouping of negativity 'justifies' the label of prejudiced attitudes (i.e., unfortunate, tragic and victimized versus lazy, selfish and violent), their point serves a broader question of association content. In particular, does a White/good, Black/bad association actually imply negative prejudicial bias? The IAT, as the authors note, shows degree of *relative* rather than *absolute* associations. Consider an IAT with categories apple/orange and values good/bad, which finds greater association between apple/good and orange/bad, relative to its inverse. Compare this with a similar IAT using apples/worms and good/bad, finding the same apple/good and worms/bad pattern of results. Both IAT results suggest relatively more positive association with apples than with oranges or worms; however, the results do not suggest similar levels of negative association between oranges and worms. That is, the IAT does not serve to metric absolute positivity and negativity (important for questions of racial bias, and often the conclusions drawn in such research realms), but rather relative associations. Participants may have a positive association with oranges that is simply more negative (while still remaining positive) when compared against apples, but a strictly negative association with worms. A traditional IAT cannot distinguish between these two types of held associations.

ALTERNATIVE IMPLICIT ASSESSMENTS: BEYOND THE IAT

Although the IAT has received the most attention from scholars searching for implicit attitude assessments, other methods to assess attitudes implicitly have also been used productively. Evaluative priming (EPM) preceded the IAT and has been used frequently in research to assess attitudes implicitly. Subsequent to Greenwald et al.'s (1998) introduction of the IAT, other investigators have introduced innovations to the IAT procedure, at least partly to overcome some of the concerns that we considered in the previous section.

Affect Misattribution Procedure (AMP)

Eschewing response latencies, the **affect misattribution procedure** (Payne, Cheng, Govorun, & Steward, 2005) is based on the tendency for affect-laden primes to influence the evaluation of a neutral target presented immediately afterward (Murphy & Zajonc, 1993). Payne et al. (2005) adapted this tendency to misattribute affect-laden primes into as a method of measuring implicit attitudes. In their procedure, participants see a consciously presented prime, followed by a neutral target (a Chinese character), and finally a masking image (created with black and white noise). For each trial, participants are asked to provide a binary decision of whether the target image was pleasant or unpleasant, relative to the average pleasantness of the target images presented.

Across six studies, Payne et al. verified that the AMP is sensitive to normatively positive and negative stimuli (as primes) in influencing the evaluation of the neutral targets. They extended this effect to the domain of implicit racial attitudes, showing ingroup bias effects, as well as moderation by motivations to control prejudice. Importantly, the AMP was robust in the face of experimentally manipulated warnings to avoid bias from the valenced primes. The authors thus argue that the AMP provides a tool akin to the inkblots of old, providing researchers a method whereby participants project their implicit attitudes onto neutral stimuli, and allowing for easy measurement that resists correction.

Personalizing the IAT

As mentioned earlier, one potential source of variance in IAT scores stems from the influence of extrapersonal factors, including cultural stereotypes and knowledge of others' opinions. These extrapersonal factors are present in memory and may interfere with one's attempt to associate labels with categories in a traditional IAT. To combat the contamination of one's personal attitude with extrapersonal factors, Olson and Fazio (2004) propose a variant of the IAT—**the personalized IAT**—to eliminate the influence of normative, non-personal associations.

In studying racial attitudes, for example, both the traditional and personalized IAT require participants to categorize Black or White faces, names, etc., to either the left or the right side of the screen using different keyboard responses. However, whereas the traditional IAT requires participants to categorize universally pleasant ('happiness') or unpleasant ('sadness') words under descriptive labels ('pleasant' and 'unpleasant,' respectively), the personalized IAT takes a different approach. Instead, participants completing a personalized IAT are provided labels of 'I like this' and 'I do not like this' and asked to categorize a number of stimuli ('soda,' 'basketball,' 'shopping') according to their personal preferences. On critical blocks, participants must associate black stimuli with a button press for 'I do not like this' and white stimuli with a button press for 'I do like this,' or vice versa.

After developing the personalized IAT, Olson and Fazio (2004) validated its use and predictive validity across four studies. They found less racial bias among White students (experiments 1 and 2), as well as stronger correspondence between IAT scores and both explicit attitude measures and behavioral intentions (experiments 3 and 4) when comparing a personalized IAT to a traditional IAT. In subsequent research, Han, Czellar, Olson and Fazio (2010) found that the personalized IAT was a more stable and less malleable instrument than the traditional IAT in measuring attitudes for which the existence of extrapersonal associations was a potentially confounding issue.

Going a step further, Vasey, Harbaugh, Buffington, Jones and Fazio (2012) investigated the predictive validity of the personalized IAT in the clinical context of phobias. The researchers administered a personalized IAT following an exposure therapy session for participants with a fear of public speaking, measuring relapse of the phobia one month later. They predicted that one way in which exposure therapy works to reduce a phobia is through changing implicit attitudes associated with the target stimulus: Thus, a measure of implicit attitudes toward public speaking immediately following the therapy session should predict its efficacy. Their results bore out their prediction, finding that personalized IAT scores predicted self-reported anticipatory anxiety, as well as actual heart rate during public speaking.

Single Category IAT

The **Single Category IAT** (Karpinski & Steinman, 2006) marks another important modification of the traditional Implicit Association Test. Recall Arkes and Tetlock's concern that the traditional IAT's emphasis on comparative or relative associations may compromise its meaning. Their concern was that the relative comparisons make it difficult to determine whether a respondent holds negative associations toward a target, or rather holds positive associations that are simply 'more negative' when compared to another target group.

The Single Category IAT circumvents this worry by removing the comparative dimension of the targets: it removes the second category target while maintaining both sides of a valenced dimension; i.e., positive/negative). The score on the Single Category IAT is calculated as a differential reaction time between associating the target with positive words and negative words. Karpinski and Steinman (2006) validated the Single Category IAT in three studies (on brand preference, self-esteem and racial attitudes), reporting predictive validity higher than either the traditional IAT or explicit measures. While the authors are careful to note its limitations—some of the flaws of the IAT may be carried over to this measure—the Single Category IAT nonetheless provides researchers a tool for independently measuring levels of positive and negative implicit associations toward a target.

Go/No-Go Association Task

Similar in purpose to the Single Category IAT, Nosek and Banaji's (2001) **Go/No-Go Association Task (GNAT)** is closely related to the traditional IAT but without the competing involvement from the second category. Much like the traditional IAT, the GNAT uses a pair of category targets (fruits and bugs, in the original study) and a pair of valenced attributes (good and bad), pairing them together in the two possible arrangements (fruit/good, bugs/bad; bugs/good, fruit/bad). However, instead of categorizing between button clicks, participants are given only one target pair (with one distracter/noise pair) and asked to provide a single type of response—Go or No-Go (that is, press the 'space' bar or press nothing). The measure cannot calculate reaction times for No-Go trials but allows for greater precision on Go trials by removing the competing behavior of categorizing the non-target pair. Using techniques from signal detection theory (Green & Swets,1966), Nosek and Banaji created a sensitivity score by calculating the difference between standardized (z-scored) hits (correct Go responses for target items) and false alarms (incorrect Go responses for distracter items). As expected, they found greater sensitivity (ability to discriminate signal from noise) for fruit/good and bugs/bad target pairs, relative to fruit/bad and bugs/good target pairs, respectively.

Quadruple Process (Quad) Model

More recently, Sherman and colleagues (Conrey, Sherman, Gawronski, Hugenberg, & Groom, 2005; Sherman, Gawronski, Conrey, Hugenberg, & Groom, 2006; Sherman, Gawronski, Gonsalkorale, Hugenberg, Allen, & Groom, 2008; Sherman, 2009) have advanced an interconnected model for analyzing the multidimensionality of performance on implicit tasks such as the IAT. While not a measurement per se, their model—the **Quadruple Process, or Quad, Model**—adds a secondary layer of analysis to existing methodology to create more nuanced data. Whereas most researchers treat automatic (implicit) and controlled (explicit) processes as two distinct issues to be handled with distinct measures or methodologies, Sherman and colleagues suggest that forms of both processes are at work in implicit task performance.

Their model outlines four processes—association activation (AC), discriminability (D), overcoming automatically activated bias (OB) and general response bias/guessing (G)—which they theorize are entangled during task performance. In their model, AC stands in for the construct researchers typically aim to asses when using implicit tasks, measuring the likelihood that an association is automatically activated on presentation of stimuli. D (discrimability) refers to effort, control and attention directed toward the task, measuring the likelihood of whether or not the correct answer *can* be (but not necessarily *is*) determined. OB represents the participant's control exerted toward inhibiting AC when explicit information in memory or environment can instead be used to make a deliberate judgment. G stands for a generalized bias—either automatic or deliberate—which may impact results. The authors suggest that G ranges from unconscious bias from handedness (faster response with one's dominant hand) to self-presentational bias by responding positively to, for example, black stimuli.

Research using implicit attitude assessments tacitly assumes that implicit measures are 'process pure'—that is, they measure, and only measure, implicit associations. The research establishing construct validity of the Quad Model (Conrey et al. 2005) supports the authors' contention that implicit task performance reflects four components rather than one. In his review of the model, Sherman (2009) concludes that failure to account for all four processes has led researchers to a state of underestimation of the controllability of implicit attitudes/associations-based biases. He further recommends viewing the multi-dimensionality of implicit task performance as a strength, rather than a weakness, by utilizing process dissociation techniques such as the Quad Model. Issues of implicit attitude malleability and, in particular, controllability, find clearer, more nuanced data through the use of such models.

Beyond Response Latencies

Measures of attitudes using response latencies have had enormous impact in social psychology. They have provided an alternative way to assess people's evaluations, especially on topics that people find difficult to report on traditional explicit assessments. However, response latency measures are not the only means of assessing attitudes implicitly. Introduced in the first chapter and then spread throughout this book, we have seen the use of measures that rely on the relatively automatic responses of the autonomic and central nervous systems. Blascovich and Mendes (2010) reviewed social psychology's long history with psychophysiological measurements to infer the attitudes of participants that bypass the need for explicit self-report. Cardiovascular activity, including heart rate and blood pressure, has been used as attitude measures, as has the perspiration at the level of the skin, measured as galvanic skin responses (GSR) or skin conductance responses (SCR). One of the more frequently used physiological assessments is electromyography (EMG) that measures subtle changes in facial musculature that people are typically unaware they are making. In one study using EMG methodology, Vanman, Paul, Ito and Miller (1997) found greater negative affect measured through brow and cheek activity when White participants were exposed to Black relative to White faces. The automaticity of such physiological responses prevents people from deliberately presenting the attitude that they feel they should have and reveals their automatic evaluations manifest in their subtle frowns and smiles. Demonstrating the predictive validity of EMG as an indicant of attitudes, a subsequent study by Vanman et al.

(2004) showed that increased cheek muscle activity to White relative to Black faces predicted participants' selection of a White candidate over a Black candidate for a teaching award.

Von Hippel, Sekaquaptewa and Vargas (2009) make the point that the use of *language* can also serve as an indicant of attitude. The range of possible ways to convey the same information through language often lets slip extra information uttered not through content, but through manner of communication. The differential use of pronouns (Agnew, Van Lange, Rusbult, & Langston, 1998), verbs (Maass, Salvi, Arcuri, & Semin, 1989) and adjective breadth (McGraw, Fischle, Stenner, & Lodge, 1996) between or within groups and individuals, provides researchers with insight into evaluations, preferences and biases. For instance, Walton and Banaji (2004) demonstrated that the use of noun labels ('is a pilot'), relative to verb labels ('flies airplanes') produces stronger, more stable evaluations of preferences of others—or even the self. Subtle behaviors such as seating distance, eye contact and speech errors have also served as indirect indicants of attitudes (Word, Zanna, & Cooper, 1974).

In summary, implicit measures are designed to assess people's automatic responses to stimulus objects. The possibilities for implicit measures are manifold, encompassing people's unscripted behavior and physiological responses. Although psychologists have been using a variety of indirect techniques for decades, the recent advent of methods that rely on response latencies have propelled the field forward. The lure of finding a path to a person's true attitude has resulted in considerable empirical research, an explosion of new methods and scoring algorithms, and controversies that have led to new insights into the meaning of attitudes.

ONE ATTITUDE OR TWO? IMPLICIT ATTITUDE VERSUS IMPLICIT MEASUREMENT

In Chapter 1, we defined an attitude as the categorization of a stimulus object along an evaluative dimension. Often, the categorizations are represented cognitively, stored in memory and affect behavior. The discussion of implicit measurement raises the question of whether there can be a single representation of an attitude object. If our attitudes toward a stimulus—whether it is group of people, a political topic or a particular individual—have different representations depending on whether they are assessed implicitly or explicitly, does that imply that we have at least dual representations of the attitude objects? Perhaps. But it is also viable to say that there is a single psychological construct that can be can be assessed with a variety of explicit and implicit measures. In this book, we have been cautious about the term 'implicit attitude' because that pre-judges the answer to an important and continuing debate. In our view, the jury is still out about whether there are separate implicit and explicit representations of attitude objects in memory (Greenwald & Nosek, 2008), each accessed by a different method, or whether there are alternative methods for assessing a unitary underlying representation.

Wilson, Lindsey and Schooler (2000) adopt the former approach in their model of dual attitudes. In their view, people hold two distinct types of attitudes and maintain them simultaneously as distinct concepts in memory. Implicit attitudes are those that are activated automatically, whereas explicit attitudes require work and capacity to retrieve. When people's experiences in life (or in a psychology laboratory) prompt them to change their attitudes about a topic or object, Wilson et al. (2000) believe that the change occurs only to the explicit attitude. By contrast, the original attitude continues to exist as an implicit construct, stored separately in memory, which affects behavior independently of the explicit attitude.

The evidence in support of dual attitudes is based on two types of findings. One considers each measure's ability to predict behavior; the other examines the pattern of correlations among measures. Greenwald, Poehlman, Uhlmann and Banaji (2009) conducted a meta-analysis of studies that measured attitudes using the IAT and behavior. They reported that the IAT showed a moderately consistent correlation with behavior in the range of approximately $r = .27$. In the same meta-analysis, they found that the correlation of behavior from explicit measures was slightly higher, approximately, $r = .36$. The conclusion from these data is that both types of measures show predictive validity in that they both significantly predict behavioral outcomes. At the same time, the correlations between implicit and explicit measures are typically smaller than between behavioral outcomes and either of the two measures. This suggests, but does not prove, that each measure assesses the attitude concept differently. In addition, and as would be expected, the IAT measure of attitudes was more successful at predicting behavior in areas that are highly sensitive, such as intergroup discrimination, whereas explicit measures were more effective in less sensitive domains such as consumers' food preferences.

The gist of the correlational findings suggests that response latency measures are reliable indicants of attitudes because, like the explicit measure, they predict behavior. They are not isomorphic with explicit measures, however, as attested to by the lower correlations with the explicit measure and by response latency measures predicting behavior better than explicit measures in certain specifiable circumstances. However, these data speak more to the use of an implicit measure as an important instrument of assessment rather than addressing whether the attitudes measured by the two techniques are represented separately and distinctly in memory. Another issue that gives pause to considering an implicit attitude as a unique concept different from explicit attitudes is that the various implicit measures rarely correlate with each other (Marsh, Johnson, & Scott-Sheldon, 2001; Sherman, Rose, Koch, Presson, & Chassin, 2003). Although Cunningham, Preacher and Banaji (2001) attribute the low correlations to measurement error, it is fair to say that the measures that are presumed to measure the same underlying implicit construct do not show a high level of consistency.

It remains a fascinating but open question whether there are two distinct conceptualizations of attitudes, one explicit and the other implicit. Resolution probably must await different types of measurement, perhaps through assessment of neural activity. Considering the current state of the data, Greenwald and Nosek (2008) conclude, "The empirical constructs *implicit attitudes* and *explicit attitudes* can reasonably be interpreted as deriving from either a single-representation or dual-representation structure. No behavior evidence can demand a conclusion that one view is right and the other is not" (p.75). We concur, and caution that the terms implicit and explicit be used for the type of measurement employed, rather than assume differences in the underlying concept.

Will the Real Attitude Please Stand Up?

An issue that has been debated since the advent of implicit measures is which attitude measurement assesses a person's *real*, or genuine attitude? Implicit measurement assesses people's automatic reactions. Explicit measurements assess people's considered evaluations. In our view, neither is more correct or real, but each may reveal different aspects of a target attitude.

Let us consider a simple example of the categorization of the stimulus object, spinach, on an evaluative dimension. Imagine that you are given a Likert scale and asked to provide your attitude on a 5-point scale where 5 is the most positive. Your first reaction might be to consider the taste of spinach. You consider that a 2, never having developed a taste for the vegetable. You may also remember that in past occasions where spinach was served, you reached for the potatoes instead. Another 2, you think. You now think of the health benefits of spinach. This green, leafy vegetable, loaded with iron and anti-oxidants, is very good for you. That would be a 5 on the scale. Returning to the Likert scale in order to explicitly categorize your evaluation, you choose a 4 as your summary evaluation.

Let's now imagine that an investigator asked you to engage in an evaluative priming procedure or a single-category IAT. Your reaction times are long when spinach is paired with 'favorable' and short when spinach is paired with 'unfavorable.' This implicit measure indicates a highly unfavorable attitude (comparable to a 2 on the explicit measure). Which is your true attitude toward spinach? We could watch to see if you eat spinach when it is offered to you, but even this would not offer a solution. You might be more likely to follow your explicitly measured attitude in a context in which you were thinking more about health and follow your implicitly measured attitude when thinking solely about hedonic pleasures.

Note, too, that automatic responses need not be purely affective. It is likely that someone primed with the concept of health might be more apt to respond automatically along that dimension. For example, if someone read a magazine article about the risk of cancer and heart disease and/or was asked to unscramble letter strings related to health, the automatic response to an IAT or EPM may be consistent with the belief about the health value of spinach than about its taste. An explicit measure might still combine the various components of the evaluation to form an overall evaluation, but the automatic evaluation may be considerably more positive.

One caveat to the argument that explicit and implicit measurements are both valid attitude assessments is when people are motivated to distort or lie about their attitude. Even attitudes toward spinach can be problematic when assessed at a convention of spinach farmers. Attitudes toward racial, sexual and intergroup relations are considerably more likely than spinach to be expressed in a context in which people feel a need to distort their true evaluations. In such a context, implicit measures can have a strong advantage, as would any other technique that encouraged honest reporting. In an interesting study, Nier (2005) used an IAT to measure participants' racial attitudes and compared their responses to their scores on the Modern Racism Scale (McConahay, 1986), an explicit measure of prejudice. There was no significant correlation whatsoever. However, when some participants were placed in a bogus pipeline procedure in which they believed that their true racial attitudes were already known, the correspondence between the implicit and explicit measures jumped to an impressive $r = .51$. In the absence of the bogus pipeline, people apparently distorted their explicit reports, resulting in the lack of correlation. When honesty of reporting was more assured, both measures revealed highly similar scores.

Different definitions of attitudes may lead to different characterizations of the relationship between implicitly and explicitly measured attitudes, but the conclusion remains similar. Consider Fazio's (2007) definition of an attitude as an association in memory between an object and its evaluation. The implicit measurement of an attitude will call up this association, which is the essence of the attitude. In some circumstances, that is all that is needed. It is the person's attitude and will likely predict his or her behavior. However, as we saw in Chapter 6, there are numerous occasions when people are motivated to be more deliberative about their attitudes (Fazio, 1990). An initial reaction to, say, spinach may then be modified by a deliberate consideration of other issues, including health, taste and past behaviors. These are known as 'downstream' considerations. They modify and adjust the original evaluation stored in memory. Given the motivation and opportunity to make the adjustment, the final evaluation reflects a combination of all of the attitude's components. The fact that one evaluation comes automatically, without reflection and/or occurs prior to any downstream modification, does not imply that the implicitly or the explicitly measured attitude is more genuine than the other. It is a matter of the social context and what it is that we wish to know.

ATTITUDE CHANGE, IMPLICITLY

The literature on persuasion that we have discussed in this book shows that attitudes can and do change. Is this explicit change or implicit change? As we pointed out previously, Wilson et al. (2000) believe that people's original attitudes do not change but rather remain intact in memory as implicit memory traces, even as people form new explicit attitudes. A growing body of research, however, shows that attitudes measured implicitly can also undergo change (e.g., Banaji, 2001; Briñol, Petty, & McCaslin, 2009). In the Quad model, Conrey et al. (2005) suggest that changes in attitudes measured implicitly should be construed as evidence against the notion of **process purity**—i.e., the notion that implicit measures assess an underlying true attitude that is immune from social influences. Similarly, various dual-process models (e.g., Smith & DeCoster, 2000) highlight the proposition that implicitly measured attitudes exist within a larger network of attitudes and associations, with different aspects being activated under different conditions. Dasgupta (2013) argues that implicit attitudes serve as a reflection of our local social environments, and thus demonstrate malleability in the face of changes to that environment (e.g., Dasgupta & Greenwald, 2001; Yogeeswaran, Dasgupta, & Gomez, 2012; Stout, Dasgupta, Hunsinger, & McManus, 2011). These interpretations all suggest that automatic, implicitly measured attitudes can and do change.

Evaluative Conditioning

One promising method of changing attitudes at the implicit level of measurement is evaluative conditioning (De Houwer, Baeyens, & Field, 2005; De Houwer, Thomas, & Bayens, 2001; Walther, Nagengast, & Trasselli, 2005), in which one leverages the associative nature of implicit attitudes to induce change. In a procedure reminiscent of classic, Pavlovian conditioning that we discussed in Chapter 3, evaluative conditioning occurs by way of repeated pairing of a stimulus to another stimulus, where the second stimulus is an attitude object previously liked or disliked. Participants come to implicitly associate the novel, first stimulus with the previous, second stimulus—as well as its associated valence. For example, Olson and Fazio (2006) conditioned participants to hold counterstereotypic implicit associations through repeated pairings of Black faces with positive words/images and White faces with negative words/images. Afterward, participants completed a Black/White evaluative priming measure, as described previously in this chapter (Fazio et al., 1995). The researchers predicted that, relative to control participants who experienced no conditioning, experimental participants would show less pro-White/anti-Black facilitation. An analysis of variance revealed the predicted three-way interaction, finding that control participants demonstrated the predicted Black/bad, White/good facilitation interaction, but experimental participants did not. In a second experiment, Olson and Fazio (2006) found that the change in the implicitly measured attitudes was long-lasting. An implicit assessment delayed by two days following the evaluative conditioning continued to show decreased prejudice on the EPM. In short, such conditioning regimens show promise in altering automatic evaluative reactions—and, importantly, do so beyond the immediate situation.

Taking the evaluative conditioning paradigm one step further, Kawakami, Phills, Steele and Dovidio (2007) leveraged embodied social cognition (Barsalou et al., 2003; Niedenthal et al., 2005) to retrain approach and avoidance tendencies toward Blacks. Embodied social cognition relies on our tendencies to associate bodily movements with certain cognitive responses. For example, when people contract their arm muscles to bring objects toward them, they experience the positive thoughts associated with "approach." When extending the arm, people experience avoidance. In Kawakami et al.'s (2007) study, participants were seated at a computer screen and told they would be viewing pictures of Black and White faces. Participants were instructed to manipulate a joystick situated in front of them in response to the presentation of each face. In the two experimental conditions, participants were told to approach Blacks by pulling the joystick toward themselves and avoid Whites by pushing the joystick away, or they were told to approach Whites and avoid Blacks. Two conditions, serving as controls, had participants press the joystick in counterbalanced sideways positions in response to the two types of faces. After completing the conditioning phase, participants completed a Black/White race IAT. The researchers predicted that, relative to control participants and participants who were told to extend their arms to pictures of Black people, participants in the approach (i.e., contract their arms) condition would demonstrate significantly reduced implicit prejudice. The data supported the researchers' prediction, finding no significant difference between the control conditions and the avoid Blacks condition, but significantly lower IAT bias in the approach Blacks condition. In several replications of their basic procedure, Kawakami et al. (2007) demonstrated implicit prejudice reduction effects with subliminal presentation of faces, with non-White faces in the training phase, and with behavioral (rather than reaction time) dependent measures of prejudice.

Directing the focus inward, Forbes (2009) employed personalized evaluative conditioning to serve as an intervention for situations of stereotype threat. Briefly, stereotype threat is the decrease in performance by individuals of stereotyped groups who are performing in stereotyped domains when their identity is made salient. Research has shown this performance decrease follows from a loss in working memory under those conditions (Schmader & Johns, 2003). Hypothesizing that positive implicit associations produce positive downstream consequences, Forbes conditioned female participants to associate math with personally liked stimuli using a modified personalized IAT (Olson & Fazio, 2004). In his procedure, Forbes adapted the evaluative conditioning paradigm to focus on gender (associating

'Women like this' and 'math' to the same button press) and assessed performance in a stereotype-threatening situation. As predicted, participants retrained to associate women with affinity for rather than an affinity for language, exhibited increased working memory and resulting increased math performance—consistent with a decrease in the experience of stereotype threat.

Associative-Propositional Evaluation Model

Gawronski and Bodenhausen (2006, 2011, 2014), drawing on both the associative properties of automatically expressed attitudes and the propositional properties of explicitly expressed attitudes, propose a framework for integrating past attitude change research with emerging research on implicit attitudes. Their **Associative-Propositional Evaluation (APE)** model proposes that attitudinal objects determine a pattern of implicit activation in memory. These reactions are affective in nature, a reaction to which implicit measures (such as the IAT or EMG) are particularly sensitive. On the other hand, people also have explicit propositional reasoning that acts separately from the affective reactions caused by attitudinal objects. Propositional reasoning, which is characterized as semantic propositions concerned with truth value, allows us to assess the validity of the activated affective associations. Figure 9.2 depicts the structural interplay between propositional reasoning and association activation according to the APE model. Gawronski and Bodenhausen (2006) point out that whereas implicit measures are particularly sensitive to assessing affective activation, explicit self-report measures are particularly appropriate for assessing the propositional validity judgment.

In their model, Gawronski and Bodenhausen suggest that attitude change, both implicit and explicit, occurs according to how two conditions are met: First, whether it is the associative or propositional process that is *directly* influenced; and second, whether those direct changes also lead to *indirect* changes in the other structure. In those cases where the associative structure is changed and those changes are accepted by the propositional reasoning, both implicit and explicit attitude change occur; if the changes are not accepted by the propositional reasoning, only implicit attitude change occurs. In those cases where the propositional reasoning is changed and those changes influence the associative structure, again both explicit and implicit attitude change occur; when the associate structure is not influenced, only explicit attitude change occurs.

As a prototypical example of direct influence on the associative structure, Gawronski and Bodenhausen analyzed the process of evaluative conditioning. According to the APE model, conditioning participants to form a new mental association—for example, pairing Black faces with positive words in the Olson and Fazio (2006) study discussed previously—directly affects the associative structure in memory, causing implicit attitude change. Direct influences on propositional reasoning, on the other

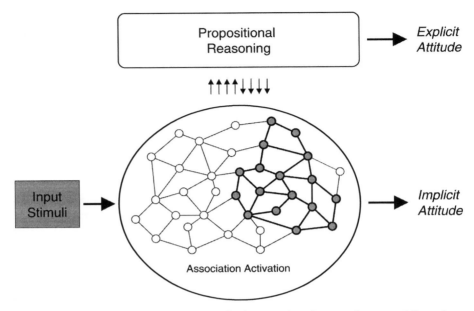

FIGURE 9.2   *Interplay between association activation and propositional reasoning according to the APE model.*

Source: Gawronski, B., & Bodenhausen, G.V. (2006). Associative and propositional processes in evaluation: an integrative review of implicit and explicit attitude change. *Psychological Bulletin, 132*(5), 692. Reprinted with permission.

hand, take the form of any classic processes through which attitudes change—e.g., persuasive communications discussed in Chapters 4 and 5 or consistency concerns (Chapter 7) such as cognitive dissonance theory (Festinger, 1957).

In a test of the indirect path prediction of the APE model between affective structure and propositional reasoning, Gawronski and LeBel (2008) had participants learn an association between positive words and 'Asia' and negative words and 'Europe.' Afterward, half of the participants wrote down their *feelings* toward the two continents, while the other half wrote down what they knew. The researchers predicted that writing down one's feelings would allow the propositional reasoning system to consider them valid with respect to the affective reaction; on the other hand, this should not be the case if one writes down their knowledge. As predicted, all participants showed significant implicit attitude change in line with previous work on evaluative conditioning; however, only those participants who wrote down their feelings also showed significant explicit attitude change.

Although the APE model is not without criticisms (see Gawronski & Bodenhausen, 2011, for review), it nonetheless provides a strong framework for understanding the conditions that lead to implicit and explicit attitude change. The model's strength lies in its ability to integrate, categorize and explain past and present attitude change literature into a straightforward framework.

SUMMARY AND CONCLUSION

Implicit measures were originally developed with the intent of providing a window with unfettered access to a person's attitude—the gold standard of attitudinal research and of particular importance for the socially sensitive topics social psychologists study. Methodology to assess participants' 'true' attitudes has continued to develop, from the bogus pipeline technique to more sophisticated response latency measures that assess implicit associations, such as the Evaluative Priming Measure and the Implicit Association Test. These measure have been extremely influential in studying attitudes that have been heretofore difficult to assess due to a variety of self-presentation concerns. Nonetheless, the IAT has not gone without significant challenges and criticism. Some researchers have questioned its predictive validity and suggested alternative measures for assessing attitudes implicitly. Others have questioned the psychological meaning of the measure, raising concerns about whether it assesses attitudes or cultural knowledge. That said, the IAT has contributed greatly to the study of attitudes—especially in the domain of racial prejudice—and enlivened debate about the nature of the attitude construct itself.

In addition to finding new ways to assess the automatic components of people's attitudes, research on implicit attitudes has also added additional depth and complexity, which revolutionized psychologists' conceptions of attitude structure. Two decades' worth of developing implicit attitude measures has taught researchers the importance of taking into account both a person's underlying, implicit associations and their outward, explicit social filters. As the research on implicit attitudes matures, so too does our modeling of attitudes in general. New theoretical frameworks, such as the APE and Quad models, take steps toward integrating implicit attitudes into a broader context. With growing knowledge about the structure and properties of implicit attitudes has come progress towards learning how to change them—a crucial step for combating pervasive societal problems like implicit racial bias.

CHAPTER 10

New Frontiers in Attitude Research
Accessing and Modeling the Brain

Gordon Allport (1935) observed that attitudes are much more complex than simple stimulus-response pairs, such as the enjoyment from licking an ice cream cone or the revulsion at finding a worm (or half of one!) in one's apple. Attitudes have different components—affective, cognitive and behavioral—and operate both inside and outside conscious awareness. Different aspects of one's attitude may guide behavior depending on myriad personal and situational variables. As complex as attitudes are, the past century has revealed a wealth of information about their structure, function and change. As with any science, however, the horizon of knowledge is ever-expanding and the depth of our understanding is steadily increasing. Part of the formidable recent gains in advancing our understanding of the attitude construct is attributable to the advances in technology that have enabled social psychologists to study attitudes in new, innovative and heretofore impossible ways. In this chapter, we will explore some of the many ways in which the study of attitudes has been evolving and provide an overview of the findings revealed by a deeper and more complex understanding of the human brain.

METHODOLOGICAL ADVANCES IN ATTITUDES RESEARCH: TOWARD A "TRUE" ATTITUDE

Since the outset of attitudes research, social psychologists have grappled with how to avoid concerns about social desirability or self-presentation. In other words, when using the most common measurement of an attitude (i.e., a self-report measure), researchers have been looking for ways to detect someone's *true* attitudes, regardless of the participant's concerns about appearing likable, normative or egalitarian. Social psychologists seek to observe participants' attitudes directly without sources of extraneous influence. As we noted in Chapter 9, Jones and Sigall (1971) described a way to elicit more honest responses about attitudes through use of a 'bogus pipeline' procedure. In essence, what they did was convince the participant that they had access to participants' true attitudes by connecting them to a polygraph (lie detector) device—if the machine could supposedly detect when participants were being deceptive, participants had little incentive to report inaccurate but inoffensive beliefs. Indeed, in their experiments—and in many subsequent studies (see Roese & Jamieson, 1993, for a review)—participants were more willing to express negative affect towards stereotyped groups that they normally might have inhibited. In this way, methodological innovation helped reach a more undistorted estimate of what an individual's attitude really was.

The bogus pipeline paradigm was only the beginning of efforts to tap into more and more accurate representations of people's attitudes. After the 1970s, these methods progressed from tricking participants into telling the researcher what they really think and feel to using proxies that inform researchers about the participant's true beliefs. As we noted in previous chapters, physiological measures of skin conductance, heart rate and blood pressure, or facial electromyography (EMG; e.g., Cacioppo, Petty, Losch, & Kim, 1986), have frequently been used to measure the body's automatic responses to certain stimuli, enabling researchers to infer mental processes based on knowledge of the physiological correlates of arousal, emotion and evaluation. Reaction time measures provide a different route to assess people's automatic expressions of attitudes, unfettered by self-presentational and other extrapersonal concerns. Today's newest methodologies, however, go even further to approach a more direct pipeline to people's thoughts and emotions. Two new technologies in particular allow psychologists to open new avenues of investigation by directly assessing brain activity. As we shall see throughout this chapter, measurements of **event-related potentials (ERP)** and the use of **functional magnetic resonance imaging (fMRI)** have made enormous contributions to the field of attitude research.

As tempting as it is to infer that, with the new complexity and precision of understanding allowed by these new measures, we have finally arrived at the ability to detect 'true' attitudes, it is important to keep in mind that these methods—advanced as they are—are still imperfect proxies for directly accessing attitude representations in the brain. Neither ERP nor fMRI directly measures neuronal firing, and, even if they did, researchers would still have to make inferences about how specific brain activations relate to evaluative processing. With that in mind, and with the knowledge that the field of neuroscience is constantly evolving, this chapter is dedicated to giving a glimpse of the current state of knowledge in the field and insight into how measurements of brain activation can be applied to the field of attitudes research. As some of the acronyms and terms in this chapter can be complex and potentially confusing, we have outlined some useful terms and rough definitions in Table 10.1.

TABLE 10.1 *Useful Terms and Definitions in Rough Order of Appearance*

TERM	DEFINITION
EEG	Electroencephalograph. A device that measures event-related potentials through recording electrical activity on the scalp.
ERPs	Event-related potentials. Positive or negative voltage deflections in the brain from a baseline in response to a stimulus.
fMRI	Functional magnetic resonance imaging. A technique inferring brain activity from blood oxygenation levels in the brain.
P300	A positive ERP waveform at 300ms after stimulus onset typically observed in stimulus evaluation or categorization.
OFC	Orbitofrontal cortex. Implicated in reward, decision-making, expectation and evaluation.
LPP	Late positive potential. A late-occurring positive ERP waveform indicative of higher-order processing, often observed in explicit recognition or facilitated attention to emotional stimuli.
N400	A negative ERP waveform at 400ms after stimulus onset, typically observed in response to potentially meaningful stimuli.
Amygdala	Subcortical structure associated with processing of potentially emotionally relevant stimuli.
ACC	Anterior cingulate cortex. Implicated in conflict monitoring and detection of inconsistency.
dlPFC	Dorsolateral prefrontal cortex. Implicated in intention, regulation and decision-making.

EVENT-RELATED POTENTIALS (ERPS) AND FMRI

If you pictured a hypothetical machine that would "read someone's mind," it is likely that you would imagine an apparatus that is quite similar in appearance to an **electroencephalograph** (EEG), *a device that measures event-related potentials through recording electrical activity on the scalp* (See Figure 10.1). This device often takes the form of a cap or collection of electrodes that adhere to the participant's head and measures **event-related potentials**. ERPs themselves are *the electrical response in the brain that is the result of a specific sensation, action or cognition.* These responses are measured as voltage deflections from a pre-measured baseline and often take the form of a wave with a positive or negative deflection. Importantly, although it is tempting to think so, these positive and negative voltage deflections are *not* indicators of the perceived valence of a stimulus; in other words, the valence of the voltage deflection in response to a given stimulus does not correspond to the valence of one's evaluation of that stimulus. Since these responses occur electrically, they can be measured within one millisecond of their actual activation (even though, typically, the first electrical response to a stimulus does not occur before 100ms), and therefore ERP provides excellent temporal resolution for measuring the various cognitive responses to stimuli. Because ERP detects electrical signals from electrodes on the scalp, however, it provides poor spatial resolution. In other words, it is difficult to localize the activation within the brain using ERP because electrical activity in the brain is by no means confined to the surface of the cortex.

Fortunately, fMRI compensates for this by reversing the strengths and weaknesses of ERP. The experience of participating in an experiment using fMRI bears little resemblance to attaching electrodes to the scalp via an EEG cap. fMRI scanners are, in essence, large and powerful electromagnets—for this reason, participants and experimenters must remove all ferromagnetic material (e.g., jewelry) from their bodies before entering the room with the scanner, lest it get attracted by the magnetic field and cause damage. The scanner itself takes the shape of a cylinder large enough to fit a human inside; while participating, participants lie on a retractable plank that fits inside of the cylinder (see Figure 10.2). Once inside, participants often view stimuli from inside the scanner and make their responses by pressing keys on a keypad with their dominant hand.

The strengths and weaknesses of fMRI are related to the mechanism by which it measures brain activation—in this case, blood flow. The logic of how fMRI works is not quite as straightforward as in ERP. **fMRI** *measures brain activity by detecting the*

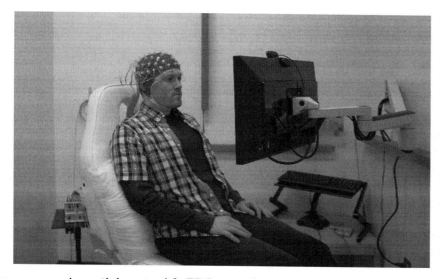

FIGURE 10.1 *A participant with EEG cap placed on the scalp.*
Note: Color version can be found in the plate section.

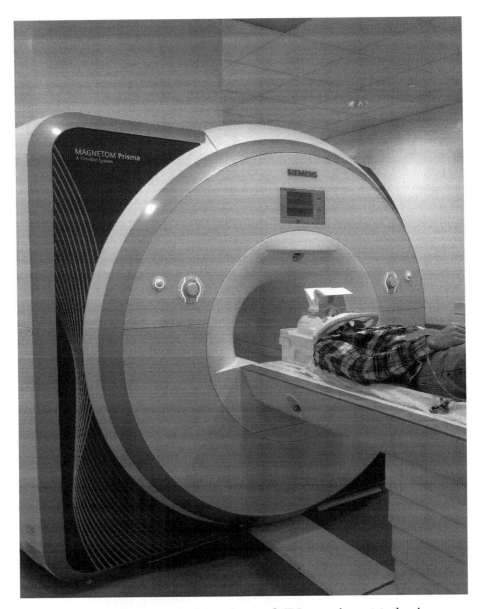

FIGURE 10.2   *A participant waiting for an fMRI experiment to begin.*
Note: Color version can be found in the plate section.

blood-oxygen-level dependent (BOLD) signal in the brain, with the inference that brain areas that are more active require more resources carried in the bloodstream. Therefore, by measuring the hemodynamic response (i.e., changes in blood flow) to different areas of the brain through detecting changes in magnetization of oxygen-rich vs.

oxygen-poor blood during some task, activation in some areas of the brain relative to others can be inferred. In research using fMRI, psychologists are often looking to examine a few specific brain areas of interest during or after a certain action or stimulus. Because normal brain function involves quite a bit of brain activity, the BOLD signal that researchers are hoping to detect is often corrupted by high levels of noise that obscure any differences in activation across areas. To remedy this, researchers use statistical techniques to eliminate noise and construct carefully controlled experiments that measure *differences* of activation across conditions, such that the normal activity of the brain can be subtracted and separated from activation in the specific areas of interest relevant to the researcher's hypotheses. Unfortunately, however, blood flow in the brain in response to activation is slow, taking up to six seconds to register a change in BOLD signal and resulting in poor temporal resolution. On the other hand, since fMRI measures blood flow in three dimensions within the brain, it has excellent spatial resolution (even up to 1mm^3). In this chapter, we will look at evidence obtained from both ERP and fMRI measures that explores the brain areas and neural networks involved in different kinds of evaluation.

NEUROLOGICAL CORRELATES OF ATTITUDE-RELATED PROCESSES

Attitudes research in the past two decades making use of novel ERP and fMRI measures has contributed enormously to the validity and robustness of the social neuroscience approach. Using a combination of these measures, the ability to infer both the timescale and location of brain activation to a very high degree has not only enhanced the precision and specificity of attitudes research, but has also enabled empirical verification of long-debated hypotheses about issues such as the automaticity of evaluative processing or the timescale of dissonance reduction. Furthermore, neuroscientific data has allowed attitude processes to be more tightly linked to (and understood in light of) other, broader social psychological phenomena and processes. This has been achieved by virtue of careful observation of which areas of activation are shared in common vs. separable between hypothetically related constructs. In the attitudes domain, in the span of a few years, ERP and fMRI data have taught us much about the interconnected automatic, reflective and regulatory components of online, real-time evaluation.

AUTOMATIC EVALUATIVE PROCESSES

Timescale of automaticity. Researchers theorized about the existence of automatic, implicit processes before any ability to construct a precise timeline of their operation was possible. With the advent of ERP, however, researchers have been given the ability to investigate novel hypotheses about the operation of automatic evaluation. As we discussed above, ERP measures have the benefit of having exceedingly precise temporal resolution. They provide an excellent way, then, to gain insight into automaticity. It is unlikely that there are many processes that operate faster than the smallest unit of measurement in ERP (one millisecond). In EEG in general, a larger delay between the positive or negative **waveform** (i.e., *a measured voltage deflection from baseline due to electrical activation in the brain*) and the stimulus that triggered it suggests the engagement of higher-order processes. For instance, while EEG may detect an ERP in the primary visual cortex 50–70ms after light from a stimulus reaches the participant's eye, recognition of incongruent or unexpected visual stimuli may elicit a positive waveform at around 300ms (or, to use the nomenclature of ERP, a **P300** waveform). In this way, one stimulus may produce a number or series of responses that each elicits positive or negative deflections: Early-occurring voltage deflections indicate processing of basic properties of a stimulus, while later-occurring voltage deflections (such as a P300 wave) indicate the workings of higher-order (but still automatic) processes. Observation of the pattern of deflections elicited by a certain psychological process, then, can give researchers the ability to discriminate between any automatic activation that may occur at a very precise level.

Most attitude theorists believe that there is at least some automaticity in the evaluations that form the basis of our attitudes. Moreover, even before the popularization of research utilizing EEG, social psychologists had long acknowledged distinctions between positively and negatively valenced stimuli and our accompanying positive vs. negative reactions to them (e.g., Higgins, 1997). Research presented in prior chapters showed that automatic responses to stimuli can have an impact on our attitudes and behavior. Consistent with this behavioral research, evidence from EEG shows that evaluatively positive and negative stimuli are distinguishable through brain activation even before 1 second elapses (Cacioppo & Gardner, 1999; Pizzagalli, Koenig, Regard, & Lehmann, 1999). This is corroborated by single-cell recordings of the human **orbitofrontal cortex (OFC)**, where processing of negative stimuli elicits activation as early as 120–160ms (Kawasaki et al., 2001) and other ERP research suggests that negative information is processed more quickly than positive information (Carretie, Mercado, Tapia, & Hinojosa, 2001). In addition to a temporal distinction between positive and negative evaluation, a robust finding in ERP research is that evaluatively negative concepts or stimuli elicit **late positive potentials (LPPs)**—*late-occurring positive voltage deflections indicative of higher-order processing*—that are lateralized on the right hemisphere of the brain. Evaluatively positive stimuli, on the other hand, elicit LPPs lateralized on the left hemisphere (Cunningham, Espinet, DeYoung, & Zelazo, 2005; Davidson, Ekman, Saron, Senalis, & Friesen, 1990; Jones & Fox, 1992). This right-hemisphere lateralization has also been observed in studies using fMRI instead of EEG, where negative evaluative processing has been linked to activation in the right inferior frontal cortex and anterior insula (Anderson et al., 2003; Cunningham et al., 2003; Cunningham, Raye, & Johnson, 2004). At least in ERP research, however, this lateralization may have more to do with the behavioral tendencies or associations than with the evaluation in question (Cunningham & Johnson, 2007).

As mentioned earlier, the ERPs for evaluatively positive vs. negative stimuli are *not* related to the positivity or negativity of the voltage deflection of the waveform; on the other hand, the magnitude of the deflection *can* be indicative of the *intensity* of the response to the stimulus (Bartholow & Amodio, 2009; Berger, 1929; Moruzzi & Magoun, 1949). In accordance with this, LPP waveforms show greater activation when participants report their true attitudes instead of misrepresenting their beliefs or preferences (Crites, Cacioppo, Gardner, & Berntson, 1995). Not only does electrical activity in the brain in response to valence and intensity register extremely rapidly, but ERP measures have also detected sensitivity to evaluative consistency. Presenting participants with stimuli that exhibit some evaluative inconsistency—for example, asking participants to evaluate a negative stimulus after having evaluated a series of positive stimuli—elicits a larger P300 wave than stimuli that are evaluatively consistent (Cacioppo et al., 1993). This P300 wave is then followed by a negative waveform at 400ms (i.e., a **N400** wave) that is normally nonexistent. In other words, when presented with a series of stimuli, we are able to rapidly and automatically recognize any evaluative discrepancy between them. The specificity of these results to evaluative consistency, however, is somewhat qualified by evidence that shows that *semantic* (rather than evaluative) inconsistency is sufficient to prompt a similar N400 wave (Morris, Squires, Taber, & Lodge, 2003). Regardless, these LPP and N400 waveforms are also greater in compatible and incompatible trials of the IAT, respectively (see Chapter 9), demonstrating the operation of evaluative processes as well as responsiveness to semantic or emotional congruence while completing the IAT (Williams & Themanson, 2011). In addition, LPP waveforms of this sort that occur after evaluatively incongruent stimuli appear to be lateralized and show more activation over the right vs. left hemisphere of the brain (Cacioppo et al., 1996).

While the broad-brush ERP findings on lateralization have been supplemented by fMRI results, individual findings about the time-course of evaluative processing and detection of inconsistency reflect a great contribution on their own to pre-existing attitude-relevant theories such as cognitive dissonance. With the advent of ERP, researchers have been able to pinpoint the time-course of mental processes with greater precision, revealing data about automatic processes—for instance, the ability to rapidly discriminate evaluatively positive and negative stimuli or detect inconsistency—that were heretofore inaccessible. As we shall see later, these data about automaticity, discriminability and lateralization from ERP experiments also feed into the understanding of theories involving reflective consideration and the regulation of our attitudes.

Automaticity, localization and function. As EEG provides us with information about the timescale of automaticity, research using fMRI has enabled attitudes researchers to link findings about localization during evaluation to broader research in decision-making, emotion and social cognition. This convergent evidence has allowed attitudes researchers to articulate coherent frameworks for the structural bases of many attitude processes. As we saw in Chapter 9, there has been much discussion about how implicit attitudes relate to explicit attitudes or fit into evaluation more broadly. Research in social neuroscience has increased knowledge about automatic evaluations dramatically. One over-arching framework for the neurological basis of implicit attitudes is Stanley, Phelps and Banaji's (2008) three-tier model. This model posits that three primary structures are responsible for the interaction between implicit attitudes and explicit/global evaluation in general. First, the **amygdala** processes automatic activation of social stimuli; second, the **anterior cingulate cortex** (ACC) detects implicit preferences and monitors whether or not they conflict with the current context and goals (e.g., see Botvinick, Braver, Barch, Carter, & Cohen, 2001); and finally, the **dorsolateral prefrontal cortex** (dlPFC) regulates the impact of these implicit attitudes for evaluation and behavior (see Figure 10.3). As we shall see throughout this section, these three brain areas (and areas functionally related to them) appear central to the complex process of forming a dynamic evaluation of an attitude object.

Traditionally, although the amygdala was thought to be specifically involved in fear processing (e.g., LeDoux, 1998), fMRI evidence has repeatedly suggested a broader role for the amygdala in processing potentially emotionally relevant stimuli more generally (e.g., Cunningham & Brosch, 2012). In particular, researchers have posited that the amygdala plays a large role in processing stimuli that pertain to the individual's current motivations and goals, and may even be activated in response to novel, ambiguous, or extremely positive stimuli (Cunningham & Brosch, 2012). This processing often occurs prior to higher-order processing in the cortex due to the amygdala's direct connection to the thalamus (LeDoux, 1998), a non-cortical brain area important for relaying sensory and motor signals to the cerebral cortex for higher-order processing. The amygdala's connections to the OFC, however, allow implicit evaluative judgments to be compared to higher-order processes of beliefs, expectations or desires, such as when comparing expected vs. actual rewards (Cunningham, Zelazo, Packer, & van Bavel, 2007).

Because of these connections that imply a certain degree of automaticity in amygdala processing, it is unsurprising that the amygdala activation in response to racial stimuli has been shown to correlate with measurements of implicit associations on the IAT (Greenwald et al., 1998). Similarly, the amygdala exhibits activation in response to subliminally presented emotional faces, suggesting automatic activation that operates outside of conscious awareness (Morris, Ohman, & Dolan, 1998; Whalen et al., 1998; Williams et al., 2006). Given the threatening content of

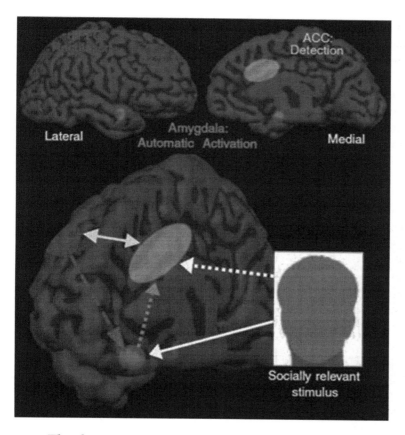

FIGURE 10.3   *The three-tier model of the neural basis for implicit attitudes. Amygdala activation is implicated in automatic evaluation of socially relevant stimuli; the ACC is implicated in the detection of socially relevant stimuli and their congruence with one's preferences; and the dlPFC is implicated in regulation of the amygdala's response.*

Source: Stanley, D., Phelps, E., & Banaji, M. (2008). The neural basis of implicit attitudes. *Current Directions in Psychological Science, 17*(2), 164–170. Reprinted with permission.

Note: Color version can be found in the plate section.

the African American stereotype, Black faces should be more (negatively) emotionally salient relative to White faces for White participants. Consistent with this reasoning, differences in automatic amygdala activation similarly occur in response to Black vs. White faces (emotionally salient due to the threat inherent in the African American stereotype) when these faces are presented subliminally (Cunningham et al., 2004).

The amygdala's specific role in evaluation has been clarified by a few studies that examine brain activation in response to the presence or lack of explicit evaluation for the same set of stimuli. In one representative study, Cunningham, Raye and Johnson (2004) presented participants with socially relevant concepts (e.g., murder, happiness, welfare) with the instructions to either rate them on an evaluative (good-bad) dimension or a non-evaluative (abstract-concrete) dimension. Previous work involving exposure to evaluatively good or bad judgments without explicit instructions to evaluate had already shown activation in the ventral striatum (Aharon et al., 2001) and amygdala (Cunningham et al., 2003). Cunningham et al.

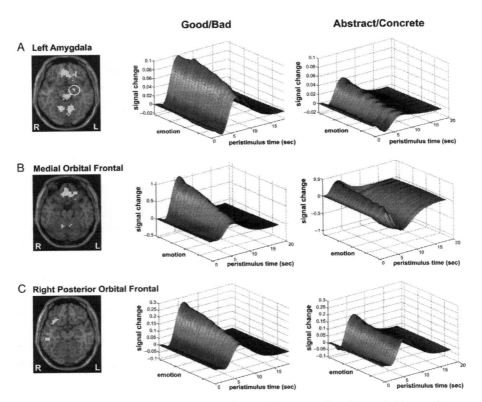

FIGURE 10.4 *Differences in the correlation between brain activity and rated emotional intensity in the left amygdala (A), medial orbital frontal cortex (B), and right posterior orbital frontal cortex (C) in response to good vs. bad and abstract vs. concrete stimuli.*

Source: Cunningham, W. A., Raye, C. L., & Johnson, M. K. (2004). Implicit and explicit evaluation: fMRI correlates of valence, emotional intensity, and control in the processing of attitudes. *Journal of Cognitive Neuroscience, 16*(10), 1717–1729. Reprinted with permission.

Note: Color version can be found in the plate section.

(2004) found similar results, identifying activation in the amygdala that correlated with participants' ratings of the emotional intensity of the stimulus and activation in the right insula that corresponded with participants' ratings of the valence of the stimulus regardless of whether or not participants were consciously given a goal to evaluate the concepts. Consistent with the three-tier model of implicit attitudes and the morphology of the amygdala (specifically its projections onto other brain structures), explicit evaluation involved activity in the lateral OFC areas, as well as activity in the ACC and frontal pole (see Figure 10.4), which correlated with participant's self-reported ratings of how much they controlled their evaluation of the stimulus. Together with the results of ERP research presented earlier, we can conclude that automatic evaluation (and activation in related brain areas, e.g., the amygdala) starts extremely rapidly and may depend on both one's goal for the evaluation and the consistency of that evaluation with previous attitudes.

REFLECTIVE EVALUATIVE PROCESSES

From our overview of the neural correlates of automatic evaluative processing, we have already alluded to the fact that automatic processing and evaluation inform downstream processing that is more conscious, controlled, and reflective. Historically, these automatic and reflective components of processing have been treated as discriminable, separable systems (e.g., as in dual-process models of attitude change; see Chapter 5). Although evidence shows that this is not always the case, fMRI research has led to the observation that each process correlates with activation in different areas of the brain, with automatic arousal being related to activation in the amygdala and reflective valence related to activation in the dlPFC (e.g., Anderson et al., 2003; Cunningham et al., 2004; Small et al., 2003). This is not to say that there is not some processing of valence that occurs automatically (as ERP research above suggests), but merely that automatic evaluations feed forward into conscious interpretations of stimulus valence in a particular context.

In parallel with ERP research, studies using fMRI to explore the neural correlates of evaluation have identified similar lateralization, such that positive attitudes are associated with activation in the left lateral PFC while negative attitudes are associated with activation in the right lateral PFC (Cunningham, Espinet, DeYoung, & Zelazo, 2005). The right inferior frontal cortex and anterior insula seem to exhibit similar lateralization, showing greater activation when processing negative vs. positive information (Cunningham et al., 2008). Although this lateralization has also been observed for approach and avoidance motivation (i.e., that left frontal brain activity is associated with approach and right frontal activity with avoidance), some contend that this congruence in lateralization results from experimental evidence confounding positive emotional valence with approach motivation (Harmon-Jones,

2004) and that approach/withdrawal motivation is the more important construct for determining lateralization since anger and dissonance (negative approach states) are both associated with relative left, not right, cortical activity. The motivational-direction model specifying that approach/withdrawal motivation, and not valence, is the determinant for lateralization of evaluative processing has been supported by other researchers (e.g., van Honk & Schutter, 2006), but some still assert the usefulness of the affective-valence hypothesis for lateralization (e.g., Koch, Holland, & van Knippenberg, 2009; for a review of the debate, see Spielberg, Stewart, Levin, Miller, & Heller, 2008).

In general, explicit evaluation appears to heavily involve the prefrontal cortex, activating the bilateral ventrolateral PFC and other areas associated with self-referential processing or mentalizing (interpreting behavior through attempting to understand intentional mental states), such as the medial PFC, dorsomedial PFC, posterior cingulated cortex, temporal-parietal junction (TPJ) and the temporal pole (Lieberman, 2007). In addition to mentalizing, areas of the frontal cortex are also commonly activated in other types of evaluation, such as that which occurs during decision-making. Here, the left posterior OFC is related to processing a stimulus' objective value, where the medial anterior OFC exhibits activation in response to making correct (i.e., successful or beneficial) decisions or evaluations (Cunningham et al., 2008). In sum, while automatic evaluative processing makes heavy use of the amygdala, conscious evaluative processes (or their interpretations of automatic evaluative processes, at least) rely on cortical areas of the brain instead, most notably the frontal cortex. The fact that the amygdala activation is commonly found in response to emotionally salient stimuli, and activation in the OFC/PFC is usually associated with decision-making and interpretation of social stimuli, suggests that not only do these two separate processes have different localizations, but they also serve different functions in forming a global evaluation.

COMPLETING THE CIRCLE—REAPPRAISAL AND REGULATION

In our discussion of automatic and reflective attitude processes, we have already touched upon how some brain areas—notably the dlPFC—are involved in the regulation of implicit attitudes (Stanley et al., 2008). Regulation and control are more sophisticated than simply suppressing unwanted, automatically activated evaluative information from influencing one's judgments, however: They involve complex integration of automatically activated information (whether it be situationally accessible cognitions/memories or emotional responses) with current goals, motivation and social context, each of which can powerfully affect behavior on its own (Cunningham & Johnson, 2007). Regulatory processes are easily observed in experiments involving sensitive topics, such as those investigating racial bias. Researchers have consistently found amygdala activation, for instance, in response to presentation of Black vs. White faces even when this amygdala activation is significantly related to measures of implicit racial bias (such as the IAT). By contrast, participants' explicit attitudes are not necessarily related to amygdala activity (e.g., Phelps, O'Connor, Cunningham, Funayama, Gatenby, Gore, & Banaji, 2000; see also Hart, Whalen, Shin, McInerney, Fischer, & Rauch, 2000). Additionally, this amygdala activity is not inevitable, but depends crucially on the processing goals of the observer. If participants are instructed to focus on identifying the basic visual features of an out-group face, no difference in amygdala activity for Black vs. White faces occurs (Wheeler & Fiske, 2005). If participants are instead instructed to individuate the targets, however, suppression of amygdala activation in response to the faces is observed instead (i.e., the amygdala shows greater activity for White vs. Black faces).

Another example of research investigating the neural correlates of evaluative regulation and control comes from a 2004 experiment by McClure, Li, Tomlin, Cypert, Montague and Montague. Beginning in 1975, PepsiCo had organized a large number of highly publicized blind taste tests between Pepsi and Coke, called the Pepsi Challenge, in malls, shopping centers and other well-trafficked public areas. The goal of this test, of course, was to show that Americans on average preferred Pepsi to Coke when they were not biased by labels or preexisting brand loyalty. If PepsiCo's argument is correct, then psychologically it would mean that Americans actually experience a stronger automatic, favorable evaluation upon tasting Pepsi vs. Coke, but regulate or control the expression of that preference either consciously, because of explicit brand loyalty, or unconsciously, due to factors such as feelings of familiarity (e.g., Alter & Oppenheimer, 2008; cf. Alter & Oppenheimer, 2009a; Tversky & Kahneman, 1973).

To explore these processes of regulation, McClure et al. administered the Pepsi Challenge to participants in an fMRI scanner, where participants tasted the beverages and provided evaluations either with or without knowing the corresponding brand. In the absence of knowledge about the drink's brand, McClure et al. found that activation in the ventromedial PFC was associated with participants' self-reported drink preference. As the vmPFC has been linked to hedonic experience (e.g., Trepel, Fox, & Poldrack, 2005), it makes sense for participants' evaluations to be related to vmPFC activation in the absence of other cues. When participants tasted the beverages with knowledge about their brands, however, activation in the dorsolateral PFC and hippocampus was instead predictive of participants' preferences, suggesting that processes related to regulation and memory were exerting influence over participants' reported preferences. Although the validity of the Pepsi Challenge has been called into question in the past (e.g., see Gladwell, 2005), McClure and colleagues' findings remain valid. Regardless of each individual American's loyalty to Pepsi or Coke, we now have strong neuroscientific evidence that experience with those brands affects their preferences, independent of taste.

In general, exercise of regulation or control over one's evaluations has been shown to involve a number of cortical areas, including the ventrolateral PFC, dlPFC, dorsal ACC, medial PFC and precuneus (Cunningham et al., 2004), although it is not yet entirely clear which of these areas may activate automatically and which only are activated in the conscious exercise of cognitive control. In considering the role of the ACC in conflict detection and cognitive control more generally, some theorists have argued that conflict monitoring may occur relatively automatically, as opposed to the more conscious processes used in the regulatory system (Botvinick et al., 2001). The same may therefore hold for the functioning of these systems in the domain of evaluation (Cunningham, Raye, & Johnson, 2004), but not much research has yet directly investigated the role of cognitive control processes in detecting inconsistencies in evaluation.

Iterative-reprocessing model. In discussing automatic vs. controlled processes and the role of conflict detection and regulation, it can be tempting to think about the dynamic process of evaluation as a unidirectional flow between recall of previous attitudinal information, initial automatic evaluation, detection of conflict and regulation, and reconciliation with conscious processes. The **iterative-reprocessing model** (Cunningham et al., 2007; Cunningham & Zelazo, 2007) presents a unifying framework for automatic and conscious evaluative processes based in a complex neural network model of how different brain areas interact to produce (and reprocess) attitudinal information. In the iterative-reprocessing framework, automatic and reflective evaluative processing are distinguishable but are linked as in a continuum rather than in a dichotomous distinction (much as central and peripheral processing, as we saw in Chapter 5). Instead of processing flowing only in one direction, from automatic to reflective, to produce an outcome, the iterative-reprocessing model posits that there is a common and iterative (thus *re*processing) set of processes involved in generating evaluative outcomes. Rather than automatic and reflective processes being completely separate, these share the same components in that automatic processing involves fewer iterations of reprocessing and reflective processes involve a greater amount of reprocessing iterations that capture a larger and larger set of contextually relevant information (see Figure 10.5). More automatic processing might include affective information about the valence or arousal of a stimulus, where reflective processing (including regulation) might change the content or properties of the evaluative judgment, which in turn may affect the automatically activated evaluation and subsequent reflective reprocessing. For example, if you were bitten by a dog when you were young, it is possible that upon hearing a dog bark you might have an intense, negative and highly arousing evaluation of the dog (and the situation). If your current goal is to rescue the dog from having its leash tangled in the bushes, however, you might modify that evaluation according to the reasoning that the dog is likely barking because it is frightened. Since you are deter-mined to rescue it, you may try to tamp down your fear. If the dog barks again, your automatic reaction may have become more positive and less arousing, perhaps lead-ing to still different conscious evaluative judgments about the dog and the situation.

The iterative-reprocessing model exhibits other nontrivial similarities with the general framework of dual-process models of attitudes covered in earlier chapters. Both dual-process attitude models and the iterative-reprocessing model assume (or infer) that humans have competing needs to form accurate attitudes and judgments—i.e., to minimize error—and exert the least amount of mental effort while doing so. Similar to dual-process models, then, there must be a set of factors that control which of these motivations wins out (or rather, to what degree each one is exerted). Variables that affect the prioritization of these motivations, just as in other dual-process models, can take the form of individual (e.g., ability, reflectivity, need for cognition) or situational (e.g., motivation, opportunity) differences. The neural mechanisms underlying evaluation in the iterative-reprocessing model are presented in Figure 10.6. Although the full neural network involved in evaluation in

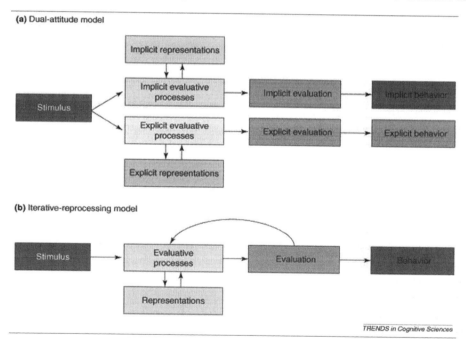

FIGURE 10.5 *A comparison of processes involved in dual-attitude (top) and iterative reprocessing (bottom) models of evaluation.*
Source: Cunningham, W. A. & Zelazo, P. D. (2007). Attitudes and evaluations: A social cognitive neuroscience perspective. *Trends in Cognitive Science, 11*(3), 97–104. Reprinted with permission.
Note: Color version can be found in the plate section.

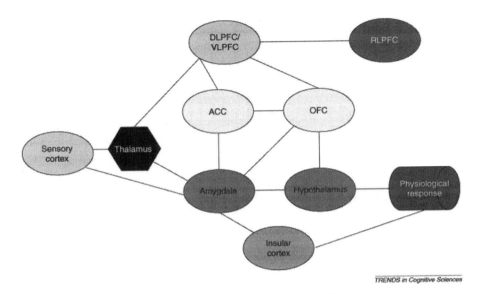

FIGURE 10.6 *Neural network underlying evaluation in the Iterative-Reprocessing Model.*

Source: Cunningham, W. A. & Zelazo, P. D. (2007). Attitudes and evaluations: A social cognitive neuroscience perspective. *Trends in Cognitive Science, 11*(3), 97–104. Reprinted with permission.

Note: Color version can be found in the plate section.

the iterative-reprocessing model is complex (see Cunningham & Zelazo, 2007), it is worth noting that the basic structure of this model utilizes the same brain areas we have previously discussed. In other words, in the iterative-reprocessing model the amygdala still initially (and perhaps constantly) processes affectively laden information, the ACC monitors conflict between context and initial evaluation and the OFC regulates the evaluative response to fit the context in case of a mismatch. Although experimental evidence directly testing the predictions of the iterative-reprocessing model is still in its infancy, the model provides a useful framework for considering automatic, reflective and regulatory processes and their effects together.

NEURAL CORRELATES OF DISSONANCE AROUSAL AND REDUCTION

One particularly fruitful avenue of investigation has been the identification of the areas of the brain that are activated in the course of cognitive dissonance arousal and reduction. Although there has been robust physiological evidence supporting the crucial role of arousal in dissonance (Croyle & Cooper, 1983; Losch & Cacioppo, 1990), the application of modern fMRI methodology to dissonance research has provided valuable convergent evidence supporting one of the classic theories in social psychology. A few landmark studies and one unifying framework have attempted to clarify how dissonance arousal and reduction function in the brain.

In an experiment replicating the induced compliance paradigm (Festinger & Carlsmith, 1959; see Chapter 7), van Veen, Krug, Schooler and Carter (2009) placed participants in an fMRI scanner and had them complete a boring task for 45 minutes. When this task was done, participants (still in the scanner) answered questions about their opinions of their experiences in the scanner and the task as well as neutral questions. Before responding, all of the participants were told to respond as though they had enjoyed the previous task and experience in the cramped scanner. Participants in the control condition were simply told that they would be paid for every question about the scanner/task for which they answered positively. The participants in the dissonance condition, however, were provided a cover story similar to the one used by Festinger and Carlsmith (1959), but adapted for the fMRI procedure. They were told that another participant was waiting in the next room and was nervous about being scanned. The participants were told that the 'waiting patient' would see their responses and, hopefully, be convinced to complete the procedure if the participants' responses were enthusiastically positive. After answering these questions in the scanner, participants left the scanner and reported their true attitudes towards the scanner and task. Not only did this experiment replicate classical dissonance attitude-change findings (i.e., participants in the dissonance condition showed more positive attitudes towards the scanner and the boring task than did participants in the control condition), but it also showed that activation in the bilateral dorsal ACC and left anterior insula predicted the amount of attitude change in the dissonance condition (but not the control condition; see Figure 10.7). This study strongly supported the predictions from dissonance theory, as it demonstrated activation in areas relating to conflict detection, negative affect, and autonomic arousal and showed that this activation (much like the self-reported measures of discomfort typical of dissonance research) predicted the degree to which participants actually changed their attitudes.

Another experiment investigating the neural correlates of dissonance used the free-choice procedure (see Brehm, 1956) adapted for use in an fMRI scanner (Jarcho, Berkman, & Lieberman, 2011). Participants first rated approximately 140 different names and 140 different paintings. As in the classic paradigm, participants then chose between two closely rated items (a hard choice) or two dissimilarly rated items (an easy choice). Unlike the original paradigm, where participants made only one choice, participants in this experiment made 80 different choices between two items. After finishing decision-making, participants then rated the items again. Replicating Brehm's results (see Chapter 7) using this paradigm, participants' attitudes changed in the positive direction for the chosen items in the difficult choice condition and changed in the negative direction for rejected items, while ratings for items that were not presented in the decision-making phase showed no attitude change

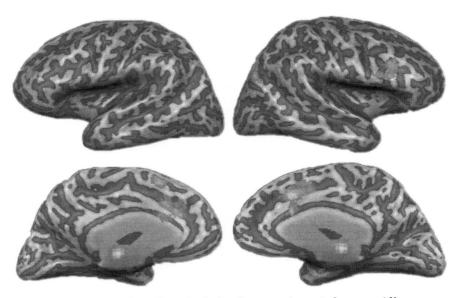

FIGURE 10.7 *The results of a whole-brain experimental group (dissonance, control) by sentence type (target, neutral) interaction displayed on an inflated cortical surface. Activations include bilateral dACC, bilateral medial frontal gyrus, and bilateral anterior insula.*

Source: van Veen, V., Krug, M. K., Schooler, J. W., & Carter, C. S. (2009). Neural activity predicts attitude change in cognitive dissonance. *Nature Neuroscience, 12*(11), 1469–1474. Reprinted with permission.

Note: Color version can be found in the plate section.

at all. Unlike the previously discussed study by van Veen et al (2009), however, participants' attitude change was predicted by activation in the right inferior frontal gyrus (IFG), medial PFC, precuneus, ventral striatum and parahippocampal gyrus while participants were making their decisions. In contrast, attitude change was negatively related to activity in the bilateral anterior insula and lateral parietal cortex. The authors interpreted these findings to suggest that the IFG may be downregulating negative arousal responses from the anterior insula, an inference supported by the fact that right IFG activity was more strongly correlated with anterior insula activation for decisions resulting in large vs. small amounts of attitude change. While both of these fMRI studies of dissonance observe activation in the anterior insula indicative of dissonance-related negative arousal, this study shows activation of areas that are indicative of regulation, suggesting that in the previously discussed study the conflict aroused through counter-attitudinal behavior may have been resolved later instead of at the moment of the decision, as in this experiment. Additionally, the authors also noted activation in areas related to self-referential thought (e.g., medial fronto-parietal areas), perhaps suggesting that participants were updating their preferences as a part of the process of rationalization. Together, these two studies illustrate the mechanisms of dissonance that are active in real time in the brain and provide convergent evidence for the pillars of dissonance theory (such as the relationship between discomfort and attitude change).

One unifying framework that foreshadowed some of the patterns of activation observed in the two fMRI experiments (Jarcho et al., 2011; van Veen et al., 2009) is the **action-based model of dissonance** (Harmon-Jones, 1999; Harmon-Jones, Amodio, & Harmon-Jones, 2009). As we saw in Chapter 7, the action-based model of dissonance proposes that dissonance is aversive because cognitive conflict stands in the way of effective and efficient goal-directed action. Blending concepts originating from regulatory focus theory (Higgins, 1997), the action-based model views dissonance as a negative emotional state, often aroused from commitment to action, that prompts approach motivation to resolve cognitive discrepancy caused by that chosen action (Harmon-Jones, Gerdjikov, & Harmon-Jones, 2008). Research investigating the action-based model of dissonance using EEG has helped elucidate the ways in which commitment may function in the brain while undergoing cognitive conflict. While dissonance, like other negative approach emotions (such as anger), seems to prompt greater left frontal cortical activity (Harmon-Jones, 2004), there is evidence that this brain region is sensitive to the magnitude of choice that participants had in performing an action, regardless of whether the actions were pro- or counter-attitudinal (Harmon-Jones, Harmon-Jones, Serra, & Gable, 2011).

These results are consistent with previous findings discussed in this chapter (and elsewhere) in which the left frontal cortex (e.g., the dlPFC) has been linked to processes involving intention, regulation and decision-making (Knight & Grabowecky, 1995; Kuhl, 2000; Petrides & Milner, 1982). Together with the finding that high vs. low choice produced more behavior-consistent attitudes regardless of whether the behavior was pro- or counter-attitudinal (Harmon-Jones et al., 2011), these findings suggest that the action-based model of dissonance perhaps has broader relevance beyond dissonance to approach-motivated responses and to commitment more generally. Supplementing findings that show the effects of cognitive dissonance in patients with anterograde amnesia (Lieberman, Ochsner, Gilbert, & Schacter, 2001) and in monkeys and young children (Egan, Santos, & Bloom, 2007), ERP evidence supporting the action-based model also supports the conclusion that dissonance can operate on a more automatic level than previously thought (Harmon-Jones et al., 2006; Harmon-Jones, Harmon-Jones, Fearn, Sigelman, & Johnson, 2008).

In summary, we have seen evidence that while automatic and reflective evaluative processing do indeed exhibit discriminable areas of activation in the brain, it is likely that these processes influence each other and that both contribute to one's attitude towards a stimulus. As is to be expected due to its role in conflict monitoring, the ACC appears to play a prominent role in theories accounting for the arousal (and detection) of cognitive dissonance. Other brain areas associated with self-regulation (e.g., the dlPFC and IFG) and self-referential thought (e.g., the OFC) feature both in observations about the process of cognitive dissonance and research focusing on regulation of evaluation or attitude expression more generally. Through the innovative use of fMRI and ERP methods, researchers have finally begun to explore the link between dissonance processes and other attitude-relevant processes involving reappraisal and regulation, as well as identify the areas of activation specific to each.

CONNECTIONIST MODELS OF ATTITUDE STRUCTURE AND CHANGE

The strength of fMRI and ERP measures is that they allow psychologists to observe direct neurological effects of a stimulus in the patterns of brain activation, whether in the form of a voltage deflection or increase in blood flow. The directness of neuroscientific data, however, can sometimes paint a deceptively simple picture of the extremely complex and sophisticated machine that is the human brain. As we saw with the neuroscientific studies investigating cognitive dissonance, researchers investigating the same psychological process may obtain slightly different patterns of brain activation across studies, even if the crucial situation of interest (e.g., being in a situation where dissonance is theoretically predicted to arise) is the same. Given the vast amount of information that the brain handles at any given moment, and the large amount of psychological processes operating within the brain, it can sometimes prove challenging for researchers to create a functional model of how the brain works with the appropriate amount of complexity to accurately reflect the patterns of activation observed in their experiments.

In light of this, **connectionist modeling** has emerged as a valuable tool that allows the researcher to artificially create and specify the properties and constraints of a model that they think reasonably resembles human behavior. Unlike neuroscientific data, these approximate models can be as simple or complex as the researchers need in order to test their hypotheses. Using powerful computer software, researchers can then conduct many repeated simulations on these models built with the goal of testing specific aspects of a psychological theory. By comparing the results of their simulations to experimentally robust behavioral or neuroscientific findings, researchers can then draw a conclusion about whether or not their model is a useful and meaningful approximation of how humans think or behave. If the results of their simulations indeed resemble empirical data from humans, it is then reasonable to conclude that the properties of the model specified by the researcher *a priori* are sufficient to produce the pattern of results found in human behavior. This, then, provides convergent evidence about process and mechanism in the observed human data of interest. In this section, we will review some innovative insights from connectionist modeling about attitude structure as well as explore how connectionist models can be applied to gain specific insight about a particular theory—once again, the theory of cognitive dissonance.

Connectionist modeling of attitude structure poses a significant theoretical challenge to traditional models of attitude structure and function. Before the advent of connectionist and **parallel-distributed-processing (PDP)** models, researchers typically conceived of attitudes (or memory traces more generally) as distinct entities that represented a specific evaluation of an attitude object. In this interpretation, encountering the attitude object (or something related to it, either through experiencing it directly or thinking of it) might trigger a memory trace of the evaluation and therefore recall one's previously constructed evaluation of the object or concept. This automatically (or willfully) activated evaluation might then undergo additional downstream revision or regulation, as per the processes described earlier in this chapter, and ultimately guide subsequent cognition or behavior. A connectionist viewpoint, however, takes an entirely different stance.

Connectionism, at least as it manifests in neuroscience and psychology, refers to the idea that mental processes and phenomena can be described through specifying properties of interconnected networks of nodes. Notably, properties that are often specified by the researcher in connectionist models include the nodes, the weights between the nodes and any sort of learning rule that specifies how the nodes change the presence or weight of the connections between them. One simple analogy for a connectionist model might be a simple model of neuronal connections where the nodes are individual neurons, the connections are synapses and the learning rule might be that the connections between the neurons (i.e., the weights between the nodes in the network) grow stronger when two neurons activate together.

In terms of how attitudes operate from a connectionist perspective, a number of researchers have attempted to perform computer simulations on connectionist models to examine certain specific properties of attitudes. From a connectionist view (Conrey & Smith, 2007), attitudes are best represented as a 'state' instead of a 'thing'—in other words, attitudes are not static evaluations that are frozen in time and stashed away in memory once created to await recall, but rather represent a complex pattern of activation that is inseparable from its context. Of course, even from a connectionist perspective, evaluative information is indeed stored in memory and recalled—the distinction is not only that what is stored or encoded depends crucially on the particular context, but also that what is *recalled* depends on the configuration of contextual and personal features currently present in the situation (and not, by contrast, a few focal retrieval cues). To be more precise, what is *recalled* is actually *reconstructed* based on the previously meaningful pattern of activation stored in memory being integrated with currently relevant situational information at hand. Consistency across situations in the attitude representation, then, is a product of experience-driven prioritization of important vs. unimportant dimensions of an attitude object. For example, if you recall your attitude towards salmon on Wednesday and again on Friday, it is likely that your attitude towards salmon would not have changed. If you recall back when you were a child, however, it is quite likely that your opinion about salmon was predicated on very different information when you saw it in a book versus when you had your first bite of it. It is quite likely, now, that your attitude towards salmon depends mostly on its taste and not its appearance or unusual mating habits. Similarly, whether you are dining at an upscale seafood restaurant or a sushi bar might influence your attitude towards salmon, as well as the attitude representation you store in memory for later use.

Some experimental evidence using computer simulations to test connectionist hypotheses about attitudes may be illustrative of the ways in which connectionist models provide useful convergent evidence for other branches of attitude research. Exploring the acquisition of attitudes and beliefs, Eiser, Fazio, Stafford and Prescott (2003) constructed a neural network model simulating approach and avoidance behaviors to investigate expectancy confirmation. By experimentally manipulating the type of feedback received after each approach/avoid decision (e.g., full feedback or feedback contingent on an approach decision), the authors sought to investigate whether or not the network could effectively discriminate between good and bad inputs. While the network perfectly discriminated good and bad inputs in the full feedback condition, contingent feedback led to misclassification of some good inputs as bad. This error was eliminated by artificially biasing the network towards approach (vs. avoidance) behavior. Since it is likely that humans do not exhibit perfect discriminability, these data suggest that the use of contingent feedback to form our evaluations and attitudes may lead to a positive bias for our interactions with stimuli (i.e., we might be happy because we interact more with the things we already like) but a persistence of negative attitudes and evaluations, such as those present in prejudicial beliefs (see also Eiser, Stafford, & Fazio, 2008). In other words, these simulations suggest that part of the persistence of negative attitudes is due to the fact that we are more likely to approach (i.e., pursue, investigate, interact with) things that we already evaluate positively and hesitant to obtain feedback about things that we evaluate negatively (even if we have no experience with them ourselves!). Even though no actual people ever participated, these computer simulations of attitude learning provide valuable insight into the process by which humans may form evaluations in the real world.

Another set of simulations carried out by Monroe and Read (2008) investigated a large number of attitude-related processes (e.g., persuasion, social influence, motivated reasoning) and their operation under the **Attitudes as Constraint-Satisfaction (ACS)** model. Given that attitudes are connected with many different facets of evaluation and with many properties of the attitude object itself, this model assumes (like many theories on attitudes, e.g. dissonance) a desire or constraint for consistency between these different facets of belief and evaluation. The idea that these different beliefs and evaluations must cohere can be represented by the concept of parallel constraint satisfaction, where the goal of the network is to maximize fit (i.e., minimize inconsistency) given the relationships between different aspects of the attitude, properties of the attitude object, etc. While the specifications of the model are complex, simulations across multiple attitude-relevant phenomena and processes illustrate that attitude structure and accompanying strength are extremely important for determining the outcome. These simulations also supported the crucial role of attention or cognitive capacity in the strength of the link between the evaluation and prior attitude (a prediction made by MODE; see Chapter 6). Finally, specifying a model in this manner (as a parallel constraint satisfaction network) allows us to view hypothetical relationships between implicit and explicit attitudes that would be very difficult, if not impossible, to observe in the laboratory. Because of the complex and dynamic nature of these processes—and how different they can seem from one another—it is theoretically meaningful to show that networks built on constraint satisfaction can account for the empirical data while simultaneously generating new insights and predictions regarding the existing theories.

Connectionist modeling of attitude networks based on constraint satisfaction has also been applied to theories of cognitive consistency, such as cognitive dissonance. In the consonance model of dissonance, the basic motivation for cognitive consistency takes the form of specifying constraints on the beliefs and attitudes that one can hold simultaneously (Shultz & Lepper, 1996, 1999). Here, the degree to which similarly evaluated units are linked together with positive weights and dissimilarly evaluated units by negative weights corresponds to the process of reducing dissonance as per constraint satisfaction. By replicating a variety of cognitive dissonance paradigms (e.g., insufficient justification, free choice and induced compliance) via simulation, Shultz and Lepper found that their constraint-satisfaction model uncovered new relationships among variables in addition to accounting for previous experimental results. Most notably, simulations of the consonance model showed evidence of spreading of alternatives in choices between two undesirable alternatives in the free choice paradigm, an effect that was unobserved at time of modeling but then experimentally replicated by the authors (see Shultz, Léveillé, & Lepper, 1995). Other connectionist attempts at modeling social psychological phenomena using constraint satisfaction criteria, such as general evidence judgments (Simon, Snow, & Read, 2004) and post-choice preference modification (Simon, Krawczyk, & Holyoak, 2004), resemble these results and echo the importance of cognitive consistency in general attitude structure. Thus, despite a wealth of pre-existing dissonance research, connectionist modeling can still generate novel hypotheses and results while providing additional evidence supporting past dissonance findings. Furthermore, through use of a more general constraint satisfaction model, the consonance model of dissonance links dissonance phenomena to the larger attitudes literature that can similarly be modeled in the same way with the same degree of success.

SUMMARY AND CONCLUSION

In this chapter, we have attempted to present a survey of the modern methodological and theoretical innovations that have greatly contributed to the study of attitudes in the 21st century. As methods have advanced and paradigms have become more sophisticated, the field of attitudes research has come closer to pursuing and observing the neurological substrates of people's attitudes. From the bogus pipeline to powerful computer simulations of neural networks, social psychologists have progressed to more powerful proxies for directly observing the process of evaluation. Research investigating ERPs has demonstrated that basic components of evaluation—e.g., valence, intensity, categorization and consistency—can happen rapidly and spontaneously in the brain. It has been extremely useful for gaining information about the automaticity and time sequence of evaluation. Data from fMRI studies form complementary and convergent evidence about localization of evaluative brain function, identifying the crucial role of brain structures such as the amygdala for automatic evaluation, prefrontal and orbitofrontal cortical structures for reflective evaluation, and the ACC and dlPFC for regulation.

The advent of connectionist modeling and computer simulation, furthermore, has given social psychologists tools to isolate variables and processes important to evaluation and has contributed a fresh perspective to the field of attitudes research. Together, these new methods have driven significant theoretical advances and spawned novel hypotheses in classic theories such as cognitive dissonance.

The dictum that is probably the most reliable in science is that nothing is static. Research questions change and the methodology changes with them. Surely, when Thurstone pronounced that attitudes can be measured, he had no inkling that people's evaluations would be assessed with changes in oxygenated blood flow or with event-related potentials measured at the scalp. Social neuroscience has opened new windows to the study of social processes in general, and attitudes in particular, that were not conceivable a few decades ago. The future will show a sharpening of our research questions and the evolution of new methods that will, in turn, help shape the questions of tomorrow.

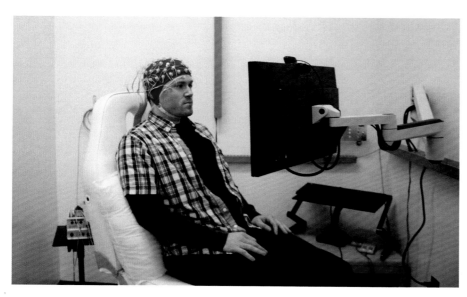

FIGURE 10.1 *A participant with EEG cap placed on the scalp.*

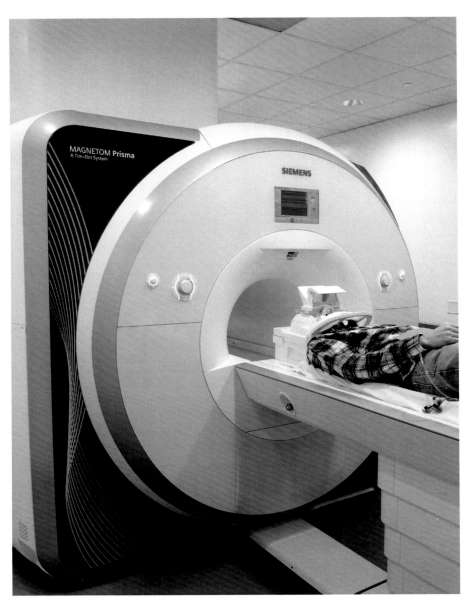

FIGURE 10.2 *A participant waiting for an fMRI experiment to begin.*

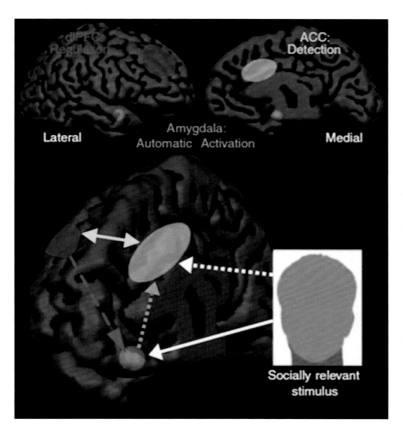

FIGURE 10.3 *The three-tier model of the neural basis for implicit attitudes. Amygdala activation is implicated in automatic evaluation of socially relevant stimuli; the ACC is implicated in the detection of socially relevant stimuli and their congruence with one's preferences; and the dlPFC is implicated in regulation of the amygdala's response.*

Source: Stanley, D., Phelps, E., & Banaji, M. (2008). The neural basis of implicit attitudes. *Current Directions in Psychological Science, 17*(2), 164–170. Reprinted with permission.

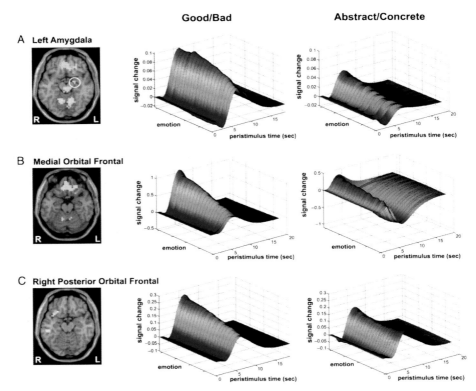

FIGURE 10.4 *Differences in the correlation between brain activity and rated emotional intensity in the left amygdala (A), medial orbital frontal cortex (B), and right posterior orbital frontal cortex (C) in response to good vs. bad and abstract vs. concrete stimuli.*

Source: Cunningham, W. A., Raye, C. L., & Johnson, M. K. (2004). Implicit and explicit evaluation: fMRI correlates of valence, emotional intensity, and control in the processing of attitudes. *Journal of Cognitive Neuroscience*, *16*(10), 1717–1729. Reprinted with permission.

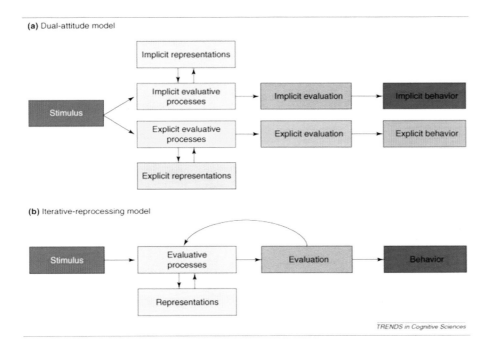

(a) Dual-attitude model

Implicit representations

Stimulus

Implicit evaluative processes → Implicit evaluation → Implicit behavior

Explicit evaluative processes → Explicit evaluation → Explicit behavior

Explicit representations

(b) Iterative-reprocessing model

Stimulus → Evaluative processes → Evaluation → Behavior

Representations

FIGURE 10.5 *A comparison of processes involved in dual-attitude (top) and iterative reprocessing (bottom) models of evaluation.*

Source: Cunningham, W. A. & Zelazo, P. D. (2007). Attitudes and evaluations: A social cognitive neuroscience perspective. *Trends in Cognitive Science, 11*(3), 97–104. Reprinted with permission.

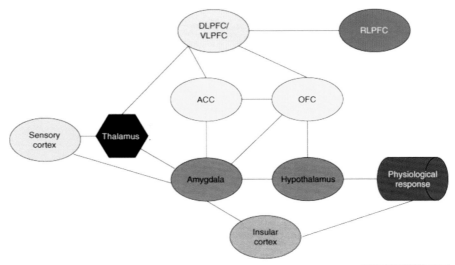

TRENDS in Cognitive Sciences

FIGURE 10.6 *Neural network underlying evaluation in the Iterative-Reprocessing Model.*

Source: Cunningham, W.A. & Zelazo, P.D. (2007). Attitudes and evaluations: A social cognitive neuroscience perspective. *Trends in Cognitive Science, 11*(3), 97–104. Reprinted with permission.

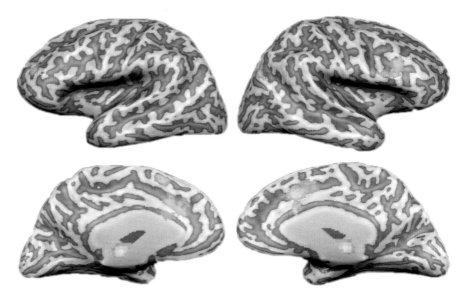

FIGURE 10.7 *The results of a whole-brain experimental group (dissonance, control) by sentence type (target, neutral) interaction displayed on an inflated cortical surface. Activations include bilateral dACC, bilateral medial frontal gyrus, and bilateral anterior insula.*

Source: van Veen, V., Krug, M.K., Schooler, J.W., & Carter, C.S. (2009). Neural activity predicts attitude change in cognitive dissonance. *Nature Neuroscience, 12*(11), 1469–1474. Reprinted with permission.

REFERENCES

Abelson, M. A. (1987). Examination of avoidable and unavoidable turnover. *Journal of Applied Psychology, 72*(3), 382.

Abelson, R. P. (1995). Attitude extremity. In Petty, R. E. & Krosnick, J. A. *Attitude strength: Antecedents and consequences* (pp.25–42). Hillsdale, NJ. Erlbaum.

Abelson, R. P., Aronson, E., McGuire, W. J., Newcomb, T.M., Rosenberg, M. J., & Tannenbaum, P. H. (Eds.). (1968). *Theories of cognitive consistency: A sourcebook.* Chicago: Rand McNally.

Abelson, R. P., Kinder, D. R., Peters, M. D., & Fiske, S. T. (1982). Affective and semantic components in political person perception. *Journal of Personality and Social Psychology, 42*(4), 619–630.

Adriaanse, M. A., Gollwitzer, P. M., de Ridder, D. T., De Wit, J. B., & Kroese, F. M. (2011). Breaking habits with implementation intentions: A test of underlying processes. *Personality and Social Psychology Bulletin, 37*(4), 502–513.

Adriaanse, M. A., van Oosten, J. M., de Ridder, D. T., de Wit, J. B., & Evers, C. (2011). Planning what not to eat: Ironic effects of implementation intentions negating unhealthy habits. *Personality and Social Psychology Bulletin, 37*(1), 69–81.

Agerström, J., & Rooth, D. O. (2009). Implicit prejudice and ethnic minorities: Arab-Muslims in Sweden. *International Journal of Manpower, 30*(1/2), 43–55.

Agerström, J., & Rooth, D. O. (2011). The role of automatic obesity stereotypes in real hiring discrimination. *Journal of Applied Psychology, 96*(4), 790.

Agnew, C. R., Van Lange, P. A., Rusbult, C. E., & Langston, C. A. (1998). Cognitive interdependence: Commitment and the mental representation of close relationships. *Journal of Personality and Social Psychology, 74*, 939–954.

Aharon, I., Etcoff, N., Ariely, D., Chabris, C. F., O'Connor, E., & Breiter, H. C. (2001). Beautiful faces have variable reward value: fMRI and behavioral evidence. *Neuron, 32*(3), 537–551.

Ajzen, I. (1985). From intentions to actions: A theory of planned behavior. In J. Kuhl & J. Beckmann (Eds.), *Action control: From cognition to behavior* (pp. 11–39). Berlin: Springer-Verlag.

Ajzen, I. (1987). Attitudes, traits, and actions: Dispositional prediction of behavior in personality and social psychology. *Advances in Experimental Social Psychology, 20*(1), 63.

Ajzen, I. (1988). *Attitudes, personality, and behavior.* Chicago: Dorsey Press.

Ajzen, I. (1991). The theory of planned behavior. *Organizational behavior and human decision processes, 50*(2), 179–211.

Ajzen, I. (2005). *Attitudes, personality, and behavior* (2nd ed.). Milton Keynes, UK: Open University Press/McGraw-Hill.

Ajzen, I., Albarracín, D., & Hornik, R. (Eds.) (2007). *Prediction and change of health behavior: Applying the reasoned action approach.* Mahwah, NJ: Lawrence Erlbaum.

Ajzen, I., & Fishbein, M. (1977). Attitude-behavior relations: A theoretical analysis and review of empirical research. *Psychological Bulletin, 84*(5), 888.

Ajzen, I., & Fishbein, M. (1980). *Understanding attitudes and predicting social behavior.* Englewood Cliffs, NJ: Prentice-Hall.

Ajzen, I., Czasch, C., & Flood, M. G. (2009). From intentions to behavior: Implementation intention, commitment, and conscientiousness. *Journal of Applied Social Psychology, 39*(6), 1356–1372.

Ajzen, I., & Manstead, A.S.R. (2007). Changing health-related behaviors: An approach based on the theory of planned behavior. In K. van den Bos, M. Hewstone, J. de Wit, H. Schut, & M. Stroebe (Eds.), *The scope of social psychology: Theory and applications* (pp. 43–63). New York: Psychology Press.

Ajzen, I., Albarracin, D., & Hornik, R. (Eds). (2007). Prediction and change of health behavior: Applying the reasoned action approach. Mahwah, NJ: Lawrence Erlbaum.

Ajzen, I., Timko, C., & White, J. B. (1982). Self-monitoring and the attitude–behavior relation. *Journal of Personality and Social Psychology, 42*(3), 426.

Albarracín, D., Johnson, B. T., Fishbein, M., & Muellerleile, P. A. (2001). Theories of reasoned action and planned behavior as models of condom use: A meta-analysis. *Psychological Bulletin, 127*, 142–161.

Albarracín, D., & Mitchell, A. L. (2004). The role of defensive confidence in preference for proattitudinal information: How believing that one is strong can sometimes be a defensive weakness. *Personality and Social Psychology Bulletin, 30*(12), 1565–1584.

Albarracín, D., Wang, W., Li, H., & Noguchi, K. (2008). Structure of attitudes: Judgments, memory, and implications for change. *Attitudes and Attitude Change*, 19–40.

Albarracín, D., Zanna, M. P., Johnson, B. T., & Kumkale, G. T. 2005. Attitudes: Introduction and scope. In D. Albarracin, B. T. Johnson, and M. P. Zanna (Eds.), *The Handbook of Attitudes* (pp. 3–19). NJ: Lawerence Erlbaum.

Allison, S. T., & Messick, D. M. (1988). The feature-positive effect, attitude strength, and degree of perceived consensus. *Personality and Social Psychology Bulletin, 14*(2), 231–241.

Allport, G. W. (1935). Attitudes. *Handbook of social psychology, 2*, 798–844.

Allyn, J., & Festinger, L. (1961). The effectiveness of unanticipated persuasive communications. *Journal of Abnormal and Social Psychology, 62*, 35.

Altemeyer, B. (1981). *Right-wing authoritarianism.* Winnipeg: University of Manitoba Press.

Alter, A. L., & Oppenheimer, D. M. (2008). Effects of fluency on psychological distance and mental construal (or why New York is a large city, but New York is a civilized jungle). *Psychological Science, 19*(2), 161–167.

Alter, A. L., & Oppenheimer, D. M. (2009a). Uniting the tribes of fluency to form a metacognitive nation. *Personality and Social Psychology Review, 13*(3), 219–235.

Alter, A. L., & Oppenheimer, D. M. (2009b). Suppressing secrecy through metacognitive ease: Cognitive fluency encourages self-disclosure. *Psychological Science, 20*(11), 1414–1420.

Alter, A. L., Oppenheimer, D. M., Epley, N., & Eyre, R. N. (2007). Overcoming intuition: Metacognitive difficulty activates analytic reasoning. *Journal of Experimental Psychology: General, 136*(4), 569.

Anderson, A. K., Christoff, K., Stappen, I., Panitz, D., Ghahremani, D. G., Glover, G., Gabrieli, J. D., & Sobel, N. (2003). Dissociated neural representations of intensity and valence in human olfaction. *Nature Neuroscience, 6*, 196–202.

Aneshensel, C. S. (1992). Social stress: Theory and research. *Annual Review of Sociology, 18*, 15–38.

Appel, V. (1971). On advertising wearout. *Journal of Advertising Research, 11,* 1–13.

Arkes, H. R., & Tetlock, P. E. (2004). Attributions of implicit prejudice, or "would Jesse Jackson 'fail' the implicit association test?" *Psychological Inquiry, 15*(4), 257–278.

Armitage, C. J., & Conner, M. (2001). Efficacy of the theory of planned behaviour: A meta-analytic review. *British Journal of Social Psychology, 40*(4), 471–499.

Aronson, E. (1969). The theory of cognitive dissonance: A current perspective. *Advances in Experimental Social Psychology, 4,* 1–34.

Aronson, E. (1992). The return of the repressed: Dissonance theory makes a comeback. *Psychological Inquiry, 3*(4), 303–311.

Aronson, E., & Carlsmith, J. M. (1962). Performance expectancy as a determinant of actual performance. *Journal of Abnormal and Social Psychology, 65,* 178.

Aronson, J., Blanton, H., & Cooper, J. (1995). From dissonance to disidentification: Selectivity in the self-affirmation process. *Journal of Personality and Social Psychology, 68*(6), 986–996.

Aronson, E., & Carlsmith, J. M. (1963). Effect of the severity of threat on the devaluation of forbidden behavior. *The Journal of Abnormal and Social Psychology, 66*(6), 584.

Aronson, E., & Mills, J. M. (1959). The effect of severity of initiation on liking for a group. *Journal of Abnormal and Social Psychology, 59,* 177–181.

Aronson, E., Turner, J. A., & Carlsmith, J. M. (1963). Communicator credibility and communication discrepancy as determinants of opinion change. *The Journal of Abnormal and Social Psychology, 67*(1), 31.

Asendorpf, J. B., Banse, R., & Mücke, D. (2002). Double dissociation between implicit and explicit personality self-concept: The case of shy behavior. *Journal of Personality and Social Psychology, 83*(2), 380–393.

Ashburn-Nardo, L., Knowles, M. L. & Monteith, M. J. (2003). Black Americans' implicit racial associations and their implications for intergroup judgment. *Social Cognition, 21,* 61–87.

Ashburn-Nardo, L., Voils, C. I., & Monteith, M. J. (2001). Implicit associations as the seeds of intergroup bias: How easily do they take root? *Journal of Personality and Social Psychology, 81*(5), 789.

Ashmore, R. D., Ramchandra, V., and R. A. Jones. *Censorship as an attitude change induction.* Paper Presented At The Meeting of The Eastern Psychological Association, New York. April 1971.

Axsom, D. (1989). Cognitive dissonance and behavior change in psychotherapy. *Journal of Experimental Social Psychology, 25,* 234–252.

Axsom, D., & Cooper, J. (1985). Cognitive dissonance and psychotherapy: The role of effort justification in inducing weight loss. *Journal of Experimental Social Psychology, 21,* 149–160.

Axsom, D., Yates, S., & Chaiken, S. (1987). Audience response as a heuristic cue in persuasion. *Journal of Personality and Social Psychology, 53*(1), 30.

Babad, E. Y., Ariav, A., Rosen, I., & Salomon, G. (1987). Perseverance of bias as a function of debriefing conditions and subjects' confidence. *Social Behaviour, 2*(3), 185–193.

Bain, P. G., Hornsey, M. J., Bongiorno, R., Kashima, Y., & Crimston, D. (2013). Collective futures: How projections about the future of society are related to actions and attitudes supporting social change. *Personality and Social Psychology Bulletin, 39*(4), 523–539.

Banaji, M. R. (2001). Implicit attitudes can be measured. In H. L. Roediger, I. N. Nairne, and A. M. Suprenant (Eds.). *The nature of remembering: Essays in honor of Robert G. Crowder* (pp. 117–149). Washington: APA.

Bandura, A. (1997). Self-efficacy: The exercise of control. New York: Freeman.

Bandura, A. (1977). *Social learning theory*. Englewood Cliffs, NJ: Prentice-Hall.

Barden, J., & Petty, R. E. (2008). The mere perception of elaboration creates attitude certainty: Exploring the thoughtfulness heuristic. *Journal of Personality and Social Psychology, 95*(3), 489.

Bargh, J. A. (1994). The four horsemen of automaticity: Intention, awareness, efficiency, and control as separate issues. *Handbook of Social Cognition, 1*, 1–40.

Bargh, J. A., Chaiken, S., Govender, R., & Pratto, F. (1992). The generality of the automatic attitude activation effect. *Journal of Personality and Social Psychology, 62*(6), 893–912.

Bargh, J. A., Chaiken, S., Raymond, P., & Hymes, C. (1996). The automatic evaluation effect: Unconditional automatic attitude activation with a pronunciation task. *Journal of Experimental Social Psychology, 32*(1), 104–128.

Baron, A. S., & Banaji, M. R. (2006). The development of implicit attitudes: Evidence of race evaluations from ages 6 and 10 and adulthood. *Psychological Science, 17*(1), 53–58.

Barsalou, L. W., Niedenthal, P. M., Barbey, A. K., & Ruppert, J. A. (2003). Social embodiment. *Psychology of Learning and Motivation, 43*, 43–92.

Bartholow, B. D., & Amodio, D. M. (2009). Brain potentials in social psychological research. *Methods in Social Neuroscience*, 198.

Bassili, J. N. (1993). Response latency versus certainty as indexes of the strength of voting intentions in a CATI survey. *Public Opinion Quarterly, 57*(1), 54–61.

Bassili, J. N. (1995). Response latency and the accessibility of voting intentions: What contributes to accessibility and how it affects vote choice. *Personality and Social Psychology Bulletin, 21*(7), 686–695.

Bassili, J. N. (1996). Meta-judgmental versus operative indexes of psychological attributes: The case of measures of attitude strength. *Journal of Personality and Social Psychology, 71*(4), 637.

Bassili, J. N. (2008). Attitude strength. *Attitudes and attitude change*, 237–260.

Bator, R. J. & Cialdini, R. B. (2000). The application of persuasion theory to the development of effective proenvironmental public service announcements. *Journal of Social Issues, 56*, 527–541.

Baumeister, R. F., Bratslavsky, E., Muraven, M., & Tice, D. M. (1998). Ego depletion: Is the active self a limited resource? *Journal of Personality and Social Psychology, 74*, 1252–1265.

Baumeister, R. F., & Leary, M. R. (1995). The need to belong: desire for interpersonal attachments as a fundamental human motivation. *Psychological Bulletin, 117*(3), 497.

Baumeister, R. F., Vohs, K. D., & Tice, D. M. (2007). The strength model of self-control. *Current Directions in Psychological Science, 16*(6), 351–355.

Beauvois, J., & Joule, R.V. (1999). A radical point of view on dissonance theory. In E. Harmon-Jones & J. Mils (Eds.), *Cognitive dissonance: Progress on a pivotal theory in social psychology*. Washington, DC: APA.

Bem, D. J. (1972). Self-Perception Theory. In L. Berkowitz (Ed.), *Advances in Experimental Social Psychology, 6*, 1–62.

Bem, D. J., & McConnell, H. K. (1970). Testing the self-perception explanation of dissonance phenomena: On the salience of premanipulation attitudes. *Journal of Personality and Social Psychology, 14*(1), 23–31.

Berger, H. (1929). Über das elektrenkephalogramm des menschen. *European Archives of Psychiatry and Clinical Neuroscience, 87*(1), 527–570.

Berger, I. E., & Mitchell, A. A. (1989). The effect of advertising on attitude accessibility, attitude confidence, and the attitude-behavior relationship. *Journal of Consumer Research*, 269–279.

Bergin, A. (1962). The effect of dissonant persuasive communications upon changes in a self-referring attitude. *Journal of Personality, 30*, 423–438.

Bernard, M. M., Maio, G. R., & Olson, J. M. (2003). The vulnerability of values to attack: Inoculation of values and value-relevant attitudes. *Personality and Social Psychology Bulletin, 29*, 63–75.

Biek, M., Wood, W., & Chaiken, S. (1996). Working knowledge, cognitive processing and attitudes: On the determinants of bias. *Personality and Social Psychology Bulletin, 22*, 547–556.

Biek, M., Wood, W., Nations, C., & Chaiken, S. (1993). *Working knowledge and persuasiveness of proattitudinal and counterattitudinal messages*. Unpublished manuscript, Texas A&M University.

Blankenship, K. L., & Wegener, D. T. (2008). Opening the mind to close it: Considering a message in light of important values increases message processing and later resistance to change. *Journal of Personality and Social Psychology, 94*(2), 196.

Blankenship, K. L., Wegener, D. T. & Murray, R. A. (2012). Circumventing resistance: Using values to indirectly change attitudes. *Journal of Personality and Social Psychology, 103*, 606–621.

Blankenship, V., Hnat, S. M., Hess, T. G., & Brown, D. R. (1984). Reciprocal interaction and similarity of personality attributes. *Journal of Social and Personal Relationships, 1*(4), 415–432.

Blanton, H., Cooper, J., Skurnik, I., & Aronson, J. (1997). When bad things happen to good feedback: Exacerbating the need for self-justification with self-affirmations. *Society of Personality and Social Psychology, 23*(7), 684–692.

Blanton, H. & Jaccard, J. (2008). Unconscious racism: A concept in pursuit of a measure. *Annual Review of Sociology, 34*, 277–297.

Blanton, H., Jaccard, J., Gonzales, P. M., & Christie, C. (2006). Decoding the implicit association test: Implications for criterion prediction. *Journal of Experimental Social Psychology, 42*(2), 192–212.

Blanton, H., Jaccard, J., Klick, J., Mellers, B., Mitchell, G., & Tetlock, P. E. (2009). Strong claims and weak evidence: Reassessing the predictive validity of the IAT. *Journal of Applied Psychology, 94*(3), 567–582.

Blascovich, J., & Mendes, W. B. (2010). Social psychophysiology and embodiment. In S. T. Fiske, D. T. Gilbert, & G. Lindzey (Eds.), *The handbook of social psychology* (5th ed., pp. 194–227). New York, NY: Wiley.

Bless, H., Bohner, G., Schwarz, N., & Strack, F. (1990). Mood and persuasion: A cognitive response analysis. *Personality and Social Psychology Bulletin, 16*(2), 331–345.

Bohner, G., Chaiken, S., & Hunyadi, P. (1994). The role of mood and message ambiguity in the interplay of heuristic and systematic processing. *European Journal of Social Psychology, 24*(1), 207–221.

Boninger, D. S., Brock, T. C., Cook, T. D., Gruder, C. L., & Romer, D. (1990). Discovery of reliable attitude change persistence resulting from a transmitter tuning set. *Psychological Science, 1*(4), 268–271.

Boninger, D. S., Krosnick, J. A., Berent, M. K., & Fabrigar, L. R. (1995). The causes and consequences of attitude importance. *Attitude strength: Antecedents and consequences*, 159–189. Mahwah, NJ: Lawrence Erlbaum Associates.

Bornstein, R. F. (1989). Exposure and affect: Overview and meta-analysis of research, 1968–1987. *Psychological Bulletin, 106*(2), 265.

Botvinick, M. M., Braver, T. S., Barch, D. M., Carter, C. S., & Cohen, J. D. (2001). Conflict monitoring and cognitive control. *Psychological Review, 108*(3), 624.

Brannon, L. A., Tagler, M. J., & Eagly, A. H. (2007). The moderating role of attitude strength in selective exposure to information. *Journal of Experimental Social Psychology, 43*, 611–617.

Brehm, J. W. (1956) Postdecision changes in the desirability of alternatives. *Journal of Abnormal and Social Psychology*, 52, 384–9.

Brehm, J. W. (1966). *A theory of psychological reactance.* New York, NY: Academic Press.

Brehm, J. W., & Cole, A. H. (1966). Effect of a favor which reduces freedom. *Journal of Personality and Social Psychology, 3*(4), 420–426.

Brehm, J. W., Stires, L. K., Sensenig, J., & Shaban, J. (1966). The attractiveness of an eliminated choice alternative. *Journal of Experimental Social Psychology, 2*(3), 301–313.

Brehm, S. S., & Brehm, J. W. (1981). *Psychological reactance: A theory of freedom and control.* New York: Academic Press.

Briñol, P., McCaslin, M. J., & Petty, R. E. (2012). Self-generated persuasion: Effects of the target and direction of arguments. *Journal of Personality and Social Psychology, 102*(5), 925.

Briñol, P. & Petty, R. E. (2003). Overt head movements and persuasion: A self-validation analysis. *Journal of Personality and Social Psychology, 84*, 1123–1139.

Briñol, P., & Petty, R. E. (2009). Source factors in persuasion: A self-validation approach. *European Review of Social Psychology, 20*(1), 49–96.

Briñol, P., & Petty, R. E. (2009). Persuasion: Insights from the self-validation hypothesis. *Advances in Experimental Social Psychology, 41*, 69–118.

Briñol, P., Petty, R. E., & McCaslin, M. (2009). Changing attitudes on implicit versus explicit measures. *Attitudes. Insights from the New Implicit Measures*, 285–326.

Briñol, P., Petty, R. E., & Tormala, Z. L. (2004). Self-validation of cognitive responses to advertisements. *Journal of Consumer Research, 30*, 559–573.

Brock, T. C. (1967). Communication discrepancy and intent to persuade as determinants of counterargument production. *Journal of Experimental Social Psychology, 3*(3), 296–309.

Burkley, E. (2008). The role of self-control in resistance to persuasion. *Personality and Social Psychology Bulletin, 34*(3), 419–431.

Byrne, D., & Griffitt, W. (1969). Similarity and awareness of similarity of personality characteristics as determinants of attraction. *Journal of Experiment Research in Personality, 3*, 179–186.

Cacioppo, J. T. (1979). Effects of exogenous changes in heart rate on facilitation of thought and resistance to persuasion. *Journal of Personality and Social Psychology, 37*(4), 489–498.

Cacioppo, J. T., Crites, S. L., Berntson, G. G., & Coles, M. G. (1993). If attitudes affect how stimuli are processed, should they not affect the event-related brain potential? *Psychological Science, 4*(2), 108–112.

Cacioppo, J. T., Crites, S. L., & Gardner, W. L. (1996). Attitudes to the right: Evaluative processing is associated with lateralized late positive event-related brain potentials. *Personality and Social Psychology Bulletin, 22*(12), 1205–1219.

Cacioppo, J. T., Gardner, W. L., & Berntson, G. G. (1999). The affect system has parallel and integrative processing components: Form follows function. *Journal of Personality and Social Psychology, 76*(5), 839.

Cacioppo, J. T., Harkins, S. G., & Petty, R. E. (1981). The nature of attitudes and cognitive responses and their relationships to behavior. In R. Petty (Ed.), *Cognitive responses in persuasion* (pp. 31–51). Mahwah, NJ: Lawrence Erlbaum Associates.

Cacioppo, J. T., Marshall-Goodell, B. S., Tassinary, L. G., & Petty, R. E. (1992). Rudimentary determinants of attitudes: Classical conditioning is more effective when prior knowledge about the attitude stimulus is low than high. *Journal of Experimental Social Psychology*, *28*(3), 207–233.

Cacioppo, J. T. & Petty, R. E. (1979). Attitudes and cognitive response: An electrophysiological approach. *Journal of Personality and Social Psychology*, *37*(12), 2181–2199.

Cacioppo, J. T., & Petty, R. E. (1980). Persuasiveness of communication is affected by exposure frequency and message quality: A theoretical and empirical analysis of persisting attitude change. In J. H. Leigh & C. R. Martin (Eds.), *Current issues and research in advertising* (pp. 97–122). Ann Arbor: University of Michigan.

Cacioppo, J. T., & Petty, R. E. (1981a). Social psychological procedures for cognitive response assessment: The thought listing technique. In T. Merluzzi, C. Glass, & M. Genest (Eds.), *Cognitive assessment* (pp. 309–342). New York: Guilford.

Cacioppo, J. T., & Petty, R. E. (1981b). Argument-based persuasion. *Journal of Personality and Social Psychology*, *41*(5), 847–855.

Cacioppo, J. T., & Petty, R. E. (1981c). Electromyograms as measures of extent and affectivity of information processing. *American Psychologist*, *36*(5), 441–456.

Cacioppo, J. T., & Petty, R. E. (1982). The need for cognition. *Journal of Personality and Social Psychology*, *42*(1), 116–131.

Cacioppo, J. T., & Petty, R. E. (1985). Central and peripheral routes to persuasion: The role of message repetition. In L. Alwitt & A. Mitchell (Eds.), *Psychological processes and advertising effects* (pp. 91–112). Hillsdale, NJ: Erlbaum.

Cacioppo, J. T., Petty, R. E., Feinstein, J. A., & Jarvis, W. B. G. (1996). Dispositional differences in cognitive motivation: The life and times of individuals varying in need for cognition. *Psychological Bulletin*, 119(2), 197.

Cacioppo, J. T., Petty, R. E., & Geen, T. R. (1989). From the tripartite to the homeostasis model of attitudes. In A. R. Pratkanis, S. J. Breckler, & A. G. Greenwald (Eds.), *Attitude structure and function* (pp. 275–305). Hillsdale, NJ: Lawrence Erlbaum.

Cacioppo, J. T., Petty, R. E., Kao, C. F., & Rodriguez, R. (1986). Central and peripheral routes to persuasion: An individual difference perspective. *Journal of Personality and Social Psychology*, *51*(5), 1032–1043.

Calder, B. J., & Sternthal, B. (1980). Television commercial wearout: An information processing view. *Journal of Marketing Research*, 173–186.

Campbell, D. T. (1963). Social attitudes and other acquired behavioral dispositions. In K. Sigmund (Ed.), *Psychology: A study of a science. Study II. Empirical substructure and relations with other sciences. Investigations of man as socius: Their place in psychology and the social sciences* (Vol. 6, pp. 94–172). New York: McGraw-Hill.

Carlsmith, J. M., Collins, B. E., & Helmreich, R. L. (1966). Studies in forced compliance: I. The effect of pressure for compliance on attitude change produced by face-to-face role playing and anonymous essay writing. *Journal of Personality and Social Psychology*, *4*(1), 1.

Carretié, L., Mercado, F., Tapia, M., & Hinojosa, J. A. (2001). Emotion, attention and the "negativity bias", studied through event-related potentials. *International Journal of Psychophysiology*, 41, 75–85.

Caruso, E. M., Mead, N. L., & Balcetis, E. (2009). Political partisanship influences perception of biracial candidates' skin tone. *Proceedings of the National Academy of Sciences*, *106*(48), 20168–20173.

Carver, C. S., & Scheier, M. F. (1981). The self-attention-induced feedback loop and social facilitation. *Journal of Experimental Social Psychology*, *17*(6), 545–568.

Chaiken, S. (1979). Communicator physical attractiveness and persuasion. *Journal of Personality and Social Psychology*, 37(8), 1387–1397.

Chaiken, S. (1980). Heuristic versus systematic information processing and the use of source versus message cues in persuasion. *Journal of Personality and Social Psychology*, *39*, 5, 752–766.

Chaiken, S. (1986). Physical appearance and social influence. In C. P. Herman, M. P. Zanna, & E. T. Higgins (Eds.), *Physical appearance, stigma and social behavior: The Ontario symposium* (Vol. 3, pp. 143–177). Hillsdale, NJ: Erlbaum.

Chaiken, S. (1987).The heuristic model of persuasion. In M. P. Zanna, J. M. Olson, & C. P. Herman (Eds.), *Social influence: The Ontario symposium* (Vol. 5, pp. 3–39). Mahwah, NJ: Lawrence Erlbaum Associates.

Chaiken, S., & Bargh, J. A. (1993). Occurrence versus moderation of the automatic attitude activation effect: Reply to Fazio. *Journal of Personality and Social Psychology, 64*, 759–765.

Chaiken, S., & Eagly, A. H. (1983). Communication modality as a determinant of persuasion: The role of communicator salience. *Journal of Personality and Social Psychology, 45*(2), 241–256.

Chaiken, S., Giner-Sorolla, R., & Chen, S. (1996). Beyond accuracy: Defense and impression motives in heuristic and systematic information processing. In P. M. Gollwitzer & J. A. Bargh (Eds.), *The psychology of action: Linking cognition and motivation to behavior* (pp. 553–578). New York: Guilford Press.

Chaiken, S., & Ledgerwood, A. (2012). A theory of heuristic and systematic information processing. In P.A.M. van Lange, A. W. Kruglanski, & E. T. Higgins (Eds.), *Handbook of theories of social psychology* (pp. 246–266). Thousand Oaks, CA: Sage Publications.

Chaiken, S., Liberman, A., & Eagly, A. H. (1989). Heuristic and systematic processing within and beyond the persuasion context. In J. S. Uleman & J. A. Bargh (Eds.), *Unintended thought: Limits of awareness, attention, and control* (pp. 212–252). New York: Guilford.

Chaiken, S., & Maheswaran, D. (1994). Heuristic processing can bias systematic processing: Effects of source credibility, argument ambiguity, and task importance on attitude judgment. *Journal of Personality and Social Psychology*, 66, 460–460.

Chaiken, S., Pomerantz, E. M., & Giner-Sorolla, R. (1995). Structural consistency and attitude strength. In R. E. Petty & J. A. Krosnick (Eds.), *Attitude strength: Antecedents and consequences*. Ohio State University series on attitudes and persuasion (Vol. 4., pp. 387–412). Hillsdale, NJ: Lawrence Erlbaum Associates.

Chaiken, S., & Trope, Y. (Eds.). (1999). *Dual-process theories in social psychology*. New York: Guilford Press.

Chapanis, N. P., & Chapanis, A. (1964). Cognitive dissonance: Five years later. *Psychological Bulletin*, *61*, 1.

Charng, H. W., Piliavin, J. A., & Callero, P. L. (1988). Role identity and reasoned action in the prediction of repeated behavior. *Social Psychology Quarterly*, 303–317.

Clark, J. K., Wegener, D. T. & Fabrigar, L. R. (2008). Attitude accessibility and message processing: The moderating role of message position. *Personality and Social Psychology Bulletin, 34*, 565–577.

Clark, J. K., Wegener, D. T., Habashi, M. M., & Evans, A. T. (2012). Source expertise and persuasion: The effects of perceived opposition or support on message scrutiny. *Personality and Social Psychology Bulletin, 38(1)*, 90–100.

Cohen, A. R. (1962). An experiment on small rewrds for discrepant compliance and attitude change. In Brehm, J. W. and Cohen, A. R. (Eds.), *Explorations in cognitive dissonance*. New York: Wiley.

Cohen, A. R., Stotland, E., & Wolfe, D. M. (1955). An experimental investigation of need for cognition. *The Journal of Abnormal and Social Psychology, 51*(2), 291.

Collins, B. E. (1969). The effect of monetary inducements on the amount of attitude change produced by forced compliance. In A. C. Elms (Ed.), *Role playing, reward, and attitude change* (pp. 209–223). New York: Van Nostrand.

Conklin, L. R., Strunk, D. R., & Fazio, R. H. (2009). Attitude formation in depression: Evidence for deficits in forming positive attitudes. *Journal of Behavior Therapy and Experimental Psychiatry, 40*(1), 120–26.

Conner, M., Lawton, R., Parker, D., Chorlton, K., Manstead, A. S., & Stradling, S. (2007). Application of the theory of planned behaviour to the prediction of objectively assessed breaking of posted speed limits. *British Journal of Psychology, 98*(3), 429–453.

Conner, M., Sherlock, K., & Orbell, S. (1998). Psychosocial determinants of ecstasy use in young people in the UK. *British Journal of Health Psychology, 3*(4), 295–317.

Conner, M., & Sparks, P. (2002). Ambivalence and attitudes. *European Review of Social Psychology, 12*(1), 37–70.

Conner, M., Sparks, P., Povey, R., James, R., Shepherd, R., & Armitage, C. J. (2002). Moderator effects of attitudinal ambivalence on attitude–behaviour relationships. *European Journal of Social Psychology, 32*(5), 705–718.

Conrey, F. R., Sherman, J. W., Gawronski, B., Hugenberg, K., & Groom, C. J. (2005). Separating multiple processes in implicit Social Cognition: The quad model of implicit task performance. *Journal of Personality and Social Psychology, 89*(4), 469.

Converse, P. E. (1970). Attitudes and non-attitudes: Continuation of a dialogue. *The quantitative analysis of social problems, 168*, 189.

Cooke, R., & Sheeran, P. (2004). Moderation of cognition-intention and cognition-behaviour relations: A meta-analysis of properties of variables from the theory of planned behaviour. *British Journal of Social Psychology, 43*(2), 159–186.

Cooper, J. (1971). Personal responsibility and dissonance: The role of foreseen consequences. *Journal of Personality and Social Psychology, 18*, 354–363.

Cooper, J. (2007). *Cognitive dissonance: Fifty years of a classic theory*. Thousand Oaks, CA: Sage.

Cooper, J., Bennett, E. A., & Sukel, H. L. (1996). Complex scientific testimony: How do jurors make decisions? *Law and Human Behavior, 20*(4), 379–394.

Cooper, J., & Fazio, R. H. (1984). A new look at dissonance theory. *Advances in Experimental Social Psychology, 17*, 229–266.

Cooper, J., & Hogg, M. A. (2007). Feeling the anguish of others: A theory of vicarious dissonance. *Advances in Experimental Social Psychology, 39*, 359–403.

Cooper, J., & Mackie, D. (1983). Cognitive dissonance in an intergroup context. *Journal of Personality and Social Psychology, 44*(3), 536.

Cooper, J. & Neuhaus, I. M. (2000). The hired gun effect: Assessing the effect of pay, frequency of testifying, and credentials on the perception of expert testimony. *Law and Human Behavior, 24*, 149–171.

Cooper, J., & Worchel, S. (1970). Role of undesired consequences in arousing cognitive dissonance. *Journal of Personality and Social Psychology, 16*(2), 199–206.

Cooper, J., Zanna, M. P., & Goethals, G. R. (1974). Mistreatment of an esteemed other as a consequence affecting dissonance reduction. *Journal of Experimental Social Psychology, 10*(3), 224–233.

Cooper, J., Zanna, M. P., & Taves, P. A. (1978). Arousal as a necessary condition for attitude change following induced compliance. *Journal of Personality and Social Psychology, 36*(10), 1101.

Correll, J., Park, B., Judd, C. M., & Wittenbrink, B. (2002). The police officer's dilemma: Using ethnicity to disambiguate potentially threatening individuals. *Journal of Personality and Social Psychology, 83*, 1314–1329.

Correll, J., Park, B., Judd, C. M., Wittenbrink, B., Sadler, M. S., & Keesee, T. (2007). Across the thin blue line: Police officers and racial bias in the decision to shoot. *Journal of Personality and Social Psychology, 92*(6), 1006.

Craik, F. I., & Lockhart, R. S. (1972). Levels of processing: A framework for memory research. *Journal of Verbal Learning and Verbal Behavior, 11*(6), 671–684.

Crano, W. D. (1983). Assumed consensus of attitudes: The effect of vested interest. *Personality and Social Psychology Bulletin, 9*(4), 597–608.

Crano, W. D. (1995). Attitude strength and vested interest. In R. E. Petty & J. A. Krosnick (Eds.), *Attitude strength: Antecedents and Consequences.* Ohio State University series on attitudes and persuasion, Vol. 4, 131–157. Hillsdale, NJ: Lawrence Erlbaum Associates.

Crano, W. D., & Prislin, R. (2006). Attitudes and persuasion. *Annual Review of Psychology, 57*, 345–374.

Creel, G. (1920). *How we advertised America: The first telling of the amazing story of the Committee on Public Information that carried the gospel of Americanism to every corner of the globe.* Harper & brothers.

Crites, S. L., Cacioppo, J. T., Gardner, W. L., & Berntson, G. G. (1995). Bioelectrical echoes from evaluative categorization: II. A late positive brain potential that varies as a function of attitude registration rather than attitude report. *Journal of Personality and Social Psychology, 68*, 997–997.

Crites, S. L., Fabrigar, L. R., & Petty, R. E. (1994). Measuring the affective and cognitive properties of attitudes: Conceptual and methodological issues. *Personality and Social Psychology Bulletin, 20*(6), 619–634.

Cronbach, L. J. (1951). Coefficient alpha and the internal structure of tests. *Psychometrika, 16*, 297–334.

Cronbach, L. J., & Shavelson, R. J. (2004). My current thoughts on coefficient alpha and successor procedures. *Educational and Psychological Measurement 64*, 391–418.

Crosby, F., Bromley, S., & Saxe, L. (1980). Recent unobtrusive studies of Black and White discrimination and prejudice: A literature review. *Psychological Bulletin, 87*(3), 546.

Crowne, D. P., & Marlowe, D. (1960). A new scale of social desirability independent of psychopathology. *Journal of Consulting Psychology, 24*(4), 349–354.

Croyle, R. T., & Cooper, J. (1983). Dissonance arousal: Physiological evidence. *Journal of Personality and Social Psychology, 45*(4), 782.

Crutchfield, R. S. (1955). Conformity and character. *American Psychologist, 10*, 5, 191–198.

Csikszentmihalyi, M., & Rochberg-Halton, E. (1981). *The meaning of things: Domestic symbols and the self.* New York: Cambridge University Press.

Cunningham, W. A., & Brosch, T. (2012). Motivational salience: Amygdala tuning from traits, needs, values, and goals. *Current Directions in Psychological Science, 21*(1), 54–59.

Cunningham, W. A., Espinet, S. D., DeYoung, C. G., & Zelazo, P. D. (2005). Attitudes to the right and left: Frontal ERP asymmetries associated with stimulus valence and processing goals. *NeuroImage, 28*(4), 827–834.

Cunningham, W. A., & Johnson, M. K. (2007). Attitudes and evaluation: Toward a component process framework. In E. Harmon-Jones & P. Winkielman (Eds.), *Social neuroscience: Integrating biological and psychological explanations of social behavior* (pp. 227–245). New York: Guilford Press.

Cunningham, W. A., Johnson, M. K., Gatenby, J. C., Gore, J. C., & Banaji, M. R. (2003). Component processes of social evaluation. *Journal of Personality and Social Psychology, 85*, 639–649.

Cunningham, W. A., Packer, D. J., Kesek, A., & Van Bavel, J. J. (2009). Implicit measures of attitudes: A physiological approach. In R. E. Petty, R. H. Fazio & P. Brinol (Eds.), *Attitudes: Insights from the new implicit measures* (pp. 485–512). New York: Psychology Press.

Cuningham, W. A., Preacher, K. J. & Banaji, M. R. (2001). Implicit attitude measures: Consistency, stability and convergent validity. *Psychological Science, 12*, 163–170.

Cunningham, W. A., Raye, C. L., & Johnson, M. K. (2004). Implicit and explicit evaluation: fMRI correlates of valence, emotional intensity, and control in the processing of attitudes. *Journal of Cognitive Neuroscience, 16*(10), 1717–1729.

Cunningham, W. A., & Zelazo, P. D. (2007). Attitudes and evaluations: A social cognitive neuroscience perspective. *Trends in Cognitive Science, 11*(3), 97–104.

Cunningham, W. A., Zelazo, P. D., Packer, D. J., & Van Bavel, J. J. (2007). The iterative reprocessing model: A multilevel framework for attitudes and evaluation. *Social Cognition, 25*(5), 736–760.

Dabbs Jr, J. M., & Leventhal, H. (1966). Effects of varying the recommendations in a fear arousing communication. *Journal of Personality and Social Psychology, 4*(5), 525–531.

Dal Cin, S., Zanna, M.P., & Fong, G.T. (2004). Narrative persuasion and overcoming resistance. In E. S. Knowles & J. A. Linn (Eds.), *Resistance and persuasion* (pp. 175–191). Mahwah, NJ: Erlbaum.

Darke, P. R., Chaiken, S., Bohner, G., Einwiller, S., Erb, H. P., & Hazlewood, J. D. (1998). Accuracy motivation, consensus information, and the law of large numbers: Effects on attitude judgment in the absence of argumentation. *Personality and Social Psychology Bulletin, 24*(11), 1205–1215.

Dasgupta, N. (2013). Implicit attitudes and beliefs adapt to situations: A decade of research on the malleability of implicit prejudice, stereotypes, and the self-concept. *Advances in Experimental Social Psychology, 47*, 233–279.

Dasgupta, N., & Greenwald, A. G. (2001). On the malleability of automatic attitudes: Combating automatic prejudice with images of admired and disliked individuals. *Journal of Personality and Social Psychology, 81*(5), 800–814.

Davidson, A. R., & Jaccard, J. J. (1979). Variables that moderate the attitude–behavior relation: Results of a longitudinal survey. *Journal of Personality and Social Psychology, 37*(8), 1364.

Davidson, R. J., Ekman, P., Saron, C. D., Senulis, J. A., & Friesen, W. V. (1990). Approach-withdrawal and cerebral asymmetry: Emotional expression and brain physiology I. *Journal of Personality and Social Psychology, 58*(2), 330–341.

Davis, L. E., Ajzen, I., Saunders, J., & Williams, T. (2002). The decision of African American students to complete high school: An application of the theory of planned behavior. *Journal of Educational Psychology, 94*(4), 810–819.

de Houwer, J. (2003). The extrinsic affective Simon task. *Experimental Psychology (Formerly Zeitschrift Für Experimentelle Psychologie), 50*(2), 77–85.

de Houwer, J., Baeyens, F. & Field, A.P. (2005). Associative learning of likes and dislikes: Some current controversies and possible ways forward. *Cognition and Emotion, 19,* 161–174.

de Houwer, J., Thomas, S., & Baeyens, F. (2001). Associative learning of likes and dislikes: A review of 25 years of research on human evaluative conditioning. *Psychological Bulletin, 127*(6), 853–869.

DeBono, K. G. (1987). Investigating the social-adjustive and value-expressive functions of attitudes: Implications for persuasion processes. *Journal of Personality and Social Psychology, 52*(2), 279.

DeBono, K. G., & Harnish, R. J. (1988). Source expertise, source attractiveness, and the processing of persuasive information: A functional approach. *Journal of Personality and Social Psychology, 55,* 541–546.

Delia, J. G. (1987). Communication research: A history. In C. R. Berger & S. H. Chaffee (Eds.), *Handbook of communication science* (pp. 20–98). Newbury Park, CA: Sage.

DeMarree, K. G., Wheeler, S. C., Briñol, P., & Petty, R. E. (2014). Wanting other attitudes: Actual–desired attitude discrepancies predict feelings of ambivalence and ambivalence consequences. *Journal of Experimental Social Psychology, 53,* 5–18.

DePaulo, B. M. & Friedman, H. S. (1998). Nonverbal communication. In D. T. Gilbert, S. T. Fiske & G. Lindzey (Eds.) *Handbook of social psychology, 4th ed* (pp 3–40). NY: McGraw-Hill.

Diener, E., & Wallbom, M. (1976). Effects of self-awareness on antinormative behavior. *Journal of Research in Personality, 10*(1), 107–111.

Dion, K. K., & Stein, S. (1978). Physical attractiveness and interpersonal influence. *Journal of Experimental Social Psychology, 14,* 1, 97–108.

Doll, J., & Ajzen, I. (1992). Accessibility and stability of predictors in the theory of planned behavior. *Journal of Personality and Social Psychology, 63*(5), 754.

Doob, L. W. (1947). The behavior of attitudes. *Psychological Review, 54*(3), 135.

Dotsch, R., Wigboldus, D. H., Langner, O., & van Knippenberg, A. (2008). Ethnic out-group faces are biased in the prejudiced mind. *Psychological Science, 19*(10), 978–980.

Dovidio, J. F., Gaertner, S. L., Validzic, A., Matoka, K., Johnson, B., & Frazier, S. (1997). Extending the benefits of recategorization: Evaluations, self-disclosure, and helping. *Journal of Experimental Social Psychology, 33*(4), 401–420.

Dovidio, J. F., Kawakami, K., & Gaertner, S. L. (2002). Implicit and explicit prejudice and interracial interaction. *Journal of Personality and Social Psychology, 82*(1), 62–68.

Dowd, E. T., Milne, C. R., & Wise, S. L. (1991). The Therapeutic Reactance Scale: A measure of psychological reactance. *Journal of Counseling & Development, 69*(6), 541–545.

Downs, D. S., & Hausenblas, H. A. (2005). Exercise behavior and the theories of reasoned action and planned behavior: A meta-analytic update. *Journal of Physical Activity and Health, 2,* 76–97.

Droba, D. D. (1933). The nature of attitude. *The Journal of Social Psychology,4*(4), 444–463.

Duckworth, K. L., Bargh, J. A., Garcia, M., & Chaiken, S. (2002). The automatic evaluation of novel stimuli. *Psychological Science, 13*(6), 513–519.

Dunton, B. C., & Fazio, R. H. (1997). An individual difference measure of motivation to control prejudiced reactions. *Personality and Social Psychology Bulletin, 23*(3), 316–326.

Dutta-Bergman, M. J. (2005). Theory and practice in health communication campaigns: A critical interrogation. *Health Communication, 18*(2), 103–122.

Eagly, A. H. (1978). Sex differences in influenceability. *Psychological Bulletin, 85,* 86–116.

Eagly, A. H., & Carli, L. L. (1981). Sex of researchers and sex-typed communications as determinants of sex differences in influenceability: A meta-analysis of social influence studies. *Psychological Bulletin, 90,* 1, 1–20.

Eagly, A. H., & Chaiken, S. (1975). An attribution analysis of the effect of communicator characteristics on opinion change: The case of communicator attractiveness. *Journal of Personality and Social Psychology, 32*(1), 136.

Eagly, A. H., & Chaiken, S. (1993). *The psychology of attitudes.* Fort Worth, TX: Harcourt Brace Jovanovich.

Eagly, A. H., & Chaiken, S. (1995). Attitude strength, attitude structure, and resistance to change. In R. E. Petty & J. A. Krosnick (Eds.), *Attitude strength: Antecedents and consequences* (pp. 413–432). Mahwah, NJ: Erlbaum.

Eagly, A. H., & Chaiken, S. (1998). Attitude structure and function. In D. T. Gilbert, S. T. Fiske, & G. Lindzey (Eds.), *The Handbook of Social Psychology* (Vols. 1 and 2, 4th ed., pp. 269–322). New York: McGraw-Hill.

Eagly, A., Chen, S., Chaiken, S., & Shaw-Barnes, K. (1999). The impact of attitudes on memory: An affair to remember. *Psychological Bulletin, 125*(1), 64–89.

Eagly, A. H., & Warren, R. (1976). Intelligence, comprehension, and opinion change. *Journal of Personality, 44,* 226–242.

Eagly, A. H., Wood, W., & Chaiken, S. (1978). Causal inferences about communicators and their effect on opinion change. *Journal of Personality and Social Psychology, 36,* 424–435.

Eagly, R. V. (1974). *The structure of classical economic theory.* Oxford: Oxford University Press.

Edwards, A. L. (1957). Social desirability and probability of endorsement of items in the interpersonal check list. *Journal of Abnormal Psychology, 55*(3), 394.

Effron, D. A., & Miller, D. T. (2012). How the moralization of issues grants social legitimacy to act on one's attitudes. *Personality and Social Psychology Bulletin, 38*(5), 690–701.

Egan, L. C., Bloom, P., & Santos, L. R. (2010). Choice-induced preferences in the absence of choice: Evidence from a blind two choice paradigm with young children and capuchin monkeys. *Journal of Experimental Social Psychology, 46*(1), 204–207.

Egan, L. C., Santos, L. R., & Bloom, P. (2007). The origins of cognitive dissonance evidence from children and monkeys. *Psychological Science, 18*(11), 978–983.

Eiser, J. R., Fazio, R. H., Stafford, T., & Prescott, T. J. (2003). Connectionist simulation of attitude learning: Asymmetries in the acquisition of positive and negative evaluations. *Personality and Social Psychology Bulletin, 29*(10), 1221–1235.

Eiser, J. R., Stafford, T., & Fazio, R. H. (2008). Expectancy confirmation in attitude learning: A connectionist account. *European Journal of Social Psychology, 38*(6), 1023–1032.

Elkin, R. A., & Leippe, M. R. (1986). Physiological arousal, dissonance, and attitude change: Evidence for a dissonance-arousal link and a "Don't remind me" effect. *Journal of Personality and Social Psychology, 51*(1), 55.

Elliot, A. J., & Devine, P. G. (1994). On the motivational nature of cognitive dissonance: Dissonance as psychological discomfort. *Journal of Personality and Social Psychology, 67,* 382–382.

Erb, H.-P., Bohner, G., Rank, S., & Einwiller, S. (2002). Processing minority and majority Communications: The role of conflict with prior attitudes. *Personality and Social Psychology Bulletin, 28,* 1172–1182.

Evans, R. I., Rozelle, R. M., Lasater, T. M., Dembroski, T. M., & Allen, B. P. (1970). Fear arousal, persuasion, and actual versus implied behavioral change: New perspective utilizing a real-life dental hygiene program. *Journal of Personality and Social Psychology, 16*(2), 220.

Fabrigar, L. R., Petty, R. E., Smith, S. M., & Crites, S. L. (2006). Understanding knowledge effects on attitude-behavior consistency: The role of relevance, complexity, and amount of knowledge. *Journal of Personality and Social Psychology, 90*(4), 556–577.

Fazio, R. H. (1986). How do attitudes guide behavior. *Handbook of motivation and cognition: Foundations of social behavior, 1*, 204–243.

Fazio, R. H. (1989). On the power and functionality of attitudes: The role of attitude accessibility. In A. R. Pratkanis, S. J. Breckler, & A. G. Greenwald (Eds.), *Attitude structure and function* (pp. 153–179). Hillsdale, NJ: Lawrence Erlbaum.

Fazio, R. H. (1990). The MODE model as an integrative framework. *Advances in Experimental Social Psychology, 23*, 75–109.

Fazio, R. H. (1995). Attitudes as object-evaluation associations: Determinants, consequences, and correlates of attitude accessibility. In R. E. Petty& J. A. Krosnick (Eds.), *Attitude strength: Antecedents and consequences. Ohio State University series on attitudes and persuasion* (Vol. 4., pp. 247–282). Hillsdale, NJ: Lawrence Erlbaum Associates.

Fazio, R. H. (2000). Accessible attitudes as tools for object appraisal: Their costs and benefits. In G. R. Maio & J. M. Olson (Eds). *Why we evaluate: Functions of attitudes* (pp. 1–36). Mahwah, NJ: Lawrence Erlbaum.

Fazio, R. H. (2001). On the automatic activation of associated evaluations: An overview. *Cognition & Emotion, 15*(2), 115–141.

Fazio, R. H. (2007). Attitudes as object-evaluation associations of varying strength. *Social Cognition, 25*(5), 603.

Fazio, R. H., Blascovich, J., & Driscoll, D. M. (1992). On the functional value of attitudes: The influence of accessible attitudes on the ease and quality of decision making. *Personality and Social Psychology Bulletin, 18*(4), 388–401.

Fazio, R. H., Chen, J. M., McDonel, E. C., & Sherman, S. J. (1982). Attitude accessibility, attitude-behavior consistency, and the strength of the object-evaluation association. *Journal of Experimental Social Psychology, 18*(4), 339–357.

Fazio, R. H., & Dunton, B.C. (1997). Categorization by race: The impact of automatic and controlled components of racial prejudice. *Journal of Experimental Social Psychology, 33*(5), 451–470.

Fazio, R. H., Eiser, J. R., & Shook, N. J. (2004). Attitude formation through exploration: Valence asymmetries. *Journal of Personality and Social Psychology, 87*(3), 293–311.

Fazio, R. H., Herr, P. M., & Olney, T. J. (1984). Attitude accessibility following a self-perception process. *Journal of Personality and Social Psychology, 47*(2), 277.

Fazio, R. H., Herr, P. M., & Powell, M. C. (1992). On the development and strength of category–brand associations in memory: The case of mystery ads. *Journal of Consumer Psychology, 1*(1), 1–13.

Fazio, R. H., & Olson, M. A. (2003). Implicit measures in Social Cognition research: Their meaning and use. *Annual Review of Psychology, 54*(1), 297–327.

Fazio, R. H., Jackson, J. R., Dunton, B.C., & Williams, C. J. (1995). An individual difference measure of motivation to control prejudiced reactions. *Personality and Social Psychology Bulletin, 23*, 316–326.

Fazio, R. H., Ledbetter, J. E., & Towles-Schwen, T. (2000). On the costs of accessible attitudes: Detecting that the attitude object has changed. *Journal of Personality and Social Psychology, 78*(2), 197.

Fazio, R. H., & Powell, M. C. (1997). On the value of knowing one's likes and dislikes: Attitude accessibility, stress, and health in college. *Psychological Science*, 430–436.

Fazio, R. H., Powell, M. C., & Williams, C. J. (1989). The role of attitude accessibility in the attitude-to-behavior process. *Journal of Consumer Research*, 280–288.

Fazio, R. H., Sanbonmatsu, D. M., Powell, M. C., & Kardes, F. R. (1986). On the automatic activation of attitudes. *Journal of Personality and Social Psychology, 50*, 229–238.

Fazio, R. H., & Towles-Schwen, T. (1999). The MODE model of attitude-behavior processes. *Dual process theories in social psychology* (97–116). New York: Guiford Press.

Fazio, R. H., & Williams, C. J. (1986). Attitude accessibility as a moderator of the attitude-perception and attitude-behavior relations: An investigation of the 1984 presidential election. *Journal of Personality and Social Psychology, 51*, 505–514.

Fazio, R. H., Sanbonmatsu, M. P., & Kardes, F. R. (1986). On the automatic activation of attitudes. *Journal of Personality and Social Psychology, 50*(2), 229–238.

Fazio, R. H., & Zanna, M. P. (1978). Attitudinal qualities relating to the strength of the attitude-behavior relationship. *Journal of Experimental Social Psychology, 14*, 398–408.

Fazio, R. H., Zanna, M. P., & Cooper, J. (1978). Direct experience and attitude-behavior consistency: An information processing analysis. *Personality and Social Psychology Bulletin, 4*(1), 48–51.

Fein, S., & Spencer, S. J. (1997). Prejudice as self-image maintenance: Affirming the self through derogating others. *Journal of Personality and Social Psychology, 73*, 31–44.

Ferguson, M. J., & Bargh, J. A. (2007). Beyond the attitude object: Automatic attitudes spring from object–centered–contexts. In B. Wittenbrink & N. Schwarz (Eds.), *Implicit measures of attitudes: Progress and controversies* (pp. 216–246). New York: Guilford Press.

Festinger, L. (1950). Informal social communication. *Psychological Review, 57*(5), 271.

Festinger, L. (1954). A theory of social comparison processes. *Human Relations, 7*(2), 117–140.

Festinger, L. (1957). *A theory of cognition.* Evanston, IL: Row, Peterson.

Festinger, L. (1964). *Conflict, decision and dissonance.* Stanford, CA: Stanford University Press.

Festinger, L. (1987). A personal memory. *A distinctive approach to psychological research: The influence of Stanley Schachter*, Hillsdale, NJ: L. Erlbaum, 1–9.

Festinger, L., & Carlsmith, J. M. (1959). Cognitive consequences of forced compliance. *Journal of Abnormal and Social Psychology, 58*, 203–210.

Festinger, L., & Maccoby, N. (1964). On resistance to persuasive communication. *Journal of Abnormal and Social Psychology, 68*, 359–366.

Fischer, D. G., & Fick, C. (1993). Measuring social desirability: Short forms of the Marlowe-Crowne social desirability scale. *Educational and Psychological Measurement, 53*(2), 417–424.

Fischer, P., Jonas, E., Frey, D., & Schulz-Hardt, S. (2005). Selective exposure to information: The impact of information limits. *European Journal of Social Psychology, 35*(4), 469–492.

Fishbein, M. (1967). A consideration of beliefs and their role in attitude measurement. *Readings in attitude theory and measurement.* New York: Wiley.

Fishbein, M. (2000). The role of theory in HIV prevention. *AIDS Care, 12*, 273–278.

Fishbein, M., & Ajzen, I. (1974). Attitudes towards objects as predictors of single and multiple behavioral criteria. *Psychological Review, 81*(1), 59.

Fishbein, M., & Ajzen, I. (1975). *Belief, attitude, intention and behavior: An introduction to theory and research.* Reading, MA: Addison-Wesley.

Fishbein, M. & Ajzen, I. (2010). *Predicting and changing behavior.* New York: Psychology Press.

Fiske, A. P. (1992). The four elementary forms of sociality: Framework for a unified theory of social relations. *Psychological Review, 99*(4), 689.

Fiske, S. T., & von Hendy, H. M. (1992). Personality feedback and situational norms can control stereotyping processes. *Journal of Personality and Social Psychology, 62,* 577–596.

Fleischhauer, M., Enge, S., Brocke, B., Ullrich, J., Strobel, A., & Strobel, A. (2010). Same or different? Clarifying the relationship of need for cognition to personality and intelligence. *Personality and Social Psychology Bulletin, 36*(1), 82–96.

Forbes, C. E. (2009). Lessons Learned from "A Clockwork Orange": How retraining implicit attitudes and stereotypes affects motivation and performance under stereotype threat. (Doctoral Dissertation). University of Arizona, Tucson, Arizona.

Förster, J. (2004). How body feedback influences consumers' evaluations of products. *Journal of Consumer Psychology, 14,* 416–426.

Freedman, J. L. (1965). Long-term behavioral effects of cognitive dissonance. *Journal of Experimental Social Psychology, 1,* 145–155.

Freedman, J. L., & Sears, D. O. (1965). Warning, distraction, and resistance to influence. *Journal of Personality and Social Psychology, 1*(3), 262–266.

Friese, M & Fiedler, K. (2010). Being on the lookout for validity: Comment on Sriram and Greenwald (2009). *Experimental Psychology, 57,* 228–232.

Froming, W. J., Walker, G. R., & Lopyan, K. J. (1982). Public and private self-awareness: When personal attitudes conflict with societal expectations. *Journal of Experimental Social Psychology, 18*(5), 476–487.

Gaertner, S. L. (1976). Nonreactive measures in racial attitude research: A focus on "liberals." *Towards the elimination of racism.* New York: Pergamon.

Gaertner, S. L., & Dovidio, J. F. (1981). Racism among the well intentioned. In J. Bermingham & E. Claussen (Eds.), *Racism, pluralism, and public policy: A search for equality* (pp. 208–222). Boston: G. K. Hall.

Gaertner, S. L., & McLaughlin, J. P. (1983). Racial stereotypes: Associations and ascriptions of positive and negative characteristics. *Social Psychology Quarterly, 46,* 23–30.

Gawronski, B., & Bodenhausen, G. V. (2006). Associative and propositional processes in evaluation: An integrative review of implicit and explicit attitude change. *Psychological Bulletin, 132*(5), 692.

Gawronski, B., & Bodenhausen, G. V. (2011). The associative-propositional evaluation model: Theory, evidence, and open questions. *Advances in Experimental Social Psychology, 44,* 59.

Gawronski, B., & Bodenhausen, G. V. (2014). Implicit and explicit evaluation: A brief review of the associative-propositional evaluation model. *Social and Personality Psychology Compass, 8*(8), 448–462.

Gawronski, B., & LeBel, E. P. (2008). Understanding patterns of attitude change: When implicit measures show change, but explicit measures do not. *Journal of Experimental Social Psychology, 44*(5), 1355–1361.

Gawronski, B., Rydell, R. J., Vervliet, B. & De Houwer, J. (2010). Generalization versus contextualization in automatic evaluation. *Journal of Experimental Psychology: General, 139,* 683–701.

Gawronski, B., Ye, Y., Rydell, R. J., & De Houwer, J. (2014). Formation, representation, and activation of contextualized attitudes. *Journal of Experimental Social Psychology, 54,* 188–203.

Gibbons, F. X. (1978). Sexual standards and reactions to pornography: Enhancing behavioral consistency through self-focused attention. *Journal of Personality and Social Psychology, 36*(9), 976.

Gillig, P. M., & Greenwald, A. G. (1974). Is it time to lay the sleeper effect to rest? *Journal of Personality and Social Psychology, 29,* 132–139.

Giner-Sorolila, R., & Chaiken, S. (1997). Selective use of heuristic and systematic processing under defense motivation. *Personality and Social Psychology Bulletin, 23*(1), 84–97.

Gladwell, M. (2005). *Blink: The power of thinking without thinking.* New York: Little, Brown & Co.

Glasford, D. E., Dovidio, J. F., & Pratto, F. (2009). I continue to feel so good about us: In-Group identification and the use of social identity—enhancing strategies to reduce intragroup dissonance. *Personality and Social Psychology Bulletin, 35*(4), 415–427.

Glasman, L. R., & Albarracín, D. (2006). Forming attitudes that predict future behavior: A meta-analysis of the attitude-behavior relation. *Psychological Bulletin, 132*(5), 778.

Godin, G., Conner, M., & Sheeran, P. (2005). Bridging the intention-behaviour gap: The role of moral norm. *British Journal of Social Psychology, 44*(4), 497–512.

Godin, G., & Kok, G. (1996). The theory of planned behavior: A review of its applications to health-related behaviors. *American Journal of Health Promotion, 11*(2), 87–98.

Goethals, G. R., Cooper, J., & Naficy, A. (1979). Role of foreseen, foreseeable, and unforeseeable behavioral consequences in the arousal of cognitive dissonance. *Journal of Personality and Social Psychology, 37*(7), 1179–85.

Goldberg, P. (1968). Are women prejudiced against women? *Transaction, 5,* 28–30.

Goldman, W., & Lewis, P. (1977). Beautiful is good: Evidence that the physically attractive are more socially skillful. *Journal of Experimental Social Psychology, 13*(2), 125–30.

Gollub, H., & Dittes, J. (1965). Different effects of manipulated self-esteem on persuasability depending on the threat and complexity of the communication. *Journal of Personality and Social Psychology, 2,* 195–201.

Gollwitzer, P. M. (1999). Implementation intentions: strong effects of simple plans. *American Psychologist, 54*(7), 493–503.

Gollwitzer, P. M., & Sheeran, P. (2006). Implementation intentions and goal achievement: A meta-analysis of effects and processes. *Advances in Experimental Social Psychology, 38,* 69–119.

Gorn, G. J., & Goldberg, M. E. (1980). Children's responses to repetitive television commercials. *Journal of Consumer Research, 6,* 421–424.

Green, D. M., & Swets, J. A. (1966). *Signal detection theory and psychophysics* (Vol. 1). New York: Wiley.

Green, M. C., & Brock, T. C. (2000). The role of transportation in the persuasiveness of public narratives. *Journal of Personality and Social Psychology, 79*(5), 701–721.

Greenwald, A. G. (1968). Cognitive learning, cognitive response to persuasion, and attitude change. In G. Greenwald, T. C. Brock, & T. M. Ostrom (Eds.), *Psychological foundations of attitudes* (pp. 147–170). New York: Academic Press.

Greenwald, A. G. (1980). The totalitarian ego. *American Psychologist, 35*(7), 603–618.

Greenwald, A. G. (1981). Self and memory. In G. H. Bower (Ed.), *The psychology of learning and motivation* (Vol. 15, pp. 201–236). New York: Academic Press.

Greenwald, A. G., & Albert, R. D. (1968). Acceptance and recall of improvised arguments. *Journal of Personality and Social Psychology, 8*(1), 31–34.

Greenwald, A. G., & Farnham, S. D. (2000). Using the Implicit Association Test to measure self-esteem and self-concept. *Journal of Personality and Social Psychology, 79*(6), 1022–1038.

Greenwald, A. G., McGhee, D. E., & Schwartz, J. L. (1998). Measuring individual differences in implicit cognition: The implicit association test. *Journal of Personality and Social Psychology, 74,* 1464–1480.

Greenwald, A. G., & Nosek, B. A. (2008). Attitudinal dissociation: What does it mean. In R. E. Petty, R. H. Fazio & P. Brinol (Eds.), *Attitudes: Insights from the new implicit measures* (pp. 65–82). New York: Psychology Press.

Greenwald, A. G., Nosek, B. A., & Banaji, M. R. (2003). Understanding and using the Implicit Association Test: I. An improved scoring algorithm. *Journal of Personality and Social Psychology, 85*(2), 197–216.

Greenwald, A. G., Poehlman, T. A., Uhlmann, E. L., & Banaji, M. R. (2009). Understanding and using the Implicit Association Test: III. Meta-analysis of predictive validity. *Journal of Personality and Social Psychology, 97*(1), 17.

Griffin, D. W., & Ross, L. (1991). Subjective construal, social inference, and human misunderstanding. *Advances in Experimental Social Psychology, 24,* 319–359.

Gross, S. R., Holtz, R., & Miller, N. (1995). Attitude certainty. In R. E. Petty & J. A. Krosnick (Eds.), *Attitude strength: Antecedents and consequences.* Ohio State University series on attitudes and persuasion (Vol. 4., pp. 215–245). Hillsdale, NJ: Lawrence Erlbaum Associates.

Gruder, C. L., Cook, T. D., Hennigan, K. M., Flay, B. R., Alessis, C., & Halamaj, J. (1978). Empirical tests of the absolute sleeper effect predicted from the discounting-cue hypothesis. *Journal of Personality and Social Psychology, 36,* 1061–1074.

Grush, J. E. (1976). Attitude formation and mere exposure phenomena: A nonarticial explanation of empirical findings. *Journal of Personality and Social Psychology, 33,* 281–290.

Guadagno, R. E., & Cialdini, R. B. (2002). Online persuasion: An examination of gender differences in computer-mediated interpersonal influence. *Group Dynamics, 6,* 38–51.

Hagger, M. S., Chatzisarantis, N. L., & Biddle, S. J. (2002). A meta-analytic review of the theories of reasoned action and planned behavior in physical activity: Predictive validity and the contribution of additional variables. *Journal of Sport & Exercise Psychology, 24*(1), 3–32.

Hagger, M. S., Chatzisarantis, N. L., & Harris, J. (2006). From psychological need satisfaction to intentional behavior: Testing a motivational sequence in two behavioral contexts. *Personality and Social Psychology Bulletin, 32*(2), 131–148.

Han, H. A., Czellar, S., Olson, M. A., & Fazio, R. H. (2010). Malleability of attitudes or malleability of the IAT. *Journal of Experimental Social Psychology, 46,* 286–298.

Han, H. A., Olson, M. A., & Fazio, R. H. (2006). The influence of experimentally created extrapersonal associations on the Implicit Association Test. *Journal of Experimental Social Psychology, 42,* 259–272.

Harkins, S. G., & Petty, R. E. (1987). Information utility and the multiple source effect. *Journal of Personality and Social Psychology, 52*(2), 260.

Harmon-Jones, C., Schmeichel, B. J., Mennitt, E., & Harmon-Jones, E. (2011). The expression of determination: Similarities between anger and approach-related positive affect. *Journal of Personality and Social Psychology, 100*(1), 172.

Harmon-Jones, E. (1999) Toward an understanding of the motivation underlying dissonance effects: is the production of aversive consequences necessary? In E. Harmon-Jones and J. Mills (Eds.), *Cognitive Dissonance: Progress on a Pivotal Theory in Social Psychology* (pp. 71–103). Washington, DC: APA.

Harmon-Jones, E. (2000). Cognitive dissonance and experienced negative affect: Evidence that dissonance increases experienced negative affect even in the absence of aversive consequences. *Personality and Social Psychology Bulletin, 26*, 1490–1501.

Harmon-Jones, E. (2004). Contributions from research on anger and cognitive dissonance to understanding the motivational functions of asymmetrical frontal brain activity. *Biological Psychology, 67*(1–2), 51–76.

Harmon-Jones, E., & Harmon-Jones, C. (2002). Testing the action-based model of cognitive dissonance: The effect of action orientation on postdecisional attitudes. *Personality and Social Psychology Bulletin, 28*(6), 711–723.

Harmon-Jones, E., Harmon-Jones,C., Fearn, M., Sigelman, J.D. & Johnson, P. (2008). Left Frontal Cortical Activation and Spreading of Alternatives: Tests of the Action-Based Model of Dissonance. *Journal of Personality and Social Psychology, 94*, 1–15.

Harmon-Jones, E., Harmon-Jones, C., Serra, R., Gable, P.A. (2011). The effect of commitment on relative left frontal cortical activity: Tests of the action-based model of dissonance. *Personality and Social Psychology Bulletin, 37*, 395–408.

Harmon-Jones, E., & Mills, J. (1999). An introduction to cognitive dissonance theory and an overview of current perspectives on the theory. In E. Harmon-Jones & M. Judson (Eds.), *Cognitive dissonance: Progress on a pivotal theory in social psychology. Science conference series* (pp. 3–21). Washington, DC: American Psychological Association.

Harmon-Jones, E., Amodio, D. M., & Harmon-Jones, C. (2009). Action-based model of dissonance: A review, integration, and expansion of conceptions of cognitive conflict. *Advances in Experimental Social Psychology, 41*, 119–166.

Harmon-Jones, E., Gerdjikov, T., & Harmon-Jones, C. (2008). The effect of induced compliance on relative left frontal cortical activity: A test of the action-based model of dissonance. *European Journal of Social Psychology, 38*(1), 35–45.

Hart, A. J., Whalen, P. J., Shin, L. M., McInerney, S. C., Fischer, H., & Rauch, S. L. (2000). Differential response in the human amygdala to racial outgroup vs ingroup face stimuli. *Neuroreport, 11*(11), 2351–2354.

Hass, R. G., & Grady, K. (1975). Temporal delay, type of forewarning, and resistance to influence. *Journal of Experimental Social Psychology, 11*(5), 459–469.

Hass, R. G., Katz, I., Rizzo, N., Bailey, J., & Eisenstadt, D. (1991). Cross-racial appraisal as related to attitude ambivalence and cognitive complexity. *Personality and Social Psychology Bulletin, 17*(1), 83–92.

Hass, R. G., & Linder, D. E. (1972). Counterargument availability and the effects of message structure on persuasion. *Journal of Personality and Social Psychology, 23*(2), 219.

Haugtvedt, C. P., & Petty, R. E. (1992). Personality and persuasion: Need for cognition moderates the persistence and resistance of attitude changes. *Journal of Personality and Social Psychology, 63*(2), 308–319.

Heesacker, M., Petty, R. E., & Cacioppo, J. T. (1983). Field dependence and attitude change: Source credibility can alter persuasion by affecting message-relevant thinking. *Journal of Personality, 51*, 653–666.

Heider, F. (1946). Attitudes and cognitive organization. *The Journal of Psychology, 21*(1), 107–112.

Heider, F. (1958). *The psychology of interpersonal relations.* New York: John Wiley & Sons.

Heine, S. J., & Lehman, D. R. (1997). The cultural construction of self-enhancement: An examination of group-serving biases. *Journal of Personality and Social Psychology, 72,* 1268–1283.

Hepler, J., & Albarracín, D. (2013). Attitudes without objects: Evidence for a dispositional attitude, its measurement, and its consequences. *Journal of Personality and Social Psychology, 104*(6), 1060–1076.

Herek, G. M. (1987). Can functions be measured? A new perspective on the functional approach to attitudes. *Social Psychology Quarterly, 50,* 285–303.

Hermans, D., De Houwer, J., & Eelen, P. (2001). A time course analysis of the affective priming effect. *Cognition & Emotion, 15*(2), 143–165.

Hess, E.H. (1965). Attitudes and pupil size. *Scientific American, 212,* 46–54.

Higgins, E. T. (1997). Beyond pleasure and pain. *American Psychologist, 52,* 1280–1300.

Hofmann, W., Gawronski, B., Gschwendner, T., Le, H., & Schmitt, M. (2005). A meta-analysis on the correlation between the Implicit Association Test and explicit self-report measures. *Personality and Social Psychology Bulletin, 31*(10), 1369–1385.

Hogg, M. A. (2007). Uncertainty-identity theory. *Advances in Experimental Social Psychology, 39,* 69–126.

Holland, R. W., Verplanken, B., & Van Knippenberg, A. (2002). On the nature of attitude-behavior relations: The strong guide, the weak follow. *European Journal of Social Psychology, 32*(6), 869–876.

Horcajo, J., Petty, R. E., & Brinol, P. (2010). The effects of majority versus minority source status on persuasion: A self-validation analysis. *Journal of Personality and Social Psychology, 99*(3), 498.

Hoshino-Browne, E. (2012). Cultural variations in motivation for cognitive consistency: Influences of self-systems on cognitive dissonance. *Social and Personality Compass, 6,* 126–141.

Hoshino-Browne, E., Zanna, A. S., Spencer, S. J., Zanna, M. P., Kitayama, S., & Lackenbauer, S. (2005). On the cultural guises of cognitive dissonance: The case of Easterners and Westerners. *Journal of Personality and Social Psychology, 89*(3), 294.

Houston, D. A., & Fazio, R. H. (1989). Biased processing as a function of attitude accessibility: Making objective judgments subjectively. *Social Cognition, 7*(1), 51–66.

Hovland, C. I., Harvey, O. J., & Sherif, M. (1957). Assimilation and contrast in communication and attitude change. *Journal of Abnormal and Social Psychology, 55,* 242–252.

Hovland, C., & Janis, I. L. (1959). *Personality and persuasibility.* New Haven, CT: Yale University Press.

Hovland, C. I., Janis, I. L., & Kelley, H. H. (1953). *Communication and persuasion: Psychological studies of opinion change.* New Haven, CT: Yale University Press.

Hovland, C. I., Lumsdaine, A. A., & Sheffield, F. D. (1949). *Experiments on mass communication.* Princeton, NJ: Princeton University Press.

Hovland, C. I., & Mandell, W. (1952). An experimental comparison of conclusion-drawing by the communicator and by the audience. *The Journal of Abnormal and Social Psychology, 47*(3), 581–588.

Hovland, C. I., & Mandell, W. (1957). Is there a law of primacy in persuasion? In C. I. Hovland (Ed.), *The order of presentation in persuasion* (pp. 1–22). New Haven, CT: Yale University Press.

Hovland, C. I., Mandell, W., Campbell, E. H., Brock, T., Luchins, A. S., Cohen, A. R., & Janis, I. L. (1957). *The order of presentation in persuasion.* New Haven, CT: Yale University Press.

Hovland, C. I., & Pritzker, H. A. (1957). Extent of opinion change as a function of amount of change advocated. *The Journal of Abnormal and Social Psychology, 54*(2), 257–261.

Hovland, C. I., & Weiss, W. (1951). The influence of source credibility on communication effectiveness. *Public Opinion Quarterly, 15*, 635–650.

Hull, C. L. (1943). Principles of behavior: An introduction to behavior theory. NY: Appelton-Century-Crofts.

Hullett, C. (2002). Charting the process underlying the change of value-expressive attitudes: The importance of value-relevance in predicting the matching effect. *Communication Monographs*, 69(2), 158–178.

Huskinson, T.L. & Haddock, G. (2006). Individual differences in attitude structure and the accessibility of the affective and cognitive components of attitudes. Social Cognition, 24, 453–468.

Hynie, M., MacDonald, T. K., & Marques, S. (2006). Self-conscious emotions and self-regulation in the promotion of condom use. *Personality and Social Psychology Bulletin, 32*(8), 1072–1084.

Imada, T. & Kitayama, S. (2010). Social eyes and choice justification: Culture and dissonance revisited. *Social Cognition, 28*, 589–608.

Imajo, S. (1996). The interactive effect of initial position and threat to freedom on psychological reactance. *Shinrigaku kenkyu: The Japanese Journal of Psychology, 66*(6), 431.

Insko, C. A. (1964). Primacy versus recency in persuasion as a function of the timing of arguments and measures. *Journal of Abnormal Psychology, 69*, 381–91.

Insko, C. A. (1965). Verbal reinforcement of attitude. *Journal of Personality and Social Psychology*, 2(4), 621.

Insko, C. A., Thompson, V. D., Stroebe, W., Shaud, K. F., Pinner, B. E., & Layton, B. D. (1973). Implied evaluation and the similarity-attraction effect. *Journal of Personality and Social Psychology, 25*(3), 297.

Ito, T. A., Larsen, J. T., Smith N. K., & Cacioppo, J. T. (1998). Negative information weighs more heavily on the brain: The negativity bias in evaluative categorizations. *Journal of Personality and Social Psychology, 75*, 887–900.

Jaccard, J., & Becker, M. A. (1985). Attitudes and behavior: An information integration perspective. *Journal of Experimental Social Psychology*, 21(5), 440–465.

Jacks, J. Z., & Cameron, K. A. (2003). Strategies for resisting persuasion. *Basic and Applied Social Psychology*, 25(2), 145–161.

Jackson, J. R. 1997. *Automatically activated racial attitudes*. PhD thesis, Indiana University, Bloomington, Indiana.

Jamieson, D. W., & Zanna, M. P. (1989). Need for structure in attitude formation and expression. In A. R. Pratkanis, S. J. Breckler, & A. G. Greenwald (Eds.), *Attitude structure and function* (pp. 383–406). Hillsdale, NJ: Erlbaum.

Janis, I. L., & Feshbach, S. (1953). Effects of fear-arousing communications. *Journal of Abnormal and Social Psychology, 48*, 78–92.

Janis, I. L., & Field, P. B. (1959). Sex differences and personality factors related to persuasibility. In C. Hovland & I. L. Janis (Eds.), *Personality and persuasibility* (pp. 55–68). New Haven, CT: Yale University Press.

Janis, I. L., & Gilmore, J. B. (1965). The influence of incentive conditions on the success of role playing in modifying attitudes. *Journal of Personality and Social Psychology, 95*, 17.

Janis, I. L., Kaye, D., & Kirschner P. (1965) Facilitating effects of "eating-while-reading" on responsiveness to persuasive communications. *Journal of Personality and Social Psychology, 1*, 181–6.

Janis, L. (1968). Stages in the decision-making process. In R.P. Abelson (Ed.), *Theories of cognitive consistency: A sourcebook*. Chicago: Rand McNally.

Jarcho, J. M., Berkman, E. T., & Lieberman, M. D. (2011). The neural basis of rationalization: Cognitive dissonance reduction during decision-making. *Social Cognitive and Affective Neuroscience, 6*(4), 460–467.

Jarvis, W.B.G., & Petty, R. E. (1996). The need to evaluate. *Journal of Personality and Social Psychology,* 70(1), 172.

Jemmott, J. B., Borysenko, J. Z., Borysenko, M., McClelland, D. C., Chapman, R., Meyer, D., & Benson, H. (1983). Academic stress, power motivation, and decrease in secretion rate of salivary immunoglobulin A. *The Lancet, 25*, 1400–1402.

Johar, J. S., & Sirgy, M. J. (1991). Value-expressive versus utilitarian advertising appeals: When and why to use which appeal. *Journal of Advertising, 20*(3), 23–33.

Johnson, B. T., & Eagly, A. H. (1989). Effects of involvement on persuasion: A meta-analysis. *Psychological Bulletin, 106*(2), 290.

Johnson, H. H., & Watkins, T. A. (1971). The effects of message repetitions on immediate and delayed attitude change. *Psychonomic Science, 22*(2), 101–103.

Jonas, E., Schulz-Hardt, S., & Frey, D. (2005). Giving advice or making decisions in someone else's place: The influence of impression, defense, and accuracy motivation on the search for new information. *Personality and Social Psychology Bulletin, 31*(7), 977–990.

Jonas, K., Broemer, P., & Diehl, M. (2000). Attitudinal ambivalence. *European Review of Social Psychology, 11*(1), 35–74.

Jones, E. E., & Sigall, H. (1971). The bogus pipeline: A new paradigm for measuring affect and attitude. *Psychological Bulletin, 76*(5), 349–364.

Jones, N. A., & Fox, N. A. (1992). Electroencephalogram asymmetry during emotionally evocative films and its relation to positive and negative affectivity. *Brain and Cognition, 20*(2), 280–299.

Jones, R. A., & Brehm, J. W. (1970). Persuasiveness of one-and two-sided communications as a function of awareness there are two sides. *Journal of Experimental Social Psychology, 6*(1), 47–56.

Jordan, N. (1953). Behavioral forces that are a function of attitudes and of cognitive organization. *Human Relations, 6*, 273–287.

Jost, J. T., Pelham, B. W., & Carvallo, M. R. (2002). Non-conscious forms of system justification: Implicit and behavioral preferences. *Journal of Experimental Social Psychology, 38*, 586–602.

Judd, C. M., & Brauer, M. (1995). Repetitive and evaluative extremity. In R. E. Petty & J. A. Krosnick (Eds.), *Attitude strength: Antecedents and consequences* (pp. 43–47). Mahwah, NJ: Erlbaum.

Judd, C. M., & Johnson, J. T. (1981). Attitudes, polarization, and diagnosticity: Exploring the effect of affect. *Journal of Personality and Social Psychology,41*(1), 26.

Kahle, L. R., & Homer, P. M. (1985). Physical attractiveness of the celebrity endorser: A social adaptation perspective. *Journal of Consumer Research*, 954–961.

Kahneman, D. (2003). Maps of bounded rationality: Psychology for behavioral economics. *The American economic review, 93*(5), 1449–1475.

Kahneman, D. (2011). *Thinking, fast and slow*. New York: Farrar, Straus and Giroux.

Kahneman, D., & Tversky, A. (1996). On the reality of cognitive illusions. *Psychological Review, 103*(3), 582–591.

Kaplan, K. J. (1972). On the ambivalence-indifference problem in attitude theory and measurement: A suggested modification of the semantic differential technique. *Psychological Bulletin, 77*(5), 361.

Karabenick, S. A. (1983). Sex-relevance of content and influenceability: Sistrunk and McDavid revisited. *Personality and Social Psychology Bulletin, 9*(2), 243–252.

Karlins, M., Coffman, T. L. & Walters, G. (1969). On the fading of social stereotpes: Sudies in three generations of college students. *Journal of Personality and Social Psychology, 13*, 1–16.

Karpinski, A. & Hilton, J. L. (2001). Attitudes and the Implicit Associtation Test. *Journal of Personality and Social Psychology, 81*, 774–788.

Karpinski, A., & Steinman, R. B. (2006). The single category implicit association test as a measure of implicit Social Cognition. *Journal of Personality and Social Psychology, 91*(1), 16.

Katz, D. (1960). The functional approach to the study of attitudes. *Public Opinion Quarterly, 24*(2), 163–204.

Katz, D., & Braly, K. (1933). Racial stereotypes of one hundred college students. *The Journal of Abnormal and Social Psychology, 28*(3), 280.

Katz, I. (1970). Experimental studies of Negro-white relationships. *Advances in Experimental Social Psychology, 5*, 71–117.

Katz, I., & Hass, R. G. (1988). Racial ambivalence and American value conflict: Correlational and priming studies of dual cognitive structures. *Journal of Personality and Social Psychology, 55*(6), 893.

Kawakami, K., Phills, C. E., Steele, J. R., & Dovidio, J. F. (2007). Attitudes and interracial interactions through approach behaviors. *Journal of Personality and Social Psychology, 92*(6), 957–971.

Kawasaki, T., Nishio, T., Kawaguchi, S., & Kurosawa, H. (2001). Spatiotemporal distribution of GAP-43 in the developing rat spinal cord: A histological and quantitative immunofluorescence study. *Neuroscience Research, 39*(3), 347–358.

Kelley, H. H. (1972). *Causal schemata and the attribution process.* Morristown, NJ: General Learning Press.

Kelman, H. C. (1958). Compliance, identification, and internalization: Three processes of attitude change. *The Journal of Conflict Resolution, 2*(1), 51–60.

Kelman, H. C., & Hovland, C. I. (1953). "Reinstatement" of the communicator in delayed measurement of opinion change. *Journal of Abnormal and Social Psychology, 48*, 327–335.

Killeya, L. A., & Johnson, B. T. (1998). Experimental induction of biased systematic processing: The directed-thought technique. *Personality and Social Psychology Bulletin, 24*(1), 17–33.

Kimel, S. Y., Grossmann, I., & Kitayama, S. (2012). When gift-giving produces dissonance: Effects of subliminal affiliation priming on choices for one's self versus close others. *Journal of Experimental Social Psychology, 48*(5), 1221–1224.

Kitayama, S., & Uchida, Y. (2005). Interdependent agency: An alternative system for action. In *Culture and social behavior: The Ontario symposium* (Vol. 10, pp. 137–164). Mahwah, NJ: Erlbaum.

Kitayama, S., Chua, H. F., Tompson, S., & Han, S. (2012). Neural mechanisms of dissonance: An fMRI investigation of choice justification. *Neuroimage, 69*, 206–212.

Knight, R. T., & Grabowecky, M. (1995). Escape from linear time: Prefrontal cortex and conscious experience. In M. S. Gazzaniga (Ed.), *The cognitive neurosciences* (pp. 1357–1371). Cambridge, MA: The MIT Press.

Knower, F. H. (1936). Experimental studies of change in attitude: II. A study of the effect of printed argument on changes in attitude. *Journal of Abnormal and Social Psychology, 30*, 522–532.

Knowles, E. D., & Peng, K. (2005). White selves: Conceptualizing and measuring a dominant-group identity. *Journal of Personality and Social Psychology, 89*(2), 223.

Knowles, E. S., Brennan, M., & Linn, J. A. (2002). Consuming resistance to political ads. *Manuscript in preparation.* Fayetteville, AR: University of Arkansas.

Koch, S., Holland, R. W., & Knippenberg, A. V. (2009). Lateralisation of diffuse positive and negative affect: Ascribing valence to ambiguous stimuli. *Cognition and Emotion, 23*(3), 587–598.

Kokkinaki, F., & Lunt, P. (1997). The relationship between involvement, attitude accessibility and attitude-behaviour consistency. *British Journal of Social Psychology, 36*(4), 497–509.

Kraus, S. J. (1995). Attitudes and the prediction of behavior: A meta-analysis of the empirical literature. *Personality and Social Psychology Bulletin, 21*(1), 58–75.

Krosnick, J. A. (1988). The role of attitude importance in social evaluation: A study of policy preferences, presidential candidate evaluations, and voting behavior. *Journal of Personality and Social Psychology, 55*(2), 196–210.

Krosnick, J. A., & Abelson, R. P. (1992). The case for measuring attitude strength in surveys. *Questions about questions,* 177–203.

Krosnick, J. A., Boninger, D. S., Chuang, Y. C., Berent, M. K., & Carnot, C. G. (1993). Attitude strength: One construct or many related constructs? *Journal of Personality and Social Psychology, 65*(6), 1132.

Krosnick, J. A., & Petty, R. E. (1995). Attitude strength: An overview. In R. E. Petty & J. A. Krosnick (Eds.), *Attitude strength: Antecedents and consequences* (pp. 1–24). Mahwah, NJ: Lawrence Erlbaum Associates.

Kruglanski, A. W. (1989). *Lay epistemics and human knowledge: Cognitive and motivational bases.* New York: Plenum Press.

Kruglanski, A. W. (2012). Lay epistemic theory. In P.A.M. Van Lange, A. W. Kruglanski, & E. T. Higgins (Eds.), *Handbook of theories of social psychology* (Vol. 1, pp. 460–482). Thousand Oaks, CA: SAGE.

Kruglanski, A. W., Derchesne, M., & Chun, W. Y. (2004). Culture, thought and the unimodel. *Journal of Cultural and Evolutionary Psychology, 2*(1), 143–167.

Kruglanski, A. W., Dechesne, M., Orehek, E., & Pierro, A. (2009). Three decades of lay epistemics: The why, how, and who of knowledge formation. *European Review of Social Psychology, 20*(1), 146–191.

Kruglanski, A. W., & Gigerenzer, G. (2011). Intuitive and deliberate judgments are based on common principles. *Psychological Review, 118*(1), 97–109.

Kruglanski, A. W., & Thompson, E. P. (1999). Persuasion by a single route: A view from the unimodel. *Psychological Inquiry, 10*(2), 83–109.

Kruglanski, A. W., & Webster, D. M. (1996). Motivated closing of the mind: Seizing and freezing. *Psychological Review, 103*(2), 263–283.

Kuhl, P. K. (2000). A new view of language acquisition. *Proceedings of the National Academy of Sciences, 97*(22), 11850–11857.

Kumkale, G. T., & Albarracín, D. (2004). The sleeper effect in persuasion: A meta-analytic review. *Psychological Bulletin, 130*(1), 143.

Lane, K. A., Mitchell, J. P., & Banaji, M. R. (2005). Me and my group: Cultural status can disrupt cognitive consistency. *Social Cognition, 23*, 353–386.

LaPiere, R. T. (1934). Attitudes vs. actions. *Social Forces, 13*(2), 230–237.

Larsen, J. T., Norris, C. J., & Cacioppo, J. T. (2003). Effects of positive and negative affect on electromyographic activity over zygomaticus major and corrugator supercilii. *Psychophysiology, 40*(5), 776–785.

Larsen, J. T., Norris, C. J., McGraw, A. P., Hawkley, L. C., & Cacioppo, J. T. (2009). The evaluative space grid: A single-item measure of positivity and negativity. *Cognition and Emotion, 23*(3), 453–480.

Lassiter, G. D., Apple, K. J., & Slaw, R. D. (1996). Need for cognition and thought-induced attitude polarization: Another look. *Journal of Social Behavior and Personality, 11*(4), 647–665.

Lasswell, H. D. (1948). The structure and function of communication in society. In L. Bryson (Ed.), *The communication of ideas: Religion and civilization series* (pp. 37–51). New York: Harper & Row.

Lasswell, H. D., Casey, R. D., & Smith, B. L. (1935). *Propaganda and promotional activities.* Minneapolis: University of Minnesota Press.

Lavine, H., Thomsen, C. J., Zanna, M. P., & Borgida, E. (1998). On the primacy of affect in the determination of attitudes and behavior: The moderating role of affective-cognitive ambivalence. *Journal of Experimental Social Psychology, 34*(4), 398–421.

Lawton, R., Conner, M., & McEachan, R. (2009). Desire or reason: predicting health behaviors from affective and cognitive attitudes. *Health Psychology, 28*(1), 56.

Lawton, R., Conner, M., & Parker, D. (2007). Beyond cognition: Predicting health risk behaviors from instrumental and affective beliefs. *Health Psychology, 26*(3), 259.

LeDoux, J. (1998). Fear and the brain: where have we been, and where are we going? *Biological Psychiatry, 44*(12), 1229–1238.

Lee, S., & Schwarz, N. (2014). Question context and priming meaning of health: Effect on differences in self-rated health between Hispanics and Non-Hispanic Whites. *American Journal of Public Health, 104*, 179–185.

Leippe, M. R., & Elkin, R. A. (1987). When motives clash: Issue involvement and response involvement as determinants of persuasion. *Journal of Personality and Social Psychology, 52*(2), 269.

Leone, C., & Ensley, E. (1986). Self-generated attitude change: A person by situation analysis of attitude polarization and attenuation. *Journal of Research in Personality, 20*, 434–446.

Levav, J., & Fitzsimons, G. J. (2006). When questions change behavior: The role of ease of representation. *Psychological Science, 17*(3), 207–213.

Levenson, H., Burford, B., & Davis, L. (1975). Are women still prejudiced against women? A replication and extension of Goldberg's study. *Journal of Psychology, 89*, 67–71.

Leventhal, H., & Niles, P. (1965). Persistence of influence for varying durations of exposure to threat stimuli. *Psychological Reports, 16*(1), 223–233.

Lieberman, M. D. (2007). Social cognitive neuroscience: A review of core processes. *Annual Review of Psychology, 58*, 259–289.

Lieberman, M. D., Ochsner, K. N., Gilbert, D. T., & Schacter, D. L. (2001). Do amnesics exhibit cognitive dissonance reduction? The role of explicit memory and attention in attitude change. *Psychological Science, 12*(2), 135–140.

Lifton, R. J. 1961. *Thought Reform and the Psychology of Totalism: A Study of "Brainwashing" in China.* New York: Norton.

Likert, R. (1932). A technique for the measurement of attitudes. *Archives of Psychology, 22*, 1–54.

Linder, D. E., Cooper, J., & Jones, E. E. (1967). Decision freedom as a determinant of the role of incentive magnitude in attitude change. *Journal of Personality and Social Psychology, 6*(3), 245.

Linder, D. E., & Worchel, S. (1970). Opinion change as a result of effortfully drawing a counterattitudinal conclusion. *Journal of Experimental Social Psychology, 6*(4), 432–448.

Loewenstein, G. F., Weber, E. U., Hsee, C. K., & Welch, N. (2001). Risk as feelings. *Psychological Bulletin, 127*(2), 267.

Lord, C. G., & Lepper, M. R. (1999). Attitude representation theory. *Advances in Experimental Social Psychology, 31*, 265–344.

Lord, C. G., Paulson, R. M., Sia, T. L., Thomas, J. C., & Lepper, M. R. (2004). Houses built on sand: effects of exemplar stability on susceptibility to attitude change. *Journal of Personality and Social Psychology, 87*(6), 733–749.

Lord, C. G., Ross, L., & Lepper, M. R. (1979). Biased assimilation and attitude polarization: The effects of prior theories on subsequently considered evidence. *Journal of Personality and Social Psychology, 37*(11), 2098–2109.

Losch, M. E., & Cacioppo, J. T. (1990). Cognitive dissonance may enhance sympathetic tonus, but attitudes are changed to reduce negative affect rather than arousal. *Journal of Experimental Social Psychology, 26*(4), 289–304.

Lydon, J., Zanna, M. P., & Ross, M. (1988). Bolstering attitudes by autobiographical recall: Attitude persistence and selective memory. *Personality and Social Psychology Bulletin, 14*(1), 78–86.

Maass, A., Salvi, D., Arcuri, L., & Semin, G. R. (1989). Language use in intergroup contexts: The linguistic intergroup bias. *Journal of Personality and Social Psychology, 57*(6), 981.

Mackie, D. M. (1987). Systematic and nonsystematic processing of majority and minority persuasive communications. *Journal of Personality and Social Psychology, 53*(1), 41.

Mackie, D. M., & Worth, L. T. (1989). Processing deficits and the mediation of positive affect in persuasion. *Journal of Personality and Social Psychology, 57*(1), 27.

Maddux, J. E., & Rogers, R. W. (1983). Protection motivation and self-efficacy: A revised theory of fear appeals and attitude change. *Journal of Experimental Social Psychology, 19*(5), 469–479.

Maheswaran, D., & Chaiken, S. (1991). Promoting systematic processing in low-motivation settings: Effect of incongruent information on processing and judgment. *Journal of Personality and Social Psychology, 61*(1), 13.

Maio, G. R., Bell, D. W., & Esses, V. M. (1996). Ambivalence and persuasion: The processing of messages about immigrant groups. *Journal of Experimental Social Psychology, 32*(6), 513–536.

Maio, G. R., & Esses, V. M. (2001). The need for affect: Individual differences in the motivation to approach or avoid emotions. *Journal of Personality, 69*(4), 583–614.

Maio, G. R., Esses, V. M., Arnold, K. H., & Olson, J. M. (2004). The function-structure model of attitudes: Incorporating the need for affect. *Contemporary Perspectives on the Psychology of Attitudes*, 9–33.

Maio, G. R., & Olson, J. M. (1994). Value-attitude-behaviour relations: The moderating role of attitude functions. *British Journal of Social Psychology, 33*(3), 301–312.

Maio, G. R., & Olson, J. M. (1995). Relations between values, attitudes, and behavioral intentions: The moderating role of attitude function. *Journal of Experimental Social Psychology, 31*(3), 266–285.

Maio, G. R., & Olson, J. M. (1998). Values as truisms: Evidence and implications. *Journal of Personality and Social Psychology, 74*(2), 294–311.

Maio, G. R. and Olson, J. M. (2000a). Emergent themes and potential approaches to attitude function: The function-structure model of attitudes. In Maio, G. and Olson, J. (Eds.), *Why evaluate: Functions of attitudes.* Mahwah, NJ: Lawrence Erlbaum, pp. 417–442.

Maio, G. R. and Olson, J. M. (2000b). What is a "value-expressive" attitude? In Maio, G. and Olson, J. (Eds.), *Why evaluate: Functions of attitudes.* Mahwah, NJ: Lawrence Erlbaum, pp. 249–270.

Manstead, A. S., & Eekelen, S. A. (1998). Distinguishing between perceived behavioral control and self-efficacy in the domain of academic achievement intentions and behaviors. *Journal of Applied Social Psychology, 28*(15), 1375–1392.

Markus, H. R., & Kitayama, S. (1991). Culture and the self: Implications for cognition, emotion, and motivation. *Psychological Review, 98*(2), 224.

Marsh, K. L, Johnson, B. T., Scott-Sheldon, L. A. (2001). Heart versus reason in condom use: Implicit versus explicit attitudinal predictors of sexual behavior. *Zeitschrift for Experimental Psychology, 48*, 161–175.

Martinie, M-A., Olive, T., Milland, L., Joule, R-V. & Capa, R. L. (2013). Evidence that dissonance arousal is initially undifferentiated and only later labeled as negative. *Journal of Experimental Social Psychology.*

Matz, D. C. & Wood, W. (2005). Cognitive dissonance in group: The consequences of disagreement. *Journal of Personality and Social Psychology, 88*, 22–37.

McClelland, D. C., & Jemmott III, J. B. (1980). Power motivation, stress and physical illness. *Journal of Human Stress, 6*(4), 6–15.

McClure, S. M., Laibson, D. I., Loewenstein, G., & Cohen, J. D. (2004). Separate neural systems value immediate and delayed monetary rewards. *Science, 306*(5695), 503–507.

McClure, S. M., Li, J., Tomlin, D., Cypert, K.S., Montague, L.M., & Montague, P.R. (2004). Neural correlates of behavioral preference for culturally familiar drinks. *Neuron, 44*, 379–387.

McConahay, J. B. (1986). Modern racism, ambivalence, and the modern racism scale. In J. F. Dovidio & S. L. Gaertner (Eds.), *Prejudice, discrimination, and racism* (pp. 91–126). Orlando, FL: Academic Press.

McConnell, A. R., & Leibold, J. M. (2009). Weak criticisms and selective evidence: Reply to Blanton et al. *Journal of Applied Psychology, 94*(3), 583–589.

McDonald, H. E., & Hirt, E. R. (1997). When expectancy meets desire: Motivational effects in reconstructive memory. *Journal of Personality and Social Psychology, 72*(1), 5–23.

McGraw, K. M., Fischle, M., Stenner, K., & Lodge, M. (1996). What's in a word? *Political Behavior, 18*(3), 263–287.

McGuire, W. J. (1961). Resistance to persuasion conferred by active and passive prior refutation of the same and alternative counterarguments. *Journal of Abnormal and Social Psychology, 63*(2), 326–332.

McGuire, W. J. (1964). Inducing resistance to persuasion. *Advances in Experimental Social Psychology, 1*, 191.

McGuire, W. J. (1969). The nature of attitudes and attitude change. In G. Lindzey & E. Aronson (Eds.), *Handbook of Social Psychology* (Vol. 3, pp. 136–314). Reading, MA: Addison-Wesley.

McGuire, W. J., & Papageorgis, D. (1961). The relative efficacy of various types of prior belief-defense in producing immunity against persuasion. *The Journal of Abnormal and Social Psychology, 62*(2), 327.

McKimmie, B. M., Terry, D. J., & Hogg, M. A. (2009). Dissonance reduction in the context of group membership: The role of metaconsistency. *Group Dynamics: Theory, Research, and Practice, 13*(2), 103.

Mendes, W. B., Blascovich, J, Lickel, B., & Hunter, S. (2002). *Personality and Social Psychology Bulletin, 28*, 939–952.

Meyer, D. E., & Schvaneveldt, R. W. (1971). Facilitation in recognizing pairs of words: Evidence of a dependence between retrieval operations. *Journal of Experimental Psychology, 90*(2), 227–234.

Millar, M. G., & Tesser, A. (1986). Effects of affective and cognitive focus on the attitude–behavior relation. *Journal of Personality and Social Psychology, 51*(2), 270.

Miller, N., & Campbell, D. T. (1959). Recency and primacy in persuasion as a function of timing of speeches and measurements. *Journal of Abnormal and Social Psychology, 59*, 1–9.

Miller, N. E. (1944). Experimental studies of conflict. In J. Hunt (Ed.), *Personality and the behavior disorders* (Vol. 1, pp. 431–465). New York: Ronald Press.

Miller, R. L., Seligman, C., Clark, N. T., & Bush, M. (1976). Perceptual contrast versus reciprocal concession as mediators of induced compliance. *Canadian Journal of Behavioral Science, 8*(4), 401–409.

Mills, J., & Aronson, E. (1965). Opinion change as a function of the communicator's attractiveness and desire to influence. *Journal of Personality and Social Psychology, 1*(2), 173.

Mitchell, A. A., & Olson, J. C. (1981). Are product attribute beliefs the only mediator of advertising effects on brand attitude? *Journal of Marketing Research, 18*, 318–332.

Mitnick, L., & McGinnies, E. (1958). Influencing ethnocentrism in small discussion groups through a film communication. *Journal of Abnormal and Social Psychology, 56,* 82–92.

Monin, B., Norton, M. I., Cooper, J., & Hogg, M. A. (2004). Reacting to an assumed situation vs. conforming to an assumed reaction: The role of perceived speaker attitude in vicarious dissonance. *Group Processes & Intergroup Relations, 7*(3), 207–220.

Monroe, B. M., & Read, S. J. (2008). A general connectionist model of attitude structure and change: The ACS (Attitudes as Constraint Satisfaction) model. *Psychological Review, 115*(3), 733–759.

Moore, D. J., & Reardon, R. (1987). Source magnification: The role of multiple sources in the processing of advertising appeals. *Journal of Marketing Research*, 412–417.

Morris, J. P., Squires, N. K., Taber, C. S., & Lodge, M. (2003). Activation of political attitudes: A psychophysiological examination of the hot cognition hypothesis. *Political Psychology, 24*(4), 727–745.

Morris, J. S., Öhman, A., & Dolan, R. J. (1998). Conscious and unconscious emotional learning in the human amygdala. *Nature, 393*(6684), 467–470.

Moruzzi, G., & Magoun, H. W. (1949). Brain stem reticular formation and activation of the EEG. *Electroencephalography and Clinical Neurophysiology, 1*(1), 455–473.

Mowrer, O. H. (1960). *Learning theory and behavior* (Vol. 960). New York: Wiley.

Moyer-Gusé, E., & Nabi, R. L. (2010). Explaining the effects of narrative in an entertainment television program: Overcoming resistance to persuasion. *Human Communication Research, 36*(1), 26–52.

Muraven, M., Tice, D. M., & Baumeister, R. F. (1998). Self-control as limited resource: Regulatory depletion patterns. *Journal of Personality and Social Psychology, 74,* 774–789.

Murphy, S. T., & Zajonc, R. B. (1993). Affect, cognition, and awareness: Affective priming with optimal and suboptimal stimulus exposures. *Journal of Personality and Social Psychology, 64,* 723–739.

Murray, S. L., Haddock, G., & Zanna, M. P. (1996). Creating value-expressive attitudes: An experimental approach. In C. Seligman, J. M. Olson & M. P. Zanna (Eds.), *The Psychology of Values: The Ontario Symposium* (Vol. 8, pp. 107–133). Mahwah, NJ: Lawrence Erlbaum Associates.

Myers, R. E. (2010). Promoting healthy behaviors: how do we get the message across? *International Journal of Nursing Studies, 47*(4), 500–512.

Na, J. & Kitayama, S. (2012). Will people work hard on a task they choose? Social-eyes priming in different cultural contexts. *Journal of Experimental Social Psychology, 48,* 284–290.

Nass, C., & Lee, K. M. (2001). Does computer-synthesized speech manifest personality? Experimental tests of recognition, similarity-attraction, and consistency-attraction. *Journal of Experimental Psychology: Applied, 7*(3), 171–181.

Neely, J. H. (1977). Semantic priming and retrieval from lexical memory: Roles of inhibitionless spreading activation and limited-capacity attention. *Journal of Experimental Psychology: General, 106*(3), 226–254.

Nel, E., Helmreich, R., & Aronson, E. (1969). Opinion change in the advocate as a function of the persuasibility of the audience: A clarification of the meaning of dissonance. *Journal of Personality and Social Psychology, 12,* 117–124.

Newby-Clark, I. R., McGregor, I., & Zanna, M. P. (2002). Thinking and caring about cognitive inconsistency: When and for whom does attitudinal ambivalence feel uncomfortable? *Journal of Personality and Social Psycholgoy, 82,* 157–166.

Newcomb, T. M., & American Council on Public Affairs. (1957). *Personality and social change.* New York: Dryden.

Niedenthal, P. M., Barsalou, L. W., Winkielman, P., Krauth-Gruber, S., & Ric, F. (2005). Embodiment in attitudes, social perception, and emotion. *Personality and Social Psychology Review, 9*(3), 184–211.

Nier, J. A. (2005). How dissociated are implicit and explicit racial attitudes? *Group Processes and Intergroup Relations, 8,* 39–52.

Nisbett, R. E., & Wilson, T. D. (1977). Telling more than we can know: Verbal reports on mental processes. *Psychological Review, 84*(3), 231–259.

Nisbett, R., Krantz, D., Jepson, C., & Kunda, Z. (1983). The use of statistical heuristics in everyday inductive reasoning. *Psychological Review, 90*(4), 339–363.

Nordgren, L. F., van Harreveld, F., & van der Pligt, J. (2006). Ambivalence, discomfort, and motivated information processing. *Journal of Experimental Social Psychology, 42*(2), 252–258.

Norman, R. (1975). Affective-cognitive consistency, attitudes, conformity, and behavior. *Journal of Personality and Social Psychology, 32*(1), 83.

Norton, M. I., Monin, B., Cooper, J., & Hogg, M. A. (2003). Vicarious dissonance: Attitude change from the inconsistency of others. *Journal of Personality and Social Psychology, 85*(1), 47–62.

Nosek, B. A., & Banaji, M. R. (2001). The go/no-go association task. *Social Cognition*, *19*(6), 625–666.

Nosek, B. A., Banaji, M. R., & Greenwald, A. G. (2002). Harvesting implicit group attitudes and beliefs from a demonstration web site. *Group Dynamics*, *6*, 101–115.

Nosek, B. A., Greenwald, A. G., & Banaji, M. R. (2005). Understanding and using the Implicit Association Test: II. Method variables and construct validity. *Personality and Social Psychology Bulletin*, *31*(2), 166–180.

Nosek, B. A., & Hansen, J. J. (2008). The associations in our heads belong to us: Searching for attitudes and knowledge in implicit evaluation. *Cognition & Emotion*, *22*(4), 553–594.

Ogilvy, D. (1983). *On Advertising*. New York: Crown Publishing.

Olson, M. A., & Fazio, R. H. (2001). Implicit attitude formation through classical conditioning. *Psychological Science*, *12*(5), 413–417.

Olson, M. A., & Fazio, R. H. (2004). Reducing the influence of extrapersonal associations on the Implicit Association Test: Personalizing the IAT. *Journal of Personality and Social Psychology*, *86*(5), 653–667.

Olson, M. A., & Fazio, R. H. (2006). Reducing automatically activated racial prejudice through implicit evaluative conditioning. *Personality and Social Psychology Bulletin*, *32*(4), 421–433.

Olson, M. A., & Fazio, R. H. (2009). Implicit and explicit measures of attitudes. *Attitudes: Insights from the new implicit measures*, 19–63.

Oppenheimer, D. M. (2006). Consequences of erudite vernacular utilized irrespective of necessity: Problems with using long words needlessly. *Applied Cognitive Psychology*, *20*(2), 139–156.

Oppenheimer, D. M., & Frank, M. C. (2008). A rose in any other font would not smell as sweet: Effects of perceptual fluency on categorization. *Cognition*, *106*(3), 1178–1194.

Orbell, S., Hodgkins, S., & Sheeran, P. (1997). Implementation intentions and the theory of planned behavior. *Personality and Social Psychology Bulletin*, *23*, 945–954.

Orne, M. T. (1962). On the social psychology of the psychological experiment: With particular reference to demand characteristics and their implications. *American Psychologist*, *17*(11), 776–783.

Osgood, C. E. (1962). Studies on the generality of affective meaning systems. *American Psychologist*, *17*(1), 10.

Osgood, C. E., Suci, G. J., & Tannenbaum, P. H. (1957). *The measurement of meaning* (Vol. 47). Urbana: University of Illinois Press.

Oskamp, S., Harrington, M. J., Edwards, T. C., Sherwood, D. L., Okuda, S. M., & Swanson, D. C. (1991). Factors influencing household recycling behavior. *Environment and Behavior*, *23*(4), 494–519.

Osterhouse, R. A., & Brock, T. C. (1970). Distraction increases yielding to propaganda by inhibiting counterarguing. *Journal of Personality and Social Psychology*, *15*(4), 344–58.

Oswald, F. L., Mitchell, G., Blanton, H., Jaccard, J., & Tetlock, P. E. (2013). Predicting ethnic and racial discrimination: A meta-analysis of IAT criterion studies. *Journal of Personality and Social Psychology*, *105*, 171–192.

Pavlov, I. (1927). *Conditioned reflexes*. Oxford, UK: Oxford University Press.

Payne, B. K., Burkley, M. A., & Stokes, M. B. (2008). Why do implicit and explicit attitude tests diverge? The role of structural fit. *Journal of Personality and Social Psychology*, *94*(1), 16.

Payne, B. K., Cheng, C. M., Govorun, O., & Stewart, B. D. (2005). An inkblot for attitudes: Affect misattribution as implicit measurement. *Journal of Personality and Social Psychology, 89(3),* 277.

Payne, B. K., Krosnick, J. A., Pasek, J., Lelkes, Y., Akhtar, O., & Tompson, T. (2010). Implicit and explicit prejudice in the 2008 American presidential election. *Journal of Experimental Social Psychology, 46*(2), 367–374.

Pechman, C. & Stewart, D. (1988). Advertising repetition: A critical review of wearin and wearout. In J. Leigh and C. R. Martin, Jr., (Eds.), *Current Issues and Research in Advertising* (pp. 285–331). Ann Arbor: University of Michigan.

Perlman, D., & Oskamp, S. (1971). The effects of picture content and exposure frequency on evaluations of Negroes and whites. *Journal of Experimental Social Psychology, 7*(5), 503–514.

Perugini, M. (2005). Predictive models of implicit and explicit attitudes. *British Journal of Social Psychology, 44*(1), 29–45.

Peters, K. R., & Gawronski, B. (2011). Are we puppets on a string? Comparing the impact of contingency and validity on implicit and explicit evaluations. *Personality and Social Psychology Bulletin, 37*(4), 557–569.

Petersen, K. K., & Dutton, J. E. (1975). Centrality, extremity, intensity: Neglected variables in research on attitude-behavior consistency. *Social Forces, 54*(2), 393–414.

Petkova, K. G., Ajzen, I., & Driver, B. L. (1995). Salience of anti-abortion beliefs and commitment to an attitudinal position: On the strength, structure, and predictive validity of anti-abortion attitudes. *Journal of Applied Social Psychology, 25*(6), 463–483.

Petrides, M., & Milner, B. (1982). Deficits on subject-ordered tasks after frontal-and temporal-lobe lesions in man. *Neuropsychologia, 20*(3), 249–262.

Petty, R. E. (1994). Two routes to persuasion: State of the art. In G. d'Ydewalle, P. Eelen, & P. Bertelson (Eds.), *International perspectives on psychological science* (Vol. 2, pp. 229–247). Hillsdale, NJ: Erlbaum.

Petty, R. E. (1997). The evolution of theory and research in social psychology: From single to multiple effect and process models. In C. McGarty & S. A. Haslam (Eds.), *The message of social psychology: Perspectives on mind in society* (pp. 268–290). Oxford, UK: Blackwell.

Petty, R. E. & Briñol, P. (2008). Persuasion: From single to multiple to meta-cognitive processes. *Perspectives on Psychological Science, 3,* 137–147.

Petty, R. E. & Briñol, P. (2009). Implicit ambivalence: A meta-cognitive approach. In R. E. Petty, R. H. Fazio, & P. Briñol (Eds.), *Attitudes: Insights from the new implicit measures* (pp. 119–164). New York: Psychology Press.

Petty, R. E. & Briñol, P. (2012). The Elaboration Likelihood Model. In P.A.M. Van Lange, A. Kruglanski, & E. T. Higgins (Eds.), *Handbook of theories of social psychology* (Vol.1, pp. 224–245). London: Sage Publications.

Petty, R. E., Briñol, P., & DeMarree, K. G. (2007). The meta-cognitive model (MCM) of attitudes: Implications for attitude measurement, change, and strength. *Social Cognition, 25*(5), 657–686.

Petty, R. E., Briñol, P., & Tormala, Z. L. (2002). Thought confidence as a determinant of persuasion: the self-validation hypothesis. *Journal of Personality and Social Psychology, 82*(5), 722–741.

Petty, R. E., & Brock, T. C. (1981). Thought disruption and persuasion: Assessing the validity of attitude change experiments. *Cognitive responses in persuasion* (pp. 55–79). Hillsdale, NJ: Erlbaum.

Petty, R. E., & Cacioppo, J. T. (1977). Forewarning, cognitive responding, and resistance to persuasion. *Journal of Personality and Social Psychology, 35*(9), 645–655.

Petty, R. E., & Cacioppo, J. T. (1979). Effects of forewarning of persuasive intent and involvement on cognitive responses. *Personality and Social Psychology Bulletin, 5,* 173–176.

Petty, R. E., & Cacioppo, J. T. (1980). Effects of issue involvement on attitudes in an advertising context. In G. Gorn & M. Goldberg (Eds.), *Proceedings of the Division 23 Program,* Montreal: American Psychological Association.

Petty, R. E., & Cacioppo, J. T. (1981). Issue involvement as a moderator of the effects on attitude of advertising content and context. *Advances in Consumer Research, 8*(1), 20–24.

Petty, R. E., & Cacioppo, J. T. (1983). Central and peripheral routes to persuasion: Application to advertising. In L. Percy & A. Woodside (Eds.), *Advertising and consumer psychology* (pp. 3–23). Lexington, MA: D. C. Heath.

Petty, R. E., & Cacioppo, J. T. (1984). The effects of involvement on responses to argument quantity and quality: Central and peripheral routes to persuasion. *Journal of Personality and Social Psychology, 46*(1), 69–81.

Petty, R. E., & Cacioppo, J. T. (1986). The Elaboration Likelihood Model of persuasion. In L. Berkowitz (Ed.), *Advances in experimental social psychology* (Vol. 19, pp. 123–205). New York: Academic Press.

Petty, R. E., Cacioppo, J. T., & Goldman, R. (1981). Personal involvement as a determinant of argument-based persuasion. *Journal of Personality and Social Psychology, 41,* 847–855.

Petty, R. E., Cacioppo, J. T., Kasmer, J. A., & Haugtvedt, C. P. (1987). A reply to Stiff and Boster. *Communication Monographs, 54,* 257–263.

Petty, R. E., Cacioppo, J. T., & Schumann, D. (1983). Central and peripheral routes to advertising effectiveness: The moderating role of involvement. *Journal of Consumer Research,* 135–146.

Petty, R. E., Fabrigar, L. R., & Wegener, D. T. (2003). Emotional factors in attitudes and persuasion. In R. J. Davidson, K. Scherer, & H. H. Goldsmith (Eds.), *Handbook of affective sciences* (pp. 752–772). Oxford, UK: Oxford University Press.

Petty, R. E., Fazio, R. H., & Briñol, P. (2009). The new implicit measures. *Attitudes: Insights from the new implicit measures,* 3–18.

Petty, R. E., Harkins, S. G., & Williams, K. D. (1980). The effects of group diffusion of cognitive effort on attitudes: An information processing view. *Journal of Personality and Social Psychology, 38,* 81–92.

Petty, R. E., Kasmer, J. A., Haugtvedt, C. P., & Cacioppo, J. T. (1987). Source and message factors in persuasion. A reply to Stiff's critique of the elaboration likelihood model. *Communication Monographs, 54*(3), 233–249.

Petty, R. E., & Krosnick, J. A. (Eds.). (1995). *Attitude strength: Antecedents and consequences* (Vol. 4). Mahwah, NJ: Lawrence Erlbaum Associates.

Petty, R. E., & Wegener, D. T. (1993). Flexible correction processes in social judgment: Correcting for context-induced contrast. *Journal of Experimental Social Psychology, 29*(2), 137–165.

Petty, R. E., & Wegener, D. T. (1999). The elaboration likelihood model: Current status and controversies. In S. Chaiken & Y. Trope (Eds.), *Dual-process theories in social psychology* (pp. 37–72). New York: Guilford Press.

Petty, R. E., Wegener, D. T., & White, P. H. (1998). Flexible correction processes in social judgment: Implications for persuasion. *Social Cognition, 16*(1), 93–113.

Petty, R. E., Wells, G. L., & Brock, T. C. (1976). Distraction can enhance or reduce yielding to propaganda: Thought disruption versus effort justification. *Journal of Personality and Social Psychology*, *34*(5), 874–884.

Petty, R. E., Wheeler, S. C., & Bizer, G. Y. (1999). Is there one persuasion process or more? Lumping versus splitting in attitude change theories. *Psychological Inquiry*, *10*(2), 156–163.

Phelps, E. A., O'Connor, K. J., Cunningham, W. A., Funayama, E. S., Gatenby, J. C., Gore, J. C., & Banaji, M. R. (2000). Performance on indirect measures of race evaluation predicts amygdala activation. *Journal of Cognitive Neuroscience*, *12*(5), 729–738.

Pittman, T. S. (1993). Control motivation and attitude change. In *Control motivation and social cognition* (pp. 157–175). New York: Springer.

Pizzagalli, D., Koenig, Regard, M., & Lehmann, D. (1999). Rapid emotional face processing in the human right and left brain hemispheres: An ERP study. *Neuroreport*, *10*(13), 2691–2698.

Powell, M. C., & Fazio, R. H. (1984). Attitude accessibility as a function of repeated attitudinal expression. *Personality and Social Psychology Bulletin*, *10*(1), 139–148.

Pratkanis, A. R. & Aronson, E. (2001). *Age of propaganda: The everyday use and abuse of persuasion*. New York: Holt Paperbacks.

Pratkanis, A. R., Greenwald, A. G., Leippe, M. R., & Baumgardner, M. H. (1988). In search of reliable persuasion effects: III. The sleeper effect is dead: Long live the sleeper effect. *Journal of Personality and Social Psychology*, *54*, 203–218.

Prentice, D. A. (1987). Psychological correspondence of possessions, attitudes, and values. *Journal of Personality and Social Psychology*, *53*, 993–1003.

Priester, J. R. & Petty, R.E. (1996). The gradual threshold model of ambivalence: Relating the positive and negative bases of attitudes to subjective ambivalence. *Journal of Personality and Social Psychology, 71*, 431–439.

Pronin, E. (2007). Perception and misperception of bias in human judgment. *Trends in cognitive sciences*, *11*(1), 37.

Pronin, E. (2009). The introspection illusion. *Advances in Experimental Social Psychology*, *41*, 1–67.

Pronin, E., & Kugler, M. B. (2007). Valuing thoughts, ignoring behavior: The introspection illusion as a source of the bias blind spot. *Journal of Experimental Social Psychology*, *43*(4), 565–578.

Pronin, E., Lin, D. Y., & Ross, L. (2002). The bias blind spot: Perceptions of bias in self versus others. *Personality and Social Psychology Bulletin*, *28*(3), 369–381.

Ramsey, S. L., Lord, C. G., Wallace, D. S., & Pugh, M. A. (1994). The role of subtypes in attitudes towards superordinate social categories. *British Journal of Social Psychology*, *33*(4), 387–403.

Ratneshwar, S., & Chaiken, S. (1991). Comprehension's role in persuasion: The case of its moderating effect on the persuasive impact of source cues. *Journal of Consumer Research*, 52–62.

Reber, R., & Schwarz, N. (1999). Effects of perceptual fluency on judgments of truth. *Consciousness and Cognition*, *8*(3), 338–342.

Reber, R., Winkielman, P., & Schwarz, N. (1998). Effects of perceptual fluency on affective judgments. *Psychological Science*, *9*(1), 45–48.

Regan, D. T., & Fazio, R. (1977). On the consistency between attitudes and behavior: Look to the method of attitude formation. *Journal of Experimental Social Psychology*, *13*(1), 28–45.

Reinecke, J., Schmidt, P., & Ajzen, I. (1996). Application of the theory of planned behavior to adolescents' condom use: A panel study. *Journal of applied social psychology, 26*(9), 749–772.

Reinecke, J., Schmidt, P., & Ajzen, I. (1997). Birth control versus AIDS prevention: A hierarchical model of condom use among young people. *Journal of Applied Social Psychology, 27*(9), 743–759.

Rhodes, N., & Wood, W. (1992). Self-esteem and intelligence affect influenceability: The mediating role of message reception. *Psychological Bulletin, 111*, 156–171.

Richetin, J., Conner, M., & Perugini, M. (2011). Not doing is not the opposite of doing: Implications for attitudinal models of behavioral prediction. *Personality and Social Psychology Bulletin, 37*(1), 40–54.

Robinson, R. J., Keltner, D., Ward, A., & Ross, L. (1995). Actual versus assumed differences in construal: "Naive realism" in intergroup perception and conflict. *Journal of Personality and Social Psychology, 68*, 404–404.

Roediger, H. L. (1990). Implicit memory: Retention without remembering. *American Psychologist, 45*, 1043–1056.

Roese, N. J., & Jamieson, D. W. (1993). Twenty years of bogus pipeline research: A critical review and meta-analysis. *Psychological Bulletin, 114*, 363–363.

Rogers, C. R. (1945). The nondirective method as a technique for social research. *American Journal of Sociology*, 279–283.

Rogers, R. W. (1983). Cognitive and physiological processes in fear appeals and attitude change: A revised theory of protection motivation. In J. T. Cacioppo & R. E. Petty (Eds.), *Social psychophysiology: A sourcebook* (pp. 153–176). New York: Guilford.

Rokeach, M. (1954). The nature and meaning of dogmatism. *Psychological Review, 61*(3), 194–204.

Rokeach, M. (1968). A theory of organization and change within value-attitude systems. Journal of *Social Issues, 24*(1), 13–33.

Rokeach, M. (1973). *The nature of human values*. New York: Free Press.

Ronis, D. L., Baumgardner, M. H., Leippe, M. R., Cacioppo, J. T., & Greenwald, A. G. (1977). In search of reliable persuasion effects: I. A computer-controlled procedure for studying persuasion. *Journal of Personality and Social Psychology, 35*(8), 548.

Rosenberg, M. (1960). An analysis of affective-cognitive consistency. *Attitude organization and change*, 15–64.

Rosenberg, M. (1965). *Society and the adolescent self-image*. Princeton, NJ: Princeton University press.

Rosenberg, M. J. (1968). Hedonism, inauthenticity and other goads toward expansion of a consistency theory. In R. P. Abelson, E. Aronson, W. J. Mc Guire, T. M. Newomb, M. J. Rosenberg, & P. H. Tannenbaum (Eds.), *Theories of cognitive consistency: A sourcebook* (pp. 73–111). Chicago: Rand-McNally.

Rosenberg, M. (1969). The conditions and consequences of evaluation apprehension. In R. Rosenthal & R. L. Rosnow (Eds.) *Artifact in behavioral research* (pp. 279–349). New York: Basic Books.

Rosenberg, M. J., & Hovland, C. I. (1960). *Attitude organization and change: An analysis of consistency among attitude components* (Vol. 3). New Haven, CT: Yale University Press.

Roskos-Ewoldsen, D. R., & Fazio, R. H. (1992). On the orienting value of attitudes: Attitude accessibility as a determinant of an object's attraction of visual attention. *Journal of Personality and Social Psychology, 63*(2), 198–211.

Ross, L., & Ward, A. (1996). Naive realism in everyday life: Implications for social conflict and misunderstanding. *Values and Knowledge*, 103–135.

Ross, M. (1989). Relation of implicit theories to the construction of personal histories. *Psychological Review*, *96*(2), 341–357.

Ross, M., McFarland, C., & Fletcher, G. J. (1981). The effect of attitude on the recall of personal histories. *Journal of Personality and Social Psychology*, *40*(4), 627–634.

Rothermund, K. & Wentura, D. (2010). It's brief but is it better? An evaluation of the Brief Implicit Association Test. *Experimental Psychology*, *57*, 233–237.

Rucker, D. D., Petty, R. E., & Briñol, P. (2008). What's in a frame anyway?: A meta-cognitive analysis of the impact of one versus two sided message framing on attitude certainty. *Journal of Consumer Psychology*, *18*(2), 137–149.

Rudman, L. A., Feinberg, J. & Fairchild, K. (2002). Minority members' attitudes: Automatic ingroup bias as a function of group status. *Social Cognition*, *20*, 294–320.

Rudman, L. A., Greenwald, A. G., Mellott, D. S. & Schwartz, J.L.K. (1999). Measuring the automatic components of prejudice: Flexibility and generality of the Implicit Association Test. *Social Cognition*, *17*, 437–465.

Rudolph, A. Schröder-Abe, M., Riketta, M., & Schütz, A. (2010). Easier when done than said! Implicit self-esteem predicts observed or spontaneous behavior, but not selfreported or controlled behavior. *Zeitschrift für Psychologie/Journal of Psychology*, *218*, 12–19.

Rydell, R. J., McConnell, A. R. & Mackie, D. M. (2008). Consequences of discrepant explicit and implicit attitudes: Cognitive dissonance and increased information processing. *Journal of Experimental Social Psychology*, *44*, 1526–1532.

Sanbonmatsu, D. M., & Fazio, R. H. (1990). The role of attitudes in memory-based decision making. *Journal of Personality and Social Psychology*, *59*(4), 614.

Sanbonmatsu, D. M., & Kardes, F. R. (1988). The effects of physiological arousal on information processing and persuasion. *Journal of Consumer Research*, 379–385.

Sanbonmatsu, D. M., Posavac, S. S., Vanous, S., Ho, E. A., & Fazio, R. H. (2007). The deautomatization of accessible attitudes. *Journal of Experimental Social Psychology*, *43*(3), 365–378.

Saucier, D. A., & Webster, R. J. (2010). Social vigilantism: Measuring individual differences in belief superiority and resistance to persuasion. *Personality and Social Psychology Bulletin*, *36*(1), 19–32.

Sawicki, V., Wegener, D. T., Clark, J. K., Fabrigar, L. R., Smith, S. M. and Durso, G.R.O. (2013). Feeling conflicted and seeking information: When ambivalence enhances and diminishes selective exposure to attitude-consistent information. *Personality and Social Psychology Bulletin*, *39*(6), 735–747.

Schachter, S. (1951). Deviation, rejection, and communication. *Journal of Abnormal and Social Psychology*, *46*, 190–208.

Scher, S. J., & Cooper, J. (1989). Motivational basis of dissonance: The singular role of behavioral consequences. *Journal of Personality and Social Psychology*, *56*(6), 899.

Schmader, T., & Johns, M. (2003). Converging evidence that stereotype threat reduces working memory capacity. *Journal of Personality and Social Psychology*, *85*(3), 440–452.

Schneider, W., & Shiffrin, R. M. (1977). Controlled and automatic human information processing: I. Detection, search, and attention. *Psychological Review*, *84*(1), 1–66.

Schuette, R. A., & Fazio, R. H. (1995). Attitude accessibility and motivation as determinants of biased processing: A test of the MODE model. *Personality and Social Psychology Bulletin*, *21*(7), 704–710.

Schumann, D. W., Petty, R. E., & Clemons, D. S. (1990). Predicting the effectiveness of different strategies of advertising variation: A test of the repetition-variation hypotheses. *Journal of Consumer Research, 17*(2), 192–202.

Schwartz, B. L., & Metcalfe, J. (1992). Cue familiarity but not target retrievability enhances feeling-of-knowing judgments. *Journal of Experimental Psychology: Learning, Memory, and Cognition, 18*(5), 1074.

Schwarz, N. (2007). Attitude construction: Evaluation in context. *Social Cognition, 25*(5), 638–656.

Schwarz, N. & Bohner, G. (2001). The construction of attitudes. In A. Tesser & N. Schwarz (Eds.), *Blackwell handbook of social psychology, Vol. 1: Intraindividiaual processes* (pp. 436–457). Oxford, UK: Blackwell.

Schwarz, N., & Clore, G. L. (1983). Mood, misattribution, and judgments of well-being: Informative and directive functions of affective states. *Journal of Personality and Social Psychology, 45*(3), 513.

Schwarz, N., & Clore, G. L. (2007). Feelings and Phenomenal Experiences. In E. T. Higgins & A. Kruglanski (Eds.), *Social psychology: A handbook of basic principles* (2nd ed., pp. 385–407). New York: Guilford Press.

Sears, D. O. (1986). College sophomores in the laboratory: Influences of a narrow data base on social psychology's view of human nature. *Journal of Personality and Social Psychology, 51*(3), 515–530.

Sedikides, C., & Strube, M. J. (1997). Self-evaluation: To thine own self be good, to thine own self be sure, to thine own self be true, and to thine own self be better. *Advances in Experimental Social Psychology, 29*, 209–269.

See, Y.H.M., Petty, R. E., & Evans, L. M. (2009). The impact of perceived message complexity and need for cognition on information processing and attitudes. *Journal of Research in Personality, 43(5),* 880–889.

Shavitt, S. (1990). The role of attitude objects in attitude functions. *Journal of Experimental Social Psychology, 26*(2), 124–148.

Shavitt, S. (1992). Evidence for predicting the effectiveness of value-expressive versus utilitarian appeals: A reply to Johar and Sirgy. *Journal of Advertising*, 47–51.

Sheeran, P. (2002). Intention-behavior relations: A conceptual and empirical review. *European Review of Social Psychology, 12*(1), 1–36.

Sheeran, P., Milne, S., Webb, T. L., & Gollwitzer, P. M. (2005). *Implementation intentions and health behaviour.* Bibliothek der Universität Konstanz.

Sheeran, P., & Taylor, S. (1999). Predicting intentions to use condoms: A meta-analysis and comparison of the theories of reasoned action and planned behavior. *Journal of Applied Social Psychology, 29*(8), 1624–1675.

Sheppard, B. H., Hartwick, J., & Warshaw, P. R. (1988). The theory of reasoned action: A meta-analysis of past research with recommendations for modifications and future research. *Journal of Consumer Research*, 325–343.

Sherif, M., & Hovland, C. I. (1961). *Social judgment: Assimilation and contrast effects in communication and attitude change.* New Haven, CT: Yale University Press.

Sherman, B. R., & Kunda, Z. (1989, June). Motivated evaluation of scientific evidence. In *American Psychological Society convention, Arlington.* Reported in Kunda, Z. (1990).*The Case for Motivated Reasoning, Psychological Bulletin, 108*(3), 480–498.

Sherman, J. W. (2009). Controlled influences on implicit measures. *Attitudes: Insights from the New Implicit Measures*, 391–426.

Sherman, J. W., Gawronski, B., Conrey, F. R., Hugenberg, K., & Groom, C. (2006). The Quad Model of impulse and self-regulation. Unpublished manuscript.

Sherman, J. W., Gawronski, B., Gonsalkorale, K., Hugenberg, K., Allen, T. J., & Groom, C. J. (2008). The self-regulation of automatic associations and behavioral impulses. *Psychological Review, 115*(2), 314.

Sherman, J. W., Gawronski, B., & Trope, Y. (Eds.). (2013). *Dual-process theories of the social mind.* New York: Guilford Publications.

Sherman, S. J., Rose, J. S., Koch, K., Presson, C. C., & Chassin, L. (2003). Implicit and explicit attitudes toward cigarette smoking: The effects of context and motivation. *Journal of Social and Clinical Psychology, 22*(1), 13–39.

Shiffrin, R. M., & Schneider, W. (1977). Controlled and automatic human information processing: II. Perceptual learning, automatic attending, and a general theory. *Psychological Review, 84*(2), 127–190.

Shultz, T. R., & Lepper, M. R. (1996). Cognitive dissonance reduction as constraint satisfaction. *Psychological Review, 103*(2), 219–240.

Shultz, T. R., & Lepper, M. R. (1999). Computer simulation of cognitive dissonance reduction. *Cognitive dissonance: Progress on a pivotal theory in social psychology*, 235–265.

Shultz, T. R., Léveillé, E., & Lepper, M. R. (1999). Free choice and cognitive dissonance revisited: Choosing "lesser evils" versus "greater goods." *Personality and Social Psychology Bulletin, 25*(1), 40–48.

Sia, T. L., Lord, C. G., Blessum, K. A., Thomas, J. C., & Lepper, M. R. (1999). Activation of exemplars in the process of assessing social category attitudes. *Journal of Personality and Social Psychology, 76*(4), 517–532.

Sigall, H. & Page, R. (1971). Current stereotypes: A little fading, a little faking. *Journal of Personality and Social Psychology, 18*, 247–255.

Simon, D., Snow, C. J., & Read, S. J. (2004). The redux of cognitive consistency theories: Evidence judgments by constraint satisfaction. *Journal of Personality and Social Psychology, 86*, 814–837.

Simon, D., Krawczyk, D.C., & Holyoak, K. J. (2004). Construction of preferences by constraint satisfaction. *Psychological Science, 15*(5), 331–336.

Sistrunk, F., & McDavid, J. W. (1971). Sex variable in conforming behavior. *Journal of Personality and Social Psychology, 17*, 2, 200–207.

Sivacek, J. & Crano, W. D. (1982). Vested interest as a moderator of attitude-behavior consistency, *Journal of Personality and Social Psychology, 43*, 210–221.

Six, B., & Eckes, T. (1996, August). *Attitude-behavior relations: A comprehensive meta-analysis of 887 studies published between 1927 and 1993.* Paper presented at the XXVI International Congress of Psychology, Montreal, Quebec, Canada.

Skinner, B. F. (1938). *The behavior of organisms: An experimental analysis.* New York: Appleton-Century.

Slamecka, N. J., & Graf, P. (1978). The generation effect: Delineation of a phenomenon. *Journal of Experimental Psychology: Human Learning and Memory, 4*, 592–604.

Small, D. M., Gregory, M. D., Mak, Y. E., Gitelman, D., Mesulam, M. M., & Parrish, T. (2003). Dissociation of neural representation of intensity and affective valuation in human gustation. *Neuron, 39*(4), 701.

Smallman, R., Becker, B. & Roese, N.J. (2014). Attitude construction: Evaluation in context. *Journal of Experimental Social Psychology, 52*, 25–31.

Smith, E. R., & DeCoster, J. (2000). Dual-process models in social and Cognitive Psychology: Conceptual integration and links to underlying memory systems. *Personality and Social Psychology Review, 4*(2), 108–131.

Smith, E. R., Fazio, R. H., & Cejka, M. A. (1996). Accessible attitudes influence categorization of multiply categorizable objects. *Journal of Personality and Social Psychology, 71*(5), 888.

Smith, J. R. & Terry, D. J. (2012). Attitudes and behavior: Revisiting LaPiere's hospitality study. In J. R. Smith & S. A. Haslam (Eds.), *Social psychology: Revisiting the classic studies* (pp. 27–41). Thousand Oaks, CA: Sage Publications.

Smith, M. B., Bruner, J. S., & White, R. W. (1956). *Opinions and personality*. New York: Wiley.

Smith, S. M., Fabrigar, L. R. & Norris, M.E. (2008). Reflections on six decades of selective exposure research: Progress, challenges and opportunities. *Social and Personality Compass, 2*(1), 464–493.

Smith, S. M., Haugtvedt, C. P., & Petty, R. E. (1994). Need for cognition and the effects of repeated expression on attitude accessibility and extremity. *Advances in Consumer Research, 21*, 234–237.

Smith, S. M., & Shaffer, D. R. (1991). Celerity and cajolery: Rapid speech may promote or inhibit persuasion through its impact on message elaboration. *Personality and Social Psychology Bulletin, 17*(6), 663–669.

Smith, T. (1885). *Successful advertising: Its secrets explained*. London: Bazaar Press.

Snyder, M. (1974). Self-monitoring of expressive behavior. *Journal of Personality and Social Psychology*, 30(4), 526–537.

Snyder, M. (1987). *Public appearances, private realities*. New York: Freeman.

Snyder, M., & DeBono, K. G. (1985). Appeals to image and claims about quality: Understanding the psychology of advertising. *Journal of Personality and Social Psychology*, 49(3), 586–597.

Snyder, M., & Kendzierski, D. (1982). Acting on one's attitudes: Procedures for linking attitude and behavior. *Journal of Experimental Social Psychology, 18*(2), 165–183.

Snyder, M., & Monson, T. C. (1975). Persons, situations, and the control of social behavior. *Journal of Personality and Social Psychology*, 32(4), 637.

Snyder, M., & Rothbart, M. (1971). Communicator attractiveness and opinion change. *Canadian Journal of Behavioural Science, 3*, 377–387.

Snyder, M. L., & Wicklund, R. A. (1976). Prior exercise of freedom and reactance. *Journal of Experimental Social Psychology, 12*(2), 120–130.

Sparks, P., & Manstead, A.S.R. (2006). Moral judgements as constitutive of attitudes in the evaluation of actions. Unpublished manuscript.

Spencer, S. J., Fein, S., Wolfe, C. T., Fong, C., & Dunn, M. A. (1998). Automatic activation of stereotypes: The role of self-image threat. *Personality and Social Psychology Bulletin*, 24(11), 1139–1152.

Spicer, C. V., & Monteith, M. J. (2001). *Implicit outgroup favoritism among African Americans and vulnerability to stereotype threat*. Unpublished manuscript.

Spielberg, J. M., Stewart, J. L., Levin, R. L., Miller, G. A., & Heller, W. (2008). Prefrontal cortex, emotion, and approach/withdrawal motivation. *Social and Personality Psychology Compass, 2*, 135–153.

Sriram, N. & Greenwald, A. G. (2009). The brief Implicit Association Test. *Experimental Psychology, 56*, 283–294.

Staats, A. W., & Staats, C. K. (1958). Attitudes established by classical conditioning. *The Journal of Abnormal and Social Psychology, 57*(1), 37.

Stanley, D., Phelps, E., & Banaji, M. (2008). The neural basis of implicit attitudes. *Current Directions in Psychological Science, 17*(2), 164–170.

Stark, E., Borgida, E., Kim, A., & Pickens, B. (2008). Understanding public attitudes toward tobacco harm reduction: The role of attitude structure. *Journal of Applied Social Psychology, 38*(10), 2615–2635.

Steele, C. M. (1988). The psychology of self-affirmation: Sustaining the integrity of the self. *Advances in Experimental Social Psychology, 21*, 261–302.

Steele, C. M., & Liu, T. J. (1983). Dissonance processes as self-affirmation. *Journal of Personality and Social Psychology, 45*(1), 5.

Steele, C. M., Spencer, S. J., & Lynch, M. (1993). Self-image resilience and dissonance: The role of affirmational resources. *Journal of Personality and Social Psychology, 64*, 885–885.

Stevens, S. S. (1946). On the theory of scales of measurement. *Science, New Series, 103*(2684). 677–680.

Stone, J. (1999). What exactly have I done? The role of self-attribute accessibility in dissonance. In E. Harmon-Jones &. J. Mills (Eds.), *Cognitive dissonance: progress on a pivotal theory in social psychology* (pp. 175–200). Washington, DC.: APA.

Stone, J., & Cooper, J. (2001). A self-standards model of cognitive dissonance. *Journal of Experimental Social Psychology, 37*(3), 228–243.

Stone, J., & Cooper, J. (2003). The effect of self-attribute relevance on how self-esteem moderates attitude change in dissonance processes. *Journal of Experimental Social Psychology, 39*(5), 508–515.

Stone, J. & Fernandez, N. C. (2008). How behavior shapes attitudes: Cognitive dissonance processes. In W. D. Crano & R. Prislin (Eds.), *Attitudes and attitude change* (pp. 313–334) New York: Psychology Press.

Stone, J. & Focella, E. (2011). Hypocrisy, dissonance and self-regulation processes that improve health. *Self and Identity, 10*, 295–303.

Stout, J. G., Dasgupta, N., Hunsinger, M., & McManus, M. A. (2011). STEMing the tide: Using ingroup experts to inoculate women's self-concept in science, technology, engineering, and mathematics (STEM). *Journal of Personality and Social Psychology, 100*, 255–270.

Strack, F., & Deutsch, R. (2004). Reflective and impulsive determinants of social behavior. *Personality and social psychology review, 8*(3), 220–247.

Strack, F., Martin, L. L., & Stepper, S. (1988). Inhibiting and facilitating conditions of the human smile: a nonobtrusive test of the facial feedback hypothesis. *Journal of Personality and Social Psychology, 54*(5), 768–777.

Strick, M., Holland, R. W., van Baaren, R. B., & van Knippenberg, A. (2012). Those who laugh are defenseless: How humor breaks resistance to influence. *Journal of Experimental Psychology: Applied, 18*(2), 213–223.

Stroebe, W., Insko, C. A., Thompson, V. D., & Layton, B. D. (1971). Effects of physical attractiveness, attitude similarity, and sex on various aspects of interpersonal attraction. *Journal of Personality and Social Psychology, 18*, 79–91.

Swanson, J. E., Rudman, L. A., & Greenwald, A. G. (2001). Using the Implicit Association Test to investigate attitude-behavior consistency for stigmatized behavior. *Cognition and Emotion, 15*, 207–230.

Swim, J., Borgida, E., Maruyama, G., & Myers, D. G. (1989). Joan McKay versus John McKay: Do gender stereotypes bias evaluations? *Psychological Bulletin, 105*, 409–429.

Tajfel, H., & Turner, J. C. (1986). The social identity theory of intergroup behaviour. In S. Worchel & W. G. Austin (Eds.), *Psychology of intergroup relations* (2nd ed., pp. 7–24). Chicago: Nelson Hall.

Tannen, D. (1990). Gender differences in conversational coherence: Physical alignment and topical cohesion. *Conversational organization and its development, 38*, 167–206.

Taylor, S. E. (1975). On inferring one's attitudes from one's behavior: Some delimiting conditions. *Journal of Personality and Social Psychology, 31*, 126–131.

Tedeschi, J. T., Schlenker, B. R., & Bonoma, T. V. (1971). Cognitive dissonance: Private ratiocination or public spectacle? *American Psychologist, 26*(8), 685.

Tesser, A. (1978). Self-generated attitude change. In L. Berkowitz (Ed.), *Advances in experimental social psychology* (Vol. 11, pp. 289–338). New York: Academic Press.

Tetlock, P. E. (1983). Accountability and complexity of thought. *Journal of Personality and Social Psychology, 45*(1), 74.

Tetlock, P.E. (1985). Accountability: The neglected social context of judgment and choice. In B. Staw & L. Cummings (Eds.), *Research in organizational behavior* (Vol. 7, pp. 297–332). Greenwich, CT: JAI Press.

Thomas, W. I. & Znaniecki, F. (1918). *The Polish peasant in Europe and America*. Boston, Badger.

Thompson, M. M., Zanna, M. P., & Griffin, D. W. (1995). Let's not be indifferent about (attitudinal) ambivalence. In R. E. Petty & J. A. Krosnick. (Eds.), *Attitude strength: Antecedents and consequences*. Ohio State University series on attitudes and persuasion (Vol. 4., pp. 361–386). Hillsdale, NJ Lawrence Erlbaum Associates.

Thorndike, E. L. (1920a). A constant error in psychological ratings. *Journal of Applied Psychology, 4*, 25–29.

Thorndike, E. L. (1920b). Intelligence and its uses. *Harper's magazine*.

Thurstone, L. L. (1928). Attitudes can be measured. *American Journal of Sociology*, 529–554.

Thurstone, L. L. (1946). Comment. *American Journal of Sociology, 52*, 39–50.

Todorov, A., Dotsch, R., Wigboldus, D. H., & Said, C. P. (2011). Data-driven methods for modeling social perception. *Social and Personality Psychology Compass, 5*(10), 775–791.

Tom, G., Petterson, P., Lau, T., Burton, T. & Cook, J. (1991). The role of overt head movements in the formation of affect. *Basic and Applied Psychology, 12*, 281–289.

Tormala, Z. L. (2008). A new framework for resistance to persuasion: The resistance appraisals hypothesis. *Attitudes and Attitude Change*, 213–234.

Tormala, Z. L., Briñol, P., & Petty, R. E. (2006). When credibility attacks: The reverse impact of source credibility on persuasion. *Journal of Experimental Social Psychology, 42*, 684–691.

Tormala, Z. L., Clarkson, J. J., & Henderson, M. D. (2011). Does fast or slow evaluation foster greater certainty? *Personality and Social Psychology Bulletin, 37*(3), 422–434.

Tormala, Z. L., DeSensi, V. L., & Petty, R. E. (2007). Resisting persuasion by illegitimate means: A metacognitive perspective on minority influence. *Personality and Social Psychology Bulletin, 33*(3), 354–367.

Tormala, Z. L., & Petty, R. E. (2002). What doesn't kill me makes me stronger: The effects of resisting persuasion on attitude certainty. *Journal of Personality and Social Psychology, 83*(6), 1298–1313.

Tormala, Z. L., & Petty, R. E. (2004). Resistance to persuasion and attitude certainty: The moderating role of elaboration. *Personality and Social Psychology Bulletin, 30*(11), 1446–1457.

Tormala, Z. L., & Rucker, D. D. (2007). Attitude certainty: A review of past findings and emerging perspectives. *Social and Personality Psychology Compass, 1*(1), 469–492.

Towles-Schwen, T., & Fazio, R. H. (2006). Automatically activated racial attitudes as predictors of the success of interracial roommate relationships. *Journal of Experimental Social Psychology, 42*(5), 698–705.

Trafimow, D., & Finlay, K. A. (1996). The importance of subjective norms for a minority of people: Between subjects and within-subjects analyses. *Personality and Social Psychology Bulletin, 22*(8), 820–828.

Trafimow, D., & Sheeran, P. (1998). Some tests of the distinction between cognitive and affective beliefs. *Journal of Experimental Social Psychology, 34*(4), 378–397.

Trepel, C., Fox, C. R., & Poldrack, R. A. (2005). Prospect theory on the brain? Toward a cognitive neuroscience of decision under risk. *Cognitive Brain Research, 23*(1), 34–50.

Turner, J. C. (1982). Towards a cognitive redefinition of the social group. *Social Identity and Intergroup Relations*, 15–40.

Tversky, A., & Kahneman, D. (1973). Availability: A heuristic for judging frequency and probability. *Cognitive Psychology, 5*(2), 207–232.

Tversky, A., & Kahneman, D. (1974). Judgment under uncertainty: Heuristics and biases. *Science, 185*(4157), 1124–1131.

Uleman, J. S., Newman, L. S., & Moskowitz, G. B. (1996). People as flexible interpreters: Evidence and issues from spontaneous trait inference. *Advances in Experimental Social Psychology, 28*, 211–279.

Uskul, A. K., Oyserman, D., Schwarz, N., Lee, S. W., & Xu, A. J. (2013). How successful you have been in life depends on the response scale used: The role of cultural mindsets in pragmatic inferences drawn from question format. *Social Cognition, 31*(2), 222–236.

Valins, S. (1966). Cognitive effects of false heart-rate feedback. *Journal of Personality and Social Psychology, 4*, 400–408.

van der Pligt, J., Zeelenberg, M., van Dijk, W. W., de Vries, N. K., & Richard, R. (1997). Affect, attitudes and decisions: Let's be more specific. *European Review of Social Psychology, 8*(1), 33–66.

van Harreveld, F., van der Pligt, J., & de Liver, Y.N. (2009). The agony of ambivalence and ways to resolve it: Introducing the MAID model. *Personality and Social Psychology Review, 13*(1), 45–61.

van Honk, J., & Schutter, D. J. (2006). From affective valence to motivational direction: The frontal asymmetry of emotion revised. *Psychological Science, 17*(11), 963–965.

van Veen, V., Krug, M. K., Schooler, J. W., & Carter, C. S. (2009). Neural activity predicts attitude change in cognitive dissonance. *Nature Neuroscience, 12*(11), 1469–1474.

Vanman, E. J., Paul, B. Y., Ito, T. A., & Miller, N. (1997). The modem face of prejudice and structural features that moderate the effect of cooperation on affect. *Journal of Personality and Social Psychology, 73*, 941–944.

Vanman, E. J., Saltz, J. L., Nathan, L. R., & Warren, J. A. (2004). Racial discrimination by low-prejudiced whites: Facial movements as implicit measures of attitudes related to behavior. *Psychological Science, 15*(11), 711–714.

Vasey, M. W., Harbaugh, C. N., Buffington, A. G., Jones, C. R., & Fazio, R. H. (2012). Predicting return of fear following exposure therapy with an implicit measure of attitudes. *Behaviour Research and Therapy, 50*(12), 767–774.

Visser, P. S., Bizer, G. Y., & Krosnick, J. A. (2006). Exploring the latent structure of strength related attitude attributes. *Advances in Experimental Social Psychology, 38*, 1–67.

Visser, P. S., & Cooper, J. (2003). Attitude change. In M. Hogg & J. Cooper (Eds.), *Sage Handbook of Social Psychology* (pp. 211–231). London: Sage Publications.

Visser, P. S., & Krosnick, J. A. (1998). Development of attitude strength over the life cycle: Surge and decline. *Journal of Personality and Social Psychology, 75*, 1389–1410.

Visser, P. S., Krosnick, J. A., & Simmons, J. P. (2003). Distinguishing the cognitive and behavioral consequences of attitude importance and certainty: A new approach to testing the common-factor hypothesis. *Journal of Experimental Social Psychology, 39*, 118–141.

Vohs, K. D., Baumeister, R. F., & Ciarocco, N. J. (2005). Self-regulation and self-presentation: regulatory resource depletion impairs impression management and effortful self-presentation depletes regulatory resources. *Journal of Personality and Social Psychology, 88*(4), 632–657.

Voisin, D. & Fointiat, V. (2013). Reduction of dissonance according to normative standards in the induced compliance paradigm. *Social Psychology, 44*, 191–195.

von Hippel, W., Brener, L., & von Hippel, C. (2008). Implicit prejudice toward injecting drug users predicts intentions to change jobs among drug and alcohol nurses. *Psychological Science, 19*(1), 7–11.

von Hippel, W., Sekaquaptewa, D., & Vargas, P. T. (2009). Linguistic markers of implicit attitudes. *Attitudes: Insights from the new implicit measures*, 429–458.

Wagner, B. C., & Petty, R. E. (2011). The elaboration likelihood model of persuasion: Thoughtful and non-thoughtful social influence. In D. Chadee (Ed.), *Theories in social psychology* (pp. 96–116). Oxford, UK: Blackwell.

Wakslak, C. J. (2012). The experience of cognitive dissonance in important and trivial domains: A Construal-Level Theory approach. *Journal of Experimental Social Psychology, 48*, 1361–1364.

Walster, E., Aronson, V., Abrahams, D., & Rottman, L. (1966). Importance of physical attractiveness in dating behavior. *Journal of Personality and Social Psychology, 4*(5), 508–516.

Walster, E., & Festinger, L. (1962). The effectiveness of "overheard" persuasive communications. *Journal of Abnormal and Social Psychology, 65*(6), 395–402.

Walther, E., Nagengast, B., & Trasselli, C. (2005). Evaluative conditioning in social psychology: Facts and speculations. *Cognition & Emotion, 19*(2), 175–196.

Walton, G. M., & Banaji, M. R. (2004). Being what you say: The effect of essentialist linguistic labels on preferences. *Social Cognition, 22*(2), 193–213.

Wan, C-S. & Chiou, W-B. (2010). Inducing attitude change toward online gaming among adolescent players based on dissonance theory: The role of threats and justification of effort. *Computers and Education, 54*, 162–168.

Wason, P. C. (1960). On the failure to eliminate hypotheses in a conceptual task. *Quarterly Journal of Experimental Psychology, 12*(3), 129–140.

Watt, S., Maio, G. R. & Haddock, G., Johnson, B. T. (2008). Attitude functions in peruasion: Matching, involvement, self-affirmation and hierarchy. In W. D. Crano & R. Prislin (Eds.), *Attitudes and attitude change*. New York: Psychology Press.

Watts, W. A., & Holt, L. E. (1979). Persistence of opinion change induced under conditions of forewarning and distraction. *Journal of Personality and Social Psychology, 37*, 778–789.

Webb, T. L., Ononaiye, M. S., Sheeran, P., Reidy, J. G., & Lavda, A. (2010). Using implementation intentions to overcome the effects of social anxiety on attention and appraisals of performance. *Personality and Social Psychology Bulletin, 36*, 612–627.

Webb, T. L., & Sheeran, P. (2006). Does changing behavioral intentions engender behavior change? A meta-analysis of the experimental evidence. *Psychological Bulletin, 132*(2), 249.

Webster, D. M., & Kruglanski, A. W. (1998). Cognitive and social consequences of the motivation for closure. *The European Review of Social Psychology, 32,* 254–270.

Wegener, D. T., & Petty, R. E. (1995). Flexible correction processes in social judgment: The role of naive theories in corrections for perceived bias. *Journal of Personality and Social Psychology, 68,* 36–36.

Wegener, D. T., & Petty, R. E. (1997). The flexible correction model: The role of naive theories of bias in bias correction. In M. P. Zanna (Ed.), *Advances in experimental social psychology* (Vol. 29, pp. 141–208). San Diego: Academic Press.

Wegener, D. T., Petty, R. E., Smoak, N. D., & Fabrigar, L. R. (2004). Multiple routes to resisting attitude change. *Resistance and Persuasion,* 13–38.

Wegner, D. M. (1992). You can't always think what you want: Problems in the suppression of unwanted thoughts. In M. Zanna (Ed.), *Advances in experimental social psychology* (Vol. 25, pp. 193–225). San Diego, CA: Academic Press.

Weigel, R. H., & Newman, L. S. (1976). Increasing attitude-behavior correspondence by broadening the scope of the behavioral measure. *Journal of Personality and Social Psychology, 33*(6), 793.

Wells, G. L., Olson, E. A., & Charman, S. D. (2003). Distorted retrospective eyewitness reports as functions of feedback and delay. *Journal of Experimental Psychology Applied, 9*(1), 42–51.

Werner, P. D. (1978). Personality and attitude-activism correspondence. *Journal of Personality and Social Psychology, 36*(12), 1375–1390.

Wheeler, M. E., & Fiske, S. T. (2005). Controlling racial prejudice social-cognitive goals affect amygdala and stereotype activation. *Psychological Science, 16*(1), 56–63.

Wheeler, S. C., Briñol, P., & Hermann, A.D. (2007). Resistance to persuasion as self-regulation: Ego-depletion and its effects on attitude change processes. *Journal of Experimental Social Psychology, 43*(1), 150–156.

Whittlesea, B. W., & Williams, L. D. (2000). The source of feelings of familiarity: The discrepancy-attribution hypothesis. *Journal of Experimental Psychology: Learning, Memory, and Cognition, 26*(3), 547.

Wicker, A. W. (1969). Attitudes versus actions: The relationship of verbal and overt behavioral responses to attitude objects. *Journal of Social Issues, 25*(4), 41–78.

Wicklund, R. A. (1974). *Freedom and reactance.* Potomac, MD: L. Erlbaum Associates.

Wicklund, R. A., & Brehm, J. W. (1976). *Perspectives on cognitive dissonance.* Hillsdale, NJ: Lawrence Erlbaum Associates.

Wicklund, R. A., Cooper, J. & Linder, D. E. (1967). Effects of expected effort on attitude change prior to exposure. *Journal of Experimental Social Psychology, 3,* 416–428.

Widman, L., & Olson, M. (2013). On the relationship between automatic attitudes and self-reported sexual assault in men. *Archives of Sexual Behavior, 42*(5), 813–823.

Williams, J. K., & Themanson, J. R. (2011). Neural correlates of the implicit association test: evidence for semantic and emotional processing. *Social Cognitive and Affective Neuroscience, 6*(4), 468–476.

Williams, L. M., Kemp, A. H., Felmingham, K. L., Barton, M., Olivieri, G., Peduto, A., & Bryant, R. A. (2006). Trauma modulates amygdala and medial prefrontal responses to consciously attended fear. *Neuroimage, 29,* 347–357.

Wilson, T. D., Dunn, D. S., Kraft, D., & Lisle, D. J. (1989). Introspection, attitude change, and attitude-behavior consistency: The disruptive effects of explaining why we feel the way we do. *Advances in Experimental Social Psychology, 22,* 287–343.

Wilson, T. D., & Hodges, S. D. (1992). Attitudes as temporary constructions. *The construction of social judgments, 10*, 37–65.

Wilson, T. D., Kraft, D., & Dunn, D. S. (1989). The disruptive effects of explaining attitudes: The moderating effect of knowledge about the attitude object. *Journal of Experimental Social Psychology, 25*(5), 379–400.

Wilson, T. D., Lindsey, S., & Schooler, T. Y. (2000). A model of dual attitudes. *Psychological Review, 107*(1), 101.

Wilson, T. D., Lisle, D. J., Schooler, J. W., Hodges, S. D., Klaaren, K. J., & LaFleur, S. J. (1993). Introspecting about reasons can reduce post-choice satisfaction. *Personality and Social Psychology Bulletin, 19*, 331–331.

Winkielman, P., & Cacioppo, J. T. (2001). Mind at ease puts a smile on the face: psychophysiological evidence that processing facilitation elicits positive affect. *Journal of Personality and Social Psychology, 81*(6), 989.

Witte, K., & Allen, M. (2000). A meta-analysis of fear appeals: Implications for effective public health campaigns. *Health Education & Behavior, 27*(5), 591–615.

Wittenbrink, B., & Schwarz, N. (Eds.) (2007). *Implicit measures of attitudes: Procedures and controversies.* New York: Guilford Press.

Witvliet, C. V., & Vrana, S. R. (2007). Play it again Sam: Repeated exposure to emotionally evocative music polarises liking and smiling responses, and influences other affective reports, facial EMG, and heart rate. *Cognition and Emotion, 21*(1), 3–25.

Wood, W. (1982). Retrieval of attitude-relevant information from memory: Effects on susceptibility to persuasion and on intrinsic motivation. *Journal of Personality and Social Psychology, 42*(5), 798–810.

Wood, W., Kallgren, C. A., & Preisler, R. M. (1985). Access to attitude-relevant information in memory as a determinant of persuasion: The role of message attributes. *Journal of Experimental Social Psychology, 21*(1), 73–85.

Wood, W., Rhodes, N., & Biek, M. (1995). Working knowledge and attitude strength: An information-processing analysis. In R. E. Petty, Richard & J. A. Krosnick (Eds.), *Attitude strength: Antecedents and consequences.* Ohio State University series on attitudes and persuasion (Vol. 4., pp. 283–313). Hillsdale, NJ: Lawrence Erlbaum Associates.

Worchel, S., & Arnold, S. E. (1973). The effects of censorship and attractiveness of the censor on attitude change. *Journal of Experimental Social Psychology, 9*(4), 365–377.

Worchel, S., Arnold, S., & Baker, M. (1975). The effects of censorship on attitude change: The influence of censor and communication characteristics. *Journal of Applied Social Psychology, 5*(3), 227–239.

Worchel, S., & Brehm, J. W. (1970). Effect of threats to attitudinal freedom as a function of agreement with the communicator. *Journal of Personality and Social Psychology, 14*(1), 18.

Word, C. O., Zanna, M. P. & Cooper, J. (1974). The nonverbal mediation of self-fulfilling prophecies in interracial interactions. *Journal of Experimental Social Psychology, 10*, 109–120.

Worth, L. T., & Mackie, D. M. (1987). Cognitive mediation of positive affect in persuasion. *Social Cognition, 5*(1), 76–94.

Wu, C., & Shaffer, D. R. (1987). Susceptibility to persuasive appeals as a function of source credibility and prior experience with the attitude object. *Journal of Personality and Social Psychology, 52*(4), 677.

Ybarra, O. & Trafimow, D. (1998). How priming the private self or collective self affects the relative weights of attitudes and subjective norms. *Personality and Social Psychology Bulletin, 4*(24), 362–370.

Yogeeswaran, K., Dasgupta, N., & Gomez, C. (2012). A new American dilemma? The effect of ethnic identification and public service on the national inclusion of ethnic groups. *European Journal of Social Psychology, 42*, 691–705.

Young, A. I., & Fazio, R. H. (2013). Attitude accessibility as a determinant of object construal and evaluation. *Journal of Experimental Social Psychology, 49*, 404–418.

Young, A. I., Ratner, K. G., & Fazio, R. H. (2014). Political attitudes bias the mental representation of a presidential candidate's face. *Psychological Science, 25*, 503–510.

Zajonc, R. B. (1968). Attitudinal effects of mere exposure. *Journal of Personality and Social Psychology, 9*(2 pt 2), 1–27.

Zanna, M. P., & Cooper, J. (1974). Dissonance and the pill: An attribution approach to studying the arousal properties of dissonance. *Journal of Personality and Social Psychology, 29*(5), 703.

Zanna, M. P., Kiesler, C. A., & Pilkonis, P. A. (1970). Positive and negative attitudinal affect established by classical conditioning. *Journal of Personality and Social Psychology, 14*(4), 321.

Zanna, M. P., & Rempel, J. K. (1988). Attitudes: A new look at an old concept. In D. Bar-Tal & A. W. Kruglanski (Eds.), *The social psychology of knowledge* (pp. 315–334). New York: Cambridge University Press; Paris, France: Editions de la Maison des Sciences de l'Homme.

Ziegert, J. C., & Hanges, P. J. (2005). Employment discrimination: The role of implicit attitudes, motivation, and a climate for racial bias. *Journal of Applied Psychology, 90*(3), 553.

Ziegler, R., Dobre, B., & Diehl, M. (2007). Does matching versus mismatching message content to attitude functions lead to biased processing? The role of message ambiguity. *Basic and Applied Social Psychology, 29*(3), 269–278.

Zimbardo, P., & Ebbesen, E. B. (1970). *Influencing attitudes and changing behavior: A basic introduction to relevant methodology, theory, and applications.* Reading, MA: Addison-Wesley Publishing Company, Inc.

AUTHOR INDEX

Abelson R. P. 29, 48, 146, 221
Abraham L. M. 87
Adriaanse M. A. 159
Agerstrom J. 151, 238
Agnew C. 249
Aharon I. 268
Ajzen I. 150–1, 154–60, 167
Akhtar O. 151
Alberracin D. 6, 110, 217
Albert R. 110
Alessis C. 91
Allen B. P. 98
Allen M. 98
Allen T. J. 247
Allison S. 29
Allport G. W. 3, 145, 258
Allyn J. 210
Altemeyer B. 217
Alter A. L. 137
Amodio D. M. 265, 277
Anderson A. K. 265, 269
Aneshensel C. S. 79
Appel V. 103
Apple K. J. 107
Arcuri L. 249
Arkes H. R. 242, 244, 246
Armitage C. J. 41, 155, 156–8
Arnold K. H. 80
Arnold S. E. 206
Aronson E. 3, 51, 83, 87, 92, 102, 109,
    182–4, 188, 189–92
Asendorpf J. B. 240
Ashburn-Nado L. 238, 243
Axsom D. 120, 185

Babad E. Y. 221
Baeyens F. 253

Bailey J. 41
Bain P. G. 155
Baker M. 206
Balcetis E. 45
Banaji M. R. 19, 233–7, 240, 243, 247,
    249–50, 253, 266–7, 271
Bandura A. 157, 161
Banse R. 240
Barden J. 139
Bargh J. A. 39, 47, 75, 167, 229
Baron A. S. 234
Barsalou L. W. 39, 254
Bartholow B. D. 265
Bassili J. N. 23, 29–30, 37, 221
Bator R. J. 117
Bauer M. 29
Baumeister R. F. 162, 218–19
Baumgardner M. H. 91
Bayens F. 253
Beauvois J. L. 191
Becker B. 16
Becker M. 29
Bell D. W. 41
Bem D. J. 169, 192–3
Bennett E. 128
Benson H. 79
Berent M. K. 29, 31
Berger H. 265
Berger I. E. 164
Bergin A. 97
Berkman E. T. 275
Bernard M. M. 213–14
Bernston G. G. 171
Bhargava M. 50
Biddle S. J. 158
Biek M. 27, 218
Bizer G. Y. 31, 129

329

SUBJECT INDEX

action based model; *see* cognitive dissonance
advertising 3, 68, 83, 89
affect 6, 47–9, 216
Affective/Evaluative Priming Task; *see* implicit measures
Affect Misattribution Procedure; *see* implicit measures
amygdala 266–9, 271
anterior cingulate cortex (ACC) 266
Aristotle 84–5
association activation 257
Associative Propositional Evaluation Model (APE) 255–7
attention 76, 109, 115
attitude accessibility 32–6, 80; attitude-nonattitude continuum 32, 37, 75; automatic activation of 37–8; *in* MODE model 163–4; model of *32; and* object appraisal 75; reaction time in *33;* rehearsal, role of 33–5, 107; relevance 75; response latency (see reaction time); stability *7*
attitude ambivalence 40–7
attitude behavior relationship: affective-behavior consistency 149, 152; crystallization of attitudes 152–3; dispositional influences 152; evaluative-cognitive consistency 152; internal 152; principle of compatibility 149–50; principle of correspondence 149–51, 153, 158
attitude components 5–7, 23, 46–56
attitude, definitions of 5, 162, 249, 252
attitude discrepant behavior; *see* cognitive dissonance
attitude formation 24, 50, 62–3, 134

attitude functions: ego defensive 59, 71–2; externalization *59, 71;* knowledge function 59, 74; need for affect 80–1; negative bias 63; object appraisal 59, 74–9; reinforcement 60; self-esteem 71; social adjustive 59, 69–70; utilitarian 59, 62, 64; value expressive 63–5, 70, 151; value relevance 65
attitude measurement; *see* explicit attitude measurement; implicit attitude measurement; physiological measures
attitude-nonattitude continuum 75
attitude object; *see* stimulus object
attitude object approach 68
attitude permanence 133
attitude representation theory 39–40
attitudes as possessions hypothesis 66–7
attitude strength: certainty (as measurement of) 30–1, 207, 221–2; definition 32; direct experience 24; durability 23, 26; elaboration 25; extremity of attitude 29–31; false consensus 28–9; formation 24; hedonic relevance 28; importance of attitude 29; need for cognition 25; pervasiveness 23; rehearsal 33, 76, 78, 163; speed (as measurement of) 30–1; stability 221; vested interest 27–8; working knowledge 27
attitude structure 46–57; Expectancy-Value models 51–3, 154; horizontal structure 55–6; syllogistic model 54–6; vertical structure 54–5; *see also* connectionist models
attribution theory 222
audience factors (in persuasion) 101,